AF244211

REFLECTION OF HOME
LETTERS FROM VIETNAM

THE LETTERS OF MASTER SERGEANT LEO DUBOIS

Edited by
Bryan Dubois

Leapin Leo Press
New Market, Maryland

Leapin Leo Press
P.O. Box 347
New Market, Maryland 21774
www.leapinleo.com

Library of Congress Control Number: 2006910991

ISBN 978-0-9790581-0-3

Cover design by H. Christopher Christner

Some names have been changed to protect privacy.

Article "City Man Wed in Texas", courtesy of the Pawtucket (Rhode Island) Times. Articles "Clerihew Knows Enemy Below", and "Jacksboro Officer in TV Interview", courtesy of the Jacksboro (Texas) Gazette-News. Fort Worth Star Telegram photos courtesy of Fort Worth Star-Telegram Collection, Special Collections, The University of Texas at Arlington Library, Arlington, Texas. Scripture taken from the New King James Version, Copyright © 1982 by Thomas Nelson, Inc. Used by permission. All rights reserved.

ACKNOWLEDGEMENTS

Thank you to the typists across America who have transcribed the letters: Jamie Daggett of California, Jeanne Crider and Karen Gunnell of Maryland, Kathy Kissell of Florida, Priscilla Savary of Pennsylvania and Elisabeth Williams of North Carolina,

to Director Juanita Damron and Delyn Lewis of the Gladys Johnson Ritchie Public Library, Jacksboro, Texas, for assistance with research in the archives of the Jacksboro Gazette-News,

to Dorothy Prunty, Ken Maurer, Kendra Parsons, Lyle Carlson, Candice Spears, Donna-Jeanne Lechak and Wanda Dyson for critique and guidance, and

to Mike Farrell of Mountain River Communications, Greenville, South Carolina, for web development, operations and good counsel.

REFLECTION OF HOME
LETTERS FROM VIETNAM

THE LETTERS OF MASTER SERGEANT LEO DUBOIS

Introduction

Like a canoe in a swift and sure current, these letters and little else will propel you through this year-long tour of duty. Only occasionally will I dip the paddle in, on one side or the other, to guide or recount a memory.

Leo is 37 when he leaves for Vietnam. At home, his wife, Don Leta, has charge of the five children, Karen, Stephanie, Lanis, Paul and me. And she is pregnant with the sixth.

Early in their marriage, war had sent him away, to Korea. Now, fifteen years later, war separates them again. This time he is not a young airman and newlywed, but a father and an experienced NCO.

See how comfortably he directs and mentors the young men under his supervision, how ably he runs his shop — communications maintenance at Da Nang, at the time, the

Leo Dubois, 1965, just prior to Vietnam

busiest airport in the world. Picture his observations of daily life on a growing airbase.

Leo's thoughts do not get far, though, before they are drawn back to home. He receives a letter. He shares a package of homebaked goods. Or he lies in the sack at the end of the day. He turns his mind towards his wife and children. Unable to touch, speak and kiss from so far, he writes himself into these letters and sends them off. Don Leta reads each and responds, then lovingly stores them away in a box.

Forty years later, we are going to open the lid of that box and glimpse a war and a reflection of home, 1965.

- Bryan Dubois

Hamilton AFB, Calif.
26 October 1965

My Darling

I made through the course here and now we're just waiting 'till 1300 to board a bus for Travis.

We had a nice quiet flight from Dallas. While getting my baggage in San Francisco, I started talking to this SSgt, also a communicator, and he's from Cumberland but used to live in Pawtucket. Since it was some 15 miles to town, some of us shared a cab to the Greyhound terminal. There we found that Uncle Sugar had a contract with them to furnish transportation to Hamilton for people coming for M-16 training. We had lunch there since the next bus wasn't leaving until 2:30.

Talking to everyone here, it seems that about 90% of us in this shipment are in comm[1]. There are 180 people in this class, and a new class starts every even numbered day. The instructors said they have to work 7 days a week except when there are 31 days in a month – then there are two odd days in a row – the 31st and the 1st – so they get the 1st off.

About half of us are NCOs[2]. I understand they're establishing a relay center there and that's why there are so many of us at once. As one of the ranking men, I have a room which I share with a CMSgt[3] from personnel. Most of the people are in open bays.

The next morning (Sunday) we got up at five for chow, with a formation at six. It was pitch black and freezing. Though it was only 48 degrees, it was so damp it cut right through you. They formed us in relays of 50 people and I was assistant to a SMSgt [4]for our group. Busses then picked us up and took us to the range, across the runway and about 5 miles away. The sun finally gets up around 7:30 due to the mountains surrounding us. The first day the thermometer climbed to 92 degrees.

The training with the M-16 is not the regular target shooting that we do with the carbine. The course is quite interesting, but they've got to cram too much in too short a time.

We started off with learning the weapon itself, taking it apart and putting it back together. By the time we finished that part, the field kitchen was set up and the coffee boiling, so we took a break. Black coffee was all they had, but it tasted good by then. We had been issued field equipment, helmets and rifles, so we just dunked our canteen cups into the kettle to get our coffee.

---

[1] communications

[2] Non Commissioned Officer

[3] Chief Master Sergeant

[4] Senior Master Sergeant

After that, one group went to the line to fire, another in back-up to fire next, another in the pits, putting up and scoring targets and the fourth in a class on weapon handling. We were second to fire, so that gave us a bit more break period. They've got a big range they're still working on. Fifty people can fire at once. I qualified as "Expert", getting 57 hit in 60 shots.

By then it was about 2:30 and we went to the class on weapon handling. In that class, the instructor asked for a track man and some A2C[5] got up. (I'm getting too old to be raising my hand to that anymore!) Next he asked for a MSgt[6] – so I got up. There were two of us, but obviously since he intended to use that airman for speed, I couldn't resist the challenge. Then he said here was an airman's chance to legally punch a MSgt. Of course, that set pretty good with the others – not me. Anyhow, he set us about 30 feet apart. The airman had no helmet, field equipment or rifle to slow him up, while I was all decked out. Then he gave us separate instructions, so neither one of us knew what the other was going to do. Whatever it was, we were both to act when he hollered, "Go".

As it was, this guy was to race at me and touch me before I could shoot him. In my case, I was supposed to have an empty rifle so that when he said "Go", I had to release the empty magazine, insert a new one and fire. Luckily, I didn't fumble and shot 3 times before he got to me. He wanted to emphasize the need for doing this rapidly and without looking at your weapon. Just another second would have made the difference. When that was over, we did our turn to work the pits and then quit at almost five o'clock. For typical Sunday evening fare, we had cold cuts in the mess hall. For lunch, we had eaten C rations. Also, they had about a 15-20 minute non-denominational church service on the range in the morning since we were unable to go to regular services.

By night time, I was just about pooped, so I didn't do much of anything but stretch out in the sack.

The next morning, it was up at five again and formation at six. This time, they left us off some distance from the training area and we had to march in. When we arrived in the area (it was still real dark), they greeted us with flares, explosions and gunfire, so that everyone had to hit the deck. Fine way to start a day! We had a couple sessions covering night fighting and different types of grenades and mortars. From that, our group had a coffee break and this time I foxed them. I had saved my powdered milk and sugar from the previous day's "C" rations, so I had a decent cup of coffee! Then we did some firing from the hip with the weapon on automatic (so it fires like a machine gun – about 600 rounds per minute). We then went to the launch area where we

---

[5] Airman 2nd Class

[6] Master Sergeant

launched grenades with the M-16. By using a special cartridge and attaching the grenades to the end of the barrel, they can be fired about 400 yards. But boy, the kick-back on that weapon will knock you on your fanny if it's not held right. I've an injury on the knuckle of my thumb to prove it. On one of the shots, you have to fire with the thumb and when it kicked, my hand wasn't just right.

Next, we went to grenade throwing, where we had to toss from different positions. Throughout the day also there was some instructor throwing practice grenades in the middle of people so that people would learn to holler "grenade", pick it up and toss it away. From there, we went to assault, where we had to attack bunkers, houses, etc., shooting live ammunition and throwing grenades. Then, right-handers had to fire left-handed, etc.

That was the end of it except for cleaning our weapons and turning in our equipment. It was around 4:00 when we got back. I wasn't feeling quite so tired this time, so I took in the movie. "Von Ryan's Express", with Frank Sinatra, was playing. Real exciting! Afterwards, I stopped to pick up a couple hamburgers and some coffee.

This morning, they could keep their 5 o'clock reveille. I stayed in bed for almost all morning, not getting up until almost 8 o'clock! By then, it was too late for the mess hall, so I took a walk to the cafeteria. It's about 11 a.m., now, and I'm due to move out at 1300 for Travis.

Hamilton is pretty but seems real old. I'll bet there's not much more than 1000 troops on the base. It sure seems that there's not much of anything going on. Crossing the flight line to the range, you have to look real hard to detect any activity. It's an Air Defense Command base.

I hope you're not having too many problems with the kids. If the girls especially can learn to just do what they know they must do without being told over and over again, it would help.

I miss you so terribly much, my love. It has always gotten me so discouraged looking ahead to a year away, though when it's past it isn't quite so bad. Even once the half-way point is reached, things get a bit easier, at least psychologically, if not in fact.

I love you and our children with all my heart. Be sweet, my love, and write real soon.

Your Leo

Tan Son Nhut
28 Oct 65

My Dearest,

First of all – let me start by saying I don't know how much of a letter this will be since I've hardly slept since around 9 o'clock yesterday morning and it's almost 9 P.M. now.

After writing you yesterday I stuck the letter in my pocket since there was no place nearby to mail it at Hamilton. I only thought about it at the last minute while in the terminal at Travis. We left for Travis by bus at 1300. There were quite a few flights at different times destined for Saigon, and it seemed that they all had different routings. A combination of Anchorage, Japan, the Philippines, Wake, Guam, and Hawaii were used. We drew a brand spanking new Boeing 707 jet contracted with World Airways. 165 of us, plus the crew, boarded for at 5 P.M. take-off which would eventually take in about 16 hours flying time though it would end at 6 A.M. two days later. Actually, when it got dark the night we left we would not see daylight until we were in Saigon. The reason it took 2 days (from the 26th to the 28th) was due to the time difference and the fact that crossing the International Dateline made us lose a day.

The first leg was 10 ½ hours non-stop, Travis to Tokyo. We only stayed on the ground 45 minutes and couldn't get off the plane. It was then around 8 P.M. Next we flew to Clark Field in the Philippines, arriving there at one in the morning. Here we had a 3 hour layover, since it had to be gauged where we wouldn't arrive at Saigon before 6 A.M. They'll not let passenger planes in here at night. I was walking to the restroom to shave when someone yelled to me. It was TSgt Gerry Cramer, who was in crypto school with me. I think you might remember that he was the one I had told you used to be a drill instructor at Lackland, and he was the clown of the class. He said he knew I was coming and thought I was already here. He had seen my name on the message that also sent him over. He had been at Clark since the night before and was scheduled to go out 1 ½ hours after us.

At 4 A.M. we took off again, arriving at Tan Son Nhut at 6:10. It was real foggy, the temperature 82 degrees and the humidity about 8 million percent. Sweat has just rolled off me all day. This is really a rat-race. They're building all over the place and it's crawling with servicemen and Vietnamese. Everything is on one side of the base, while we're on the other side.

One of the first things we find out is that at Tan Son Nhut only up to SSgt can eat in the mess halls. NCOs must get their chow wherever they can find it – NCO Club, snack bar, etc. NCOs' draw extra for this as well as for quarters, for Tech's and above live in government quarters in downtown Saigon.

While sitting around outside awaiting transportation to the 1964th Comm Group I ran into Wilkerson from the gym and Airman Fisher from our outfit. Both of them are going to Cam Rahn Bay, the real hot place they're abuilding – remember the one where the temps reached 135 degrees.   I also saw MSgt Davis who was in the Personnel Section at Ellsworth.   Then this other guy walked by and pointed to me and said he remembered me from somewhere.   I knew right away who he was.   He used to work in personnel at Orlando.   He said they sent bunches of the Orlando personnel here.

When I finally got to the Comm Group, I didn't get to do much processing.   I'm supposed to see about pay in the morning.   I'll not be staying here, but will leave in a couple or three days for Da Nang.   That's where the big Marine Base is also.   I'll probably be in the 1972nd Comm Sq, however, keep sending mail to the 1964th Comm Group until this is firm and I have an APO number for you.

I went to eat at the NCO club, and that's a rat race too.   It's packed since that's where most of the NCOs eat.   Then who should I see at the table but Sgt Walker and his boss—MSgt Coker who was at school and at the NCO Academy with me.   He was the one who had nosed me out of the Academic award.   Coker's been here six months and already has his new assignment.   He asked and got Lackland.   Walker didn't get the concurrent tour to England he desired but did get his first base of choice, Homestead in Florida.   He only has 32 days to go.

I hope you can make out this scribbling, my sweet.   I'm writing while lying on an upper bunk in the transient area.   I'm going to cut this off now but will write again tomorrow night to bring you up to date on matters of pay as I can get them resolved.

Somebody is out working as I can here explosions in the distance.   It must be another SAC raid.

Bye-bye, my sweet.   I love you so very much and think of you constantly. Take good care of yourself and let me hear from you real soon.

Your loving husband,
Leo

Tan Son Nhut
29 Oct 65

Hi Honeybunch,

Well, I'm still just sitting here.   On the 4th I'll be going up to Da Nang. Today was almost all wasted.   I reported for processing as told and other than getting a couple minor things signed off I was waiting to get my pay taken care of. About 10:30 they said there was too much backlog and to come back at one o'clock.   At one they had us all in and were giving instructions for about an hour when he said that people going to Da Nang had their own finance set-up and we'd be paid up there.   I wasn't without fussing that I did at least get travel pay and dislocation allowance out of them.   I'm enclosing $200 and will send more when I finally get to Da Nang. I'll get it to you as soon as I possibly can. The address you can write to now is:

1972 Comm Sq.

APO San Francisco 96337

Boy, you have to stand in line for everything. It seems that's all I've done since I got to Hamilton. Lines for the bathroom, showers, chow, etc. After I got money from finance (after standing in line, of course) I stood in another line to get money orders before getting in line for chow. By then it was past 6 o'clock. I just got back and took a shower.

Saw Sgt. Kelley, who used to be Wing Sgt. Major in Orlando. He's with the Office of Protocol, 2nd Air Division, here in Tan Son Nhut. He said Sgt. Bowles, also Orlando, as well as a couple others were here. I didn't get to talk to him but for a minute, but he said he was coming TDY to Da Nang in a couple weeks and he'd look me up.

I think the heat and humidity takes as much out of you as anything. I was sweating at breakfast and I'm still sweating at 8:30 at night.

Its morning now and I want to get this off in the mail. I laid back a bit last night and out I went. Be sweet my love, and remember that you mean more to me than anything in this world. I'll be so glad when this is over with.

Your Leo

Tan Son Nhut
31 Oct 65

Hi Honeybunch,

Didn't get to write last night as I was pooped. Boy this climate really saps it out of you. For lack of anything else I went to the movie last night and slept thru the last 10 – 15 minutes. Excerpts from Oliver and Hardy movies called the "Laughing Twenties" were playing. I got back to the hut around 8 P.M. and started reading a story in Argosy. I read less than 3 pages and woke up this morning.

Mass here is said in the Vietnamese AF Chapel. I went to the 0900 Mass after breakfast at the club. I'm enclosing a few articles. Sgt Gerish shown launching a grenade with the M-16 was one of our instructors at Hamilton. Another shows Sgt. Savery. I guess that's why he's a chief – moves up to the front.

These people here at Tan Son Nhut have got it knocked, especially Techs and above. Besides drawing $2.57 a day for rations and $77 a month for rent, they have no real hardships. Saigon is nearby and that's where they spend most of their time as far as I can see. They get things here which are mighty hard to come by up-country. I was talking to some people from Da Nang and they said to make sure I had plenty of blades, shaving cream, tooth paste, and the like – that it was sometime quite hard to come by up there. The PX here has cameras, tape recorders, radios, jewelry, etc. Even tho the selection is not great, they do have these things. There's supposed to be a big Navy BX in Cholon, sort of a suburb of Saigon even though it's a separate city.   They supposedly have many fine French restaurants there where big steaks cost 100 piastres. The rate of exchange is 118 piastres to the dollar. I don't know yet if we ration in the mess hall or separately at Da Nang. I hope it's separate since I won't eat $2.57 worth a day. Another thing that surprised me is that civilian clothing is authorized. As a matter of fact blues, 1505's or civies must be worn when going into Saigon, and they encourage civies. I don't figure I'll have to worry about that.

Nov. 1st is Vietnamese Independence Day and I understand you can hardly move around in town. This morning's paper said all traffic was halted for about 4 hours yesterday as they threw up road blocks everywhere while they had a practice military parade.

I can guess that Paul must be getting into more every passing day. You know it's only been 8 days since I left and already I find myself thinking (or trying to think) of how everyone acted and looked. I'm really anxious to hear from you, but I don't expect I'll get any mail until I get to Da Nang since my orders have been changed.

I'll have to write to Mom today, as I haven't done that yet. You take care and let me hear from you often. I love you more than I can ever say. Be sweet, my love.

Leo

Opps!   I don't know where I put that clipping about Savery.

Tan Son Nhut
3 Nov 65

My Darling,

Sometimes one has to wonder if anyone knows what's going on. Here I've been sitting for a week and they still don't have me scheduled out for a trip. A couple of guys I've come here with just left this evening for Bien Hua. After two flight cancellations they finally went by bus. Bien Hua is only 26 miles the other side of Saigon, so you can imagine what it'll be like trying to get me within 41 miles of the North Vietnamese border.

There's just nothing to do but swelter. Sleep is not the best here either. We're in a transient area and our building has 76 bunks. When I first got here there were but 3 of us in this building. They've been coming and going at all hours ever since. I mention this now because as I write another bunch is coming in.

The nights are not the most comfortable. Besides being so humid, we sit right next to the ramp and runway and they're going all the time. Worse is the alert pad right near by. When they start and pull out with those F-105's there's one heck of a blast. They're usually off before dawn every morning. I guess just about every morning I awoke sometime before 5. After that, it's just twisting and turning until I finally roll out. There's no getting away from a daily shower so I usually shave at night, too, so as to avoid the mob in the morning.

There were a couple of blasts in rapid succession this morning and I learned later today that the VC had blown some building about 400 yards from the main gate. I don't know what kind of a place it was, but obviously it went off prematurely and no one was injured.

I was talking to a TSgt down here from Da Nang and he said in all likelihood we'd be in tents when we first got up there. They're supposed to be doing considerable building all over.

Good night, my love. I think of you constantly and miss you more with each passing day. The nights get particularly bad when I just lay here and think. Be sweet, my happiness,

Your Leo

5 Nov 65

Hi Sweet,

Just a quicky note 'cause I want to get this off to you as soon as possible.

Got a few more dollars from them but still have some coming which I can't draw until I get to Danang. Leaving Monday, 8 Nov, at about 1500. Ever since I got here no mail for me. It's all (if any) being forwarded to Danang.

Make sure any future mail to me is addressed as on this envelope.

Love you loads & loads,
Your Leo

Tan Son Nhut
6 Nov 65

Hi Sweetheart,

This is your old grizzly husband, now 37. "Happy birthday to me; happy birthday to me; happy birthday to meeeee, happy birthday to me!"

I took my first ride into town today and it was more like a thrill ride at an amusement park. It's only about 4 – 5 miles into Saigon, but the trip takes over an hour one-way. The Navy runs the main BX there and I wanted to see what they had. They're quite complete, even having tailors from Hong Kong. You select the material and they fix it up. I'd like to pick up a camera while I'm in this country since it has to be seen to be believed. They have a large variety of cameras – mostly Japanese. Maybe after my pay gets squared away, I'll be able to swing one. I don't know whether it would be better to get one for snapshots or an automatic movie camera.

Anyhow, I never saw so many bodies in my life. The streets, which are not the widest to start with, are full of taxis and military vehicles, with a sprinkling of private cars, trucks and busses. Remember now, they're full of these vehicles. Now, on top of that, add thousands of motorcycles and motorscooters and tens of thousands of bicycles and you get an idea of the congestion. It gets to be survival of the fittest, particularly at intersections. Many of the bikes are pedicabs – like a buggy with a bicycle pushing it. Though I rode this Navy bus, you can get a cab outside the main gate and take this ride for about 20 piastres (18 cents). With taking the bus in, visiting the BX, and then riding back, the morning was shot.

Well, I don't have too much longer in this place. I'll sure be glad to be able to empty my duffel bag at last. They just keep pouring into this place. It seems they're coming in much faster than they're leaving.

This afternoon I went out the main gate with a couple guys here. They wanted to get themselves one of those Aussie campaign hats. I ended up doing most of the transaction since the shop owner spoke French. He ended up showing me the pictures of his eight kids. He spoke quite good French. He claims to have spent four years in the French military and was one of those at Dien Bien Phu where the French met that disastrous defeat in 1954.

These are quite small people. Very few are much taller than I, and few less are as heavy. The women are real slim, generally. You wonder what holds them together. Downtown is pretty much like any oriental city, particularly off the main streets. It seems everyone and his uncle sets up his own shop on the sidewalk.

As I can figure now, NCOs living in Saigon will be drawing about $160 more than I will per month and won't be as much under the gun. Generally, my pay should be

Base pay	$409
Quarters	114
Combat Pay	65
Family Separation	30
Overseas Pay	22
Clothing Allowance	6
Income Tax (nopay)	20
Rations	77
Total	$ 743

Out of that will come social security and any allotments. I should be able to get a clearer breakdown once I get to Da Nang.

Had a bad night last night. Woke up at 3:45 and couldn't get back to sleep. It's a good thing I had hit the sack about 8:30. I laid there for a while, then got up and had some coffee. There's a hut back here used as a snack bar and its open 24-hours a day. I laid back down and could do nothing but think of you and the kids the rest of the time. I miss you all so terribly much. One thing I do know for sure, nothing short of an all-out war will ever separate us again. I often think of what a wonderful thing it was to have met you and loved you. I'll never stop loving you, my darling. Be sweet and give all the kids a big sugar for me.

Your loving husband,
Leo

DA NANG AIR BASE
12 Nov 65

My Darling,

It must seem like quite some time since I last wrote. The rat race seems to be over, at least that part of waiting around for things to get done.

To go back to Saigon, I was scheduled to depart on a flight at 1600 Monday, 8 November. I got out to the terminal around 1300 and began my wait. There were 38 of us, plus cargo, scheduled for this C-130. That's the aircraft whose tail end sticks up and the back opens up. Anyhow, they posted the board to show that the plane hadn't arrived yet, that it was delayed at Da Nang by bad weather. Well, we waited and waited until around 8 P.M. when they said they would give us another aircraft. Finally, at 9:30 we all got on a bus to go out to the aircraft. We got there and there was no one around and everything was dark. They had decided that our destination was still weathered in and we couldn't land anyhow.

Back to the terminal we went. They told us we could come back the next day and either get a new booking, which would mean about 4 or 5 days more at Tan Son Nhut, or we could come in and put our name on the standby list, in which case it would be a hit-or-miss proposition. What made it so bad was that everybody flies out of there – Army, Navy, Marines, Air Force, Australians, Vietnamese, Koreans, etc. Now, we couldn't do this until the next day and they wouldn't open the terminal until 5 A.M. The standby list is good for that day only. If you're unsuccessful you must go thru the same routine each day, plus which it's on a first come, first served basis.

Well, by the time I got back to the transient area and checked out some bedding it was almost midnight. Having been there some 12 days already, I had decided to take my chances and try to get out as soon as I could. At 4 A.M. I was up-and-at-em and headed for the terminal. Got my name on the list (12th) and continued playing the waiting game. There were four flights out at 0730, 1330, 1345 and 1600. At about 3 P.M. I was called and placed on the 1600 flight. Naturally it was late in coming in and we finally got airborne at 9:30 that night. We stopped at Qui Nhon for about 30-40 minutes, at Pleiku only to discharge passengers and then on to Da Nang, arriving here at 11 P.M.

I called for transportation and was picked up by a couple guys from the Comm Center who were going for midnight chow. So I went to chow with them. In the interim, one of them got the FSgt[7] up and he came over and got me fixed up for the night. I'm now living in a tent but the First Shirt said tomorrow (Saturday) he'd have me in a barracks. There are tents here between just about every building.

The Sq Commander (Maj Leary) just got here too. There are some 200 people in the outfit, with more coming. I swear I haven't seen so many TSgt's & above as there are in Vietnam. I think they're all here! My boss is the Chief of Maintenance, Lt. Carol. He seems to be a go getter a la Lt Murphy and not like Lt W__.

As you might know, I'll not be near any crypto equipment. Shades of Ellsworth, they haven't got a Maintenance Control other than in name so I was put in charge. I've got 3 Staffs, 1-A1C and 1-A2C. I've only been at it 2 days but it looks like I'll be getting some backing. I told him if he wanted it to remain only a recording and coordinating agency we could run it the way it was; but if he wanted to control maintenance I had to have more people, more room, more this and more that. He seems all for it. As a matter of fact, he was talking to the Seabees ten minutes later trying to get them to put up another Quonset for us.

---

[7] First Sergeant, informally called the "First Shirt" or "Shirt". The First Sergeant is the senior enlisted member with the designated responsibility for the morale, welfare and conduct of the enlisted men in the squadron.

This is a Vietnamese base and plenty of activity. The artillery is booming away right now and fighters are going hunting. Most of the air strikes from here are directed to North Vietnam. Marine and VN guards are all over the place and one of the first things they told us is not to go walking around outside the compound at night if you want to stay for a full tour. Going out after dark and before dawn has to be by vehicle.

Lo & behold, before departing Tan Son Nhut I saw somebody else I know and I was surprised. Who do I see standing there in spankin new fatigues and looking lost but TSgt Costello from Personnel Assignments @ Ellsworth? He is the one we had to see when we got assignments and the one I called twice from Jacksboro. I remembered then that the second time I called he wasn't in and the Airman told me he was processing. I had assumed he was processing for discharge & reenlistment and had no idea the he too had been caught. He told me they also got CMSgt Renfro, the Division Sergeant Major and many others from Ellsworth. I had also seen an article in the Tan Son Nhut base paper about Sgt Loy who used to be in the medics at EAFB. He flies air rescue in choppers. The article said that 2 of the 4 who had the job before him had been killed in action and on his first mission the wounded man he was carrying to the chopper was killed by the VC before he got him aboard. I didn't know the guy but I had heard his name mentioned at Ellsworth.

Hon, it's getting a bit late now so I'll cut this off in order to get it on the way but will write again tomorrow. I can't tell you how wonderful it was hearing from you. When I got here, 3 letters were waiting, postmarked the 29th & 31st Oct & 5th Nov. The next mail had one marked 27 Oct and two today were 2 Nov and 8 Nov. Now that they're addressed to the 1972nd they should be getting here better. The one dated 8 Nov got here in 3 days since today is the 12th and one day was lost in crossing the international date line.

As nice as letters are, and though I wouldn't want to be without them, they make me miss you and the kids all the more. Be sweet, my love, and remember that I love you more than I can ever say. Tell Steph and Lanis I'll write to them real soon (Bryan too!).

Your Leo

Da Nang
Sunday, 14 Nov 65

My darling,

I missed again; I intended writing last night but ended up falling asleep shortly after eight and didn't wake up until almost 10 o'clock this morning. Our regular duty days are for 10 hours, Monday thru Friday, plus Saturday morning. Saturday afternoon everybody had to work in a big equipment moving program. We've got all this stuff scattered about in the area and it all had to be straightened out. The sweat nearly poured so that by the time we quit I was dead. I could feel all those long-quiet muscles throbbing.

When processing in, I was interviewed by the Chaplain and he nearly flipped when I told him I had done some commentating. He's Father Sinclair, and he's leaving next week. His replacement, Father Roberts, got here about the same time I did, but I haven't met him yet. I went to Mass at 1700 tonight, and was I surprised. They do it entirely different here, even to the point where anyone going to communion puts a host in the ciborium as he enters. Also, the whole congregation sings most of the Mass. Particularly impressive is that all sing – and loud. Maybe it's just that there are only men so they don't feel as self-conscious. Really though, it comes out pretty good.

I was just going over your letter again to see if there were any question you asked that needed answering. Some I may have answered before you asked, so you maybe reading things for the second time.

First off, everyone I have shown that clipping to (about the Saigon Warriors) really got their laughs. So much of it is true, though I'm afraid as always points are stretched a bit. I'm afraid they won't have too much in that vein to write about if they visit Da Nang.

I think it's a good idea to ask Doug & Sybil to be godparents. I know they would love to be, even though I'm afraid Sybil might get too excited, even by proxy!

While I think of it, and since in one of your letters you mentioned the Bishops, one of the guys I've been hanging around with here, Sgt Grenier, is a graduate of the school in Keasler Air Force Base. He was stationed at March AFB before getting shipped here. He said he guessed that business of a controlled tour at some stateside base didn't get very far. He's from New Hampshire. Anyhow, Bob could end up here as he feared.

You mention not seeing Da Nang on a map. They usually have one in the Stars & Strips showing where the latest major actions took place. I'll have to enclose one with this note.

Sgt Coker knows he'll go to Lackland because it's a special assignment (instructor duty) and is handled by different procedures. We forecast after we've been here 5 months, which means March for me. You can ask for two overseas areas (consecutive tours overseas are given preference, if available), two bases, one state and two geographical areas (northeast, southeast, etc.) I figured on asking for Ellsworth & Minot!

Today I moved from a tent into the barracks, and I don't know if I'm any better off or not. I'm on top of a double bunk, and there are four of us in an area approximately 12 x 12. Cramped, to say the least. The nights are fairly nice here, but the days are hot & humid. Unlike what the Saigon Warriors have in line of BX, ours doesn't have much of anything. One of the guys is going to Saigon next week and he's getting orders from everybody. He's going to get me some towels, I only brought 4 and taking a shower every night uses them up pretty quick like. Techs & above have to eat at the NCO club here also. Their food has been quite good, and reasonable, as we can make a little extra on the deal which carries us through for drinks & snacks. The club isn't the fanciest, but it works out o.k. They're enlarging it somewhat now.

One thing I want to mention is to make sure you mention to me when you get any money from me. In your letter of 4 Nov you said you received some. I also sent $240 on 5 Nov and I want to make sure it gets there. The last letter from you was written the 8th, so I'm sure you wouldn't have it by then.

There's really not too much that you could send me other than anything homemade. There is one thing you could include in any package, and that's Air Mail envelopes. They're pretty hard to come by. Sgt Grenier's wife sent him a package and he was going around shaking his head. He had told her of the shortage of vegetable and fruit here and she sent him half a bushel of McIntosh apples, a couple cabbages & some carrots! We've been eating! As a matter of fact, I've just been eating an apple. Postage cost her $18. Ridiculous.

You mention Mineral Wells not stocking Celontin for Karen. I wonder if they would have it at Carswell; or maybe you could get some from Sheppard when you go there.

Tell Bryan I was glad to hear he took his shot like a soldier. He must really be getting to be a big boy. Daddy took another shot here—but I had to take it in the bottom like a baby! We have to take Gamma Globulin for protection against hepatitis. Shots have to be taken every 4 months and the dosage is ½ cc for every 10 lbs of weight. That meant 8 ½ cc for old lard-butt – half in each cheek! Let me tell you that's a lot of medicine and a mighty big needle. We also take a pill each week for malaria.

They just opened the finance section here of Da Nang in a tent. I'll be checking them out Monday or Tuesday. They didn't get any paperwork until Friday, so probably not much has been done. I'll get some more money to you as soon as I can. Finance here will mail any amount we designate directly, so I may do that instead of an allotment. The allotment may not start until 1 Jan or 1 Feb, and I'll have the same drill to go through to stop it. I'll see about that real soon. I should be able to send somewhere around $600 a month, starting 1 Dec.

Goodnight, my love. I'll be going to bed now and will surely miss snuggling up to you, under the pretense of keeping you warm. I love you, love you, love you, my darling. Sweet dreams and may God watch over you all ever so closely,

                                                          Your Leo

Da Nang
16 Nov 65

My Darling,

It's so nice to get another letter from you. This one took a little long (it was postmarked the 10th) and was the one in which you included Mom's letter.

I checked with Finance today and got a little money (my travel pay). The last I had sent you ($240) was my regular base pay up to that time. We only get paid here once a month, so I will send you $850 on the 1st of December. This includes my regular pay plus some back combat pay, quarters allowance, etc. Subsequently, you should get at least $500 per month. I hope to be sending $540 or so, but I really can't gauge it right this minute until I see what it'll cost me here since I have to buy my own meals. Laundry is something else I understand has gone up here, though I don't think it's too bad. The BX – or what we call a BX has prices just as high if not higher than in the states on regular necessities. The Navy owns it but the Army – AF Exchange Service is supposed to take it over 26 December. Thereafter, merchandise will be brought directly here. Right now it goes to Saigon, then here, and I guess quite a bit of the better stuff is being shortstopped for the Saigon Warriors.

Let me know in your next letter whether or not you want me to make out an allotment. It wouldn't start until 1 February and then I wouldn't be able to allot but about $475, the rest I've have to send you. I heard Finance would mail any amount home we wanted, but I was advised against it. The MPO has to be made out here and sent to Tan Son Nhut (3-5 days delay) since only Tan Son Nhut can make out checks. Then, Tan Son Nhut would take 3-5 days more to get them out. If you want me to make out the allotment, I'll start it in February and make the last check for 1 October. Come to think of it, that's probably the best thing to do; otherwise, if I somehow was incapacitated you would still be getting the allotment.

Saw somebody else from Ellsworth yesterday. Walked into the club for lunch and saw TSgt John Hill from 8214. He is in Guam and spends one month there and two here, on and off. He said he expected Sgt Immel in at Guam the day he left. He didn't know Kirchgasler, I guess, or didn't remember him. Since he's on an unaccompanied tour to Guam, he has an 18 month stretch. However, for TDY to Vietnam he gets one month taken off for every two months he spends here. He's due to go back in February or March. Last night, I was sitting in front of the barracks with Grenier and John came over. He had just received his stateside assignment and he was all discouraged. Still being in SAC, he had to ask for six SAC bases. He requested Barksdale, Carswell, Blythville and 3 other southern bases. His assignments: Westover. He had never been anywhere north outside of Ellsworth. He didn't feel quite so bad by the time he left.

Forgot to mention another thing I did when I got here—got my hair cut down! Haircuts are 25¢. It sure feels better in this climate. It'll grow back by the time my tour is up—maybe. Also weighted myself yesterday and lost 6 lbs, but I feel pretty good. Haven't missed a shower each night though, with this clammy weather. It's been particularly bad today since it rained on and off all morning. When it rains, let me tell you it pours. And then, like someone shutting the faucet, it'll quit. So out you go and some so-and-so will turn the faucet on full blast again.

Poor Mom, she worries so much about everything. I would say keep the $100 and spend it as you see fit. I'm sure it gives her a thrill to send it, and she might feel hurt if we didn't accept it. I'll be keeping this letter open until I get to the post office in the morning and will send a money order for $40 to help until I can draw my pay on 1 December.

My shop is about ¼ mile from here and transportation is by footmobile. It's not bad mornings and evenings, but coming and returning from lunch is a chore in this heat. Fatigues are not the coolest clothes, either.

Boy, I've been writing (re-writing) just about every instruction they've got here and adding a few. The Lt seems to be behind me – so far. Now, if I can just keep him buffaloed for 11 more months!

Nothing else is news but shop stuff, honeybunch, so we'll quit for now. I wish so much I could be with you all; not only to hold you close and hug you, but to help you with all the things you must take care of by yourself. One thing for sure – "Rots of ruck" to them if they ever want to separate us again. Good night, my dearest, I love you so very much.

Your Leo

Da Nang
18 Nov 65

My Dearest,

I know I won't get this finished now as I'm on my lunch break, but I just received another letter from you and when I do I want so much to talk to you and see you that I immediately do the next best thing, which is writing.

Haven't heard from Bob as of yet so I don't know how much luck Marie has had in getting him to put that letter in an envelope like she said she would. Even so, they probably have my old address so it would take longer to get here. My mail now comes direct to Da Nang, so service is a bit better. Likewise, outgoing mail used to go to Tan Son Nhut first but now it goes from here to Okinawa and then to the states. The letter I got today took 4 days. 4-5 days seems about average.

You say Marie mentioned Commendation Medals. Actually, what happened was that Schooley prepared his and Bob's in draft form before he left. I then got them fixed up and on their way after they had departed. I then took care of Hancock when he left. The last one I did was on Lewis. If I hadn't taken care of the last two, no one else would have. Just before my leaving, as a matter of fact, the day I got the word, Dorrough had moved down to the Chief of Maintenance with me. When I checked out he said he would write one up on me and see that it got out. Haven't heard anything yet, but it usually takes some time.

I think when I do get the chance (and enough money) I'll buy a good movie camera. That would be better here, especially in viewing the terrain and the people. Then I could send the film off for development with your return address. Likewise, it would be nice if you get an instamatic. I enjoyed the girls' school pictures and I know there'll be many changes in them all before I get back. When you do send some, don't forget yourself (and keep your eyes open!). The only ones I have of you now date back to Korea and Holy Cross!

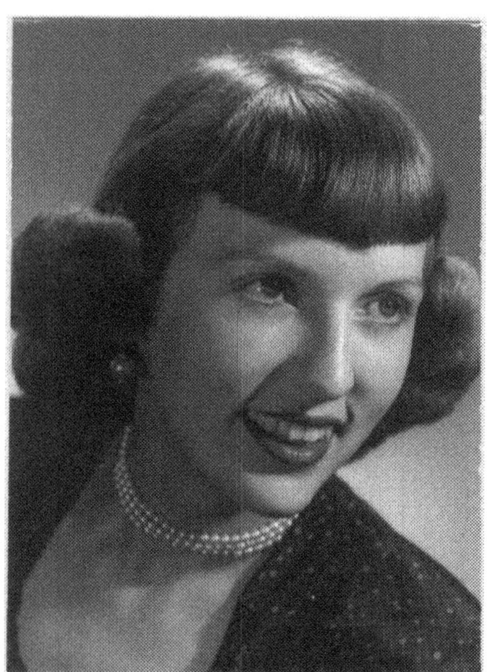

Don Leta around the time of Korea

I wrote to Mom again yesterday and also dropped a few words to the people back at Ellsworth. Haven't heard from Mom, other than the letter you forwarded.

Back to taking pictures again, I don't know when I'll get back to Saigon. It may on business. I would like to get some pictures there however, since no place can be quite like it. I haven't seen the city of Da Nang yet, so I can't compare. Da Nang is the second largest city in the RVN. I might get into town some day.

After we've been here 4 months, we can put in for R&R. We can either go in country, the Philippians, Okinawa, Bangkok, or Hong Kong. If I could afford it, I'd like to get to Hong Kong, or as second choice, Bangkok. I could probably get some good clothes cheap in HK.

Time to go back to the pits. It's a hot walk. We work out of tents and Quonset type buildings. See you later.

Made it through the rest of the day without much excitement. As a matter of fact, I didn't get much done at all this afternoon. There was quite a bit of artillery being fired up into the hills shortly after supper. As long as it's "outgoing mail" they can keep it up as long as they wish.

Of late here, it's been pouring late at night and then on and off in the morning. It has cleared by noon but then you can imagine how hot and sultry it gets. I hope to get up to Marble Mountain tomorrow to visit the transmitter sites we have up there. They say you can see quite a bit when it's clear and then you realize how many rivers and waterways crisscross this terrain.

I don't know if I mentioned it before, but make sure that if you have to get a hold of me in an emergency to contact the Red Cross first thing. That's the quickest way to get word here. You might get their number for quick reference and also let your folks know about it.

Good night, my love. Miss you terribly and think of you always,

Your Leo

20 Nov 65

My Dear Lanis,
You've probably been thinking that I would never be getting around to writing to you. Well, you see, I finally made it.

I'm sending you two Vietnamese coins like I sent Stephanie. After I wrote to her, however, I realized I made a mistake. The small coin (1 Dong) is worth almost 1¢ in American money, not 12¢ like I told Steph. It takes 118 of them to make one of our dollars.

I wish I already had a camera so you could see what the people look like and what the country is like over here. I'll be sending movies home. I can look out back of where I live and see the Vietnamese kids playing almost all the time. There's one thing that you'll notice here, and it can be seen in most countries like this, and that's the bigger kids taking care of the little ones. Over here it's natural for them to do this, and it reminds me of the fuss sometimes when we try to do it in the States.

Lanis

I hope you're still doing as well in school as when I left. I understand you all are about ready for tests again. Many of the children here don't go to school, and may never get to go. There are a lot of Americans that have classes for the Vietnamese, especially to teach them to speak English. The biggest thing holding back these people is that they don't have education. Those who are able to go to school will get all the jobs and run the government, but there are not enough of them. Those who have no schooling have to work hard and they make about 60 piastres (Vietnamese dollars) a day. In our money, that's just about 50¢.

Sugar bun, you know what I've told your sister, and I mean it for you too. I hope you will help your mother all you can at home. The first thing is to obey and do what you know you should do. After that, helping take care of your brothers and doing other jobs around the house, without a big fuss, will be lots of help. Everyone needs to do some playing – but there are other things which must be done first. There are people here who are 20 years old and seldom have had the chance to play. They've known nothing but war – their houses burned, bombs falling, their families and friends killed. The people of the United States talk a lot, but they can never really know how lucky they are until they come to places like this and see how people live.

I hope you'll have a chance to write me pretty soon, as I would like to hear how you're doing. You be a sweet girl now and help your mommy all you can at home. I love you very much and sure hope this year goes by fast so we can all be together again. You say some prayers for us all.

Your Daddy

20 Nov 65

Hi Skinhead,

I figured it was about time that I wrote a letter to the big boy of the house. Mommy tells me that you've been a pretty good boy most of the time. I write to you because you're pretty big, but Paul will have to wait until he learns to talk.

Since you haven't seen me for a long time, here's a picture of me so you'll see what I look like now:

Now, were fighting some bad guys over here and I saw a couple of them the other day so I took their picture. Here's

what they look like:

Really, though, there's a PW camp here.

I hope you've been a good boy with your brother and that you've been helping to take care of him. He's just little you know, and so we have to watch him pretty close so he doesn't get into trouble.

I'm putting some money in here for you. This is the kind of nickels we use in Vietnam. You tell your Mommy that means she has to buy you a candy bar next time she goes to the store.

I'm very glad to hear that you've started brushing your teeth and drinking plain milk. You keep being a good boy and say a prayer for me.

I love you,
Your Dad

Bryan – also called "Skinhead"

21 Nov 65

My Dearest Don Leta,

It was my intention to write last night since I had received a letter from you, but it ended up being such a hectic evening with communications troubles that it went by the boards.

First off, around 5 o'clock we lost all circuits in a cable. Come to find out the Marines had laid a string of explosives to dig a channel for drainage and even though it was 30-40 feet from our lines, the shock snapped them. To top it off, it was really pouring. It's now more than 24 hours later and it hasn't hardly stopped. We must have gotten 15-20 inches. People were out digging up the cable to lay a temporary throw around it and they're still at it. On top of that, some of our radar gear went out and a plane crashed landed in the storm while coming in.

You asked about living conditions here, so I've enclosed a rough sketch of the area. Everything is enclosed in the cantonment area, with exception of the PX which is out the main gate, about ½ mile away. It's between us and a Marine battalion.

There's really not too much else of interest to mention today. Things have been kind of gloomy with all the rain. Of course there's more to the cantonment area, more barracks and tents, but really it's not too big. I would say about the size of 3 football fields. Also, outside each building or group of tents are sandbagged bunkers where we take cover if necessary. Our gear is hung ready from the end of the bunk.

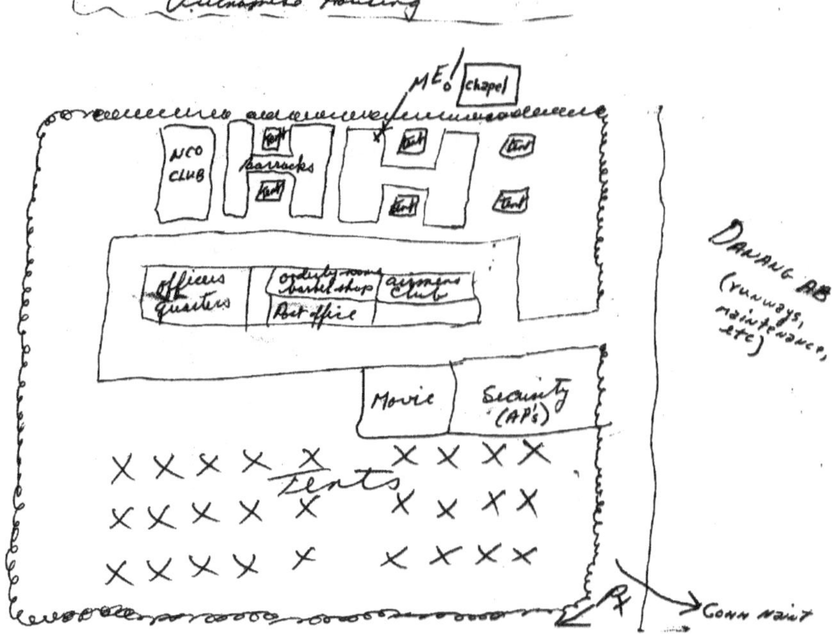

I couldn't sleep around 4:30 Friday night. There were mortars being fired and I could hear small arms fire and automatic weapons. I stood out the back door and could see flares falling where the firing was coming from. They were four or five miles away.

One of the surprising things here is the lack of current news. Everything we get is at least a day old, more often two. We get the Stars & Stripes, when it gets here, or the Saigon Post, a Vietnamese paper. It's published in Saigon, so we never get it until the next day.

We have Sunday mail delivery and today I got a letter from Mom. She didn't say too much other than she had said in her letter to you. She also wanted to know if there was anything she could send me. Really there's nothing unless it's home baked stuff. I did mention to you that when you send anything to include airmail envelopes, didn't I? Now I can't remember. I had brought some from Tan Son Nhut and it's a good thing because they haven't had any here since I arrived. Isn't it ridiculous? I can't get that at the PX, but their shelves are loaded with civilian sox, thermos inserts (no thermos), Fasteeth, Polident, and brass trays!

By the time you get this I will probably have my first month done—eleven to go. I'll sure be glad when the World Series comes around!

Sgt Grenier went up to Monkey Mountain tonight. We have some new equipment half way up and he took some of his troops up there in the pouring rain yesterday. In the early hours of the morning they called him. They had made their way back to the base of the mountain where tents are set up. Grenier said he had all sorts of confusing reports of the generators going out and they thought they were getting sniper fire, that they could see the tracers. He took a couple more men and went up there to spend the night.

It's 5 minutes past lights out, so I'll quit for now, my sweet, I love you, love you, love you, my darling.

Your Leo

23 Nov 65

My Dearest Don Leta,

A batch of mail came in today, so I thought I might be getting a letter from someone but no luck.

I had meant to tell you in my last letter that the allotment I made out starts 1 December (with you getting the first check in January). The amount will be $400 in as much as I'm restricted on the amount of money I can have out in allotments (can't include subsistence, combat pay, etc.) That should be o.k. to take care of you until I can mail money orders. I should be able to send at least another $100 each month, which should get to you about the 4th or 5th of each month. Also I can't quite agree with what Finance says I should draw, so I'm going to see them again this afternoon.

I'm at work right now. I came back from chow a bit early hoping to catch the re-broadcast of the Clay-Patterson fight. The way the last few championships fight have been, I'll miss it all if I'm two minutes late.

The sun is out today, the first time since Thursday. It had been raining from Friday until sometime last night. Going to chow yesterday morning entailed walking in about a foot of water. The front part of the club (inside) had about 6 inches of water. Real nice without boot or overshoes. It's a new experience to eat French toast and drink coffee with your feet in water!

Last night I went to the movies, the first since I arrived at Da Nang. Charles Boyer, Rock Hudson & Leslie Caron were playing in "A Very Special Favor". It was good for a few laughs. Most of the time I've just been sitting out front gabbing or in the sack reading, except for the first night when I went to the club, and last Friday which was free steak night at the club. They have free steak every other Friday. A couple of us usually go to the club around 7 o'clock and have coffee (free coffee at the time), and wait for the club card drawing. The first night they call one card number for $5. If nobody claims it, the next night they call up to 2 numbers for $10, etc., until someone's number is called who is present, and the next night they start over again.

24 Nov 65

Wouldn't you know it; I had to go out just before fight time and didn't get back 'till midway in the 11ᵗʰ round. As it was, I caught the 12ᵗʰ and final round, so I can't say I missed the fight.

I wanted to finish this letter last night but I got called out and had to go to work. It was almost ten when I got back and by the time I had my shower that was it.

Nothing new and exciting happened today either. I laid down on the sack and was about to go for supper at 6:45 when Sgt Hill came in. He returned the sewing kit he borrowed from me when he went to the NCO academy. In it was still a dime a guy who had used a button or something (at the academy) had put in there. John also told me he had just received word that he made Master! I can just imagine how this would go over with the Ellsworth troops. He only has 2 ½ years in grade.

A whole bunch of cookies came in from the states today and were distributed to each squadron. They were all in coffee cans. Our batch in maintenance came from some school in Warren, Pa. Some of them had notes in them from the kids who sent them. There was one in the can we had in our section, including a school picture of the girl. Her name is Lucinda and she looks to be about 12 or 13.

Anyone who got a note is supposed to write them a thank you note. I though it was real cute that she started the letter "Hi handsome (I hope)," I was telling everyone how I'm continuously amazed at such coincidences – that it should be in <u>my</u> can! The troop I've got on duty tonight is writing to her. It was probably meant for him since he's a rather good looking 6 footer – with hair! I thought I might write her a note tomorrow too – maybe send her a little souvenir like VN money. Everyone is enjoying the cookies – sampling from other sections, etc.

All for now, my sweet. You know what you can do for me – real soon – send me some pictures of you. I miss you so and would so enjoy them, especially at night when I must admit, even though surrounded by people, it gets a bit lonely. There is one thing I can't for the life of me remember if I've told you lately – I love you, love you, love you – forever.

<u>Your</u> Leo

25 Nov 65

My darling wife,

I may not be writing too much tonight since it's almost eleven and I'm yawning even as I start this. We didn't get back 'till just a while ago but I got a letter from you today so I want to write at least a few lines.

Grenier was going to Monkey Mountain with some mail and supplies for 4 of his troops up there so I rode shotgun for him. They're installing a new radio relay station half way up the hill and his troops have to guard it since there are not enough AP's and the Marines wouldn't be able to do it. They first went up there during the big rains last weekend and the first night I guess they shot at everything in sight. Grenier went up himself for a couple nights because he figured they were so jittery they'd probably end up shooting each other. The jungle around there is real thick. I don't think you could walk in 5 feet without having to cut your way thru. He said the last night the mosquitoes liked to kill him. His lips were swollen from mosquito bites and lots kept flying around his head. What he figures they thought they saw were probably monkeys, since they're all over the mountain.

Your telling me of the things the kids have been doing sure makes me miss them. The biggest thing, of course, is Paul's antics since this is all new stuff for him. I lay here and think that when I get back the girls will be going on 13, 11 and 10, Bryan will be 5 and Paul 2, with yet another I'll not have seen. That's not so bad, but I'll be almost 38! One good thing—you'll still be 29!

I got a letter from Chippy also today. He really didn't say a heck of a lot. He sent pictures of David and Paul that I thought were real cute. I think Paul looks just like Chip. Since they didn't ask for them back, thought I'd send them on to you and you can return them in a later letter.

You asked a couple questions. First, about the allotment, I will stop it in October; that is to say, October will be the last month that they'll take money from my pay. This money is the allotment check that you'll receive in November. Secondly, my month of return will be October, regardless of when I got

Uncle Chippy and Auntie Florence, cousins David, Marianne and Paul in Rhode Island

over here or to work. Overseas time starts and stops with your departure and arrival on the mainland. Theoretically, I could come back anytime in October, but usually they keep it pretty close to the date you left – which in my case is 26 October.

Also, I do draw an extra allowance for my meals (like the Warriors), but I do not get the cost of living allowance techs & above get in Saigon. Here we live on base. At Tan Son Nhut, Techs and above either live in hotels or on the economy (a bunch of them get together and rent a place) – real rough – and they get paid extra for it. Now quite often people think almost everything is happening in Saigon, but that's far from fact. The thing is that all dispatches come out of Saigon (they have the only 2 papers in the Republic of VN), and everything, almost, is reported in relation to that area. You note sometimes where it says this or that happened "30 miles north of Saigon", "180 miles northeast of Saigon", or "300 miles northeast of Saigon". Really, they're getting up into this territory.

We have our own private way of thinking of some of those people back there. Now I'm straying. I was talking to you about allowances. My total pay now is $640 per month, of which I allotted $400 and will send you a minimum of $100 by money order. I figure my chow at costing between $2.50 & $3.00 a day. Next month I'll get $11 raise (longevity). I figured on holding back a little extra for getting things like a camera and film, unless you let me know you really need it. Towards the end of the month, I'll send you any extra I may have. Like now, with payday Tuesday, I've got a little extra which I'll send along shortly.

I'm going up to Monkey Mountain with Sgt Grenier this weekend – probably Saturday afternoon. It's been pouring again and those troops of his have to stand guard in the rain. They've built themselves a bunker with sandbags, so were going to lug some materials to put a roof over their heads. It won't be completely enclosed since they have to see and be able to fire out of it, but it will at least keep the worst of it off their heads.

Gee, how I wish I was back with you, honeybunch. I want so much to hold you close to me. Not only that, but what probably bothers me more than anything is that I can't be there to help you with anything – the house, the yard, the kids. Even at that, I feel like when I get back I'm just going to want to sit on the couch with you next to me (<u>real</u> close) and all the kids around and just stay there for about 48 hours! You've made me so very happy, my darling, and how I've enjoyed and relished these years with you. I'm ready to come back for another 5 years or so of the same. I just could go on and on, my love, trying my best to in some way tell you how much I love you, how terribly much I miss you, and what you've meant and still mean to me, but regardless of which way I turn it or try to say it, it always comes out that my Don Leta is really and truly My Happiness.

Your Leo

28 Nov 65

My darling,

I have two letters from you to answer today. The one you wrote 18 Nov didn't get here until yesterday. It was the one with Karen's letter enclosed. It got mis-sent to Guam. I also heard from Bob Bishop. His letter had my old address and it took 5 days to get to Tan Son Nhut, and another 7 days to get to Da Nang! Real good service out of those warriors.

There wasn't time to write last night. Friday night the troops on Monkey Mountain shot up the place. They called in the strike team from the base of the mountain and a Lt. Col. went up there with about 20 men. They sprayed the whole jungle with every weapon they had. The top of the mountain has the Da Nang Tropo site, a big relay with huge antennas through which all our circuits go. Everybody working there lives in a cantonment area at the base of the mountain. Both these areas are fenced and guarded. About half way up the mountain is where all this trouble has been. There we're installing a radio relay connecting us with Thailand. A couple giant parabolic antennas have been set up. There are a couple army vans with relay equipment and some AF vans with the new gear. Civilian contractors are doing the installation, but the equipment is manned by the Army and AF. The Army stuff is only there until our gear is complete. There's no sweat in the daytime, but at night there's only 2 Army troops in their van and one airman in the AF vans. Since I told you before we couldn't get guards, our own radio relay people have to do the guard work.

The old man was quite perturbed when he heard of all the shooting going on, and no one has hit anything yet. I'm sure the boys are so shook up that they're firing at shadows. We've heard stories from them about seeing people up there, monkeys with orange faces (probably baboons), apes up to 200 lbs and mountain lions. I expected elephants, too! Anyhow, Saturday night Grenier and I went up and sent all but the operators down to base camp. We had some field phones connected to the vans where we could get word to the operators. We settled down in the sandbagged bunker with our M-16's and everybody's ammo, looking like a couple of Mauldin's G.I. Joe characters. It was a raw rainy night as usual and we were wearing field jackets. Over that Grenier had a poncho and I had foul weather pants and top. With our hoods up and steel helmets on we had to laugh at each other as we settled down to wait.

It was about 6 PM by then and getting dark rapidly. We had spotted the trails through the jungles but in no time they were gone and we only had a general direction. The rest of it is so thick no one could possibly come through it. Throughout the night as flares were fired at Da Nang East or near the base of the mountain we'd catch some of the light and be able to scan the area quickly. Periodically, the Marines were firing mortars somewhere on the mountain. After it got real dark, Grenier and I took turns moving about the area so we could see what a body looked like. I swear it was so dark and the clouds hung so low that we couldn't make out a body more than 15-20 yards. We had told the operators not to come out of their vans unless we told them to evacuate 'cause anything moving out there was fair game. It seems that every time a mortar went off or flares lit the area this colored boy in the Army van would call us and want to know what was going on. He was still thinking of the previous night's shooting. We sat there all night and didn't see a thing. Oh, if we wanted to, we could of imagined all sorts of things. Foliage on trees moving in the wind, jungle noises, the tricks your eyes can play on you at night—all can make one jittery.

We had to show these kids that they were their own greatest enemy. In the week they had been there, they've fired over 4,000 rounds and have never been fired upon in return. We were either not going to shoot wild or get something for our efforts. Though we didn't see anything, they have previously picked up suspected VC in that area. I think this may have settled them down somewhat.

We were picked up at daybreak and came back to base. It was 9:30 by the time we breakfasted and showered. After being up 26 hours or so, I was ready for the sack. I woke up in time to make Mass at 1700.

I'm glad to see the girls did so well in 6-week tests. Karen amazed me with the 92 in math, even though I must say I was surprised at her low English grade. I should say Lanis & Steph are doing well, with one of them narrating the class play and the other president of her class. That's pretty good for new kids in school. I don't know, maybe so much homework hurts rather than helps Karen. I'm a strong believer that you can get saturated by too much to the point where really you're only spinning your wheels and not learning anymore.

I was happy to hear that you like the doctor who checked you. Perhaps he's right and we should strongly consider an hysterectomy. Definitely something will have to be done about your legs also. Gee, how I wish I could be with you during these next few months my sweet. I know there's no good time for us to be separated, but it seems with everything happening that this is one of the worst times. It all the more convinces me that I must take steps to see that we're not apart like this again. When this is over with, I feel we'll have done our duty and others can help carry the load.

Rain again yesterday and today, though not downpours like last week. I think the sun has been out only 3-4 hours in the past ten days. It sure makes things dreary. It's past 10 o'clock now and I've got to get ready for the sack. Good night, my love. I'll lie down again and think about you—about us—and the things we've done together. Though a poor substitute, thinking of having you in my arms again at least helps a little to soothe the pain of being parted. I love you so very, very much, Don Leta.

Your Leo

30 Nov 65

My Dearest Don Leta,

There's not too much new to report since my last letter. Things are starting to take shape at work now and as things become more familiar they're a bit easier to work with. Midway between the barracks and work we have a building housing our radio relay gear, switchboards and terminals. They're in the process of extending both ends of the building and we're supposed to move into one end when complete, probably some time in January. AIR CONDITIONED, too! Right now, where we're at is so crowded and there are so many people in and out and around that sometimes it's almost impossible to get anything done.

This morning I sent $850 in money orders which I hope you've received by now. I got paid $964. Enclosed is the check I received as close-out of my account @ Ellsworth AFB, so you can add that to the till. Don't worry, I'll be holding on to enough so that I won't have to be going looking for any.

Well, tomorrow we'll start on December. I'd rather say that's my 3rd month here, even though the third month won't start until the 26th. At least I can say I've got 10 more paydays. Also, Saturday I'll reach the 18 year mark (with an $11 raise).

Tell Bill that I wouldn't have spent Thanksgiving hunting had I been home. If he really wants something to shoot at I'll fix him up. It's open season around here year round.

I'm afraid this isn't much of a letter tonight, honeybunch, but there's just not much to report. I guess Grenier's problems were taken care of. The Marines are taking over security of the site on Monkey Mountain. Yesterday was our first day of sunshine in ages, while today was about half & half.

Good night, my darling. I love you and miss you something terrible and can hardly wait until I hold you close again. You really are the most wonderful person in the world.

Your loving
Leo

3 Dec 65

My dearest Don Leta,

A letter from you yesterday and a cake today, so things are looking better since a couple of slack days. There was no mail delivery (coming in) for a couple days. They were utilizing all available aircraft to bring in ammunition. A load of candy also came in today, sent by some organization in California. Last week, AFRS radio said the 1972nd Comm at Da Nang was going to get

Christmas packages from some church group in Nashville, Tenn. – razors, blades, shaving cream, etc. I guess they're shuttling quiet a bit of stuff over here.

You remember my telling you of Grenier and me on Monkey Mountain. Well, the Marines came up and surveyed the situation. They've put barbed wire all around, dug foxholes and built a couple more bunkers – plus, they've got 15 men on guard duty. They said that's what they decided was needed to give it proper security since it's all jungle but for the road. Kind of glad no one decided to come snooping around while just the two of us were there.

You asked if we've used the sandbagged bunkers yet – heck, I haven't even looked inside! There's always something going on in one direction or another, but nothing on the base proper. Last July was the last time the cantonment area came under fire, even though they hit the east part of the field in October. I sleep pretty good now, except for the early morning hours at which time I often wake up, turn over, and go back to sleep.

No rain today, but it got hotter – or at least muggier. It's a heck of a place to be slopping in mud and yet have the trucks go by and blow dust in your face. The mud gets real deep and gooey and then the surface dries and turns to a fine dust.

The Stars & Stripes is a daily – but the day we get it is another story! The last couple days we got them the same day they were dated, which is the exception rather than the rule.

The brass trays are the type with stands to use as tables. They have different sizes up to about 5 ft in diameter.

I got a letter from Dorrough also. He said the nomination for my AFCM (Air Force Commendation Medal) had come back because of errors and had been resubmitted. Further news from Ellsworth: Becker made MSgt, Fruits made TSgt and Fritsch made TSgt (he's the one you said was always home). I thought Ed Rossley would of made it before Becker. Spencer made it through the NCO Academy and Lex Thorp was getting ready to go. Sgt Roger's oldest boy had an unfortunate accident. It seems he was on a scouting trip in the hills and a rock either falling or pushed off a cliff fell on his foot. He lost the front 1/3 of his foot and was in Fitzsimmons Gen. Hosp. He was 14 years old. Sgt Rogers was on leave now, and understandably was quite shook up. The troops in Comm. took up a collection and sent the boy a gift.

I thought Clark went to Vandenberg, at least that's what Ann Fisher told me when I was at Tan San Nhut, but Dorrough says he came to Vietnam. Another promotion: Robozzi to Master. They're going to Maine.

That's about the news from this end, honeybunch, except for one thing – I love you. Do you know, I can honestly say that there's not been one single night since I left that I did not go to sleep without thinking of you. Oh, it'll be so nice to see you again, and talk to you, and hold you. I miss my girl so very much.

Good night, my sweet.
Your Leo

P.S. Enclosed are a couple items from S & S. I'll be sending some of these along as I write. Da Nang AB is rated the busiest combat military base in the world. It is among the top 5 airports in the world on amount of traffic handled.

5 Dec 65

My Darling Don Leta,

Your old Dad hit the mail jackpot yesterday—3 letters—one from you, one from my cousin Marie and one from Mom.

Boy, that Marie. I don't know what she thinks I'm doing here, but on the other hand, her suggestion on how to get out of here sounds like her—and don't think it hasn't been tried by a few. I'm enclosing her letter so you'll see what I mean.

Mom didn't have too much news. She said she mailed a box to me last Saturday, including a fruit cake she made. She said she put newspapers in the box to fill it and one of the papers has her cousin Beatrice's son's picture. He was getting the Purple Heart for being wounded here. He's an Army Captain.

There's one piece of the cake left and I'm saving it for myself. Sgts. Grenier & Carter and myself ate some last night. We went to the club and got paper cups of coffee and sat on what we call our "patio" and ate. This patio is a strip of cement about the height of a curbstone which runs across the front of the barracks. We can be found sitting there any night that it's not raining too hard.

I got a charge out of Bryan's reaction to the letter I wrote him. I'll have to write again. The gum is something Grenier said he did for his youngest and so I figured I'd try it.

No, I don't wear one of those "Go-to-Hell" hats. You interpreted right when I said I went with a couple guys when they bought one. They're heavy, they're hot and they soon look sloppy. A lot of these troops figure this makes them pretty rough, I guess, but I think I'll be able to survive without one.

Today was my first time in Da Nang, and I haven't been missing anything. After being in Saigon with its teeming rat-race, this was like going to some village. Da Nang has upwards of 135,000 people, almost all of whom are refugees rather than natives. I was only there about 4 hours and saw most of it.

That's the excitement for now, my love. I still continue to miss you something awful and I love you with all my heart.

Your Leo

7 Dec 65

My Beloved,

It's been pretty nice again today, two days in a row now, but right now it's pouring. I went to the early show tonight (6PM) and then had some coffee at the club. I took another cup of coffee out with me and was just about to set out front when down it came. So, I'm back to my letter writing 30 minutes sooner than planned.

There's not been too much going on, pretty much routine the last few days. As a matter of fact, night firing seems to have lessened a bit, too. Really, the hardest thing is probably trying to do without things you normally took for granted in the states. At work, our biggest problem is transportation. Where we had 30-40 trucks at Ellsworth, here we have 4 and they're all limping. As a matter of fact, we had 5 until about 10 days ago when one just died. About 5 months ago, two of our wire people got this 6-by out of salvage and, by either building parts or trading whiskey to the Marines for them, they got it running.

Sgt. Grenier finally got his hold baggage today and he has a movie camera. Since there's no telling when I'll be able to latch on to one up here, he said I could borrow it. I'll go down to the PX tomorrow and see if they have film and mailers. What I'll do is send them to the states and request they forward them directly to you. So, as I take pictures, I'll carry a little notebook to let you know what each scene is and send it on to you as I finish each roll. You can probably post them on to Mom afterwards. I should be able to get some good pictures not only of the country and the people, but also the military activity. When I go out to the RAPCON or TACAN sites we cross the runway and I can get good shots of the jets taking off on missions.

Ran into another old Carswellite trooper. Having coffee after breakfast yesterday morning, this guy and I kept looking at each other. He's MSgt. Greene, formerly of the 492nd. He's flying on C-130's and was here TDY out of Japan. He left Carswell in 1953. I don't know for sure if his picture is in that yearbook at home.

No rush, but when you send me another box, here are some hard to get items you could include: Oral B-40 toothbrush, flints, a package of single edge blades, and if you can pack them good, 60 watt light bulbs. I use the light in my wall locker to keep things from getting moldy.

At nights, I just sit or lay around wishing I could be helping you, my darling. I know how hard it must be for you to be doing everything by yourself, because you kept going all the time even when I was there. Maybe that's it—you kept busy so that I wouldn't have so much chance to get after you! Seriously, honeybunch, I'll be so happy to be able to help you again before too very long. The more we go on, the more convinced I become that the time is coming close to call this quits and find ourselves someplace where we can settle down and stay together. Then, if my boss says I have to leave my family, I can use the phrase famous in Vietnam: "sorry about that". I love you so much my wonderful, sweet wife.

Your Leo

9 Dec 65

My Dearest,

I do hope that all went well and you've received the money I sent you. That's another problem with this long range business, an answer to a question or word on anything takes about 10 days to go one way and then back again.

No mail today, but did get a letter from you yesterday, plus a letter from Theresa and a card from Mom. While I think of it, another thing for any package coming this way—8mm film. They've got stacks of 8mm film here, but typically it's all in magazines and everyone wants the spool or reel. The brass trays they have here are $10.50 – either round or oval. The great big ones are $21.50. Legs are separate. They may be cheaper in Bangkok or Hong Kong. Another thing many people buy here are precious stones. A ruby, emerald or star sapphire about this size (maybe a little larger) costs about $10. The Lt. I work for had a friend take a ring home for him with a star sapphire and his father had it appraised at $75. It had cost him $12. With my long experience with stones (well…….I found an agate & babysat when you went to the rock shop!), I'd probably pay a fortune for a chip off the Rock of Gibraltar.

Things have been quite active hereabouts the last couple days with some heavy fighting south of here. Grenier just stopped by as I was writing the last paragraph. He just went for another penicillin shot – 2 a day for 5 days due to infected tonsils. While he was there, they brought in 4 dead Marines. Yesterday a Vietnamese regiment was just about wiped out and today the Marines cornered the VC and they're having quite a battle. The jets and choppers have been making a continuous circle – taking off, hitting the enemy, coming back, reloading and off again. The Vietnamese have a hospital just across from our maintenance area and all day long they're in and out, just long enough to unload casualties and they're off again. And here we sit at times moaning 'cause there's no cold water, or we're crowded, or the PX doesn't have any film.

One of the guys reminded me that it's been a month today that I arrived at Da Nang. I hadn't even given it a thought since it's the 300+ days to go that I've been counting. Right now, my closest aim is for April, about 120 days, when I'll be forecasting. We forecast during our 6th month. Any idea where you'd like to go? I'm asking you because I intend to take you with me!

Last night was real miserable. I was tired and went to bed about 9:30. It was almost 1AM before I fell asleep. Once I was in the sack, I was wide awake and try as I might, I just couldn't get to sleep. I can feel it tonight, though, and in just a bit I'm going to give it another try. Good night, my darling. It may be sounding like a broken record, but I love you, love you, love you.

Your Leo

11 Dec 65

My Darling,

I've got to make it up to you today, since it's been three days since I've written. The first night there just wasn't too much to say, and the second night I was running around quite a bit getting people together to work on communications outages.

One of the troops in our outfit cracked up last night. He's a young airman and quite a few people have been concerned because of his past actions. He worked at the radio tower and at night he would drive his shift buddy boo-boo. Kept talking how he had to be always ready – that's what they taught him in Strike Command. Sgt. Carter, who hangs around with Grenier and I, is asst NCOIC in charge of that shop and he said a couple of days ago he found this wire running with their cables in the trough, and the wire was taped at both ends – in other words, it was just a telephone wire with nothing hooked to it. This airman said: "Shhh…that's Top Secret…..something I learned in STRIKECOM…..don't touch it and don't tell anyone about it." The other A1C he works with said he used to get mad because he wasn't ready and joining him in all his safeguards against the V.C. At night this guy would put all outside lights out, just turning them on and off occasionally to fool the VC. He would string up all sorts of wires with pieces of metal, etc. so noise would be made by anyone trying to penetrate. About ten times a night he would string field phones out into the bushes and hook them up to the speaker in the radio room. Then he'd go out there and watch for the VC. A while back he filled the bottom of a truck with sandbags 'cause it would protect him if he ran over a mine. Some of the guys said he would be awake at all hours of the night, flashing a light on and off and laughing. The night before last, the kid he worked with said 2 or 3 times he sat down and cried because his buddies had to go out flying against the enemy. Big tears would sob down, and then he would laugh his head off.

Last night, around 7:30, they were both on duty. An Army Sgt. has just gotten off his helicopter and came in to the tower to use the phone to call his outfit for transportation. He carried a bag and an M-14 rifle. As he went to use the phone this Airman L__ took his rifle and went to the other end of the room. They figured he was just looking at it. He checked and inserted the clip and put a round into the chamber. As the guy completed his call, he pointed the gun at him and told him he was his prisoner. He then told the other airman to call Security, that he had captured a VC saboteur. His co-worker told him for gosh sakes to quit fooling around, that he (the Sgt) had to go since a jeep was coming for him. Again he told Amn Steiger to call Security and when Steiger refused, Airman L__ said, "I thought so; you're a VC, too." He then had him lock the door and alternately putting the lights on and turning them off, he had them go from one room to the other, having them sit, stand, lay, on and off. He then took them outside and had them sit in the mud, then stand, again on and off. When Steiger tried to tell him again to cut it out, L___ said, "I'm going to kill you." That's all Steiger, who's a nervous kid, needed. L__ then had them lie in the mud and was trying to call the guards on the nearby flight line. He also called to a couple of VN Air Force types who were on the top deck of the tower, but they weren't about to come down. He laid a pipe across the legs of the prone troops. Shortly he fired 3 times. Steiger said he didn't know if he fired at them or somewhere else, because by that time he and the Sergeant were both digging their nails into the dirt. He fired again 2 or 3 times. By then, people had heard the shots and they were surrounded by about 15 marines and guards. An AP came to L___ and L___ turned the gun on him. The AP told him who he was and to turn that thing away from him. By then the Provost Marshal, Col. Phillips had arrived and L___ told him they were VC and that the bag the Sgt carried contained a bomb. The Col checked the bag—full of dirty laundry.

By then, Sgt Carter and a couple of others who had been notified by our telephone operator arrived. When Carter saw that one of the guys clawing the ground was Steiger he said, "Hell, this ain't right, that's the man on the shift with him." They carted L___ off to the hospital where they kept him overnight and shipped him out Air Evac to Clark this morning. I think Steiger is still shaking. It's probably a good thing it was him and not one of the NCOs like Carter who probably would have sounded off and not be around to talk about it afterwards.

The Commander just formed an NCO Advisory Council composed of the First Sgt, two from operations and Grenier and I representing maintenance. The personnel officer called us together to tell us what kind of things we would handle – morale, welfare, discipline, etc. He said we were hand-picked! That they didn't want "yes men".   Then he told us how we'd meet with the Commander and discuss problems, policies, etc. Right off I disagreed and the FSgt joined me. If we're going to be objective we've got to discuss these things by ourselves and then advise the Commander. Him sitting there will cause some people not to voice their true feelings. He didn't take too kindly to that—but at least he knows he won't have "yes" men. After the meeting he asked the First Shirt what happened and Hodgson told him we'd report to the Commander, that he could read it then.

I just thought of something: I love you. God, how I want to be with you again. I'm afraid you'll probably find some of my letters a bit jumbled, running from one subject to the next with no semblance of order, but it's just that no matter what I may be thinking of at any one time, I keep remembering you and how much I miss you.

On to other subjects, temporarily! I had gotten Karen's letter with the poems before I got your letter saying she was sending them. I had no idea she had written them, so I had to re-read them. She sure has done amazingly well – I was really surprised. By gosh—we may have <u>ANOTHER</u> genius in the house. She says she does well in English except at test time. I'm sure the problem she has is that she doesn't take time enough to understand what the question or the assignment is. That's the easiest way in the world to goof a test. Even the smartest will miss if they're not careful.

You asked about the monsoon season here. We're in it now. It rains from October to about March in the northwestern part of VN. Down south, around Saigon, it's from April to September. The last few days haven't been too bad, most of the rain falling at night.

I was surprised to hear of the other promotions since Dorrough had only mentioned those I told you about. They sure did well, then – 2 Masters and 7 Techs. I was glad to hear especially that Graham and Zimmerman made it. Boy, it shows you how it goes – Becker and Minkler at one time both worked for Rossley. I personally think, based on what I've observed at Ellsworth, that Ed should have made it over both of them. Hearing things like that make me even think that I won't make E-8 next cycle…yuk, yuk.

We've still been getting all sorts of goodies to eat. I don't think the flood of things coming in here has ever been seen by an army before, and from people all over the country. It does a lot towards negating the actions of the many cowards and ignoramuses parading for "peace". There are also many items like tobacco, pipes, flints, lighters, pens, writing paper, books, etc., which we have set aside. We plan on wrapping all of these and passing them out at a little Christmas party our outfit is planning for around the 19th. I'll probably get something like chewing tobacco and have to find the old farmers in the outfit to trade with.

Honeybunch, Korea was nothing like this, as far as I felt. I missed you then, and as much as I may have thought how awful it was being separated from you, it was not 1/10th as bad as it is now. Then it was being away from someone I loved. It's more than that now, if you can understand anything being more than love. It's more like being cut in half; you're so much a part of me and of my whole life. I have no fear of cracking up myself, thought heaven knows I could at times come close to it as I think of you. As a matter of fact, that's what helps me and makes me so sure all will be well – the knowledge that before too very long the two halves will be once again be one. The wonderful recollections of our years together make every little act between us, everything we've done together and for each other, seem so important to me now. I don't know, maybe in a way this separation will have it's good points in that respect. We're not perfect, my darling, and because of this I know that at times I've hurt you, either by doing things I shouldn't or by not doing things I should have. But, I do swear to you, never was it with the intent of hurting you. I love you and respect you too much to ever do that.

My beloved, I can sit here and write a volume trying to let you know how I feel about you, but it could not come near expressing my full feelings. Only by taking you bodily into the depths of my heart and soul, so you could see with your heart and soul, can I ever hope to express my love. I long once again to hold your hand, to take you in my arms and hold you close, to just come up behind you, as so often in the past, and hug you and kiss your neck. Surely the physical attractions are strong – the feel of you lying naked beside me as I try my best to make you happy and content, and this probably will always be. But much greater than this is just being together in our lives. To come home from work, maybe one or both of us tired or grouchy for any of a hundred reasons – but still we're together.   To have worries about buying this or that, and where's the money coming from – but still we're together. To worry about the children's behavior, their schoolwork, their health—but worry together. To laugh at things any one of us say or do – to laugh together. The perfect examples are the things you tell me about what Paul and Bryan doing; there's something missing….we're not enjoying it together. Just writing to you I realize one of my greatest failings toward you has been in telling you "I love you" repeatedly. This was fine, but it wasn't enough. I should have tried to explain it more fully, if possible. The many times when you've needed me to reassure you, to express some of my thoughts and feelings, I failed you. Instead I would retreat in my shell and say nothing. My pride has been my biggest fault. Regardless of what I may say and do, I still fear certain things. One of these is that when you needed my help perhaps I was incapable of making the right decision or saying the right words to you – so I kept silent.

Perhaps this short while we've been apart, and the conditions here, have already helped me mature in this respect. I hope so.   I never want to be in a position where I cannot offer you my whole being, for whatever your needs. I've occasionally called you My Happiness. Though I should have explained my feelings years ago; what I've said here is what I've meant. But I didn't have the confidence that I could utter the right words, so I let it slip by with that one phrase. My darling, you mean absolutely everything to me, apart or together, and you always will. I will tell you personally one day very soon how very much I love you. I will tell you over and over again so it will never be possible for to ever forget or to ever doubt why you, and only you, are my happiness.

Your Leo

13 Dec 65

My dearest Don Leta,

The hardest part of this assignment to a combat zone is the feeling that in some way you could take a greater part but are in some way prevented. Still, every now and then someone sneaks off on a mission, mostly as a machine-gunner on one of the helicopters. In a way it's ridiculous, since unqualified people manning these weapons put everyone else in jeopardy, plus which if anything happened it would be "not in the line of duty" since it's forbidden. I think in many cases we have to close one eye to these happenings, however, especially after a day like today when 6 planes loaded with bodies of Marines left Da Nang. This was a result of the melee which is mentioned in the enclosed clipping, and which is still going on.   The "light" or "moderate" casualties we read about don't always tell the full story.

Not much new workwise, except that shades of stateside, we're expecting a Pacific Command (Hawaii) inspection next month. That really shakes the heck out of me! But of course we have to go thru all sorts of ridiculous and silly routines to try to satisfy them. That's like trying to get the pig pen spotless 'cause the Secretary of Agriculture is coming for lunch.

I did want to write tonight, my darling, even though you can already see there's not much to enlighten your day. As times go on, I am more and more sorry and feel so helpless than I'm not with you – to help you with all the little things that have to be done day in and day out. Maybe my saying I want to help you is just an excuse and what I really mean is that I want to be near you – but regardless, I would help you if I were near, so that's all that matters. Don Leta, I love you so very much. Can you possibly understand? Do you think it possible in any way that there could be any doubt in your mind? My love, you and you alone mean more to me than anything, and I mean anything, in this world. I want to much to be able to speak these words to you. I hope, my sweet, that you don't think old dad is depressed and discouraged. Far from it. Rather, it's more that I'm happier for the opportunity to stop and meditate on what really counts for me in this world. Yes, I get discouraged and a bit disgusted at times. All of us do. But more often are the times, for me, when I rejoice at what has been given me – wonderful children and a mother for which I can truly find no equal – an understanding mate, an exemplary mother, and a loving girl.

You're just going to turn around now and say I'm being silly, or I'm exaggerating, or I'm getting battle-weary. That's not the case, Don Leta, believe me. It's just that I've been so long …these many (yet few), years when I should have told you this. Let it stand for now that I love you – God how I love you – and I hope and pray that I can come back to tell you and show you, over and over and over again, how very much you mean to me.

Yours, now & forever,
Leo

14 Dec 65

My dearest,

Just a few short lines tonight, since there's really not too much to report. I note in the paper that they salvaged the mail that went down here 8 Dec. and that it had all been forwarded on to the states. I can't remember if I had one in there or not. If you did get a letter later than usual, you know now that it's been in an accident.

A bit of activity here last night and this morning. I guess there were snipers firing on the planes as they were taking off. Pretty soon all aircraft were taking off, landing, and flying about without lights. Then about 4 A.M. the mortars started laying down a barrage about 1 ½ miles from here, in the area the sniper fire was coming from. Fortunately it was outgoing mail, but it sure sounded for a bit like it was coming in to our back yard, especially when waking up to it.

I haven't been to a movie in well over a week. It must be true; they're just not making many good ones any more. This weekend we had a Beatles movie. It sure hurt me to miss it! I intend to go tomorrow night, however, since there's a good old timer on that I've already seen – The Bridge on the River Kwai.

I'm sorry that the picture of me didn't turn out as well as you expected. Oh well, you can't get a diamond out of a plain old rock! It sure did take them a long time to get that thing done, didn't it? Still don't know when, if ever, I'll be able to get movie film here, much less a camera. If things don't improve much in the BX once the Air Force takes it over after Christmas, I may not be able to pick up a camera until I go on R&R to Hong Kong or Thailand around August or July.

Still 316 days to go, and here I am straining to get below 300. Then, my next goal will be forecast time in March, about 90 days from now. Other than special assignments or consecutive overseas tours, people are getting their assignments from 45 to 75 days prior to rotation. I notice in the AF times that they've put a firm restriction on holding people in VN beyond their normal return date. It used to be they could hold you until a replacement arrived and had been in place for 5 days. This caused some people to be extended up to 3 months. Now they say no one will be retained in Vietnam beyond the normal tour of 365 days.

Things have been hot and heavy in my section the last couple of days, which is good. Keeps you busy and helps the time go by. Each day itself seems quite long, even though the week goes by fairly quick since we don't get much of a weekend. Right now I put in an average of 65 hours a week on the job.

That's it for now, sugar. I always miss you and love you so very much. I must now go to what I like and hate – bed. I'd like to lay quietly and think of you and yet hate it because think is all I can do. Be sweet, my love.

Your Leo

16 Dec 65

My darling,

A heavy mail day with Christmas cards, but not too much to report to you otherwise. I received cards from Mother & Daddy, Mom, Theresa, her Gary, Aunt Nellie and Masie and also my cousin Frank (Masie's brother).

I slept pretty late this morning and when I got up it was pouring. Finally made it to work by 0845. I had hit the sack around 1145 last night and just couldn't go to sleep. At one o'clock I got up and had a smoke and then tried again. By 2 o'clock I was still wide awake so I sat outside for a while, finally going back to bed sometime between 2 and 3.

There isn't much getting in the Christmas spirit around here, what with the weather and conditions. I understand the Vietnamese Catholics celebrate quite a bit, but there sure isn't much of anything in the line of decorations. The people here are mostly Buddhists.

Work has been going fairly good, but I think they should concentrate on doing the job instead of spending time on "stateside" type projects. We still have many of the little irritants that go in this game and they wouldn't hurt a thing by doing away with them in a zone like this.

Go to get my beauty sleep, my darling, and dream of my sweet girl back home. I love you great big bunches and basketsful and miss you so. Good night, my love.

Your Leo

18 Dec 65

My Beloved,

After receiving a nice letter from you at lunch time, as well as a card from the Bishops, my day was really complete when I got back tonight and there was another letter from my honeybunch.

It's just past 7 o'clock Saturday night, and I just took a shower. It was a full day today and the old dad's muscles can feel it. We spent the afternoon putting up Christmas decorations. We placed loudspeakers around the area and are playing taped Christmas music on it. The tape we have plays for 7 hours. We also built a billboard type affair, 16' x 16', and it was a job lugging it around and getting it up. I'll have to see if one of the guys here can get me a picture of it. We were up to our ankles in water and mud trying to get it up inasmuch as it's been raining quite a bit. It looks something like this:

That's supposed to be a green wreath with red holly berries and a red bow. Anyhow, it looks fairly good.

Here I had sent out 10 Christmas cards and wanted to get 9 more today, but unless the PX has any left over tomorrow I'll be out of luck. Da Nang has been placed off-limits until after Christmas, especially since the VC have an anniversary coming up the 20th. I had gotten some Vietnamese cards and wanted to get more. So, unless I can get some tomorrow at the PX, I guess you won't know how much I love you!

Another thing we had to get done today was put up a 20' x 40' tent for our Squadron party Sunday. Boy, if you don't think that's a dirty job in this kind of weather. Those things are real heavy in dry weather, let alone wind or rain. All told, 3 prs. of sox, 2 sets of fatigues and 2 pairs of shoes since this morning. The party is from 10 to 2 tomorrow over in our maintenance area – steaks, beans, etc. Which reminds me – Grenier and I were both complaining. He told me eating beans and hot dogs was ritual with them on Saturdays (did you ever hear of anything so ridiculous?) We've had hot dogs 3 times (tonight was one) but have yet to see a bean since leaving the states. Now I thought sure we'd have beans here. How do they expect us to ever beat the VC?

Boy, I hope I get some pictures from you pretty soon now that you have that camera, especially when you are telling me so many of the things that Paul has been doing and getting into. It sounds to me like he's definitely going to be a boy too. I know getting some recent pictures will make me all the more homesick but I don't care. I'd like some shots of all the kids, but especially I'd like some of their wonderful mother. Maybe it'll be different when I get home, but I feel that if I saw you now I'd probably hug you so hard I would crush you.

Tomorrow I'm going to do a bit of letter writing. I want to write Mom and all the kids again. I had been waiting to hear from Lanis but she hasn't written though I've heard from her sisters more than once. I'm going to scold her if I don't hear from her pretty soon. I'll definitely have to write to Bryan since he kept that blank sheet from one of my letters to write to me.

It was nice to hear of Daddy getting that promotion and raise. Mother didn't mention it, probably figuring you would since she said you probably gave me all the news. Like you say, working out of town probably helped. It can get sometimes that you do a job well and they begin taking it for granted. Only when someone else gets to see it that it's realized the work is being done better than by others.

Yes I would rather have cake or banana bread than candy. We can occasionally get candy at the PX, but pastry is almost non-existent, as I mentioned previously that we've only had some 2 or 3 times since I've been here. Amn Tapscott, the clerk in maintenance, got a fruitcake from home and brought it in to work this morning. We had it with coffee – one time around is all it made.

<u>I</u> <u>love</u> <u>you</u>

That was just a reminder since I haven't told you in a page or two. Gosh but I miss you, Don Leta, more even than I thought I would. As much as I've said I loved you, I don't believe I fully realized myself how deep that love goes. It's a funny thing here. I'll bet that, without exception almost, I could point out the ones who really left something of themselves behind. With many, it's as if they couldn't wait to get away so they could raise a bit of hell. I don't see how some of them can act the way they do, as if it's a big ball, when actually they sit in the face of death. To leave a place like this without the feeling that you've done your best should haunt some people forever. But, I guess it doesn't bother some people; they really don't know what they're living for, other than their own good times.

Good night, my wonderful and sweet Don Leta. Oh my darling, how very much I miss you and, if it's at all possible, my love for you grows with each passing day. I swear I never realized I could even love anyone as much as I do you. Be sweet, my darling.

Your Leo

19 Dec 65

My dearest Don Leta,

Though it's still early afternoon, I thought I would write to you now and finish it later tonight after I see if any mail has come in. I shouldn't get any after two from you yesterday, but I can still hope. Really, with all you have to do, I don't see how you can write as often. As much as I savor your letters and look forward to them, I'll understand perfectly well if you skip a few days.

We were scrambling around a bit at about 1 o'clock this morning. The siren went off and it was a rat race in the dark. In about 5 minutes a truck came around saying it was an accidental tripping of the alarm – so back to bed.

I just came back from our Christmas party – not too much excitement. We had steaks, beans (at long last!) and salad with soft drinks and un-spiked eggnog. Like I say, things were rather subdued. I picked up a bunch of candy and gum which I just distributed to about 30 kids back of our place. That's something else I'll have to take pictures of if I can ever get some film. Everybody got sets – combs, nail file and nail trimmers (2 of each), plus which, I got some writing paper, razor blades, pens and a nice PINK towel. There was all sorts of stuff and more will be coming until about mid-January. I've never seen anything like it. Most of the stuff today was from New Jersey, West Virginia, and Tennessee. Ah yes, I got a bunch of soap too. There were all sorts of things – cigars, insect repellent, tobacco, pipes, tobacco pouches, <u>baby oil</u>, gum, candy, cookies, fruitcake (which we had with the meal) shaving lotion, creams and razors, games, books, a Virginia Ham (which we've taken to the orphanage). Everyone also got toothpaste and a toothbrush, which we received by the case.

We've had scattered, very light drizzle so far today, so though it's overcast it's not too bad.

Well, I wasn't too surprised at no mail today. Just have been laying around most of the afternoon, reading a bit. Just came back from chow and now I've got to get with my letter writing, though there's nothing new.

There's a bunch of country music types with guitars just out back and all they've been doing is singing those sad country songs – where the guy is always pining for his girl or his horse, or both. If they go according to form, they'll sing about 5 or 6 hours, quitting around 11 or 12 tonight.

Got's to get busy on other letters, my darling, so will leave you for now, missing you so very much. How awful it sounds to say there are 56 days down and 309 to go. Some day these figures will be reversed, but by then 56 days to go will seem like 309 to me. I think one of the happiest days of my life will be the day that first let's me hold you again – even though you've given me so many happy days already: when you accepted me, when you married me, when you brought forth our wonderful children and the many, many days in between. My Don Leta, I love you, love you, love you – with all my heart and soul.

Your Leo

21 Dec 65

My dearest,

Just a little note right now during my lunch break inasmuch as I didn't write last night. Went to the first show, John Wayne in The Sons of Kate Elder, and then got embroiled in a big hairy game of hearts. No mail yesterday, other than a Christmas card from Dorrough, and none at noon today, so there's not too much to report. We get two mail deliveries per day, including Sundays. Still haven't received the package Mom sent around the 15th of November. It should get here pretty soon.

Still haven't gotten letters off to the kids as I wanted; will have to get with that tonight. Things are going fairly well at work. I do have some construction work to do since I want to build a new console for our new location. That way, I'll only have to nail it together when we're ready to move in sometime in January.

Today we got a day of sunshine. The first we've had in quite some time, or so it seems. It had been drizzling out most of last night. Things have still been pretty quiet here – just the regular boom-boom of outgoing mail. I was down to the hangar for coffee this morning and they were getting ready for some VIPs. I understand Gen. Ky and Ambassador Lodge were due in. Couldn't hang around to see the show, however.

That's about it for now, my sweet. I want to get this into the afternoon mail. I'll write again tonight if I get any mail this P.M. Just so you don't forget, I love you. You know, as I think of it, there are but very few days that have gone by since we've been together that I haven't said that to you. My Don Leta is just the most wonderful person in the world and I love her and miss her so very much. Until a little later then, be sweet my darling.

Your Leo

21 Dec 65

My dearest wife,

Got another wonderful letter from you this evening, so you get two letters from me today.

I didn't do too much since my noon-time letter, just back to the pits and chow. Did go to the first movie tonight (twice in a row now) and saw Rod Steiger in "The Pawnbroker".

One of our troops had an accident this morning. This SSgt who works in radio was out checking the gear in the North Mobile Tower and on his way back, just before dawn, the brakes on his truck gave out. He hit a fork lift and then ran into a Vietnamese guard shack. The VN guard received two broken legs. None of our people were hurt. Of course, in typical fashion, everyone is concerned with the safe condition of all trucks now. It's forever locking the barn after the horse has been stolen.

You mention in your letter about your legs bothering you again. Had you ever decided what to do once the baby comes? Or will you be putting if off a bit until I get back and we get settled somewhere. I guess that will probably have to be the thing since someone will have to be chasing after the pack. Gee I wish I were there to help you with them now. Then perhaps you'd be able to sit at least occasionally and rest up.

I hope after Christmas you'll be able to send me some film. There are so many times I see things I'd like to take pictures of so you could see what our place is like and the different things around here. You'd never believe it of an advanced airfield in a combat zone, but you can take pictures right on the flight line. You'd never hear of that in the States.

I got a charge out of this SSgt Carter, who bunks with Grenier and plays cards with us. He's been in about as long as I have. He's from East Texas and has that old dry humor. We were in the club one night and he had tears running out of my eyes when he told one guy "You're so ugly you have to sneak up on a can of beer to get a drink." What makes me think of him is that we were sitting out front a while ago and you could hear the regular thud of outgoing mail. He said: "I wish those guys would cut that out. Don't they know that if they write enough letters or knock on the door long enough they're liable to get an answer?" He's the one who Airman L__ worked for and had gone out when L__ cracked up. To hear him relate it that night was a classic. Airman L__, by the way, is at Walter Reed Hospital now.

Well, my darling, it maybe slow going but the days are going by one by one. Before we know it, it'll be Christmas and into 1966. Then March and forecast time and then the slide down the bottom half of the tour. There's a fair possibility that I'll be leaving before the 26th of October, but how much before is anyone's guess. As it stands, no one is to stay more than 365 days, which means I'm supposed to be stateside by the 27th. Good night, my love.

Your Leo

23 Dec 65

My Darling,

No mail today, but I did get the girls' letters yesterday. I had one of those days yesterday and ended it beering it up at the club – about 8 of us. And wouldn't you know it, we start having all sorts of power problems at our radio relay and both Grenier and I ended up at the shop from 10 o'clock 'till almost 1 in the morning. He had to keep adjusting equipment and I was running around trying to round up electricians and power plant personnel from Civil Engineers. Sure hated to get out of that sack this morning.

This has been the third day of sunshine, and it got a bit hot. The nights have been pretty good for sleeping.

I really enjoyed the letters from the girls. Karen surprises me with the long and interesting letters she writes. I think she's going to be like her mother in that department. There were a couple of things especially that I got a chuckle out of. In thanking me for the Christmas money she says: "As you know, I _love_ money." And Stephanie saying "we've been so-so."

Things have remained relatively quiet hereabouts. Still get the regular thumping of outgoing mail and roar of aircraft. All those dudes who can't wait to get to town have been finding it kinda hard with town off limits until after Christmas. This restriction to the base has ended up in much sitting around out back and griping and drinking beer. It's much quieter around here when they cut out for the town bars.

There just isn't very much new happening to tell you about, honeybunch. I did see Santa Claus today, but didn't have a chance to sit on his lap or let him know what I wanted for Christmas. Some guy from Special Services was dressed up and driving around in the back of a pickup. I'm afraid he didn't generate too much enthusiasm among the G.I.s, though the Vietnamese were eyeballing him. Speaking of Christmas, I had told you about the big billboard decorations we put up. The seven of us who did it had our pictures taken in front of it this morning for possible inclusion in the AFCS paper. I hope I can get a copy of the picture.

Well, my sweet, I must say good night again this awful way. I want so much to be with you when I say it. How long away it seems yet. Sixty days gone and 305 to go! At least, I try to console myself by saying that 305 is the maximum – it could be a few days less than that. I'll say it over and over, my Don Leta, but I love you so very much. You and the children are my whole life, and without you nothing much would be worth while. Take good care of yourself for me, my love, especially these next few months until I can come back to you. It's such a helpless feeling to want to tell you so much and to want to help you with everything and yet not be able to do anything tangible towards that end. The one consolation is that one day it'll be over with and we'll be together again. Sweet dreams, my happiness.

Your Leo

23 Dec 65

My dear Lanis,

My goodness, I was just about to give up that you were going to write to me. But I was real happy to receive your letter, to hear of your school Christmas party and of your shopping trip into town.

I hope you got everything you wished for at Christmas, and that you have a nice holiday season. Throughout it all, try not to forget what it is we are celebrating, and not to think of it only as a good time for us.

There are many children here for who Christmas is a special time, too, because on that day they might get a little bit more rice in their bowls, or maybe a clean pair of pants or a dress. Americans are the luckiest people in the world. Most of the time they have nice houses to live in, enough to eat, warm clothes, and many toys. When I get to take some pictures here, you'll see how people live in other parts of the world. Our garage outside is a better house than many of them have.

I know the rest of the time I'm away you'll do all you can to help your mother and get along with your brothers and sisters. Especially, mommy needs help in looking after the little ones. Be sweet, my Lanis, and let me hear soon of the Christmas you had. Give everyone a big hug & kiss for me.

Loads of love,
Daddy

23 Dec 65

Hi Pal,

I've been waiting to get another letter from you, but I guess you've been too busy playing lately. I hope you got a lot of nice presents and toys for Christmas, and that your brother Paul did too. He's not a big boy like you yet, so sometimes he's going to be getting after your toys, so you remember to try and play with him as much as you can.

Daddy still has a lot of work to do in Vietnam, so it's going to be a long time yet before I can come back home to play with you and Paul. Don't you forget now, you're the daddy of the house so you're going to have to help mommy by being a good boy and helping watch after your brother.

I love you,
Daddy

25 Dec 65

My Beloved,

This is one of the happiest days of the year for mankind, heralding the birth of the Prince of Peace. Yet, it is probably one of the saddest days I have ever known. I've put off this letter all day, though hardly a minute passed without my thoughts being with you. It was like I couldn't bring myself to sitting down to write, because that would make me concentrate on this thought all the more, and I felt too weak to cope with it.

Christmas here has generally been false time for celebration – with the majority of the people drinking and carrying on, trying to convince themselves that they were having a ball. We were scheduled to work right through Christmas day, but when word of the 30-hour cease fire was passed, we converted to skeleton crews. Starting early yesterday, just about everyone started "celebrating," it going on into the early morning hours. I'll bet there weren't more than 7 or 8 sober people, including Grenier, Carter and me. Perhaps we would have been better off joining them!

On Christmas day things were pretty quiet, what with all the hangovers. Also, it turned into quite a somber day – a few minutes of sunshine in the morning and heavy rains in the afternoon. Even though I was up well past midnight (2 A.M.), I couldn't sleep and I didn't go to midnight mass. I waited until 1300 so that I could attend a Christmas Mass celebrated at the base of Hill 327 by Cardinal Spellman. It was quite a sight. A couple Air Force busses ran us out there, an area occupied by Marines. It was quite gloomy, and the ground wet and soggy. It was a sight not soon to be forgotten, lines of people receiving Holy Communion with slung rifles and hanging bayonets. Cardinal Spellman arrived by helicopter, and as I watched him make his way to the improvised alter, I venture to say this will be the last Christmas Mass he'll be able to say among his troops. He walked feebly, held on either side and you couldn't help but wonder if he'd make it. What made the celebration particularly touching was a Vietnamese chorus—men, women and children. They would each sing hymns in Latin, like one responding to the other. It was especially beautiful when the girls and women came in. In typical Oriental voice, high pitched and clear as a bell, you were tempted to close your eyes and try to see the angels singing.

The sun shone briefly over the silent field as the Cardinal moved ever so slowly through the ceremony, never leaving his one position at the center of the alter. Throughout it all, MPs kept scanning the hills for any sign of unnatural movement. After Mass, Cardinal Spellman removed his vestments and stepped forward to address his soldiers. You could hear a pin drop as he said how honored he was that the Lord had allowed him to come here once more, and that he knew that this could well be his last. This old mans' voice fell on all sorts of people, clean and dirty, combed and unshaven, and yet not a murmur. The second he finished and turned, the skies opened and rain fell by the bucketful.

Free Christmas dinners at the club today and I didn't eat until I got back from Mass — about 3 P.M. The rest of the afternoon was quite uneventful until 5 o'clock when I received a wonderful letter from the sweetest girl in the world.

Sugar bun, I'm sorry if in some of my writings I give the impression that I may doubt that you love me as I do you. This is not it at all. What I am trying to do, in my own clumsy way, is trying, through the inadequacy of words, to make you feel how strongly and deeply my love is for you. I'm deeply flattered and honored to know that you feel you couldn't re-marry if we were no longer together, and let's face it, every man likes to hear this since it feeds his ego. However, I know it means more than that to us. It goes much deeper and is really a way of saying we could never replace each other. The thing is, and you probably feel the same way, that I know I love you so much and it's so much inside of me and growing, like a child, that it's impossible to believe anyone else could feel the same. This is what's making this year's separation so hard — to not be with you while my love continues to grow. I don't want to sound like I'm sorry for myself; rather, I'm saddened by this increasing feeling of two persons becoming more and more like one and being unable to be together, physically, to enjoy it. We are together, my happiness, in all other ways and that is what must sustain us through these days. Oh, my Don Leta, I love you so very much.

Things sure seem unnatural today — too quiet. No jets flying or guns booming. A few choppers and light observation planes have gone aloft, as well as an occasional transport, but that's all. This morning one of the observation planes kept circling the Marine & Air Force areas and the city of Da Nang. It was one of those rigged out for propaganda flights — P.A. system with large amplifiers — and it was playing Christmas carols. You couldn't hear the plane hardly and yet this music was coming out of the sky quite clearly.

Tomorrow is Sunday, so this will be the first 2-day weekend we've had. Also, restriction comes off tomorrow, so many people will make themselves scarce hereabouts. This morning, the First Shirt came in with orders for people gong back home—7 or 8 of them — and woke them all up with a "ho, ho, ho" and gave them their orders as a Christmas present. We've got a fine F/Sgt (MSgt Hodgson), and he's retiring when he goes back around August.

That's about it for now, my sweet. It must be the thought of it being Christmas that he made this day so sad for me. But the time is passing by, however slowly, and the day will be with us in the near future when we can live again. Good night, my angel, and take extra good care of yourself for me.

<u>Your</u> devoted Leo

26 Dec 65

My Darling Wife,

We're back to the old routine again. I've just returned from the 1700 Mass, and the thumps of mortars and cannons are resuming their regular tempo. (I love you.)

I've just finished writing to Stephanie regarding her latest episode at school that you told me about in yesterday's letter. I told her I want a letter back from her as soon as possible. (I love you.)

Got another sweet letter from my honeybunch today, as well as a card and note from Butch (affectionately signed "Stink") and a letter from Mrs. Houle, Aunt Nellie's neighbor. She's a good old soul, and lives with her half-blind brother in the same fire trap on Benefit Street. Christmas was also her birthday (she was 71). Mom had told me how she was praying for me, so I had sent her a Christmas card and note. She has an exceptionally good hand for a woman that age. (I love you.)

It's too bad about all the trouble you had with the Ward order. I don't see why all that stuff couldn't have been ordered concurrently with the request to transfer the account. I should think a company that size would employ some type of communication like teletype or telephone to expedite. I'm sure they must or they'd never get some orders out. Oh well, next year we'll have no such trouble! Yuk, yuk!! (I love you.)

I was in the club having coffee (5 cups at this one sitting!) when this guy came up and asked if I was at Carswell years ago. I didn't recognize him. He's TSgt Moss – used to be in the 11th Bomb Wing. His wife is from Ft. Worth and he was stationed there 7 ½ years. He left there in 1952, also for Korea. Says he's going back there to retire. He said he didn't know it when he was going with her, but his wife was a good friend of Bruce Dresnell's wife. Said the last he heard, Bruce was in Okinawa and he thought maybe they were separated. I don't know if he meant legally or because of military necessity. Later he and the guy he was with were sitting right behind me in church. After church they headed for the terminal. He was just passing through. They had come from Bangkok and were headed back for their home station (Pleiku) where he's been for 9 months. It seems everyone's been here longer than I have! I'll be glad when I can do like I'm being done to now – say to someone, "What? Ten more months to go? I'd shoot myself if I had that long to do." (I love you.)

In your letter today, you say I sounded depressed or worried. Heck don't you know that's always been my natural state? You also added "Wish there was something I could do to cheer you up." Now that you mention it, there is something. Since a problem I've had occasionally was getting or (staying) asleep, you could come over here and climb into the sack with me. I know that would cure me, since I always fell right asleep the moment you lay next to me *!* (I love you.)

I didn't even pay attention to my sack when I came in. I just got up for a minute and spotted a letter there from Burchinal. Grenier must have checked the evening mail while I was at church. Will take a short break to read it in case there's any news. That was quick, only a Christmas card. (I love you.)

I'm sure Vi meant the 30th that John would retire. All retirements are as of the 30th, except those in February. Actually, I enclosed Zimmerman's 75 – Perryman was the rating official but I wrote that for him, too. I know that I gave him an outstanding rating all the way. I was glad to see both him, Fruits and Graham make it. (I love you.)

I don't know if Bob Hope will be up this way. He's in Saigon now and someone said they heard he was coming up to the Marine camp at Da Nang East (Marble Mtn) the 28th or 29th. If I have to fight the mob, I'll just have to struggle through this tour somehow without seeing him. (I love you.)

Grenier just stopped by (he had checked mail) wanting me to go to the movie, but I declined. Frank Sinatra in "Von Ryan's Express". I saw that in Tan Son Nhut, so you see where we stand on the list for certain things. Good movies are few and far between. On Christmas day they showed "The Revenge of the Gladiators" of all things, and everyone I know who saw it said it was putrid. (I love you.)

Well Sugar Plum ('cause you keep dancing through my head), that'll be it for this time. Just remember, if some of my letters leave you with the impression that I'm depressed, try to overlook it. Mostly it's because of the loneliness and the malady I caught through you – I'm lovesick!

Your loving
Leo

27 Dec 65

My Darling,

Just a short note tonight, since I didn't get any mail today and there's not much to report. It's been kind of gloomy, weather – wise. You never know, really, from one moment to the other what kind of day it's going to be. Today we got on and off drizzle and tonight the stars are out. It may or may not be raining by morning.

The Army – AF Exchange Service took over the BX from the Navy yesterday and everyone's been waiting to see what changes come about. Of course, we can't expect miracles right off but things should be better since stuff will be shipped directly in to Da Nang instead of to Saigon for parceling out to Da Nang. It irritates me all the more when I think of how they had cameras, etc., at Tan Son Nhut and in Saigon, while up here you can't get film, much less cameras.

The roster of eligibles for E8 & E9 came down (up) from Tan Son Nhut yesterday and typically my name was missing, so the Squadron added it on. It's not surprising as messed up as things seem to be. I'm trying to find out if a copy of my last APR is in my records since Dorrough wrote that they made one out on me the day I left. The only thing is that they probably mailed it to the 1964th at TSN, while all my personnel records are being maintained at Wheeler in Hawaii. If I ever get everything together at one place again at one time I'll be lucky!

The last letter I wrote I enclosed a poem written by a kid on this base. Almost every day there are a bunch of poems written by G.I.'s, their girls or relatives printed in the Stars & Stripes. Parts of that one, however, said so much of the things I've written to you that I felt. Actually, this wouldn't be too bad a tour for me. I'm probably as safe as anywhere in Vietnam, if only I could see you and be with you occasionally. That's what really hurts – being separated. But, we've got to be realistic about it I guess (there's not much more we can do). At least, like the moron who hit himself on the head with a hammer because it felt so good when he stopped, this separation won't be all bad because it'll be so nice to be together again.

Here it's been a long short time (64 down – 301 to go) and it's going to sound mighty monotonous soon, if not already, but I'm just going to have to keep writing of how much I miss my darling wife and our children, and how I love you all so terribly much. So often I lay here and think – mostly of two things. First, different times when we were together and things we did together, and secondly trying to picture our reunion. Regardless of what I envisage it as being like, I know it'll be something entirely different and infinitely more important, because it'll be real.

Good night, my beloved. My last thoughts tonight, as they are every night, will be of you.

Your loving Leo

29 Dec 65

My Darling,

Took a break and came to the shop to do my writing tonight. Had some work to do also, so got that out of the way. I think I'll be coming in more at nights for a while since this place gets to be such a rat race here during the day that we can't think, much less get anything done. I figure on going to the movie (late show, 9:30) after this letter. It's a little after eight now.

There was no mail yesterday and not much to report, so I skipped a day writing. Did get a letter from Doug today, plus another sweet one from my honeybunch. Doug was saying how thrilled he was that we asked them to be godparents and how they were getting nervous as the time got closer for them to have a baby of their own. He says they're already wondering if they'll know what to do with it. He complained about the snow on the ground (23 inches so far) and said he nearly died when they told him January & February were the worst. I'd trade for a little of his snow right now — that would mean being away from here.

Well, we made it to the first milestone — 299 days to go, maximum. Really, I hope to get out of here the first part of October, so it might be less yet. At least, there's no harm in hoping.

I think that sending the movie camera can probably wait. Really, it's no good without film and there'd be no trouble in my borrowing one if I can just get a hold of the ammo. When you get to send some film, I'll shoot a bunch right off. Grenier sent for some too, so we've got an agreement that whoever gets some first will share it. I don't know when the BX will ever have some. When they do, it'll probably go before I get the word.

The pictures of Paul sound real cute. I'll be anxious to see them, as well as those snaps of the kids you took. Make sure there's some of their mommy too when you send them to me. Also, tell the developers it's for me so they'll rush it through! Pictures will help so much make me feel closer to you. There'll probably be all the more loneliness too, but I'll still buy the chance to see you all again.

Saw Sgt Hill at chow a couple nights ago; he had been down to Pleiku for a couple days. He ran into Sgt Silvey down there. He'd been there since August — NCOIC (Noncommissioned Officer in Charge) of 8th Aerial Port Squadron. They're the ones who schedule all the transport (personnel & freight) movements.

I guess there isn't much news tonight either. It's been raining steady all day, nothing uncommon. There should be about 3 or 4 more weeks of this weather, then the hot weather takes over. The nights have been fairly comfortable, however. From what I hear, I'd better pick up a small fan somewhere for the hot weather. We can get them on the market for about 3 dollars. No good back stateside (they're 50 cycle instead of 60) but do the job here. I'm still keeping my brush cut, since that's the only way I'm comfortable.

See ya later, my love. Gonna cut out now, if I can get this beat up truck going. Don't dare walk back at night as the VN guards will shoot at anything that moves. I love you 37 times more than the last time I wrote, and miss you 6 zillion times more.

Yours forever,
Leo

31 Dec 65

My Darling,

Here it is, New Year's Eve, and I don't have any reservation at any of the big night clubs. Yesterday I invited Carter & Grenier and their wives to the house. We don't have a basement, but there's a big upstairs. It's only 8 PM now, but I can see this will be a quieter time than Christmas Eve. For one thing, it's payday and many of the troops have cut out for town. Tomorrow's a regular work day for us, though many outfits will be on Sunday schedule.

The lines were too long at the Post Office today, but will send you $200 soon as I get money orders. I hope the $400 allotment check got to you O.K. Let me know. I should hereafter be sending you at least $200 monthly in addition to the allotment. Also got my W-2 statement. They don't have the forms here yet, so if you get one first, sign it and mail it to me. If I get it first, I'll fill it out and send it to you for signature and mailing. We paid $158.76 income tax, all of which we'll get back.

After a lapse of a couple days, I received your letter of the 26th telling me of the Christmas you all had. I really enjoyed the letter and how I wish I had been there – for so many reasons. Especially, I got a charge out of your telling me Lanis & Bryan got that G.I. Joe Combat Commander set, but that Bryan doesn't have much chance to play with it. We've had so much stuff here from the states – cookies, candy, soap, toothpaste & brushes, etc., that we loaded a whole pickup (just our Squadron) and took it to the orphanage. They were sure thrilled to receive it. Also, every payday we all kick in a bit and send them some money. Outside of what they get from the G.I.'s, all they receive is 2,000 Piastres (about $18) from the government – and that's the monthly allotment for the orphanage, not each child. Last month they got over 12,000 P. from us.

297 days to go and things have been pretty routine – rain the past 3 days and real overcast and damp right now. Had to go through about 4 inches of mud to get into the shop today. The sun did peek through for about 15 minutes this afternoon but has been hiding since. It wasn't raining for a while Wednesday night so 3 of us (Sgt McGraw, who works for me and A1C Tapscott, our clerk) had a feast squatting out front. McGraw got hold of a can of B+M beans and a can of Spanish rice. I got some crackers and coke from the club and Tap had 3 cans of Vienna sausage. It was better than a steak dinner. As you can see, pens cut out pretty quick. Finished two of them since starting this letter. Of course, these pens we got for Christmas weren't Parker 51's.

Grenier got some movie film today, so if it gets decent this weekend I'll have a roll to mail out by Monday. I'll make sure to jot down what I'm shooting so you'll have a running commentary.

Not much else, my love. Thought this would be a longer letter, but like this year it's coming to a close. I hope the next year zips by – 'till October – and then drags. I love you and miss you more than I can say.

Your Leo

Christmas and the New Year

Paul, Grandparents Lanis and Ila Hughes,
Bryan, Karen, Lanis and Stephanie

Gifts, feasts and the needs of others, these subjects were easily joined in my father's view of life. Leaving the shops at Christmas time in our later years, my father would always produce some money to put in the Salvation Army kettle. He told us to always do so, in gratitude for the work the Salvation Army did among the troops overseas.

That Christmas in Jacksboro, Texas, we walked three houses down the road to the home of my mother's parents, Lanis and Ila Hughes. The coffee table in this picture bore our few gifts. We opened presents and had dinner together.

By the time the account of our Christmas Day reached Vietnam, my father had already shared a New Years feast: canned beans, crackers and Vienna sausage. "It was better than a steak dinner."

The orphans of Vietnam made several appearances in these letters. And they were an object of instruction in the years after. My father would admonish us: Remember the orphans! A squadron can do more than a government. But more valuable is an individual's decision to give his time and treasure.

My father taught us to enjoy simple food together, shun extravagance, and care for the orphan.

3 January 1966

My dearest wife,

It was so nice getting a letter from you again today after a short lapse. No mail at all came in Saturday, 1 Jan, but I did get a letter from Mom yesterday. Today was good though, since besides your letter I got those from the kids plus a Christmas card and note from Lt Murphy. He included a cartoon strip from the AF Times (Beetle Bailey) about a Lt with peach-fuzz on his face. He said "of course, that's only 2nd Lts." He mentioned another promotion I hadn't heard about, Sgt Lewis made Master. I've been wondering if the package Mom sent will ever get here. She mailed it 18 November, but nothing yet.

I enjoyed the letters from the kids – and Bryan's pictures. It sounds like they enjoyed Christmas and all did pretty good.

I must admit I did get a bit disturbed, however, over the way you've been feeling. Gee, Don Leta, I realize you know how I feel about not being with you during this time, especially as the time for the baby approaches. There still would be certain periods of depression, I know, but at least I like to feel that you could lie on my shoulder and we would see it through together. You can't imagine how helpless I feel during this period. I know that this separation is harder on you than on me. Not that this is one of the best places to be, but in addition to your condition you have five children to look after. Even when we were together, I know what a task that is. Coughs, colds, wheezing, fevers, etc.; I perfectly well understand how you must have little time to rest. I probably could carry on under the burden you must carry for about half the time you can. I do firmly believe that everything has a purpose for being, however, and such as this separation has brought me to more fully realize my responsibilities and to appreciate my wonderful wife and family, the Lord has likewise sent you these trials to strengthen you – as hard as that may be to understand as we struggle through them. Please be brave, my love. I worry continuously about you, especially as time draws nearer to the delivery date. I worry as I've never worried about anything in my life, for without you, Don Leta, I just don't know what would become of me. If you must let certain things go to get a few minutes rest, let them go. And what's more, don't be staying up to all hours to write to me. Just scribble "I love you" on a piece of paper and send it on. That will tell me all I need to know.

Sweetheart, I know any work on your legs will have to wait until we're settled somewhere and I can make sure you can stay off your feet for some time. As for the hysterectomy, that will have to be as you see fit, as far as when it should be performed. I fully agree that we have all we can possibly handle. You've been so wonderful to me, my darling, in that respect. Even more, perhaps, then I had the right to demand. That you have borne these children proves your love and has made me love you also all the more, for though I can never fully understand the patience and pain you must endure in giving life, I can appreciate it fully. By these actions you have also given me – us – life. Verily, there are not an overabundance of wives who have done so much for their husbands and families, and I consider myself one of the most fortunate husbands. There is absolutely nothing I would desire more, my happiness, than to be with you as you brought forth our sixth child, thereby saying to me – "there is proof of my love." Don Leta, I love you so very, very much.

Regardless of what is decided, I vow to you that our family is complete. Any further adventure in this area would only be a denial of my love and respect for you. If I must treat you like a sister at times, that is how it will be, though heaven knows it won't be easy. To be realistic, knowing how much I desire you now, and how this will be multiplied many times before we're together. I do not say this lightly. I think of you constantly and in many ways, not the least of which have been those in which we have been physically united. Under no circumstance would I want these times to be undone, regardless of our six consequences, because I've felt at those times that we were so much part of each other. However, I know that steps must be taken, and if abstinence is the answer for awhile, that's what it will be. I will do anything for you, my darling.

I do hope you can send me some pictures of you and the kids pretty soon. Get another roll of film and have someone take a whole bunch of you – I want them so badly. My heart aches at missing you, my most wonderful, darling, lovely wife. Please, honeybunch.

<u>Your</u> Leo

"Our Six Consequences"

There recur in these letters themes of military and family duty and of my father's longing for rest. The duty having been borne, it is time for Leo and Don Leta to rest and let the others carry the load.

They bore not just their share of duty, but a double measure. Nearly twenty years in the service, my father vows not to be separated from his wife by military duty again.   And in this letter, anticipating the birth of the sixth child, "I vow to you that our family is complete."

A little more and it will be time to rest. But my father writes with qualifications. He refrains from issuing an ultimatum to his Authority. Leo could not bear military separation again "unless it was a matter of national survival".[8]   Though they will have a conversation in these letters about a hysterectomy, contraceptives and abstinence, he reminds Don Leta, "the rhythm method not withstanding, it was God's will that we had the latest, as well as all the others". [9]

The Lord never called my father and mother to a contest of national survival.   But the Lord did choose to go beyond "six consequence". He sent a seventh child, Mathew, to also bless their days on earth.

"Like arrows
in the hand of a warrior,
so are the children
of one's youth."

"The Seventh Consequence"
Mathew, born 1968

---

[8] Aug 30, 1966; also Nov 6, Dec 11, 1965 and Jan 21, 1966.

[9] Jul 25, 1966; also Nov 28, 1965 and Jun 17, 1966.

4 January 1966

My dearest,

Another uneventful day, though work kept me fairly busy. Not much mail came in today, mostly because of bad weather this A.M. which kept quite a few flights grounded. I did get those money orders, however, and sent those off as soon as I could. Hope you received them by now.

Haven't been to the PX since the Army-AF took it over, or even some time before then. A couple guys in the office went today and they said there was much more stock than before. I'm going to try to get down there tomorrow. Still have been waiting for some decent weather to take movies – hope maybe tomorrow. Grenier's going to let me have a couple rolls until I get some. Still none in the BX.

There are more people coming in here all the time – planes and people all over the place. Within the next month we're supposed to get in another fighter wing – some 1200 people. They're really beefing up during this lull in the bombings up north. They may be planning on increased activity in that area if current efforts to bring about negotiations prove fruitless. A year ago there were only 23,000 U.S. personnel in Vietnam and the outlook now is for something like 400,000 by summer. Our Squadron had 39 people in July and we're now over 200 and growing.

Providing it's not raining, Grenier and I have been playing catch out back of the barracks for a bit after supper. He had his wife (she's in base housing at March) send him his gloves and a ball. They own a house in Alaska and that's where he's going to forecast for. They were stationed there during the earthquake this past year. As a matter of fact Carter was with him there also. Carter's the one with the dry wit from East Texas that I've mentioned before. Grenier had gone from there to March and was only at March 3 or 4 months when he got orders for VN. He's originally from N. Hampshire and they have 3 boys.

This has been a week to get things done since the Chief of Maintenance is on R&R to Hong Kong. Less rig-a-ma-role getting things out of the way. They're sure moving slowly on that building addition we're supposed to occupy. Originally we had hoped (too optimistically) to be in there by the 1st, but now it looks more like the end of this month.

Got's to try to get out another letter or two tonight, honey bunny, so I'll be cutting this short. If I don't watch it, I'll be letting the correspondence pile up on me. I might as well come clean – since you no doubt already realize it. The real reason I married you was to take care of the letter writing for me! This other stuff like how much I love you and what a wonderful girl you are is true enough, but that's only an excuse for the real reason!

Be sweet, my love, and take extra good care of yourself for me. I find now that I can no longer say that I miss you more and more, because I've reached that point where it's impossible to miss you any more than I do. Likewise, my love for you is so great that I don't know what could be done to increase it. Good night, my happiness.

Your Leo

6 Jan 66

My dearest,

It was so good to hear from you again today. A nice long letter too. No letter mail yesterday, but I did get Mom's package that she had mailed 17-18 November. It must have been on one of the slower boats!

There was quite an assortment of stuff in the box. Some of it, like candy, will go mostly to the kids, while cake will be eaten at the shop. I've been eating everyone else's. Surprisingly, it all came through pretty good except for a box of mixed nuts which were still edible but getting a bit soft. Besides the nuts was a fruitcake, a can of hard candy, a box of Fanny Farmer candy, 12 packages of Italian candy (nougats), 10 pkgs of gum, 2 bars of soap, a carton of cigarettes, a can of instant coffee, cream and sugar substitute, a carton of Kents, a sack of figs, canned potato sticks, a plastic carton of assorted mints and 3 cans of boned chicken. It was packed with the Pawtucket Times and 3 Argosy magazines. I thumbed through the magazines last night and got a charge out of the back cover of one of them. It looked like Angie must have been picking the winners of the next day's races!

I'm afraid I had a pretty quiet New Year's Eve, even though I don't see where you get that crack about my usually going to bed early on that date! If I remember correctly, this time I was in the sack sometime around 10 o'clock. As a matter of fact, Grenier and I are, or have been, a couple of the odd balls, among a few others. We usually go to the club once or twice every night for coffee. There's only been a very few times that we've had more than 2 beers. Let me tell you, though, there are some that you'll always know where to find, night after night. Boy, I just can't figure it. Without exaggerating, I'll bet there's about 10-15 in our Sq alone who blow up to $100 a month drinking – just about all of them married too.

Here I am helpless again as you tell me about problems with Stephanie. I don't know what a doctor will be able to do since she clams up so when you try to talk to her. There's no doubt that she is smart, she's proven that often enough. It may be, as you say, that she someway felt slighted when we paid too much attention to Karen or turned to Karen for some of the more responsible or adult tasks. I don't really know what I'd do, but I wish I were there with you anyway.

I wouldn't worry too much about Bryan being tied to his Mother's apron strings. I had always heard that boys were usually more affectionate towards their mother. Additionally, there's no question of dividing it now. It's like he's lost one so he's trying to make sure the other one doesn't slip away on him. It'll probably be hardest on him when you go to the hospital for the baby.

Yes, Bob Hope and his troop performed here. They had it out at Hill 327, where Cardinal Spellman said Mass. It was scheduled for 3 P.M. and since only 25% of our people could go, I let some of the troops go. As it turned out, it rained and Bob Hope didn't arrive until almost dark. It was around 8 P.M. by the time the show was over. There's really no place around for them to put on anything like that except in the open. The secure areas are so crowded there's no one place big enough. The guys tell me Martha Raye and her troupe had come on the base but only put on a show at the Airman's Club. That only took care of about 1/3 of the Airmen – none of the NCOs or officers. Hugh O'Brien was here last month. All he did was visit each club a few minutes and sign autographs. I didn't tear myself away to get his autograph – how will you ever forgive me!

Three of the guys going home in April got their assignments today. Sgt McGraw, who works for me, got his first choice of Alaska. Another got his first choice of Japan and the third his second choice of Denver. The great majority seem to get their 1st or 2nd choice. Another 90-100 days before I'll be forecasting. That's the next milestone for me. It makes it easier to take than aiming for a rotation date 291 days away.

That's it for now, sugarbun. Want to see if maybe I can get another letter or two out of the way tonight. Then have to take a shower and hit the sack. I love you just loads and bushels full. Be sweet, my darling.

<u>Your</u> Leo

8 Jan 66

My Darling,

Did get a letter from my girl yesterday, and one from Theresa, but didn't get to do any letter writing. Thought I would get at this earlier this evening since it's Saturday, but as it turned out it's now 9:30 PM and I'm taking a short break. We had a cable go out this afternoon so there's all sorts of activity trying to restore it. I'll have to go back after a bit to check on progress, but will try to get a bit of writing done first.

Gosh, it sounds like just everyone is sick back there. I sure do hope everything has straightened itself out at least to let you catch your breath. It's awful that I must be away during these times. I know there's nothing I could do about the illness, but at least I'd be there to help you keep up with things. It's awful to be sitting here unable to do anything. I'll tell you it would really be awful if I didn't know I had such a wonderful and courageous wife and mother. I love you so much, my Don Leta.

I hope to finish the roll of film I'm half through and mail it to you Monday. You'll have to get it developed as there are no mailers here. I'm logging the scenes as I take them so you'll know what is what. The first shots, with all the kids, only show about 1/3 to 1/2 the number who are sometimes out back. Every single one knows at least 5 English words: "Hey…you give me candy."

Got to figuring things out at work today – finance wise. I should be able to send you a total of $600 minimum from now on. This will still leave me enough to pick up a few things as I run across them and also put a bit aside in case I have the chance to hit someplace on R&R around July or August. That shouldn't be too bad once the last car payment is made in March, though I know there'll always be more bills popping up.

They've brought some heavy stuff in here since Christmas and when they first went off we weren't sure what was happening. We had gotten used to the dull thuds of outgoing mortar. Fortunately it's still outgoing, but now there's considerably more noise and you can feel the shock waves and concussions when they fire salvoes from the big howitzers. We still have plenty of in-country action, but the halt to flights up north has made quite a difference in the number of jets taking off, especially in the daytime. We keep seeing in the Stars & Stripes about all the efforts being made to bring about negotiations, but nobody is overly enthusiastic over believing it'll come about. At least, no one talks about it.

Will write again tomorrow, my love, conditions permitting. I long for the sight and feel of you and think about you and the kids day in and day out. Take care of yourself for me, my darling.

Your Leo

8 Jan 66

My dear Lanis,

Just a little note to let you know I received your letter in which you sent me your first poem. I thought it was pretty good for anyone's first poem. I don't think I even though of writing one when I was your age. As a matter of fact, I don't think your daddy was ever too good at that.

We've had about 3 days without rain now. It's a little hot and dusty, but not too bad yet. Yesterday, after work, I shot half a roll of movie film out back of the barracks. Sgt Grenier gave me a roll of film and let me use his camera. I will take the rest tomorrow and mail it home.

You take care of yourself, the other kids, and your mother. Be sweet.

Loads of love & kisses,

Daddy

9 Jan 66

My Beloved,

I sweated it out today and it paid off in another sweet letter from my girl tonight. As a matter of fact, I was halfway through your letter when I had to go out. This airman had just come in from Tan Son Nhut with some equipment. I picked him up and got him squared away 'till morning, so it's still only 6:30 or so now.

This has been about the fourth straight day without rain. The weather has been real nice – warm in the daytime and just comfortable at night. I finished the first roll of film and was going to take more this afternoon but it was Grenier's turn to use his camera! If it's nice tomorrow I'll try to get some shots down around where I work – or hang out.

I hope the kids are feeling better. Your letter today indicated there had been some improvement. There's been quite a bit of virus and flu type illnesses hereabouts but I'm holding my own. A month or so ago I came down with something or other for about 3 days, but don't know what it was. As soon as I'd eat anything I'd get all sorts of cramps in my stomach. Got some liquid on sick call, but don't know if that took care of it or if it just ran its course. Outside of that, I'm just getting grayer each day!

Saw John Hill this morning. He leaves next Friday. Says he goes back to Guam and as far as he knows will be there until around 1 March.

At this point I took a break for a while. Grenier was out back and told me to come out and watch the rats. One had just strolled up to within 4 or 5 feet of him and then turned away. We see them around quite a bit once it gets dark. The rats here get as big as small cats. Another thing we watched were bats. They also start flying all over the place once it gets dark. I stayed out there a little too long now the darn mosquitoes have nibbled on my ankle. Cuss .... Cuss!

There's no getting away from it even in a combat zone. We're due an inspection the 19th of the month. Pacific Comm Region (Wheeler AFB) has a team coming to all bases in Vietnam to see that we're not sluffing off on all the ridiculous paperwork just 'cause we're here. Oh well, I guess it gives them something to do – getting away from the rigors of life in Hawaii, not to mention the opportunity to draw a month's combat pay. In typical fashion also, some of these jewels around here are all excited about getting this and that done before the inspection. I'm afraid I've been through enough of these not to get a coronary attack. I suppose after they're done S.E. Asia Comm Region out of Clark will want their turn at bat, and then Comm Group in Saigon will be wanting their turn.

This has been a bad weekend for three Squadron Troops. Two maintenance men, both out of the cable shop and one operations man all went home on emergency leave. One's (got interrupted again, tell you about it in a minute). Anyhow, one's father died and another's father was quite sick. I don't know why the third went.

Back to my latest interruption. Grenier just came in and got me. He said, "come here, I want you to see something before I go to bed." I thought he was pulling my leg and probably wanted to show me something Carter, who bunks with him, was doing. Right next to his area is a washroom with a sink, cleaning supplies and toilet paper. Up across the top was a small, beat up satchel that hadn't been there before. I got a chair and Grenier climbed up to see if there was anything marked on it or if he could tell what it was. I told him to listen to it, but there was no noise. He handed it to me and I took it where nobody was around. When I opened it, real easy like, there were only papers in it. It looked like a bunch of test papers of Vietnamese in their English class. I don't know how it got there, unless it belonged to one of the houseboys. Have to check that out tomorrow. We were particularly leery because there were Vietnamese in the barracks today doing some work. Strange suitcases don't make too good bedmates.

So much for now, my sweet. Will try to write again tomorrow. <u>I love you</u>.

Your Leo

11 Jan 66

My dearest wife,

This was a real good day for me, what with both a letter and package from my girl.

12 Jan 66
Lunch break

Well, my intentions were good. Waited a little late to start this letter last night. I quit to break up a fight in the tent next door and before I could get going again we lost our lights so I didn't get any more written.

Three of our troops, all operations types, were wounded from a thrown bomb in town last night. That's the first such incident in some time. I guess there were 5 of them together when this thing went off. One of the taboos was being violated – that is keeping out of groups. They're not so tempted to use their munitions if there are only two people involved.

Everything came through real good in the package. Polished off half a banana bread last night and I'm eating some now. Grenier like to went crazy over it. Said it was exactly like his wife's. Will be saving the beans until I have a big urge again.

I can imagine what it must be like putting Bryan through the mill with those tests. I would imagine the hardest thing would be keeping him on liquids for a full day when he's not feeling sick.

As for Stephanie, I'm just not sure. There's so much medical people don't know about behavior, much less we laymen. One of her biggest problems is probably that she's too much like her father in that many things she'll shy away from because she's afraid to fail. Like she often mentions her tetherball prowess because she could beat most of the kids, or when we'd hear of or see good grades on her papers, but bad ones would be hidden. She may feel we expect too much all the time. It may be right that we need to be patient with her and encourage her to do some of these things we never called on her to do before. That's one of the reasons I wrote her a second letter praising her for helping you and making Karen's birthday cake, etc. She may be needing more of that. I don't personally feel that she's living in a dream world, even though there may be some relationship between bed wetting, stealing, etc. and her feeling of being an equal member of the family. I still think one of her biggest challenges is to develop the ability to accept defeat at times and come back stronger. That's why I say she's too much like me in that respect. Here I am, 94 years old, and I'm only beginning to realize that there are times when I'm just going to have to go ahead with something even if there's a good chance of failure. Otherwise, one will never know for sure if he did the right thing. I agree with the doctor that right now the best thing is to try a little extra in treating her more like someone ready and willing to accept responsibility. Though I know Steph is as smart as a whip, she lacks confidence. Like you mention her making tea and being kind of sloppy in the kitchen. She probably makes herself nervous because she's not sure she can do it right.

I'm going to cut this off for now, my sweet. Gots to get back to the pits. I have considerably more to keep me going now since we reorganized and all the maintenance shops are directly under me.

For me to tell you how much I miss you and love you seems so easy and yet so difficult. You're my life, Don Leta.

Your Leo

13 Jan 66

My dearest,

I'm just taking a bit of a break here at work to try getting a few words to you. I don't know if any mail came in for me this evening as I didn't get to chow until 6:30 at which time the mail room was closed. It's almost 7:30 now and I'm back at the shop trying to catch up on paperwork that I had to let go today because of a bunch of other problems. To top it all off, some General is visiting us tomorrow. He wasn't due to get here until Saturday, but as you might know, he'll pop in right into the middle of a rat race.

There's not too much new with me, other than I've sure been putting away that banana bread. I know it didn't last long at home, and watching myself I can see why. It sure is good. There's still half of one left and I've hidden it.

We did have a bit of excitement last night as a B-57 blew up and crashed at the end of the runway. Grenier, Carter and I had just come back from the club, somewhere around 9 o'clock and we were sitting in front of the barracks. All of a sudden the sky lit up in back of the barracks. At first we thought it was a flare, but they had never been that close so we went out back to see. By then, fire engines, AP's, ambulances, etc. were heading toward the end of the runway. For about 45 minutes it burned and ammunition kept going off. At one point the bombs detonated and let me tell you that everything shook. This plane was loaded when taking off so no one could get anywhere near it while it was burning and there was still live ammo aboard. The pilot and navigator were killed and if anyone else had been anywhere nearby they would have had it.

Looks like the rains are done. It's been hot, dusty and humid for 5 straight days. You'd have to be here to see how it can be so dusty and humid at the same time. The temperature has stayed below 90° but it's muggy; and without rain the fine dust blows. All I keep hearing is wait until it really gets hot – where you can sit in the deepest shade and sweat. I'm in no rush.

Say, while I think of it, would you please send me your (our) telephone number and area code, just in case I can ever get a call through. If I can make it to Norton in California they can dial you direct on government leased lines. The trick is catching it when the line is available.

Back to work now, my love. Will keep at it until about 9:30 or so and then quit for the night. Be sweet, my darling and take good care of yourself for me. I miss you and love you terribly.

<u>Your</u> Leo

15 Jan 66

My Beloved,

I feel awful about being so irregular with my letters this past week or so. I'm writing tonight but I don't know what kind of a letter it'll be 'cause I'm just pooped.

Got a letter from you yesterday and another today. My intention was definitely to write last night, but, like all good intentions …… It had been a full day to start with, ending about 6 P.M. Then, almost 8 o'clock, Lt Carol got a hold of me. I finally got back to the barracks at 11:45. I needed a shower, but instead I accepted a shot of vodka and hit the sack! I sure didn't feel like rushing off to work this morning – but sleeping in Saturdays is not exactly the rule here. Anyhow, I had a chance to get a cup of coffee and take it to work with me! It turned out to be another doozy and I finally got back here about 6:30. It's 7:30 now and I still haven't had that shower. Will do so after this letter and then hit the pad. One thing, it does make the days go by, though the dates are still dragging. Gee, honeybunch, I never knew 365 days could take so long to go by. Now have 82 down – 283 to go, at most.

I definitely would go ahead and get someone to clean house – two days a week if necessary. Heaven knows you have enough on your hands just keeping up with things much less getting into these hairy cleaning programs. I would much rather you go ahead and spend the money for that than taking the chance of just running yourself down.

You mention putting money in savings. That's good if you can do it, but I would make sure there's enough where you can get your hands on it quickly if necessary. Definitely, however, put some aside each month for someone to help with that housework – and start it as soon as possible. You'll probably need it for some time after the baby arrives also. As for savings, the amount, etc., I'll leave that up to you as you know what you need for expenses monthly. Right now I've got to get more fatigues, shoes, combat boots, shorts & T-shirts, but by 1 April I believe I'll be able to increase money orders to you up to $250 per month without too much strain.

No, I don't need a baseball glove or anything like that. Grenier has two gloves and we just toss the ball around out back for about 30 minutes after supper, if we're both around.

I guess I'd have to agree with you about leaving Paul in his crib for now. I know with everything else, there'll hardly be enough time to keep him in a bed, especially if he gets to carrying on with his brother.

Steph's letter was included in today's mail. I think the big thing now is not to expect any major changes overnight. We'll just have to work with her as much as possible and pray that things straighten up. I'm just so sorry that I'm not there to help now, what with all the other problems you must face. Some day soon, my darling, this will all be behind us.

There's just a slight cloudiness tonight; still can see stars. Last night we got our first rain in about a week – a shower lasting 30 minutes or so. It came down fairly heavy. The days seem to be getting warmer, but the nights have been staying quite comfortable. I'm afraid that isn't going to last.

Saw and said goodbye to John Hill yesterday morning. He was in the club for breakfast – was leaving on a morning flight to Saigon. From Saigon he was going to catch a hop to the Philippines and then Guam. I wish the heck I was ready to go back. Actually, I shouldn't say it that way because I am ready – but I wish Uncle Sugar was ready too! The troops returning in August started forecasting today. That means two more months before I get my paperwork in. That's my immediate goal.

I'm going to get cleaned up and in the sack. Didn't have time to shave this morning so you can imagine what I look like. You can expect letters more regularly than the last few days, if only things would settle down. I shouldn't kick, however; there are many troops in the paddies tonight who are not having a chance to write. This should be a hectic week what with the PACOM IG (Inspector General) due in Wednesday. If they write us up for ridiculous stateside reasons I think I'll personally throw them out!

Good night, my love. I miss you and love you more than I can say. I'm so anxious to be getting some pictures of you and the kids soon. I've just been looking again at the few I have — and they make me so lonesome for you. It's true that one can be lonesome though surrounded by people. I know.

Your loving husband,
Leo

18 Jan 66

My Darling,

I'm just going to try to knock out a quickie note during my shortened lunch break so I can get something off in this afternoon's mail.

We worked right through until almost midnight last night on last minute items that we hardly have time for during normal operation around here. Then it was up at 6 A.M. and back at it. This morning the Commander was around with some Colonel and other officers from Southeast Asia Comm Region out of Clark AFB. Now the PACOM inspection team arrived about 11:30, so they'll be with us the next couple days. I'm just waiting for the mail room to open so I can check mail and then back to the pits.

I received the pictures you sent and really enjoyed them. I've looked them over many times already. Paul really does look like a character, especially the one of him & Bryan in the tub and the one where he's eyeballing the Christmas decorations.

I hope tonight I have a couple minutes to sit down and write to you. Depends on what kind of crisis is generated next.

Bye-bye for now, my sweet. I love you and miss you much, much, much.

Your Leo

19 Jan 66

My dearest Don Leta,

At last there's a chance to sit and write to you without having to scribble out quick notes. They finished the inspection today and are holding their critique tonight. They're scheduled to depart tomorrow morning. One of the guys on the inspection team told me they built more duplexes out at Bellows—in case I was interested!

Things have been relatively quiet hereabouts of late, other than our usual nighttime firing and a few small skirmishes. Everyone is restricted to the base again for 3 days, 21-23 January, while the Vietnamese celebrate the lunar new year, known as Tet. I guess it's quite the celebration in Vietnam. Fireworks (mostly firecrackers) are plentiful and understandably make a number of people nervous. Everybody from out of the province goes back home, etc. One of the traditional things, it seems is for everyone to paint the inside of their houses a new color. As you've probably heard, there's been some sort of truce agreed upon during this period.

Boy, it really sounds like they put Bryan through the mill with those tests at Wolters. I'm kind of surprised to hear there were so many x-rays involved. You didn't mention it, but when are you supposed to get a reading on the results? I hope they can do something about it. Had you mentioned about having it done for Stephanie, or were you going to wait and see what develops with her?

You'll probably know something about Mother's condition by the time you get this, or I should hope it's not overly serious and she doesn't spend too much time in the hospital. What ever it is, I hope she has it taken care of without putting it off.

I intend to have a cup of coffee, take a shower and hit the pad after this letter. Though it is only 7:30, I'm ready. This past week I've been going quite a bit and I feel pooped—like I can't get rested up. By the time I've hit the sack it seems I was burned out and sluggish. I might as well face it, old man Time is gaining on the old dad!

Stopped again to look at the pictures you sent me. Though I've only had them a few days, I'm already getting them dog-eared. I wish I could just grab you all out of it. 279 more days still seems like such a long time when I think of how long these 89 days away from you have been. Tapscott, our clerk, is going to Seattle, his first choice, and got his port call of 5 February today. That means only 2 more weeks for him here, the lucky stiff. People leaving in March, including Sgt McGraw, my Senior Controller, are all expecting their assignments any day now. I'll be glad to see them all go, 'cause that'll mean I'm getting that much closer.

Good night, my happiness. I'll lie down again tonight, as every night, thinking of you. That's how I'll finally fall asleep, with my wonderful girl on my mind and in my heart. I love you so.

Your Leo

Friday, 21 Jan 66

My Beloved Wife,

There are time that even before I sit to write to you, nothing of news is on my mind, but only the teasing feeling of loneliness and longing for you. After having spent those six weeks apart while I went to the NCO Academy, I had no idea whatsoever that these past 3 months could be so long. At least, on that last trip I knew it would all be over in a short time, while now what has already passed must be endured another 3 times before 12 months are completed.

I've read and re-read your last two letters, those I received yesterday and today, and I've taken out the pictures I have over and over again. I've come to Vietnam with but one thought in mind: to do the best I could for what is a good cause. Towards this end I have had but one prayer, that I have the strength to serve with honor. My guiding words are, and remain, that.... "greater love than this hath no man, than he who lays down his life for his friend." Through all this, little did I initially realize that the greatest suffering I would be asked to endure would be the separation from my loved ones. Don Leta, I know we will make it through this one, but I could not stand even the thought of having to do it again. I pray that some type of solution or ending is found, for escalation would probably mean extension of duty. If this must be, then so be it, but I can never miss you more than I do now.

It's strange how at certain times I get to feeling so melancholy. This usually gets when I spend too much time thinking, instead of finding some way to keep busy. I did have ways to get out of that and keep busy today as we ran into a multitude of problems with our power. A scheduled change from base power to emergency power didn't come out too good and we were kept hopping a good part of the day getting facilities and circuits back on the air.

Those pictures of Paul are real cute. He sure looks like he has dark eyes. I feel like I could just hug him. He does look like he could be a handful and a half when turned loose. I got the letter with Paul's pictures today and the one with Mom's pictures yesterday, though the first letter was written 2 days after the other. Quite the mail service!

Boy, last night was something else. I lay on the sack somewhere around 6:30 and woke up at 9:30. By then the Vietnamese were starting their celebration of Tet with fireworks. It was sporadic until midnight, and then everything broke loose, and it kept on till morning. They have no elaborate fireworks like roman candles or aerial displays; it's almost all firecrackers. The part that shocked me is that most, or at least a great part of it is done indoors!

The object of it all supposedly is that they're chasing the evil spirit out of the house so they can start the year with a clean slate, so to speak. They have strings of firecrackers that won't quit, either. Some are 3 deep on each side, 12 feet long, like this:

They're each 2 inch salutes, interspersed with 4 or 5 inch ones. Let me tell you it's a long blasting string. If you remember what the finale is like at fireworks displays in the states, try to imagine it 2 or 3 times as bad, and lasting from midnight to 6 A.M.! It must have been 1:30 or so by the time I went to sleep, and I woke up in the morning to the sound of more fireworks.

I think I may already have mentioned it, but you ask in one of your letters about buying a table and chairs. Of course do so. As far as that goes, get anything else we might need while you can. In case there's any loot left over, here's a couple of clues for any package you might send in the future:

> 2 pairs black shoelaces-24"
> 40 banana breads/apple cakes
> Canned beans/brown bread
> No more chocolate—this climate is murder on it.
> One old spoon and fork.
> As much of you as possible.

Made it to the movies tonight, the first in over a week. They just haven't had much of anything on. This was "A Shot in the Dark", a comedy with Peter Sellers, and I haven't laughed so much in ages. I even had tears from laughing so much. Of course it was silly, but a welcome break in the routine.

I've got to get with it and take a shower and hit the sack again. Here it is time for lights out already—as a matter of fact, they just went out, but I still have a lamp.

As you've mentioned previously, my darling, I sort of hate also to get to this part of the letter because I feel so inadequate when trying to say how much I love you and miss you. More often than not I will have to stop here, close my eyes and try to picture the times past when we were together –How very wonderful were those times, and how little did I realize it then. Perhaps it will be like that again, but I can't imagine it anything but finer, if possible, since I can so much more appreciate it now. To see you, to talk to you, hold you, kiss you—oh my love, I want you so very much. It's really strange how a thought can be both wonderful and sad at the same time—like thinking of having held you close and being unable to do it now. And the many times I've

laid down and found myself reaching into emptiness, looking for you—hoping to touch you and to have you hold me —only to find it wasn't to be.
Don Leta, my love, I miss you in so many different ways.

Take real good care of yourself for me my love, until I return. After that I will take care of you forever

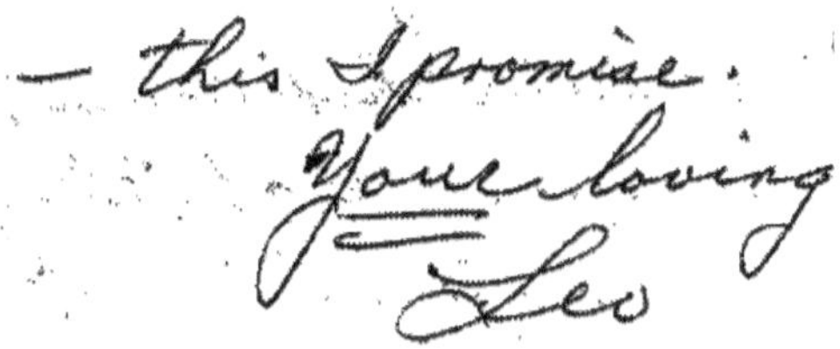

Sat, 22 Jan 66

My Honeybunch,

There's not very much news to report – nothing exciting happened and there were no mail deliveries – but figured I'd scribble a couple lines anyhow.

I am enclosing a poop sheet on some more insurance I have now; a new type insurance which only recently went into effect. So now, besides the Mass Mutual Policy, I have $5000 NSLI and this $10,000 Group Life. The first policy is the one I've had all along and cost $3.60/mo., while this new one is $2/mo., both of which are taken out of my check by Uncle Sugar. This new plan is term insurance, so there will be no dividends. File this with my papers.

Both yesterday and today have been kind of dreary – rain and clouds just about all the time. I'd like to see a bit of sun tomorrow since it's an off day. There are many tears and gnashing of teeth by some of these poor troops – they've extended the restriction to the base for another three days. It seems like some of them will never last the tour having to suffer so!

Like I said, sweet, no news to report. I can say how much I love you and miss you, but that's not news. I do want so much to be with you and how I wish it were possible for me to be there, especially from now until the baby comes. I want so much to be able to be near you at that time and tell you how wonderful you've been and how you've made me so very, very happy. Goodnight, my darling.

Your Leo

MEMO ROUTING SLIP | *Never Use for Approvals, Disapprovals, Concurrences, or Similar Actions*

		ACTION
1 TO Mrs Dubois	INITIALS / DATE	CIRCULATE / COORDINATION
2		FILE
		INFORMATION X
3		NOTE AND RETURN
		PER CON-VERSATION
4		SEE ME
		SIGNATURE

REMARKS

I

LOVE

YOU

FROM MSgt Dubois

DATE 30 NOV 65

PHONE FALCON 6106

DD FORM 95 1 OCT 60   Replaces DD Form 94, 1 Feb 50, and DD Form 95, 1 Feb 50, which will be used until exhausted.   o48—16—78279-2   GPO

22 Jan 66

My dear Lanis,

I was very happy to get another letter from you yesterday. It made me especially feel good when you told me that you and Stephanie had been working almost all day and that neither of you had to be fussed at all.

No matter where I looked, on the paper or in the envelope, I couldn't find the picture you said you were drawing of the whole family. You must have either forgotten to draw it like you said, or you forgot to put it in the envelope. I was anxious to see it because I wanted to see if Mommy was still as skinny as when I left or if she's been eating too much and getting bigger!

Mommy mentioned you girls had finished your mid-term tests and I hope you all did well. But, if some of the grades didn't come out too good we must not get discouraged. It just means we'll have to work a little harder to bring them up. Your Daddy sometimes had good grades, and sometimes they weren't so good, so I had to get busy.

You and your sisters keep trying to be good and help your Mommy like you said in your letter. It's getting closer to when the new baby will be here, so everybody will have to do a little more. Give everyone a big hug and kiss for me.

Your loving Daddy

25 Jan 66

My dearest Don Leta,

No letters were written by me last night but I have a very strong reason. I was too lazy! I heard from you yesterday, after having received Karen's letter the day before.

We did have a bit of activity hereabouts last night, or rather this morning, from around 12:45 A.M. to 0230, but went back to sleep afterwards. Only one round on the base did any damage.

Karen did get to be the first to tell me of the snow you all had, so I guess she can rest easy. I did read in today's paper of the big heavy snows they've been having back there, especially in the northeast. I guess I won't be seeing any of that stuff, this winter anyhow. Oh well, 272 more days and we'll see.

I still haven't decided where to forecast for. I intend to go through the listing of bases in the next couple days to see if you have any preference. You mentioned a dry climate while having trouble with the kids and their allergies, asthma, etc. Also, your last letter, after watching movies, made you long somewhat for Hawaii, it seems. There are 3 drawbacks to that, even though I wouldn't mind another 3 years there. First, it would require 2 extra years since

I'll have 14 months (18 if I should make Senior) to go and the tour is 3 years; secondly, I'd like to get to the east and see Mom & all after this tour and that would be one heck of a trip back and forth cross-country with 19 kids; thirdly, and far from least, I'd fear being assigned to PACOM Region Headquarters at Wheeler instead of at the Hickam Base Comm or CINCPAC. That would mean I'd be going out quite often on inspections like this team that just came through here. They hit all Pacific bases – Hawaii, Guam, Phil, Japan, Korea, VIETNAM, etc. Vietnam alone is taking them 24 days. They're always back & forth across the ocean.

Well, sugarbun. I started this early tonight and didn't get by the first page. I laid in the sack, clothes on and all and went to sleep. I guess being up last night sapped a bit out of me. Grenier woke me up at 9:30 and we went for coffee, so I feel better now. One trouble is getting coffee after 9:30, which is when they clean the urns. I'm still hoping to get a hold of an electric pot so I can at least boil water and have instant coffee after that time. I saw Sgt Green, who I mentioned to you before as being at Carswell, and he flies in and out of here from Japan all the time. He's stationed in Japan. Yesterday he said if I ever wanted anything from there to let him know and he'd get it for me, so I think I'll let him pick one up for me, as well as some items of clothing I can't get the right size of here.

Good night for now, my love. I'll be thinking of you all the time as it has been since I left you. I love you so much and miss you terribly. Take good care of yourself, my darling.

Your Leo

"Leapin Leo" played ball for the champion Carswell Bombers ball team. Carswell Air Force Base, Fort Worth, Texas, 1950 – 52. Photo courtesy, Fort Worth Star-Telegram.

26 Jan 66

My Darling,

No big news today, but did want to write a few words to my honeybunch. I've been keeping pretty busy, which seems to have helped with the time in a little way, anyhow. My sections are scattered around on both side of the runway, so it sometimes gets a bit awkward to get around to all of them when I want to. They're still working on our buildings, but I hope it'll be finished in 2 or 3 weeks. I'll probably move my SMC in there sooner, before they're completely finished, because the Lt. is getting kind of eager.

Well, after Monday there'll only be 8 paydays to go. With today shot, there are 271 days. The first three months are always supposed to be the hardest and I hope this is true since they're already behind me. At least I can look ahead to forecasting in less than two months, and hope I ship out the first part of October rather than around the 26th.

Airman Tapscott, our clerk, has but two days to go before he boards the plane for home. His DEROS[10] is 12 February but he's leaving here the 29th. He'll fly to Saigon and catch a plane there for the states. The next one in our area to go will be TSgt Daily, also a crypto man, who works in our Quality Control Section. He leaves in February for a consecutive tour to England. The following month, SSgt McGraw, my Senior Controller, leaves for what he hopes is Germany, though he hasn't received word on his assignment yet. He should be able to get it since he's a teletype man and they can go just about anywhere.

It's joy time again—already. Gots to get 2 or 3 more shots tomorrow or Friday. You get them fast and often in these parts. One kid who's been here a while skated through the last 4 months or so and they caught up with him yesterday .... 9 shots worth!

Like I said, sugar, not too much new. I just keep counting the days and they seem so long, though the weeks seem to go by fairly fast. Guess that's because there's so little to the weekends. I love you with all of me, my sweet, and couldn't ever think of another to replace you in any way. My love for you just keeps on growing and, though I try to pass a little to you through these letters, the bulk will just have to wait until we're together again. Good night, my happiness.

Your Leo

---

[10] DEROS Date of Expected Return from Over Seas

27 Jan 66, Thurs.

My dearest,

A letter from you today brightened up an otherwise tiring day. It's slowly getting warmer all the time, though there was a bit of breeze to go with it today. The mosquitoes will never quit, though. I get bitten as much in the office as anywhere. They particularly like to congregate under desks and in corners and bite into ankles, or rather right above them.

Lo and be hold, there's a floorshow on at the club tonight. Big Deal! They had one about a month ago – lasted all of 40 minutes. No one place is big enough, so what they do is put on 3 shows – Airmen's Club, NCO Club and Officers Club. I missed the last one – too crowded anyhow. All I heard afterwards was how awful it was. So tonight I'm not even making an attempt. Went for a cup of coffee at 7:30 and it was already crowded though the show isn't 'till 9 P.M. I said "Good luck to you all" and took my coffee with me.

You've mentioned a number of times about Karen needing more clothes. My gosh, with all you've got to take care of and get done around there I don't know why you insist on having to do the sewing for it. Why don't you just go out and buy her 30 or 40 dresses? Seriously, honeybunch, you ought to not try and do so much at this time, and since there are a couple dollars extra, use them to take up some of this labor. I don't want you to be running yourself into exhaustion trying to keep up with all of this. You've got to slow up and take it a bit easier wherever you can. Having Mrs. Middleton come in at times is a step I that direction,

Don Leta's parents, Ila and Lanis Hughes of Jacksboro, Texas, 1965.

but you should do more where necessary. Buy some of these things for the kids instead of making them. The extra cost will be well worth it if it means you'll be able to get a bit more rest.

I thought the kids' grades were real good, though I was disappointed in Karen's marks in English and Lit/Spelling. I thought she would do better than that in those areas. As for Social Studies (History), that couldn't bother me less. As a matter of fact, they have a nerve listing that Social Studies. She might just as well have a course in Vietnamese History for what good it'll do her! I guess Lanis will surprise us the most. We always knew and said how sharp Stephanie was, while Lanis didn't ever seem to understand anything she was told. But I guess she's really the most aggressive and will go after what she needs. Her grandpa Lanis will probably go around saying he expected it.

I hope you're not having too much more trouble with the car. I would like to eventually trade it in for one with a more powerful engine, maybe a 12 passenger! I don't know why they didn't check it after putting in a new thermostat. It must be that the lines are clogged somewhere and the hot water is just not circulating.

Gee, you're telling me about the little one getting active and wiggling so much brings back so many memories. How I wish again I could place my hand on your tummy and feel the activity. Of course, you realize that's just an excuse. What I really mean is that I'd just like to place my hand on your tummy, and all over again. I don't really know why that keeps coming to mind, because heaven knows that's not all I think about you. To be perfectly frank, (and maybe I shouldn't be in a letter), it's not been only a few times that I've dreamed of holding you again, kissing your breasts and moving to every part of you. I've tried so often to remember how wonderful you made me feel; often, I know at the expense of some part of you. But I don't want you to think that's all that remains with me. Just your presence, or the thought of it, is what makes me feel the best. God, how I want to take you again, but more than that, I just want us to be together. Oh my darling, lovely, sweet Don Leta—there's so very, very much I want to tell you when we're together once more. Maybe you'll say the mortars landed too close to him – but I hope not. It just makes me so angry and so helpless feeling to sit here and write what so much I want to say to you – even though I may not utter a word. Don Leta, understand this: You, and you alone, mean more to me than anything in this world. I love you, respect you and honor you above all else. You, and the children you've so generously borne us, are my whole life. Love – if we can ever understand its deepest and fullest meaning – is what I have for you.

Your Leo

29 Jan 66

My Dearest,

Just a brief note tonight to let you know how much I love you and miss you. I didn't receive any mail from anyone yesterday or today, so there's nothing to report in that line.

Work keeps going pretty strong, and I don't look for any let up soon. As a matter of fact I've got my whole day planned for Sunday – work. No matter where we are, however, it always makes one wonder if half the things we must do are really necessary. The Chief of Maintenance thinks the way to solve any problem is to put in longer hours. Heck, I'll put 268 more days any way they want. My hair (what's left) is hanging in my soup. I haven't even had time to get a haircut. Usually I run into town and get one for 30 piastres. There's a barber shop in a cubbyhole in the cantonment area, but they have only 4 barbers for some 3000 personnel. I can't fight those lines. In town they do a pretty good job using the old fashioned hand type clippers. The best part is that every haircut is automatically accompanied with a scalp, shoulder and neck massage as a matter of routine. They also make your neck crack by twisting it each side and up. I hope none of them are VC!

Like I said, my love, there's not much to report from this side of the world, except that there's someone here who missed you something awful. His thoughts in any free moment are of you and his family. All he lives for is the time to come when his commitment here is completed and he can come back to your warm embrace. That's right, he's

Your Leo

29 January 66

Hi Pal,

    I got a letter from Karen the other day, and she sent me another letter and picture from you. You sure do make scary pictures! Everytime I get one it makes me jump up and go hide under the bed!

    Mommy told me about all the tests you had to take at the hospital and especially how good you were when you had to take shots. She said you take shots just like a soldier. That's real good. I guess me and you are the best shot takers there is.

    You must be getting bigger all the time. I wonder if I'll be still able to throw you up high 3 times when I get back. I hope you're still being a good boy all the time and helping to take care of Paul.

    Bye bye for now. Give everybody a big hug and kiss for me.

Daddy

1 Feb 66

My Dearest,

I'm cheating a bit and writing this on duty while I have a couple minutes of relative quiet. Two letters from you yesterday and I was already to write last night when I got called out. It was 12:30 by the time I finished, so I just took a shower and hit the sack. Today I got another letter from you and one from Lanis, including the pictures of Texas winter so I'm bound and determined to get a letter off to you in some shape or form. If something else comes up I'll just cut this short but I will get it off.

Heavy snow in Jacksboro, Texas, 1966. Bryan, Paul and Grandpa Lanis Hughes

I really enjoyed the snapshot of you and the kids, especially the shot of where you caught Paul doing his unauthorized climbing. Boy, I tell you, looking at those pictures of all of you makes me think all the harder how wonderful it'll be to get back home – home being wherever you all are.

Speaking of back home, I did some researching on where I'd have the best chance for on assignment in the states so I'd have at least a fair chance of getting one of my choices come forecast and assignment time. But now that I'm looking for the list, I can't find it. I take it back. It was a few sheets down in this pad. Though not necessarily any of my choices, these places I'd have the best chance of getting. Let me know if there's any place at all you'd have a preference for. I'll go anywhere – the only requirement I have is that we're together.

 Scott, Ill – Headquarters AFCS
 Hanscom, Mass – Detachment 1, HQ AFCS
 Tinker, Okla – Central Com Region (Ugh!) That's also home of the 4th Mobile Comm Group, and these guys are forever TDY – in and out all the time)
 Westover, Mass – Eastern Comm Region
 Hamilton, Calif – Western Comm Region
 Langley, Va – TAC Com Region
 Waco, Tex – Deputy TAC Comm Region
 Show, S.C – Deputy TAC Comm Region
 Anderson, Md – Comm Group
 Wright – Pat, O. – Comm Group
 McClellan, Calif – Comm Group
 March, Barksdale, Westover,
 Offutt – SAC Headquarters

While I think of it, I got a card from Butch today, with a picture of the Americana Hotel at Miami Beach. I've just got to quote his message:

"I am also on a 'vacation'. You keep things going in South Vietnam and I'll keep things going in South Miami. Not much time to write as we are moving out – to cocktails at the pool. Your buddy in war and peace – Stink."

I had written him telling him I knew about all draft dodgers like him who heard LBJ would not draft them if they had enough kids, and that I knew he was making darn certain they'd never get him. What a character.

You asked about the attack on Da Nang. The Air Base is where we are, but it covers quite a bit of ground and quite often Da Nang East and Marble Mountain, where the bulk of the Marines are, is all taken as part of the Air Base. Most of the action thus far has taken place in the Marine area, though we've received a few shots. We're about as safe here as can be, considering it's Vietnam. That was part of the trouble last night. We have MPs all around the perimeter and they use portable radios for communications. Well, action had barely started last night when their base station went on the blink. These units are taken care of by a civilian Motorola man under contract and are monitored by one of our TSgt's. My controller couldn't reach either one so we were in a pickle 'cause everybody was hot under the collar. I got Lt. Carol out and Col Phillips of the APs got our commander, Maj. Perry. In the meantime, I rounded up 3 of our radio troops, 2 out of the club and one who was at work, and we went to check it out. The set was locked and only the two I mentioned before had keys. Really we weren't supposed to touch this stuff, but with VC in the area you don't bother about fine print in the contract. We had tried putting the base station antenna on a portable and that work fine, but for only half the net. While I was calling Lt Carol to let him know I was going to break into the unit unless he ordered otherwise, he got word the AP's had found TSgt Gouck in town and were bringing him out. When he finally got here, we opened the unit and one man, A1C Striger, was familiar with the set and got it squared away. That took care of that hectic period. As it turned out, the Marines got hit pretty bad, but they did surprise that VC setting one of their mortars and got it before they could start firing.

Airman Striger that I mentioned above was the one on duty with Airman L___ when he went berserk. We had another A1C crack this weekend, but not as violently. He had been acting a bit odd, according to some who bunk with him, for about a week, or since the last attack. Saturday afternoon he walked out the gate of the cantonment area with his hat in his hands. The AP told him to put his hat on, and he didn't seem to hear him. The AP went up to him and again told him to put his hat on and again no response. By then he noticed that the airman just seemed to be starring off into the distance. He took him to the Medics, who checked him out and called the Commander. They said it was no put on act, that he really had flipped. Didn't know who or where he was. They air evacuated him first thing Sunday. You watch people around here and really wonder what goes through their minds. That's one of the reasons I'd just as soon keep working. Even playing cards or catch gives you something to do and keeps you from thinking too much.

Speaking of cards, after more than 3 months I finally found some cribbage players – 3 of them. This MSgt Demaree, who runs my radar section, had a board on his bunk. I asked him if he played, and if he did I'd give him some free lessons since I was the world's greatest cribbage player. He immediately said no, that he was the world's greatest. By then, two others heard us and, the silly fools, both thought THEY were the world's greatest. They we're going on shift, however, and didn't have time to play. Demaree and I sat down and I proceeded to show him all I knew. He promptly whipped my butt three straight! I kidded him saying "Hell, you don't care what kind of APR[11] you get, do you." Eight more months to go – I'll get him yet!

I had read about Don Massengale[12] winning the Coosley tournament in the Stars and Stripes, but they didn't have too much coverage so I enjoyed the clipping you sent. I though sure you'd be watching the final round on T.V. I remember some tournaments where he'd start out strong and then fade in the stretch. Maybe this was just what he needed to give him a bit of confidence. I did see, however, that in his next tournament he faulted early and didn't make it into the finals.

It would perhaps be better if you got both the spring and mattress when you decide to purchase. It probably wouldn't be long before the spring went too, even though it may be serviceable today. Do what you think.

Don't be worrying too much about me, honeybunch. We're relatively safe, in this area and when there's activity in the area we head for the bunkers or other safe areas. I'll probably never see a VC that I'll know except when I go by the POW area. There are thousands of Marines, Vietnamese and AP's here taking care of the old Dad.

Today is rapidly coming to a close, and that bring us one more day closer together. It's now, I hope, a maximum of 265 days to go. I love you deeply, my happiness.

<u>Your</u> Leo

---

[11] APR Annual Performance Review

[12] Don Massengale, pro golfer from Jacksboro had his best year on the PGA Tour in 1966.

2 Feb 66, Wed.

My Darling,

Things were a little slower today so I had time to catch my breath. There's not much news to report, however, so this will probably be more of a note than a letter. Also, there were no mail deliveries here today, so there's still less to talk about.

Thought I might go to the movies tonight, but it was too crowded and I don't dig fighting those mobs. The theater seats 300 and there's normally a show at 1300 and three shows in the evening – 1730, 1930 and 2130. Tonight there are only two showings due to the length of the movie – The Unsinkable Molly Brown. With about 2500 troops on post, the place is often filled to capacity each showing.

We had another guy go on emergency leave today. I've never seen so many – real, imagined or planned. Some I can sympathize with, but others come up with the damnedest reasons and I wonder about them. We end up with quite a few where they get Dear Johns – their wives want a divorce. I can't imagine things were any too solid in their marriages to start with. Probably neither of them had guts to do anything about it so the first opportunity when they get parted they get brave – the cowards.

I hope to get the money order tomorrow. I'll send $185 this time inasmuch as I want to send something for Karen and Stephanie's birthdays. Also need to get a few things at the BX – haven't had a chance to get there in about 10 days.

The sweat is just pouring off me now and I need to hit the shower. Have to wait there also because of the crowd. The water is shut off during the day, so there are about 200 guys wanting to shower at night. I wait, most of the time, 'till around 2300 which is about the average time I hit the sack.

Again, my love, don't worry about what you hear or read about hits at Da Nang. Most of the action is taking place some distance from us. We all shake our heads in wonderment when someone gets a clipping from a stateside paper. One of our teletype men got one the other day from guys in his old outfit that had a big black headline "Da Nang Air Base Bombed". It may sound like something to the folks back home, but here those things afford us an opportunity to laugh at how minor incidents can be blown up to show major action. Your old dad has too much waiting for him at home to let anything bother him here.

Be sweet, my love. As you lay down tonight, close your eyes and imagine me by you. I'd be holding you close and telling you how very happy you've made me, what a wonderful person, wife and mother you are, and how very, very much I love you.

Your Leo

Fri, 4 Feb 66

My Sweet Don Leta,

Another day closer to my honeybunch – actually, two days since I didn't write last night. I did get a letter from you but skipped writing until today because I hadn't picked up the money order yet.

Things have been fairly routine the last couple days – hot, muggy and busy, so there's really not too much to report. The reason we've been so busy all the time is that this base keeps expanding – more and more outfits, with their personnel and equipment, means more and more communications needed. We're taxed to our limits and can't hardly keep up with it. In addition, we're assuming comm responsibility for both Hue and Dang Ha, near the North Vietnam border so that's more headaches. We'll be setting up detachments and assigning people up there shortly.

Just last night Grenier and I were commenting on how many new faces there were around here. The more new faces I see, the better I feel. I'm just waiting 'till I can look around and not see anyone who was here when I came. Then I know it's my turn to rotate. From the looks of things, if this business keeps up much longer there are many, many troops who can expect to do a year stateside and then head back here. Noticed in an old issue of the AF Times (the newest one here is dated 12 Jan) where the new assignment manual now allows the AF to curtail the overseas assignments of personnel on long tours (overseas with their families) and send them to Vietnam upon or before completion of that tour. That way, some guys figuring they'll get out of it by doing 3 years somewhere like Germany, and then maybe extending for another year, may find themselves only doing two or maybe the three years there, and then their families shipped to the states and them to Southeast Asia.

This Squadron alone got 23 new people in last month, and 18 more due in this month. In the corresponding time, there are only 8 leaving. I understand that, starting in March, bookings will be made right out of Da Nang for flights back to the states, either by Pan American or Air Force C-141 jets. I hope so, that'll save a bunch of wasted time in going down to Saigon and then flying out of there.

Boy, I've been reading about the snow and cold weather back in the states and I almost start shivering. There have been quite a few pictures of snowbound areas in the Stars and Stripes. I sure hope it doesn't last too much longer down where you all are since that barn you're in is so cold. At least I hope it's well over with by the time the little one comes. With everyone crowded into two rooms now for sleeping, I don't know where you'd put the baby, except maybe in a dresser drawer! I wish I was there to keep you warm at night!!!

The next package you send with date nut loaves et al should arrive about the right time as Grenier got a package from his wife yesterday with banana bread and brown bread. He got a larger can of brown bread. I didn't

"That barn you're in"
Our house in Jacksboro, Texas

know they had two sizes. We've already polished off one of the banana breads. We're waiting for tomorrow to open his brown bread and my beans – it's Saturday. By the way, her banana bread was moist but not as tasty as yours – couldn't hardly taste the bananas.

Well, my love, that time has come again. It must seem so repetitious to you but again I say that I miss you so very much and love you with all my heart. How wonderful it'll be for us all to be together again, regardless of where that might be. I think I could get to stay anywhere. Just as long as I know we'll be together. Good night, my darling, and sweet dreams. I know mine will be, because they'll be of you.

Your Leo

Sun., 6 Feb 66

My Darling Wife,

Lo and behold, I had a day off today—well, at least all but for 2 hours this afternoon. That's the first day off in two weeks. It came on my 104th day – 261 to go. As you see, I'm still counting every stinking one of those days.

Again, there's not too much to report, honeybunch. No mail has come into the outfit in a couple days now and there's always the moaning and gnashing of teeth when that happens. To top it off, this weekend has been one of on-again off-again rain and cloudy skies to add to the dreary atmosphere.

We still haven't moved into our other place yet, and the way these Vietnamese laborers move there's no telling when it'll be done. Originally it was to be done by Christmas. They're just now putting in electric power and lights. They still have to paint and put in the air conditioner. No kidding, this guy and I were going to chow one day when I told him to hold up a minute. There were 26 VN laborers digging a ditch for a foundation. For one minute we checked them and there were 12 shovels full of dirt put out.   Four of these were by the same man! They don't exactly strain themselves.

Don't know how long that banana bread Grenier received was in transit, but we were just going to finish it a while ago and it had gotten all moldy. I know I should have eaten it on him faster.

Well, sweetheart, I know this isn't much of a letter, but there's just not much going on. I suppose it's just as well that there is no excitement to write about 'cause "no news is good news" in many an instance. If there's no excitement here until I leave it'll be O.K. with me. Good night my beloved. My thoughts remain with you always. Right now I was just thinking of sitting near you, with your head resting on my shoulder. How I wish that could soon be. I love you with all of me.

Your Leo

8 Feb 66

My dearest Don Leta,

My good intentions went for naught again last night. I thought I would be writing a couple letters and ended up moving instead. We keep getting people in all the time and since a bunk became available in the top three barracks I got in there. It's a bit quieter, as things go around here, and not quite as crowded. I'm in a single bunk instead of a double, and next to Sgt Hodgson, our first Sergeant.

We've really been having a crazy mail schedule. Yesterday I got three letters – one from you, one from Claire and one from Mrs. Houle, Aunt Nellie's neighbor. I told you I had sent her a Christmas card and the old soul keeps writing and asking that I answer. These 3 letters were postmarked 2 Feb, 25 Jan and 12 Jan, respectively. Today I got one from Mom and another from my girl, this one postmarked 31 Jan, 2 days before the one I received yesterday. A whole bunch of people got mail yesterday dated 12 and 13 Jan. It seems a bag marked for APO 96337 got sidetracked in Saigon and was forwarded to Georgia!

None of the relatives seemed to have too much in the line of news, except that I guess Mom hadn't been feeling too good. Of course, she's been hearing things about Da Nang also and I guess that worries her. If I were a Marine or one of the 1st Calvary troops she might have cause for more concern, but as it is I guess I'm probably as safe as anyone in the country right now. I always said I was a lover, not a fighter.

It really looks like everything is happening, health-wise, around Jacksboro this year. Besides the Dubois and all their troubles, now Mother not being well and Mary coming down with her troubles, it's going to be one rough time. All the more reason I wish I were there to help out. I should think Bill would get to see the light pretty soon and start pitching in a bit. I should think he'd have been clued in by someone by now. Things are not going to take care of themselves all the time — he's going to have to do some of it. Maybe they should nationalize the guard and send him here so I could talk to him!

Well — I'm surprised you admitted to me that you found a grey hair. With what you've been telling me about Paul, however, I guess I'm really not too surprised. Maybe you ought to go ahead and secure that stool from him before it really gets to be his private property like some of them hang on to their blankets! He might as well learn it now, 'cause heavens knows it'll be harder yet keeping up with him this next couple of months.

I got a call a couple minutes ago, honeybunch, so I'll be shortening this letter to mail it before I go out since I don't know if I'll have time to write anymore by the time I get back. It's a personal problem (family) with one of my SSgt's and I think he's been given the run-around by both the Red Cross and our fine considerate headshed[13].

Tell Bryan I got his latest picture of a skeleton and it sure looks like the other pictures he sent me, and that I'll write to him again soon.

Boy, I'll tell you there's no such thing as an 8-hour day or 40-hr week in a place like this. As best I can recall, this past week was close to 80 hours. I was out at 4:45 this morning and don't know when I'll get back tonight, at least it makes time pass, and that's what I'm looking for — time to pass. It'll bring me that much closer to my wonderful Don Leta and our children. I'd like to keep writing now because I'm feeling real gushy and mushy! I love you so much, my darling. Be sweet and be extra careful to take care of yourself for me.

Your Leo

10 Feb 66, Thur.

My Darling,

Here it is 10:20 and I'm finally going to get a letter written. We moved into our new area yesterday and things are still in something of a turmoil, so I came in tonight to do some paperwork that I had to put aside trying to get everything else done.

No mail came in to the outfit today, though did get a letter and pictures from Chippy and a letter from my honeybunch. Didn't write last night — took a night off from everything and went to the movie, my first in some time. It was pretty good for laughs — "The Americanization of Emily" with James Garner and Julie Andrews.

Boy, I don't know about the heater on that darn car. It used to give out pretty good heat so it was good at one time. I don't see where the switch and wiring would have anything to do with it since the power is on and the fan

---

[13] headquarters

works. That's all those electrical connections do. It's too bad that's the only place around there or I'd say take it somewhere else and let them look at it.

As for that big W-2 for $39 we got from Ellsworth, just save it in case there's any question on our return. Since it won't make any difference in taxes, I shouldn't think they'll question it, but if they do I'll just plead ignorance.

Sgt Carter came down with something or other last night. He thought he might have gotten a case of the flu or something. I jumped on him tonight because he's been in bed all day with a slight fever, headache, cold sweats and chills. He'd better get his butt to the medics tomorrow because these are malaria symptoms if I've ever seen them.

While waiting for the movie last night, Grenier and I were talking to this guy in aircraft maintenance who came over with us. He was telling us of 7 or 8 in that batch who have already left us for the states or medical evac to the Philippines for one reason or another. I'd just as soon sweat out my tour the full way and go back for good. One guy, I know, just worked himself into a medical condition. He was a MSgt Collins and worked on the flight line. He was across from me on the C-130 that took us into Da Nang. I would see him every now and then when I was out on the line and he was going harder than any of his airman – and he was about half the size of many of them. The nut used to put in 16 – 18 hours a day regularly. He ended up with a bad case of pneumonia and had complications.

A very snowy winter in Jacksboro
Don Leta, Paul and Bryan

Wouldn't you know it, I just got a call from Lt Carol about one of my troops. He's the one I came in and talked to for 3 hours a couple of nights ago. Now he's turned himself in to the medics claiming violent headaches. I'm still not sure about this guy, though he seems to have family troubles. The more I talk to him, however, the more confused I would become. It was at the point where it couldn't be figured out whether there was trouble at home or whether he or someone at home was trying to get him out of Vietnam. I'm telling you, some of these cases are a mess. I think I told you before of this other SSgt in our teletype section who had come to me crying in the NCO club, saying I had to help him. Another one with wife trouble. When I get out I think I'll become either a psychiatrist or a marriage counselor!

And so to a close comes another day and another chapter in the life of Leo, Boy Warrior. Let me tell you I'll be ready to think of settling down and worrying about my own problems once I get through this tour. I've never had so many things to do and to remember as I do now.

Good night, my sweet. I'm going to finish this and head for the pad. I'm glad I took my shower before coming down here. It's probably superfluous for me to say so, but I miss you terribly. You know, when I lay down now I still immediately think of you, but now I've been doing it so long and so regularly that is almost seems real. I dream of all the wonderful moments past and soon to be. How easy it is during those sleepless instances for me to tell you and to show you how much I love you and how very very much you mean to me. In a way, I should have had quite a bit of practice by the time I'm back home, even though it'll all be in my mind. You're just such a wonderful person and I thank God time and time again for having made you all for me. It may be kind of silly in a way, my beloved, but sometimes I almost fell like crying because I can't really fully explain how I feel deep inside me. I won't go that far, but it's just that you've meant so much to me all these yesterdays, mean so much to me today and will mean more and more to me with each tomorrow. Be sweet, my happiness – and please take extra good care of yourself for all of us. We all need <u>you</u> above everything else.

<u>Your</u> loving Leo

Fri, 11 Feb 66

My dearest Don Leta,

Starting off late again tonight. I went back in to work from 7 to about 9:30, then went for coffee and back to the pad.

Got a letter from Vivian today and I enjoyed her descriptions of some of Gale's actions and comments. It sounds like she must be quite a character.

Also, got a letter from my honeybunch today, as well as a Valentine. Don Leta, I love you and miss you so much and I hope my saying so as often as I have in these letters doesn't wear too thin as the result of these repetitions, but gosh I could just fill pages and pages just repeating I love you.....I love you. Still it wouldn't be enough. This is without doubt the worse period of my life in some way, and surprisingly being in a combat zone has little to do with it. What makes it so bad is being apart from you and the kids. When I get back I'm going to give up all my nights at the bars and out with the boys bowling or playing cards! I'm going to spend all the time right close to you. You'd better plan on getting everything done in the daytime while I'm at work, 'cause you'll have few free moments when I'm home. As a matter of fact, you may have to call someone to try and get me to work some nights and weekends so you can get some work done and/or rest! Oh Don Leta, if only I could explain how I feel. I'm sad that we're apart, and yet so terribly happy that you're my girl, my wife, my children's mother, my happiness, my love, my everything. I think if I saw you now – no, I'll change that to <u>I know</u> if I saw you now I'd be unable to utter a word. I would just hold you close to me for some time before I could say anything. Perhaps that would say more in itself than I could with mere words. I don't' know, but words seem to be so inadequate at these times, but like now, that's all we have. I love you, my dearest.

You know what makes me appreciate you all the more? All the things I come across here, either hearing of or seeing the actions of so many of these people. You just know there can't be much real love betweens some people by observing how they act when they're apart. Let's face it – whisky & women are plentiful and many are after one or the other, or both. When I was in the other barracks, the bunk under mine was occupied by a MSgt with 5 kids. He stayed there a couple nights a month and the rest of the time was with some bar girl who had two kids. I know he kept $400 a month for himself, yet he was very faithful in writing every other night to his wife. We don't speak too much to each other. Of course, it's really none of my business, but it seems such a shame, once one has known true love, to see this. I'm not blowing my horn or anything, but I couldn't face you or the kids, or even myself, if I behaved like that. Honestly, there are some of us here like Grenier, Sgt Chisum (his wife's in Waco) and FSgt and others who seem kind of odd to some people 'cause we're not "living it up." Oh well, enough of that. I'm not guardian of people's morals. There's only one woman for me – my honeybunch.

You know, here I've been ranting on and I haven't even given you any news. It must be that there is none. I take it back, I ran into Silvey going to chow this noon. I just saw him a few minutes as he was on his way to a meeting. I'll probably get to see him tomorrow. He's down at Bien Hoa, this side of Saigon, and he's due to rotate in August.

Would you believe it, I'm actually in a hurry to get to bed. That's because the minute I'm there I'll close my eyes and try to imagine our being together again. It's still so far off, it seems. I almost wish you were there to meet me in California, even though it'll probably only be a few more hours before we're together. You see, I've changed my mind and decided I wouldn't stay in San Francisco for a week or so and have a ball before going on to Texas! Again, my beloved, I love you and miss you more than words can convey. My every minute, every breath, every thought is dedicated to bringing us closer to one another. I desire you in every way. The wonderful companionship you've given me – gosh, just everything about you – has spoiled me so that now when we're apart I finally realize how important it was. Dearest, I'm the happiest man in the world; it's all because of you.

Your Leo

13 February, Sunday

My Beloved,

As you can see by the color of ink I'm using, this will be a hot passionate letter. Since there's been no mail for me the past two days, there's nothing to comment on in that direction. I've just finished another of my favorite pastimes, looking for the umpteenth time at pictures of you and the kids. Gosh, how I wish you could just step out of the pictures and come to me.

Don Leta, here in the early 1950s

When leaving the club after chow tonight I had another guy ask me if I came from Ellsworth. He said he remembered me from church. He's TSgt Hutson, from Civil Engineers, and he's just been here a short while. I just spoke to him for a few minutes since it was starting to sprinkle. He's from somewhere in south Texas and his family is now in Fort Worth. Says he hopes to get back there, though he's thinking of asking for a consecutive tour to Europe after this. This guy's already put I his 20 years, so he must be a glutton for punishment. Good luck to him!

Work keeps going pretty hot and heavy. Though today I was off, I did manage to get a couple hours in on problems this morning. Boy, I'm telling you, this place is growing so fast it's just about impossible to keep up with it. More people, aircraft and equipment coming in all the time. There is one good sideline effect – some people will get to go home about a month early. That's both to make room and, when the activity is over-strength, because the replacements are in early. Many guys scheduled to rotate in May and June will be advanced from 2-4 weeks. With my luck they'll probably be undermanned by October!

Six months ago the Comm Sq had 38 people. Today we have 196 and the First Sgt (Hodgson) was telling me today that our outfit has 100 more people due in within the next two months.

Hodgson, Grenier and I went into town this afternoon. That's the first time I've made it there in almost a month. We all went in for haircuts. Afterwards we shopped a bit. I picked up a bedside lamp to use when lights were put out. Hodgson was looking for a brass seal stamp – the kind used to put a seal in wax on letter, documents, etc.,—but he couldn't find the kind he wanted.

I, also, wish the baby would come early for you so that it could be done and over with, but I sure hope it doesn't come so quick as to catch you unprepared! Not using it as an excuse to get back, but how I wish I could be with you at that time. As usual, I probably wouldn't be of much help but at least I'd be there. You've been so good to me, honeybunch, even though so many times I wondered why. I love you with all my heart and live everyday only waiting to be back near you and the children. Take care of yourself for us, my happiness,

Your Leo

x x x x x x x x x x

(passionate kisses)

Mon, 14 Feb 66

My dearest Don Leta,

How nice it was to hear from you today, especially since there hasn't been any mail for a couple days. It was a double treat with the enclosed colored snapshots of you and the kids. It's so nice to get pictures. Please don't stop sending them, though I must admit looking at them only serves to accentuate the pain I feel in my heart at being so far from you. Actually, any place not right near you would be too far, whether it would be just a block or these 10,000 miles. I think the pictures all came out rather good too – they're quite clear and have good coloring. Especially – my favorite—is the one of you with Karen and Bryan on Karen's birthday. Hmmm, my

honeybunch really looks good enough to eat in that one! I'm telling you, I don't ever want to be away for any length of time again.

I was glad to hear that Stephanie seems to be acting a bit better now. I suppose what she does need is a bit more attention and a few more pats on the back. Now I sure hope Karen straightens up and starts accepting a bit of responsibility. Surely, she's old enough now to know better. She'll also need a bit more self-control from the size she's getting to be. Heck, I wasn't that heavy at her age. I suppose she still lays back instead of taking part in some of the more active type games.

Still going pretty strong at work. I've just about got all my console up and working now, and I do believe it's the best in Vietnam. Now if the VC would just leave it alone! Speaking of VC, activity has been fairly quiet again in these parts of late – just outgoing mail. Of course, the jarheads are always getting into a skirmish or two on their patrols, thereby not allowing any build-up of forces around us. With as much strength as there is in this area now, it'd probably take a full size army to take this place. I thought there were a lot of aircraft before – now there's twice as many, I swear. Pretty soon they'll have to start double – decking them too.

I want to get a couple other letters written tonight, sweetheart, so I'll be cutting this off – but it'll not mean I'm thinking of you less. Looking at those pictures of you again, I don't know when I'll get to sleep tonight. I know I'll just keep reaching over trying to find you there. Let me tell you, my imagination has been working overtime! I just keep picturing all the different ways in which we will first see each other again. If I keep on like this for this full tour, perhaps the safest thing will be for you to have bodyguards around – but they'd better be big ones! I love you, my dearest, with all my heart. Oh, Don Leta, how very hard I try to tell you this – and how very inadequate these words seem to be. About all I can say is that you're my whole life.

Your Leo

14 Feb 66

Hi Pal,

My goodness, I got some more pictures you sent me and they sure do look like skeletons. Even the picture of daddy that you drew looked like a skeleton! One of the guys took a picture of me looking over the fence and this is what it looked like :

There's still a long time before daddy can come home because there's still a lot of bad people here, but in about 250 more days I'll be back so me and you and Paul and our new baby can play together. Maybe I will play with your mommy a little too! You be a good boy and write to me again some time. Loads of love, Daddy

17 Feb 66

My Darling,
     The days are not as bad as they once were. When I first got here, I really didn't know for sure what was going on, so I more or less felt my way around. Now, however, I'm afraid I'm getting to know what's going on and the more I pick up or initiate myself, the bigger the job gets. This expansion is something else. Until 1 November, this used to be a Detachment, at that time it became a Squadron, and on 1 March we'll have two detachments of our own – at Hue (pronounced "way") and Dong Ha – both near the N. Vietnam border.

     So with all this, the days are kept pretty full. It's the nights that drag,

especially if I don't get called out, which for a while there was not very often. But the nights give me more time to think – and sometimes that's not too good, in a way. Like now, I received some more snaps from you and gosh, how I miss you all. Everyone got a laugh of that one with Paul standing on the box and Bryan inside. After seeing that other one where you caught him on the clothes hamper, people think you must just follow him around with camera in hand.

     The shelling has been pretty heavy tonight. They must be keeping Charlie loose. Earlier, after supper, we could see and hear fighters dropping their loads in the distance. Speaking of supper, tonight they had stew at the club, and as usual everyone, practically, turned their noses up at it. Instead I had pea soup & crackers, 'cause I had something up my sleeve. Went to the PX yesterday and they had small (7 oz) cans of pork & beans and small cans of fruit cocktail, so I had that with Ritz crackers. Really living it up!

     Haven't seen any of your newspaper friends around. Every now and then there's a notice on the bulletin board that such and such a correspondent is in the area and would like to talk to people from his area or state. All I know is none of them ever asked for me!

     I guess as we get older we realize all the more that problems never cease. It just seems that everything is being crammed into this year, what with all the kids' little illnesses, your condition, my being away, and now Mary needing surgery, mother being delayed on hers and now Mom back with asthma in addition to her other troubles. Without wanting to seem odd and hard, I'm fairly well resolved that Mom will not get any better. Operations such as she's had at her age don't usually cure anything, they only arrest it for a while. I only hope that nothing happens while I'm here, though.

Everything else is about the same, I guess. I've been wanting to write a few more letters to people, but never seem to get to it. Gonna make a maximum effort in that direction for this weekend. Good night, my love. I miss you so much and love you more than I can say.

<u>Your</u> Leo

19 Feb 66

My dearest Don Leta,

Today was an especially good day. I had worked right through mail call last night and didn't get to check mail, but today there was both a letter and package from my honeybunch. I wondered at first about the package, 'cause the wrapping was just hanging from it, but everything came through in fine shape.

My gosh, I sure didn't expect so much cake all at one time. It really won't last too long, however, since we already polished off a banana bread. I'll bring one of them into work Monday – and I give about 10 minutes!

Everything has been about the same here-abouts, sweetheart. Work has been pretty steady, with quite a few rush periods and very few slack periods. Hardly any rain any more and the sun is out quite a bit. Nights have also been fairly well the same, pounding away to varying degrees 'till I finally get to sleep. Tomorrow is Sunday and I plan on taking advantage of it and stay in the sack.

In one of your past letters you had asked about the water shortage here. We have the water shut off during the mornings and afternoons because the pumps can't handle all that's called for. I understand they had a shortage this time last year too, and there were about one fourth as many people here. They've put in an additional pipe, but it's not too much help. A couple teams are supposed to be coming up from Saigon to dig those wells. You wouldn't think it would be so dry in an area that gets over 80 inches of rain in about three months.

Do hope the kids are behaving a bit more, especially this last month. I can just imagine what it's like going around like you do and still trying to keep up with all of them. Time is still dragging, but at least now I don't actually count every day – just every other day or so! Right now there're 248 more until 26 Oct, and I do hope to skip out a few days before the. Right now I'm looking forward to the next milestone, next month. By then I'll be close to 200 days and just a couple weeks or so from the halfway point. Talking to Sgt Hodgson last night, he said before too long we'll have more than 300 people in Comm alone. I hope so, then maybe I'll be able to skip out sooner – however,

I'm not counting on anything. The one barracks we've got was built to accommodate 60 people, and there are 138 in there now. Others are in tents.

Doesn't look too good for my ever getting to Hong Kong. There's hardly any more trips out of here between now and October. We only get a few spaces anyhow. The plane starts in Saigon, picking a few up at Nha Trong and Da Nang on its way. The trips to Bangkok are getting almost as bad, so I may end up not going anywhere. I noted in the paper where Hawaii was being considered as an R&R spot for VN personnel. I don't think I'd care to go that far just to spend five days. The only thing about it is that it would be a change from this place. Oh well, we shall see. If nothing else comes up, I may consider a trip to Taiwan (Formosa).

I'm sitting here writing and the radio is reporting how Cassius Clay has been reclassified as fit for military duty and how he says he doesn't believe in wars unless declared by Allah himself. Some people sure have it rough!

Be seeing you, honeybunch. Gonna take my shower and just stretch out on the sack for awhile and burp banana bread. Now, that makes a nice opening for a paragraph in which I'll say how much I love you. You see what war does to a guy!

I do miss you and love you so very, very much, Don Leta. It's repetitious but I want it to be. I want to remind you of my love for you every day of our lives. Be sweet, my darling, and take extra good care of yourself for us. We need you more than you'll ever know.

Your Leo

Sun, 20 Feb 66

My Honeybunch,

There must be something in the air to make me feel the way I do today. I've just lazed around all day long; can't seem to get any pep up or anything. Guess I should have gone to the club or ran around the block or something. Otherwise I just lay there and think—and not much can be gained that way. It's just that it seems so long to go yet – not even a third of it done until Wednesday. Oh well, not too awfully long ago it didn't seem I'd get below 300 days either and I'm now up to 247.

Just about finished a date-nut loaf today. It's not going to have the chance to get moldy with me! This afternoon I also got a letter from my girl and one from Florence and Chippy. Their three kids had drawn Valentines which I thought were cute.

I could just picture Stephanie when she came home with that box of Valentine candy from her boyfriend. And since the boy couldn't make it to that Scout party for Karen, I would check up on him. The fact that he had art lessons could lead to his asking her up to his place to see his "etchings"! You know what that could lead to!! Seriously, I guess it's a good thing some of the others couldn't make it either or she would have been quite dejected.

Yes, compared to the Army and Marine troops in the field, we've got it made. We don't have water all the time, and it's not always hot, but it's there. We're as crowed as can be but still have bunks and a roof over out heads. And the meals are ready for us and we don't have to eat c-rations all the time.

Did you know where Mari Nelson's husband was going? You said Southeast Asia, so that could be Laos, Thailand or Vietnam. I'd imagine it would be Vietnam, though it could also be Thailand. You didn't say whether you'd seen them or not. Make sure he has my address if perchance he comes to Da Nang. My number's in the local phone directory with the rest of the bigwigs. We have a couple F-105 outfits in here periodically, though most of ours right now are F-4C's and F-5's. They keep coming in and out of here so often, though, that you can't keep up with them. Many of the Squadrons from further south come up here for 90-120 days at a time on TDY to fly missions up north since this is the largest and northernmost major base. Boy, you think we've had rackets in the past from B-36's and B-52's, try some of these fighters from this close to the flight line. I often unconsciously find myself lowering my head thinking one of them is coming in one end of the barracks and out the other.

Got to see one and talk to another guy I was at Hamilton and Saigon with. MSgt Lytle is stationed at Saigon and was up here on business for a couple days so we dumped a few at the club. Also got a call from MSgt Oliver at Bien Hoa about some equipment he needed and I was shipping to him, so we also reminisced a bit.

Not much new outside of that, my love, except that I wish this was all over with – but that's not new. I just want so much for us to be together again. I can see how some of these guys here might crack up if they don't watch themselves. I don't remember if I told you about what happened to the Sgt O___, who worked for me. He's the one who had some type of wife problem, but nobody knew for sure what, and the one I spent some time talking to at night a couple weeks ago. I think I told you he turned in to the medics complaining of severe headaches over his problems. Well, they checked him out and evac'd him to the Philippines. Now he's left there and they've sent him back to the States, so he won't be back. I don't know if he went to a hospital there, or what.

Gots to take my shower now and then back to the empty, unfriendly bed. Oh, how I yearn to reach over and feel you there! I miss you so terribly much, my darling wife. You'll probably get so tired of my chasing after you when I get back that you'll be ready for me to go on another remote tour! But, I'll fool you – I'm never going to leave my sweetheart and children again. I love you, darling.

Your Leo

Troop Trouble

Throughout these letters occur instances of the theme I call "Troop Trouble". Leo calls it "my children acting up".   In addition to the technical work with the radio gear, a troubled soldier could turn up at any time, day or night.

Here, a Sgt O___ has unspecified wife-trouble. Elsewhere, a wife leaves. A wife has a car accident. A wife has a breakdown. A wife goes blind.

Among his men are fist fighters, a knife fighter, a whorehouse brawler.   Others need emergency leave or compassionate reassignment.

Then there are the "operators" and "string-pullers", who manipulate the system to get out early. A troop shoots himself in the leg. Men get drunk. Men get in debt. And an otherwise fine man slips up at the end of his tour and gets a reprimand.

Grabbing the troublemaker by the collar—or staying up late to counsel a worried kid—this was the senior NCO's job.

21 Feb 66

My Darling,

Just a short LOVE note tonight as it's getting rather late and I just finished another letter.

Got a letter from Theresa today and one from a Mrs. Julia Muller back in Pawtucket. I couldn't imagine who that was – figured it was probably one of my many old flames telling me to come home, that all was forgiven! Turned out she's a president of the American Legion Ladies Auxiliary in Pawtucket. Back around December I had written the Legion in Washington because they had an article in the paper saying they'd send hometown papers to people in Vietnam free. I guess they forwarded all requests to the local posts. Anyhow, she said things had been delayed due to inclement weather and no buses running after 6 P.M. Therefore, no meetings, but they were having a meeting in March and would take care of it then. At that rate, I should get 2 or 3 copies before shipping out.

There's just no news at all, so it's probably just as well that it's getting late. There was some action a few miles from here this afternoon just before quitting time. Saw more fighters scramble at once than ever before. Understand the Marines engaged the VC and had run them out into the open. If that's so, they must have got a few today.

Well, my lovely, wonderful, delicious, sweet, darling honeybunch – it's off to the sack again. Love you just oodles and bucketfuls. How very wonderful it will be to hold you close again. The dream goes on and on but, someday, I'll open my eyes and it'll be true. All I wait for now is that day.

Your Leo

23 Feb 66

My Darling,

Once again there's not too much news to report, but I guess no news is good news. Got your letter today about Mother's operation, and it sounds like it was quite serious. I do hope she's progressing properly. I should think an ordeal like that will take some time for her to really get on her feet again.

I haven't been quite up to snuff myself the last couple of days and will be turning in to sick call tomorrow. This darn sinus is acting up and making me miserable. Probably part of that too, but I have a sore throat and some pain a little below the neck, like when there's croupy coughing. I've been sniffling, got a headache and been sneezing on and off all day. Old age creeping up.

Got a cute letter from Stephanie's class today. The troops here got a charge out of it too. Of 24 who wrote, 8 told me about her boy friend, James Jonas. I got some chuckles, to wit:

All start with Dear Sgt Dubois:

".... James Jonas gave Stephanie a box of candy. Stephanie likes James very much and James likes Stephanie very much."

".... Stephanie has a boy friend his name is James Jonas he is a very nice boy she got a box of candy from him."

".... We were in a play and Stephanie's boy friend had to put his arm around her and James said, "If we put it on for the hole 4th grade he isn't going to do it.""

".... Stephanie is a good tetherball player she beats almost every one."

".... I like Stephanie very much and so do you."

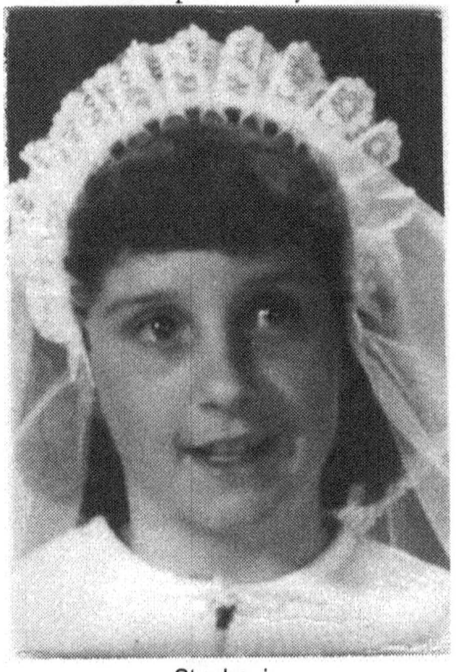

Stephanie

They were all signed "love", "with love", "your friend", etc., but Stephanie's started and ended real formal with "Dear Father" and "Sincerely Yours".

Gosh, I'm so far behind in my letter writing it's pathetic. It's just that I've felt so poop at night of late. Half the time I'll stretch out on the sack, clothes and all, and just fall asleep. I did that for a bit yesterday and then kept waking up all thru the night. Think I'll talk it over with my psychiatrist and see if he doesn't think maybe I should go home.

We've got more inspectors in – this time from Group at Tan Son Nhut. Three more days of that baloney. Besides that, they're all bothered because higher headquarters says I can't be in this job, that I ought to be in Crypto. They had gone in a while back to get authority to use a 306 (crypto) in the job instead of a 304 (radio) like the manning document said. PACOM (Hawaii) said disapproved, but they were sending it on to AFCS headquarters in the states for final word. We never did hear from AFCS. They ought to know they (higher HQ) can't beat this racket. They'll assign me to crypto, on paper, but I'll still be running SMC. It's just a vicious circle. I doubt that I'll ever see a piece of that gear again!

Not much new otherwise, honeybunch. More of the guys are getting their assignments and orders this week. We'll lose quite a few between now and May, then another batch in June—July. After that, the next big bunch is scheduled in OCTOBER!

Good night, my dearest. I still think of you most every night before going to sleep. I miss you so and how I wish I were there to help you this next month. You're a wonderful and courageous mommy-bunch, and I love you all the more for it. Be sweet, my love, and take extra good care of yourself for me.

Your Leo

Sat, 26 Feb 66

My Dearest,

Got a wonderful letter from my honeybunch today, plus one from George Zimmerman. I'm in the shop right now where I just had the enclosed pictures taken. Worked until 6 P.M., went to chow and then came on back. Sgt Hooper, one of my Crypto people, has a Polaroid camera so Grenier and I each bought a roll of film and he shot them for us. I'm sending a couple to Mom and there's a couple more I'm sending out to have reproduced. I'll forward those on later.

George gave me the poop on a few more of the 821st people. Dougal has retired and they have a Lt Col Owen there now. "Gomer Pyle" Lt W__ went PCS to Keesler and Lt Murphy is now Chief of Maintenance. Rogers is working in CMC and plans to retire in July, while Sgt Roope's retirement is being held up for medical reasons – ears. SMSgt Smith, who had taken over Radio after Williams left, was processing for Germany so they put Zimm in charge of that section. Actually, Zimm says Lt. W__ relieved Smith last Nov 15th and put him in charge. Sgt Smith had told him off too many times in front of the troops. Spencer left for Thailand and TSgt Hall, who worked in QC, was going to the Philippines. Rodrigues, in the Orderly Room was going to Spain and Sgt Wood to Vietnam. Minkler went to the Philippines on a remote tour in his additional AFSC of carpenter and Sgt Corkey was coming to join us here. George says he's still sweating. They're pulling radio people who came back in March 65 and he's been back since May 63. He says Personnel told him SAC must have forgotten to put his card back in once he was relieved from that June shipment. When he had records check last month just about everything was goofed up so all machine runs were corrected. He figures they'll get him now for sure. Oh yes, he said Sgt Whipple also had an assignment, but he didn't know where to.

Yes, I told you about getting that letter from the 4th grade class. I was hoping to pick up a little something Vietnamese for the class to send when I answered. I'll have to look around a bit. Of course, I was most happy to hear you received good reports on Stephanie from Mrs. Prunty. I hope she keeps it up without getting too cocky.

I will have to have that "man-to-man" talk with Bryan, but I'm not sure that I'll be able to resolve the problem of his "peanut" getting stiff. If I remember real good, I think I've had that problem once or twice myself!

Sometimes I think it would be wonderful to get caught up here and just take it easy for a while, but in a way I guess its better this way. I keep busy all the time and don't have as much time to think about being lonely. Didn't get any writing done last night as it was 11:30 before I left here for the barracks. It will be somewhere around ten tonight before I cut out, but at least I'll have written a letter or two. We just keep growing here, taking on more and more every day. We're about to assume some more equipment the other side of the base, plus all service to and on the City of Da Nang and the Marine enclave at Da Nang East.

There's really not much new to report from these parts, however, outside of shop talk. Things have been fairly quiet in this area of late. Of course, this is prime rumor country as any remote or isolated station is, and we're always hearing of "someone in the know" saying that we're all going to be extended here, no more discharges or retirements for the duration, tours are going to be changed to 18 months, people are going to be released 3 months early, the VC are staging a major attack, the VC have left the area, Cassius Clay is coming over here to end it all, Cassius Clay is not coming over here so it'll help us all. The easiest thing in the world is starting a rumor in places like this. The thing is people want to believe anything that will reflect a change in the status quo, so they grasp at every thought, regardless of how serious or absurd.

Well, today is my anniversary. It was on the 26th four months ago that we left the states, so the tour is now officially 1/3 over. Since Tuesday will see March with us, I'll be able to say "only 7 months to go". It's a long hard road, but one day we'll reach the end of it and be home. March is also forecast month, so we'll be forecasting sometime around the 20th. Guess I'll put in for Hanscom, Westover, and the northeast, and then sweat it out. (Just spilled coffee on here so it's hard to write in spots. Will just skip around it.)

Guess I'm just about run out, honeybunch, so will knock off for this time. I love you so dearly, my darling, and only look forward with eagerness and anticipation at the time when we can again be as one.

Your Leo

28 Feb 66

My Dearest,

As you'll note, I've cheated you a bit on money orders again, though this should be the last month. I splurged and bought myself an 8 transistor portable so I could get some news and ball scores, plus sweet, soothing music to dream by! Blew $16 on it. Might keep it, or might peddle it off before returning. It doesn't play too badly.

No mail yesterday, but did get a sugar note from my girl today. I'm back at the office now—it's about 6:45 – and will try to get a couple or three letters out. Things haven't changed too much hereabouts. Still keeping pretty busy through the day and parts of many nights. If I'm done soon enough, I might take in the 9:30 movie tonight.

The Major was telling us today that they will shortly be running flights to Hong Kong from Da Nang, so I may have a chance to go after all. Seems Pan American has been contracted for this service. Also, people leaving here on rotation must now go to Saigon and catch a flight out of there. There's often a two or three day delay there. They'll soon be running directly out of here on flights to the states, so we should be better off in that area also. I imagine that will begin as soon as the new runway here is finished.

No – it's not gone yet (head hanging in shame). That roll of film is still sitting in my locker. I thought you might ask about that again! I will definitely get that out this week….. I will, I will, I will!

We were all set to take a trip up to Dong Ha and Hue yesterday, but cancelled out when word came through the night before that the airport was closed due to VC activity. I don't know if I'll be able to get up there now, though Grenier and the Lieutenant may be going up in a few days.

Well, just a few more hours and I can cross this month off and say it's forecast time. It really doesn't seem that it was too awfully long ago that forecast time seemed to be so far away. Now my next goal is 25 April – 56 days away. That will be the official half-way mark, though in reality it may be a few days more than half, provided I get out of here before 26 October.

I'm telling you, it can't go by fast enough for me. The days now are going by in fairly good fashion – I mean they're not dragging – but the weeks and months are something else. How glad I'll be when this tour is over with and I can spend some time in the PEACE and QUIET which I just know will be at home. I love you, Don Leta, great big bunches, and I'll be missing you something awful until I can actually see you and hold you again. Be sweet, my dearest, and make sure you take extra good care of yourself for us.

Your Leo

2 Mar 66

My Happiness,

I took another night off last night and didn't get any letter writing done, even though I had received that combination letter from you, Stephanie and Bryan. Went to the late movie (it stunk!) since there wasn't much of a crowd. About 20 or 30 minutes prior to show time there were a number of loud blasts, bunches of them at once, so that movie line melted down to nothing. I happened to be in the Orderly Room, and it sure sounded like incoming heavies. CWO Robinson, our Operations officer, called and found out it was some new friendlies nearby. By then there was no line at the movie, so went right in.

Grenier's going up to Dang Ha and Hue tomorrow. I'm at the shop now and the Lt just said that he (Lt) and I would go up in a couple weeks. It's supposed to be real pretty around Hue. That used to be the capitol in the old days of Indo China. There are supposed to be a number of colleges and Buddhist and Catholic seminaries there.

It's getting warmer and warmer each passing day, with very little rain now. The nights haven't been too awfully bad yet, however. It gets particularly oppressive after lunch. I've been taking siestas at lunchtime, laying on the sack for 30 minutes or so. But boy is it ever rough getting up. I sleep pretty good nights, except for every now and then when comes up one of those twist and turn nights.

Guess it'll be during the second part of the month that we'll forecast. We have a few people leaving this month and the next, with larger groups in May and June. Sgt McGraw, who works for me, leaves in a couple weeks – going on a consecutive to Germany.

Did finish all that eating stuff you sent. It sure didn't take long for mold to set in. A couple of them started but trimmed it off and ate it up. Took a couple to the shop, where their life span is from 10 to 15 minutes! When you're all settled again after the baby and do send some more, better just hold it down to a couple. Those things are not quite so "critical" anymore since I can now occasionally pick up a goody or two at the PX.

That's all the exciting news from the other side of the world. Like last night, leaving the movie I said "What the hell are we doing in Asia?" Little did I ever dream of this in my younger (long ago) days. Little did I dream also that I would be so much in love with someone that separation would be so very difficult. But it's passing by, and though it still seems so far, it'll soon be here and over with. I wait anxiously, though not too patiently, for that day. I love you, Don Leta.

Your Leo

4 Mar 66

My Dearest,

While things have quieted down a bit, thought I would scribble a few words. Was going to write earlier tonight (last night) but had some problems. It's now almost 3 A.M. and I figure it'll be around 5 A.M. before I get off. That'll give me time to clean up, breakfast and get back.

Had left work and just finished chow when we had a cable go out. The first 4 – 5 hours were quite hectic, inasmuch as this was an important line (they all are when they go out) and everybody and his uncle wanted to know what was going on. The cable runs through a ditch and we discovered a fire burning where some Vietnamese were burning trash. The troops put out the fire and found about 10 feet of cable melted down.

No mail today – very little came in. Don't know that I would have had time for it until now anyhow. Outside of the excitement tonight everything has been routine – a minor crisis every few minutes. Grenier spent about half the day trying to get up north without success, so he's supposed to try again tomorrow.

I'm sitting here again wondering how anyone can get so lonesome for anyone when there's so much going on all the time. I'll tell you, it's beyond me, even though that seems to be the way I go around. Gosh how I miss you, Don Leta. All I seem to do is go around in a dream world. Dream of what used to be – dream of what it will be like again. Just dream, dream, dream. Really, I think that's a good part of this tour – if there is a good part – that I can at times shut it off and think of us together. Sometimes it seems quite fuzzy, sort of unreal. Then, at other times I can imagine it all so clearly. I often see you working in the kitchen, or sewing, or sitting at the table – and me not letting you alone for too long at a time. If only I could come up on you now and kiss you as I've done so often before. At most, 235 more days then we'll see. I just think we'll go into hibernation the first few days! I can keep writing this over and over a million times, but I know it still won't say it half as well as just my holding you close for a few quiet seconds. I believe this strongly and intend to test this theory as soon as I can. I want you so much, my beloved, and I'm so very, very happy and thankful that you're my very own sweet honeybunch. You've given me my whole life by being what you are, and there's no doubt that you are really and truly my happiness. Thank you, my dearest, with all my heart.

Your Leo

6 Mar 66

My Dearest,

Skipped writing a couple days again since there was no mail nor was anything exciting going on. As a matter of fact, there were no mail deliveries for three days. We were going through another one of those cycles where all available aircraft were tied up hauling ammo. Whenever they haul explosives they can't carry anything else.

Did get two letters from you today, however, which was a nice ending to that brief famine. I really enjoyed the pictures Mom sent you of the boys. I'll return them in the next letter inasmuch as I want to show them to the guys at work first. Seeing Paul in that pictured as compared to some of the recent shots you sent me really shows how fast they grow.

When you have a chance again, you'll have to include a picture of the new dining room set so I can see what it looks like. I was going to say send a picture of the new mattress also, but I guess I can wait for that!

Was glad to hear that mother was coming along fairly well. Boy, there sure is a bunch of illnesses, etc., what with mother, you, Mary, the kids—and now old grandma and Bill's father acting up again. Sure makes one stop and think, I remember how my mother used to tell me, "Just wait 'till you're grown up and have a family". Well, I don't know about growing up, but I do have the family (and a half!) And am now ready to start saying the same to our kids. I suppose there'll be a lot more problems, that is! And we'll probably never really be free of it. Gotta start learning to grow old gracefully.

Grenier called me from Dong Ha yesterday morning and said he probably couldn't get out of there until Monday. He did get back yesterday afternoon, however, after having hitched a ride on the Jolly Green Giant; a big AF helicopter. They had gone up on a C-45 to Hue and from there to Dong Ha by Huey chopper. He said he didn't have time to look around but Hue looked real nice. It's a real old city, built by the Chinese hundreds of years ago. There's much tradition attached to that city. On the flight from Hue to Dong Ha, the crew pointed out North Vietnam to them—a distance of about 10 miles from Dong Ha. He said Dong Ha is nothing but an outpost in the middle of nowhere. Everything is sandbagged, and the site is only about one acre. It's surrounded by five circles of barbed wire, with mines planted between each row of wire. The troops claim just about every night some of the mines are set off by dogs getting out there. Our antennas are banged up a bit from bullet holes and shrapnel. We'll shortly be taking over those sites (Hue & Dong Ha). Right now they're manned by TDY people from the 1st MOB at Clark, but they'll all be transferred to us PCS.

Well, I did it last night—got half bombed out—from drinking that is! Really, I didn't get drunk, but was feeling mighty high. They had these four guys playing country music at the club and about 8 of us spent the night there. I wasn't that bad off since after they closed (11pm) four of us played hearts until almost 1 o'clock, and I won every game. That should hold me for another four months. I kept saying "it's about time I get a call". Twice since we've been here, Grenier and I started to get a bit high, and both times we ended up working because of some crisis or another, but the third time we made it through the night. I was still up at 8 this morning, but Gren didn't make it until 11.

Well, honeybunch, I'd better quit now that you know how I'm fighting this war. It's a good thing I didn't get drunk 'cause this Marine invited me to go along with them in the morning—they were going on a fire-fight. Told him I was a confirmed coward! Or like TSgt A__, who runs my radio section and is colored said: "I've got a color problem—a yellow streak down my back." About a month or two ago I used my ration card to get this marine a bottle of whisky, and now every time he sees me he either wants to buy me a drink or take me out on patrol! What a way to return a favor!

Hope you haven't put on too many more pounds, honeybunch, though after this is over with you can go ahead and get big and fat as you want to. That'll make your mother happy and also there'll be more of you for me! How I wish we could just wave the magic wand and everything would be over with—the baby, this tour and our being apart. My gosh, I love you so much, Don Leta, that I don't know what I'd do if we were together and had to be separated again for anything but the shortest of period. I've always been a dreamer of sorts, I guess, but I don't want to go on too much longer with only these dreams of the past and hopes of the future to keep me company. I need the real life mommybunch. I miss you, miss you, miss you and love you with all my heart. Take extra good care of yourself for us, my sweet.

Yours Leo

8 Mar 66, Tues.

My Happiness,

I don't have much news to pass on to you again today, except that I miss you and love you something awful—but that's not news. Oh, Don Leta, if you only knew—I don't know, maybe you do—but the worst thing about all of this to me is not the mortar attacks or any fear of what might happen, but the utter loneliness that comes from one being separated from his love. I'll tell you, very few free moments come about here when my thoughts are not entirely with you. This is becoming ever more so with each passing day, particularly now when our newest is becoming due. To think that you and I, two really inconsequential beings, all considered, are responsible for this miraculous event is almost too much to believe. As once again I look at the enclosed pictures, I think how really it's too much to believe. Don Leta, you've made me so very, very happy. I know many things will be just as they were before we parted, but I expect also that certain things will be changed when I return. For one, I will never allow you to forget how much I love you, and how very much you mean to me. There's so much I want to say to you, that it even bothers me that I must wait until we're together again, for I could not possibly write the words which would be even passably adequate. As we come closer and closer to the mid-way point, I look forward to the second half passing faster—until that last few days. Oh, how I do love you, my Dearest.

Did receive a letter from you today, as well as one from Mom. She didn't have an awful lot of news, except that she wished you were around so some of them could help with the coming of the little one.

Everything has been its steady, confused self around here. Keep working every day and get called in on the average of every third night. Other than that, I sometimes go in on my own so I can catch up on a bit of the paperwork. Unexpectedly, Grenier went to Hue this evening. They had generator problems and he dropped some belts to them—literally—right out of the plane. He was back within a couple hours.

That's it for now, my darling; I do hope you're taking care of yourself. I think I'm more nervous myself than for any of the others with the little one coming, because I won't be somewhere around. Don Leta, I won't ever start trying to say it again, but I just don't know how to let you know how very, very, very happy you've made me and how proud I am that you're all mine. You are and will always be the only one who can ever mean so much to me. Be sweet, my love—my happiness—and believe me when I say that I'll be with you at all times in spirit if not in person. If only I could but hold your hand, if nothing else.   Wait for me, my darling, I have so much to say to you.

I am, forever,

your Leo

9 Mar 66

Hi Mommybunch,

There's not much news to report tonight, so this will only be a shorty. After work and chow tonight I came back to the sack and read a bit, but before I knew it I had konked out. Woke up about 8:45 and went to the club for some coffee. Its almost ten now, so did want to get this quickie out. Took a run over to the shop because I had seen an article in today's Stars and Stripes that mentioned a Jacksborite and wanted to send it on.

My name's been in the last 3 or 4 papers also, and the troops have been riding me about it. It's those articles about that W. E. B. DuBois Club, which has been listed as Communist-run by the government. I told them I was Secretary—Treasurer.

Saw in the Air Force Times this week (23 March issue—takes a while to get here) where I've got it made for E-8[14]. They're making a grand total of 8 in my AFSC[15] in the whole Air Force. Good thing I didn't stock up on stripes!

Like I said, sweetheart, no news. Oh yes, there is one big piece of news—I love you great big bushels full and still miss you like anything. Hope you're not feeling too bad these last few days. Even though it's been some time, it seems not so very long ago, in some ways, when you still had about 4 months to go. How I wish I could be with you now, my darling. Here I can only sit and worry about you and hope that everything goes well. Make sure you don't stretch it too thin and wait too long before heading to the hospital. Take good care of yourself, my love. You're my whole life.

Your Leo

---

[14] E-8 The 8th Enlisted Rank, Senior Master Sergeant. Leo is an E-7, Master Sergeant

[15] AFCS Air Force Specialty Code; Leo's AFCS was 306 Crypto Maintenance

Senior Master Sergeant

Promotion to Senior Master Sergeant (SMSgt) was the most difficult and competitive enlisted promotion to attain. Congress limited the number of Senior Master Sergeants to 2% of the active strength of the Air Force. The number allowed in any given specialty was further limited. Over-staff conditions sometimes developed, virtually freezing one's chances for promotion for years. In today's letter, Leo has learned only 8 new slots have been approved throughout the entire Air Force for people in his specialty, Crypto. It looks like it will be another frozen-out year.

11 Mar 66

My Darling,

Got a nice sweet letter from my baby today, as well as letters from Karen and Stephanie. For a while I didn't think I'd get a letter out tonight, but looks like I'll make it after all.

Don't exactly know what's going on in these parts today, but Da Nang had been put off limits again until further notice and there's been considerable activity around the base. Took a walk to the BX this afternoon and there were a lot more people along the way than usual. All the bunkers were manned, which is not usually so during daytime hours. As usual, if something happens in our back yard we'll have to wait a couple days to read about it in the paper. Oh well, I guess if we have to read about some of these things then it couldn't have been too bad for us.

It got kind of overcast and misty yesterday and then rained lightly last night, but it was quite cool and nice sleeping. Today was on and off with the sun, and after having rain that made it kind of muggy. It's not bad tonight though; actually it's rather nice, with only scattered clouds.

I noticed in the Air Force Times (about 3 issues old) where they gave housing forecasts for statewide bases. Looked for Hanscom, but it wasn't included, so I really don't know if they're closing it or not. Westover did list a four week wait, while Pease had no waiting list. I'll have to check to see if Hanscom is being closed or not. I don't figure we'll be forecasting until about the 20th or so.

Glad you all enjoyed the pictures I sent—and what do you mean my hair cut short makes my nose look longer! Actually, I don't know that it'll be long when I get back. Maybe at least it'll be on its way to growing back in. But I'll tell you, in this climate I'm not about to fight it. It's so much easier to keep clean and so much more comfortable with just that "fuzz." Maybe I'm just getting lazier.

Speaking of lazy, got a charge out of the way Karen ended her letter with comments on that L-A-Z-Y bit I had written her. She noted:

> "P.S.: When you write back mention at least one thing that doesn't have to do with:
> 1. Being good
> 2. Helping
> 3. Obeying
>
> I think you already got the message to me in all the other letters."

So, she obviously has the message—but listening to it is something else.

Don't imagine I'll be getting rid of this radio for any "small fortune". Actually, it's a pretty good little set. It's AM/FM so I can get both AM stations and shortwave by flipping a switch.

Leo titled this photo
"Yankee Imperialist Warmonger"

Carter, Grenier and I sat out back of the barracks last night having our coffee and I had the radio so we could hear the 10 o'clock news. At 9:30 we listened to Radio Peking, a propaganda broadcast of the old Axis Sally and Tokyo Rose type and it was a riot listening to some of the things being done by us "imperialists" and our Vietnamese "puppets". This radio has 8 transistors and brings in quite a few Asiatic stations but there's not much use listening since it's all Greek to me. Outside of getting AFRS (Armed Forces Radio Service—which we re-transmit from Comm Sq) there are no English language programs other than Radio Peking at certain hours.

Hearing in your letters about all the problems back home, I can see how they must be worrying you when wondering about the kids while you're in the hospital. How I wish it were possible for me to be there with you, my sweet. I know it'll work, out, however. Again I feel so helpless that you must carry this burden by yourself. I love you so much, Don Leta, and that's what makes it so difficult to have to see you go through this alone for both of us. Believe me, there's never a day that goes by that I don't think of that. All I can offer now is the promise that, once this is over with and we're together again, we'll stay together if anyone in this world can. I love you, my dearest, with all my heart and soul.

Your Leo

13 Mar 66, Sunday

My Sugarbun,

There's now 225 days to go until DEROS. If I get out of here like they are now, perhaps it'll be cut down to closer to 200. Oh well, no harm in wishful thinking, though I'm not counting on it any, that way, if I don't stay the limit it'll be a present.

This has been a pretty quiet weekend, everything considered. Of course, the city is still off limits and all the shack rats are moaning and groaning. It looks like they had all of a sudden doubled the number of NCOs on this base when one goes to chow. There are so many strange faces—guys you don't normally see because they're usually making it for town first chance they get.

Gave my old aching bones a workout of sorts this afternoon. Sgt Chisum (his family is in Waco—believe I mentioned him before) picked a game with the Army Signal Company (like our Comm Sq) across the way, so we were out practicing today. What a bunch of flub dubs we are! We're supposed to play them next Sunday. Let me tell you it's hot playing ball out here—hot and dusty.

Nothing much new going on here. Victor Charlie still isn't bothering us, which is OK with me. As many people as there are around here, they don't have much chance to get too big a group together, I guess. About the only time they can move in force is at night—there's just too much air activity in the neighborhood during daylight hours.

Thought there might be something to write about this weekend—but drew a blank. I didn't even get called out today. Did get one telephone call from my Controller on some call he received from Tan Son Nhut, but I put off any action on it 'till tomorrow. I signed McGraw's clearance yesterday. He works mids tonight and leaves tomorrow night. His DEROS was 1 April and he had a port call for 23 March; however, he could catch a flight to Okinawa the 14th, so I'll let him go.   Hope someone will let me go if I can get a flight out of here early! I'm just about ready now!!

That's it for now, honeybunch. Gee, I'm getting as anxious as you are I guess about the baby getting here (there). I pray everything goes good for you. I want so much to be with you, my love. If there's anything I wished to be over with it's this tour. And the whole thing about it is that, for us at least, things here are not so bad. Of course, it's not statewide living, but we're not without necessities. It's just this business of being in the middle of everything, and still being lonesome. I miss you and the children terribly. Never will I ever forget this separation. The one thing I keep thinking, over and over again, that I want more than anything else is to once again hold you close in my arms. I live from day to day for that moment, my beloved Don Leta.

Yours Leo

15 Mar 66

My Beloved,

There's not much to report, other than job irritants, and I'm afraid that wouldn't make too good reading. Haven't received any mail for a couple days, so there's nothing to comment on from that end either.

There is something I found out, come to think of it. Last week one of the guys showed me where I made the Air Force Times. They had a list of people from 15th Air Force who were awarded the Commendation Medal. That was in the 23 February issue of the Times, but I haven't heard anything officially as yet.

The word came out today for people returning in October to forecast between now and the 28th of the month. Will get that done some time this week. No one seems to know whether or not Hanscom is closing, so unless I hear otherwise I'll probably put in for Westover and Pease. I think I'd rather get Hanscom, however—for one thing it's not SAC—but I'll keep checking to see if anyone knows anything about plans for that base. I remember talk previously about 8th AF Headquarters moving from Westover to Pease. And from talking to some people there still seems to be something going on about it.

Things are still in somewhat of a mixed up state hereabouts. Of course, you no doubt know all about Ky relieving General Thi as I Corps Commander. It's caused a bit of rumpus on the part of the Vietnamese around here. There have been demonstration ever since in town—a big part of the reason for it being placed off limits. Indications are that these demonstrations will go on for a while yet. Doesn't phase me any, except that I'd be due for a haircut this weekend and had to think of fighting the base barbers—3 of them for over 3,000 troops in the immediate area alone. Guess I'll just get it trimmed and see _if_ and how fast the top grows back out. The hottest weather is yet to come, so I may just get it cut right back off again.

The local situation caused more troubles. None of them showed up today, so everything they've been doing has been taken over by the GIs or gone undone. A lot of the construction projects were being done by Vietnamese laborers. Also, PX[16] minus helpers, no barbers, no laundry, no KPs[17], no houseboys. War is hell!

Guess that's about all my gripes for today. Put McGraw on the plane last night. He caught one going to Okinawa and was going to book a flight out of there for the states. We've got about another 10 people or so leaving next month.

Got quite a bit of outgoing mail last night and all day today, but things have been pretty quiet so far tonight. Got off work at 5 o'clock and was walking to chow with Grenier when we passed the movies and there was no line, so we went right in and ate later. Real excitement!

Was thinking that yesterday was your day at the doctor's again and since you were supposed to get examined, maybe you have some idea of how

---

[16] PX Post Exchange, the term for a retail store on an Army base

[17] KP Kitchen Police, kitchen help

much longer there is to go. I know it's nothing compared to you, but I'll sure be glad when it's over with and you're back on your feet. Maybe then the worst will be passed, even though I know it won't be any picnic with an itsy bitsy one on top of the other five. To think, this one will be around six months old before I get to see him/her. Goodnight now, my dearest. I'll say it over and over, but it hasn't lost any of its meaning—I miss you terribly and love you with all my heart. Take extra good care of yourself, my happiness.

Your Leo

16 Mar 66

My Dearest,

The radio is carrying the latest launching[18] as I get my writing done tonight. It's 11:10 PM now and I'm in the shop. Imagine I'll be here yet until two or three in the morning. Again there won't be too much to report on the news side, honeybunch. No mail today and no big crisis—just the usual bunch of little ones!

Ended up quite noisy in the field last night, but as usual don't know much of what was going on. Lots of outgoing stuff for a while, plus quite a bit of small arms fire but it was quite a ways off and soon ended with no more from that end.

Went ahead and got my forecasting done this morning. Since Hanscom was still on the list, I went ahead and listed it and Westover 1st-2nd, with New Hampshire as my state, so that takes care of Pease also. Really, all I'm wanting is a place where we can be together again. Saw in the paper recently where 25% of the people who forecasted for March return asked for consecutive overseas tours to other areas. Let me tell you there's not that many people normally wanting to go from here to Germany, Japan, etc., but they're mostly hoping they'll be free for a three year accompanied tour and then rotate to the states. They're not even safe there anymore, however. The AF has served notice that they may be drawn from other overseas areas and sent here, even before their tours there are over. They'd just send them to Vietnam again and return their families to the states. Rot's of ruck!

Gonna have to go to supply and order some boots. One pair of my brogans is falling apart on me. All they've got on hand are sizes 7 and below or 12 ½ and above—as might be expected. It takes about 6 weeks when they order them for you. If I'd known what I do now, I wouldn't have brought

---

[18] Gemini 8. Planned as a three-day mission, a bad thruster cut the mission short and they returned the same day. The mission tested rendezvous, docking and re-entry capabilities. The Gemini 8 crew was Neil Armstrong and David Scott.

anything but traveling uniforms and fatigues in the line of clothes. Won't wear 1505[19]'s or blues I know until it's time to go back.

This letter is taking some time—it's 12:20 now. Get off on first one thing then another. Been wondering all day how you've been, whether the baby was due about now, etc. With no mail in three days I get to wondering. Don't get me wrong, I'm not complaining. Heaven knows I'm hearing from you much more often than I thought I would—what with all you have to do by yourself, you must be dead tired once the Indians are all sacked out. Guess you just spoil me.

Got to cut this off, honeybunch. More problems. Love you, love you, love you.

Your Leo

18 Mar 66

Dearest E-8 Wife,

After having worked until 3 A.M. Thursday morning, when I got back and had taken a shower last night I laid on the bed and that's all she wrote. Didn't wake up until the next morning. Also, hadn't received any mail yesterday, so there's really not too much to report.

Did get two letters from my honeybunch today, however. One of them had been delayed a bit because you forgot to add 96337 to the APO. Also received a package from Mom yesterday. I shouldn't be needing anything else since the PX is now getting a bit better on snack goods.

I was glad to hear both that mother was doing well and that you had found somebody to help when the baby came. I can well imagine how that must have preyed on your mind. Don't worry too much about the expense for now. Not this pay day but the next I'll be sending an extra $100 home each month since the April pay day will make me an extra $56 richer. The raise for the promotion is $51 and there's $5 more for quarters. I really wasn't counting

---

[19] 1505: the designation for the tan Air Force uniform introduced in 1965.

too much on making it this time since there were only 8 being made in crypto in the whole Air Force. MSgt Green, a new radio man who joined us about 3 weeks ago also made it in our outfit. Got called in to the Orderly Room this A.M. to get the word. There was a message in from PACOM with the list of communicators in S.E. Asia who had made it. The only other one I knew was MSgt Lytle at Tan Son Nhut. We came over together.

The promotion extends my time in the Air Force 4 months. My discharge date is 4 Dec 67, but anyone getting promoted to MSgt or above must agree to serve two years in that grade in order to get it. The extra money now, plus the extra $20 or so in monthly retirement pay makes it well worth the extra four months. After 20 years, I won't quibble over that. It does pose one other problem here locally. I'm not authorized here now, so I'm sweating out they're moving me to Saigon. They've already started on writing up justification for an E-8 slot in the manning for crypto here, but don't know how far they'll get with it. What I'm hoping is that by the time they arrive at a decision I won't have enough time left to make a transfer worthwhile.

Grenier went up to Dong Ha and Hue again this morning, this time for about five days. I still haven't made it up there. Don't know when or if I ever will.

Lately we've been sitting out back at night and getting our jollies by listening to Radio Peking on the shortwave band of my radio. They reported how more than 16,000 American Imperialist aggressors had been slain the first two months of this year, and all the great victories the Vietnam Liberation Forces (VC) had racked up! Sometimes they almost make you split a gut laughing.

Thought there would be a lot more to write after two days, but I guess not. Did spent the afternoon traveling – to Monkey Mountain and Marble Mountain. Looked over some relay sites we'll be taking over shortly. Marble Mountain, also called Da Nang East, sits right on the China Sea. It's nothing but sand – and hot. The Marines are there with their helicopter pads. When there's an attack on Da Nang, it's usually this place that gets hit the hardest. The big attack of last July was primarily on this facility.

That's it for now, my honeybunch. I just keep waiting for word that the baby has come. I expect a letter anytime now that you've had your check-up and maybe some word on when to expect the baby. I miss you terribly, my love, and would give anything to be with you right now. I'll love you more and more every day, I just know that. Though I may not be able to say it on paper, I hope to prove it for the rest of our days once we're together again. Take good care of yourself, my dearest.

Your Leo

20 Mar 66

My dearest Don Leta,

Got a real sweet letter from my girl today and since I have a few minutes, figure I would go ahead and start writing. It's 1:45 Sunday afternoon and I'm at the shop waiting for a meeting which was scheduled for 1 o'clock. Typical!

Didn't get to do any writing last night since we had another go 'round. One of our troops, a SSgt, shot himself in the leg with a .45, so things were in quite a turmoil for a while. Still don't know how it'll all turn out. To top it all off, he was the Squadron Safety NCO! Shades of Lt C_______!! When he was Safety Officer he was picked up for going 100 MPH and also broke his foot. That job must be jinxed.

Sgt Green and myself are going to get together to throw a little beer bust when our promotions become effective 1 April. The one thing I'm sweating out now is their having me sent to Saigon. I don't know how they can ever justify my staying up here, except that I won't have that long to go. Hope they have another E-8 or E-9 at Saigon who came here after I did. Then I can cry "overage" and they'll hurry up and send me home early. JOKE!!!

Da Nang is still off limits, and I have no idea when they'll open it again. Last Friday all the hired help walked off at noon to go on a general strike and demonstration in town. They were all back Saturday morning, however. I'm afraid everyone being kept here will generate more problems, what with everything being so crowded. Had to hunt around for a chair to sit on while I drank coffee. It takes a restriction like this for us to fully realize how crowded things are.

Nothing much is new hereabouts, honeybunch. We had our meeting (NCO Advisory Council) done and over with in a little over an hour. Was going to go to the movie but took one look at the line and changed my mind. Can't see fightin' them.

Your letter today, after your visit to the doctor's, sounded like it was almost time. Hope it's not too far off. Tomorrow I guess would be your next appointment. I had never mentioned it – actually I hadn't even thought of it – but I wondered how I would get the word. You (or someone) could write, but you could also advise the Red Cross and they would get the word to me. The last couple days, when someone says the First Sgt was looking for me or something, I automatically think that word has come.

I hate this thinking of how long to go yet, less than how much has passed, but still it seems far away. Well, another 10 days or so and we can chalk another month off. As of now, there's a <u>maximum</u> of 219 days to go. I'm going to miss you terribly each and every one of those days. I love you, my darling, with all of me. You have, and continue to make me so very happy.

Your Leo

20 Mar 66

Hi Pal,

Boy, it's been a long time since I wrote to the little man of the house. I hope you're still being a pretty good boy and listening to your mommy. I saw some pictures of you and Paul, and you both look like you're getting quite big.

I didn't send any gum this time because our mailman said it's hard on his stamping machine. I guess you'll just have to get your gum from mommy.

Since I'm getting really skinny now, I'm sending you another picture of what I look like. Give mommy a big hug and sugar for me.

Loads of love, Daddy

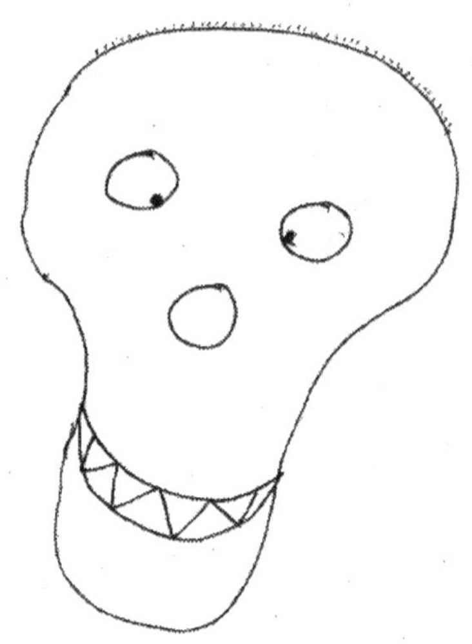

21 Mar 66

Hi Sugar Girl,

Today was a good day – got both a letter and package from my honeybunch. I had gotten the letter at noon mail call, but didn't know about the package. One of the guys had picked it up and put it on my desk. It was about 4:30 before I thought of it again, so I opened it, remembering there was banana bread included. I told everyone I had banana bread and cut one up. Knowing how it was in the past, I purposely checked the clock. From the time I started cutting until it was all eaten and crumbs were wiped off the desk took 3 minutes and 20 seconds! A new record. I left the other in the box – didn't dare mention it.

With this and what Mom sent, I don't figure I'll be needing anymore, except maybe a couple of banana breads or apple cakes occasionally. I believe I mentioned to you that the PX has been getting a few things in lately – crackers, canned fruits, beans, jams, etc.

It's been 5 days since you wrote the letter which came today (actually 4 days because of the loss of a day crossing the International Date Line), and I've been wondering if anything had happened yet. You were mentioning some slight contractions and what not. Gosh, by the time I get the word he/she will be out of diapers! We should be so lucky.

Boy, I can see what it'll be like when reading more of Paul's exploits, like him going in and out by himself and figuring ways to climb on the dishwasher. I'm sure sorry I'm not there to see him at this point. Even though they cause heart palpitations and more gray hair, it's really something to see them growing and exploring. Maybe what we need is another girl so we can relax a bit. I remember with the others how there were times when we couldn't see how boys could get into any more than they did!

Snuck out last night and figured I'd get into the 9:30 movie. Against my usual practice, I went and stood in line for about 20 minutes. Finally got my ticket and waited some more 'till they opened the doors. Finally the doors swung open and I was carried away on a sea of humanity. All of a sudden, a notice caught my eye: "Due to non-receipt of mail, the movie scheduled for tonight will be shown Monday and Tuesday. Tonight's feature is Elvis Pressley in 'Girl Happy'!" I had previously made up my mind that I was going to make a big sacrifice and pass that one up. Oh well. I killed a couple hours anyway.

Routine day today—no major crisis—and only got called to the phone once tonight. The rest of the night the FSgt, a couple of others and myself just sat on the edge of the bunks like old ladies and gossiped. I did get my curiosity settled on one item. This old FSgt just across from us always gets two cartons of cigarettes. Then he sits on his bunk and opens them all. He takes each pack of Pall Mall, takes out cigarettes, and puts in Salems. The Pall Malls he took out he puts in the Salem pack. Hodgson (our FSgt) then told me the story. This guy likes Pall Malls, but he also likes a filtered menthol cigarette. So he alternates, one of each. That's why he meticulously sits there and puts ten of each in each pack!

I imagine, having made SMSgt, it'll be more likely that I'll get Westover than Hanscom, if I get either of my choices. You mentioned about wanting to check with Family Services about those bases. I don't know if they have anything here or not. Heck, no telling now when you'd be getting there. Maybe, if you had the chance, you could write to family services at both bases, telling them I'm "pending" assignment there from VN and since you're not at a base maybe they could send you some poop. John Hill was going there, as a matter of fact he was supposed to leave Guam in March, and he told me he would send me some info since that was one of the places I was going to forecast for. <u>Maybe</u> he won't forget. One of our teletype people, A1C Labranche, went to Hanscom last month. I was going to get his address and have him check to see if they've authorized a 306 (Crypto) E-8. They may very well be since it is a TAC Comm Region HQ. I know they'll have authorized one at Westover since it's both Eastern Comm Region (AFCS) and 8th AF HQ (SAC). The question is whether they'll have any vacancy coming up. By the way, after getting this promotion I checked on freeze dates for E-8's and E-9's in my AFSC. As of the last issued list, those who came back in September '65 are already on the freeze list. Good luck to 'em!

Guess I got to rambling on tonight. Here I am on page 5 and I haven't even told you how much I love you. There's not many days or nights that I've skipped telling you – except maybe the very few times I was in one of my grouchy moods. Not the few times I was grouchy – 'cause that's more than a few – but the few times when I missed telling you. I know it's no more than you—but I'm sure anxious for the baby to come and to hear that everything is all right. I'm more anxious about this one I guess than when I was around, because then at least I'd be there – somewhere. At least when Lanis came everyone was in fairly good health and there were no boys to keep up with – or after. The last few days, especially, as the time grew nearer I got to counting the days again, and let me tell you that doesn't help it go by any faster. How I wish I could be right there by you through this.

Good night, my dearest. My last thought tonight, as almost every night since we've been parted, will be of you.

Your Leo

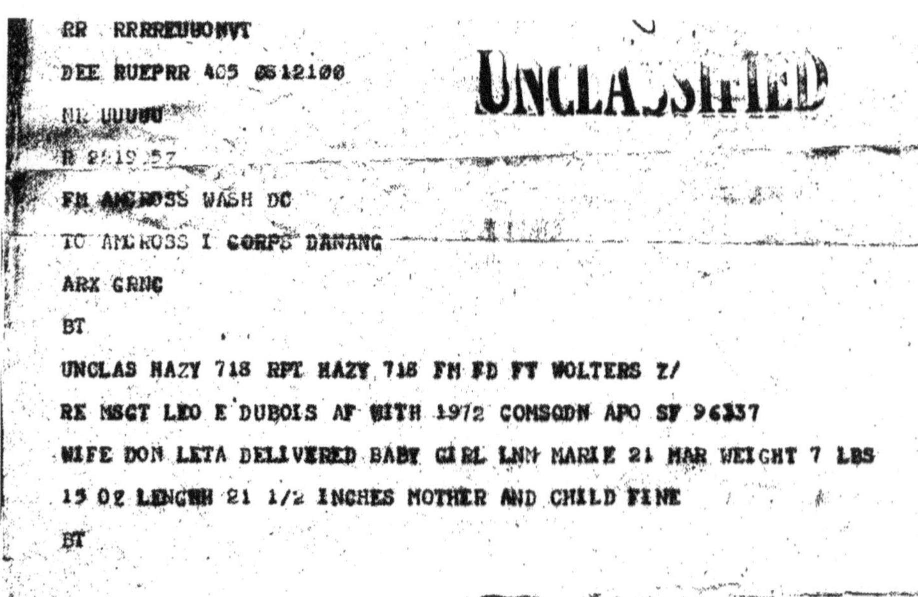

```
RR  RRRREUUONVT
DEE RUEPRR 405 0612100
NR UUUUU
R 2219 57
FM AMCROSS WASH DC
TO AMCROSS I CORPS DANANG
ARX GRNC
BT
UNCLAS HAZY 718 RPT HAZY 718 FM FD FT WOLTERS Z/
RE MSGT LEO E DUBOIS AF WITH 1972 COMSQDN APO SF 96337
WIFE DON LETA DELIVERED BABY GIRL LNM MARIE 21 MAR WEIGHT 7 LBS
13 OZ LENGTH 21 1/2 INCHES MOTHER AND CHILD FINE
BT
```

24 Mar 66

My Beloved Don Leta,

How happy and relieved I was this morning to get a call from the Red Cross telling me that Lynn Marie had joined the clan and that both of you were doing well. I wondered if maybe it had happened since it has been three days without mail. So now three things have happened within 5 days – I got the promotion notice, the baby came and so did the paperwork on my Commendation Medal. The old man is supposed to present it to me at Commander's Call Monday.

We had another one last night – of all times since I wanted to write you again then. About 1:45 in the afternoon we started getting calls on bunches of circuits and telephones going out. Checking, we found it was all in the same cable. Sure enough, one of our cables had been cut, and when that happens just about everything breaks loose. Sometimes there's hardly time to get the coordination, etc., to get the job done because you're forever on the phone to everybody and his uncle telling them what happened, what's being done, etc. It was almost midnight by the time everything was squared away and by then I just took a shower and conked out. It had been a particularly miserable day to top it off – the hottest we've had yet. Someone said it was 107°, though I didn't hear any confirmation. Today was another hot one. It's not too awfully bad once the sun drops, but from 9 A.M. to 4 P.M. it's hot and heavy.

Some more of the guys leaving shortly got their assignments. MSgt Scheicrn, our Wire Chief, got his 2nd choice of F.E. Warren; SSgt Brinlee, in Radio, had asked for Perrin and got Dyess. He's from E. Texas. SSgt McCranie, also in Radio, got his 1st choice of Robins, Ga., four blocks from his home. MSgt Smith, the teletype chief, got his consecutive tour to Okinawa. His wife is either Okinawan or Japanese.

The town is still of limits, and from what I've been hearing, this could last for some time yet. One of the local shack rats came back to the base. He said there just wasn't any authority left in town. The QC (Vietnamese Military Police) had either left or changed to civilian clothes and joined the demonstrators or left the area. The White Mice (Nationalist Police, so called because they wear all white uniforms) were also nowhere to be found. There hasn't been a Vietnamese on the base for 3 days. Gots to wash some clothes tomorrow! That's another thing. Water is only on certain hours. It went off tonight, unannounced, with a bunch of guys standing nicely soaped in the showers. It won't be back on until 5 in the morning.

You know, I had been thinking about it, and I'm just as happy we had a girl. The only thing is, I should think she'll get spoiled more than a boy would have, what with three older sisters. I don't imagine Bryan and Paul will be too impressed once the novelty wears off.

How I wish I were there to hold you now, my love. You've been so sweet and good to me all along and you're the most precious person I could ever know. It's just such a shame also that I won't get to see the little pumpkin until she's about 7 months old. I'm real anxious now to hear from you about it all, which of the kids she looks like, et cetera, and how her mommy is doing. I'd give anything to be there. I'm trying as hard as I can. I forecasted last week and have asked the people in personnel every day since if my assignment has come in yet! I'm telling you, I'd take any old place at all, just as long as we're all able to be back together again. I miss you so terribly much, Don Leta, I keep thinking that after a while I'll more or less get used to it and resolved to our being separated, but as each day passes I don't think it'll ever happen. I keep thinking of you and missing you as much as ever.

Be real careful now, honeybunch, and take care of yourself. I hope you don't go rushing into things. Take full advantage of any hired help you can get for as long as possible, 'cause when I get back I'll put you to working enough. Love you, love you, love you.

Your Leo

26 Mar 66

My Darling,

Things are still pretty quiet – as much as they get quiet around here, and there's really not much news to report. I had to go in for a while last night, but things look safe so far tonight.

Today was a frustrating kind of day. It was one of those where you seem to be running all the time, from one thing to another, and when it's all over with, you wonder what got accomplished. Restriction to the base seems to be getting to some people. Got into four different personnel problems today. I have been sweating out a big brawl or something at one of the clubs or around the barracks. There are so many with nothing to do at night that they just go and booze it up. Then, everything is so crowded, and hot. So far we've been fortunate that nothing like that has happened.

One of my Masters is getting a letter of reprimand. Originally, the old man wanted to give him Article 15 punishment. Last night he got a snoot full and then got into an argument with this SSgt who's half loaded all the time. This was 1:15 in the morning, so quite a few people were aroused. This morning, I guess the CO had gotten a report on it and told the Lt. About 9 AM the LT asked me where he was. Heck, I thought he was in the shop. I had to go get him out of bed. By 10 o'clock he still wasn't in the shop. He had turned over and gone back to sleep. I was somewhat irritated by then. To top it all off, he goes home in less than a month. He's done such a good job here that I was already writing the recommendation for commendation.

A couple of us were listening to Radio Peking tonight. I'll tell you, sometimes it's a riot. I got a charge out of an article in the paper a couple days ago. It said how two were wounded in a raid by the VC. This Army Sergeant heard on one of these propaganda broadcasts how 112 had been killed and 200 wounded. He said he was all confused since nobody told him if he was one of the dead or one of the wounded.

Is Lynn walking yet? You know, I've been trying to picture the little thing – trying to remember what the others looked like. I'm so anxious to hear from you. You've gotten me so spoiled by writing often that when you take a couple days off to have a baby it seems like forever. Guess it seems all the more so since I'm so eager to get news from you.

Now I hope you can someway catch some catnap, what with having to do all the getting up with Lynn Marie. If only I were there to help you, honeybunch. I want so much to, and there's nothing I can do. I love my wonderful, sweet wife more than anything. The days are moving so slow towards our reunion.

I miss you Don Leta. You've been so good to me and you've made me so very, very happy.

Your Leo

Mon, 28 Mar 66

My dearest,

It'll be nice when I can sew on those SMSgt stripes; then I'll be able to sit back and relax a bit. Right now I know it's us MSgts who are doing all the work. Oh well, if it wasn't like this I suppose time would drag by all the more.

It was real nice getting a letter from you today and hearing all the details leading up to Lynn's entrance. With all the activity you've been up to, including right up to the time you left for the hospital, it's about a wonder the baby wasn't a month early. Also got an Easter card from Theresa and letters from Mother and Lanis. I guess you hadn't seen Lanny's letter but she tells about you being in the hospital but the baby hadn't come yet. She said "I'm so excited". Also, "when you give me the $9.00 for my birthday, I think I should get $1.00 to grow on".

Had the Commendation Medal presented to me at Commander's Call today. Major Perry also mentioned that this had been a full month for me since besides that I had been promoted and had another baby. He then told the others, especially the younger ones, that I was setting the example and he wondered how many of them could do as well – this was my sixth! That brought a few moans, groans and guffaws.

Let me tell you, I wasn't disappointed at another girl. Another boy would have been nice, evened things up, but just as long at the baby and its sweet mother were well was all I was concerned with. I'm just sorry I wasn't there when she came, or that I won't be there to hold her (at 3 in the morning!) for some time.

Mother's letter was included with Lanis's, and after the first couple sentences I could almost have said what else she would say. I must write her and Daddy after this letter. She said how she had wanted a boy since that's what you said you wanted, and she told Daddy that when he came home. He said it didn't make any difference to him as long as it was the last one. She then told Daddy that she knew that was the way Don Leta felt also, etc. The thing was that she never mentioned herself as originating any of these sentiments – but that everyone else thought that's how it should be. I'll have to write if only to relieve her!

Six more of the troops got their assignments today. They all go back in July. Three got their first choice and three got their second choice. All had asked for consecutive tours. Two to Japan (one is married to a Japanese and one to a Korean) and one to Germany got first choices. Another got Spain and two got Germany, all second choices. Many of these communicators (about 60%) are requesting consecutive overseas tours – hoping, I guess, that things will be squared away here before they have to come back. I'm afraid that if this business here lasts too long they're going to find themselves a bit surprised. Knowing what I know now, I'd sure dread the word that I had to come here for another tour. Two years from 1 April and that's it!

Not much news I'm afraid, honeybunch. I don't do exciting things like have babies and what not. I just keep worrying right now, as I near the halfway point, that I'll be getting so anxious to rejoin you that it'll make time drag. I don't need that. I want so much to get back with you – as soon as possible. You've made me so very happy, my dearest, and I'm worth so little here without you. Pray that it will not seem too long now for either one of us; that we can just sit quietly together some night soon, after the children are down, and think that now that it's over, it was worth it in some strange way. I love you, Don Leta.

Your Leo

30 Mar 66

My Dearest,

More dreariness the last couple days. Must be getting old. It seems to have been those days when you keep going all the time and when you stop to look back nothing's been done. Guess I'm practicing for E-8.

Speaking of E-8, I still don't know what they're going to do with me now that I'm not authorized here. No word has come down yet from higher up, though I expect some will before long. Then again, they may just skip over it and decide to just let me ride out my tour.

Some of us got called in to the Commander's office to get the latest on local happenings in Da Nang. The city has been off limits now for three weeks and it seems like things are not getting any better. The Vietnamese have set up barricades all over and their demonstrations have taken a bit of the "Yankee Go Home" tinge. Among all their problems, the Buddhists have been clamoring for a return to civilian government and we're being blamed for the inflation that has set in. The poorer people can't afford the prices anymore. Of course, the fact that each VN is trying to make a buck has nothing to do with it. Like a while back, the Mayor of Da Nang had decreed that the local beer would be sold for 16 piastres instead of the 40 that was being charged. They could charge anything they wanted for American beer (which they weren't supposed to have in the first place!). The very next day, there mysteriously appeared a complete drought of local beer — you couldn't get one anywhere. Slowly it came back — again at the original 40 piastres. It seems that getting all they can is a way of life here. Stealing is the fault of the one who gets stolen from. It's a matter of practice, in the market area, to bargain for everything. Nothing has a price marked. They start at a ridiculous price like $10 and you offer $1. It's then back and forth until you agree on a figure. In other words, they'll charge every thing the traffic can bear.

Back to my tale, the Marines didn't help matters any with the locals by running one of the blockades. Now the word is that we don't go through town for anything. Since we have responsibilities at Monkey Mountain, Da Nang East and certain city areas, that means it'll all have to wait until things calm down. Guess the FSgt will have to go up to Monkey Mountain by chopper to pay the troops tomorrow.

I noticed in the attached clipping that Ed Rossley has gone down to Lackland to help rewrite the 5 and 7 level tests for his field. They're supposed to use the sharpest people in those areas to write these tests, which is something of a paradox. He's sharp enough to do this, but it's the others who get the stripes. Hope he makes it this June. I guess he must have missed some of the cold blast. Wonder what Joan did?

Got a letter from Mom today, but she didn't have much in the line of news. She said she had waited to write until she had the latest doctor's report. She talked of your calling her after Lynn came.

Like I said, honeybunch, there's not too much news – but I haven't been thinking of you any less. I can imagine you'll be pretty well pooped now what with having to get up nights with Lynn and all. I sure hope she isn't a colic prone baby and that she'll learn early to sleep through – but that'll probably be asking too much.

I'll tell you these days are moving slowly. Each day seems to zoom by, but every time I count what's left it seems like time is crawling. There's 208 days 'till DEROS now, so I figure about 195 until I leave here – providing my replacement is in. I'm trying all I can to push these days along – I want so much to be with you again, my sweet. I love you, love you, love you. You've made me so very happy.

Your Leo

DANANG, RVN
3∅ MAR 66

My dear "old" Lanis,

Happy Birthday, sugar, even though it's a bit late.

I received your letter that you sent along with Grandma Hughes's letter and it was good hearing from you again.

You asked how long it would be before I came back home. Well, right now it should be about 194 more days. So far, I've been away from home for 171 days. Pretty soon it'll be about half over with.

Mother has been giving me some fairly good reports on all you girls. I hope you keep it up, especially now that the new sister is with us. Mommy will need all the more help.

Be a good girl, pumpkin, and God Bless You. Give everyone a big hug + sugar for me.

Your loving Daddy

1 Apr 66

My dearest Don Leta,

Even as I start and wonder what I'll tell you about tonight, as just about always, the first thing that came to me was how much I love you. Now I know it's beyond me to explain, and heaven knows I've tried, at least to myself, just what I mean when I say I love you. Really it's a strange thing since there's no definite thing to point to and say "that's why I love her". Mostly, it's a combination of many things, I guess. It's wanting to go to you when things go wrong, just to know you're also concerned; to hold your hand in front of people; to help where I can around the house; to take care of our children. It's kissing you when you're busy, or when you're sleeping; wanting to get home from work 'cause you'll be there; or appreciating everything you do day in and day out. It's being happy that you're the mother of our children; wanting to spend all of my days with you; your concern at all times for the welfare of me and the children, often without consideration for yourself; baking something that you know I like, and generally making ours a home instead of a house. It's that unexplained something that makes me want you more than any sexy Hollywood star; your warmth at such times, and your understanding of what makes me content. It's the times afterwards when you just lay in my arms, like you belong there. It's even when you're grouchy, or yelling at the kids, or griping at me 'cause I goofed, or worried or hurt. That's odd, isn't it, that even you're being hurt contributes to my loving you. Then, I know what hurts you and I'm sorry and love you for it. Don Leta, I've tried before, I'm trying now, and I know I'll be trying many times again to tell you how I love you, but as always I feel I can't penetrate that magic shell which surrounds the meaning of love. But I promise I'll never stop trying. As I think of it, the closest I believe I'll ever come is when I first get to hold you close again. My darling, if you told me to prove my love by remaining in Vietnam, I would do it – and believe me that would tear into me as no shrapnel could. I don't know why I ever got off on this tangent – guess it's because it's so much on my mind, and really it's a losing proposition. I've read this over and it seems like it possibly could do as an introduction to the subject, once it was polished up some. I do love you so much, my darling.

Got a real nice letter from you today – the one you wrote once you had word of the promotion. Also did get a letter off to mother and daddy yesterday. Tried to put mother at ease a bit (gently) by assuring her that this would be the last.

Ila and Lanis Hughes with daughters
Mary (left) and Don Leta
From the mid-1940s

Now I hope those Protestants Bill and Mary don't goof things up! As far as we're concerned I know we're done in that department.

Sgt Greene and I went to the BX yesterday and loaded up on cigars. We got the old man to agree that Saturday afternoon would be a holiday. We're buying the beer and Sgt Horn, our Chief Operator (telephone switchboard) is getting hold of some steaks from the Marines. So, tomorrow afternoon we'll celebrate a bit.

The old man nominated me to Group today to sit on the promotion board for Techs and Masters which will meet 19 April for about a week – in Hawaii! This is only a nomination, however, so there's no telling whether or not I'll be called upon. That wouldn't be too hard to take.

We had another cable break last night, but my chief controller took care of me. It happened about 1 A.M. so he went in and got things moving. He called me at 6 A.M. to tell me about it and let me know it was all repaired. Otherwise, I would have been up another 40 hours or so before seeing the sack again.

It's sure nice to be into another month again. I've got a tendency, once the month gets here, to write the whole thing off at once. Now I can say it's six months to go! Gee, I'm so anxious, sugarbunch. Do you know it often takes ages for me to finish a letter to you? As little as I've written, it's taken me almost 1 ½ hours so far. It's just that I stop so often to just think about you – and us. Right now I'm trying my darnedest to pull from the past memories of snuggling up with you. Must admit, too much slips away over a period like this, and what's left is pleasant, though not too substantial.

Good night, me beloved. I'm still going to try remembering – 'cause it's been so wonderful with you.

Your Leo

3 Apr 66
Sunday

My Happiness,

It was such a nice day today, and I spent it all just lazying around. All, that is, but about an hour or so when I had to get some people together about a problem. It was warm but there was a light breeze. Sitting outside for a while it seemed impossible that people in other parts of this land were plodding through rice paddies, up in the mountains or in the jungle, intent on doing battle. Here's a bright sunny day, and off snarls a jet, bombs prominently hanging on its underside. From the other side comes a helicopter, doors open and the machine guns plainly seen pointing out – and then another, and another. You watch and wonder where they'll set down. If it's the flight line, you don't pay too much attention, but if they drop straight down the road you know there are casualties and you automatically count the number of them coming in. Big battles you don't hear about for a couple days later are foretold by counting these arrivals. It makes some of us wonder, sometimes, why we should be so fortunate as to remain here within our little circle of relative comfort, where for others to come here a day or two is a great period of rest and relaxation.

Things don't seem to be quieting any in Da Nang. It was reiterated that anyone leaving the base for any reason would automatically be given Article 15 or Courts Martial'd. Most Vietnamese are back at work on base, but there's considerable political activity in town – nothing threatening this base, however. They just want to make sure it stays that way by no one getting involved. It's going on a month that town has been off limits now, and all the shack rats are really hurting! Poor souls!!

No mail in a couple days – understandably. I know you'll really have your hands full now with that houseful, so don't worry, I'll be expecting no where near as many letters hereafter. Realistically, I'll be glad to get one letter a week from my honeybunch. Only wish I was back with you so letters wouldn't be needed at all. Gosh how I miss you, Don Leta. It still seems so awfully long to go yet – over six months. I know it wouldn't be half so bad if I just didn't miss you and love you so much – but I wouldn't change that in any way. I know I'll probably be just about speechless when we see each other again, even though there's so much to say – so much I want you to know.

Green and I never did get to throw our promotion party. As a matter of fact, we both ended up working well past quitting time Saturday. We plan on having it next weekend – and this time we'll have help. Sgt Telthorster (never heard that name before) came to the outfit about 3 weeks ago. He's in operations. Yesterday a message came in that he made CMSgt[20]. Since promotions were effective the 1st, he was really caught by surprise.

---

[20] CMSgt Chief Master Sergeant (E-9), the highest enlisted rank.

There's not much to report, sweetheart. Things just keep going their slow, plodding way. I'm getting to believe that Sundays are not so hot here when you're off duty. At least, not for guys like me. It drags too much, and gives me too much time to think. Like now, I've figured there's 205 days to 26 October – maybe around 190 before I leave here. This whole day, which seems to have lasted 110 hours, only chopped one measly day off the total. Oh well, maybe tomorrow will fly by and I'll feel better because it passes without my having had much time to count it.

You make sure to watch yourself and take extra good care for me. I love you so very much, my dearest.

Your Leo

4 Apr 66
Monday

My Dearest,

How nice it was hearing from you today. I received your long letter this morning. I say long because it was started the 27th, finished the 28th and mailed the 29th. I'm just pulling your leg now, not complaining. I imagine that's how it will be for some time with what little time you'll have free.

It sure sounds like you had a hectic time back home. No wonder that time in the hospital seemed to do you so much good, with everything else going on, both before and after. I sure do hope Lynn does settle down and doesn't become too colic bound.

I can just picture how happy the boys were to see their mommy again – they're just like their father will be, I'm sure. I won't make Bryan's mistake of saying how big you've grown, however! I'm anxious to know how the boys, especially Paul, are reacting to the baby in a few days. For one thing, I imagine they'll be keeping a close eye on you to see that you don't skip away again.

No, I'm afraid I haven't gotten too much skinnier, just a little itty bitty bit. Weigh about 165 now. I'm waiting to see what I'll melt down to come the hot weather, though. Today was around 103°, but out on the flight line it was 117°. There was another article in the Stars and Stripes recently talking about weather and in one part it mentioned 134° at Da Nang!

Looks like the town will be staying off limits for quite some time yet. Today they were setting up more tents and all the civilians moved on base. There were quite a few – construction people building new runways, buildings, power plants, etc., and they were staying in hotels and houses in town. The scuttlebutt was that there were incidents at the hotel where most of them were staying, though I don't know for sure. I know a few of them since they did some work for us (the building we're in, for example) so I'll try and get the latest gossip!

Not much new at work. Everything keeps going its normal merry way – only 4 or 5 crisis a day! There is one thing that's getting to be a pain, however, and I can see where it'll be getting worse as time goes by. They're trying to get too much like stateside, thought this is nothing like it. We're getting right back to the paper wars – letters, forms, documents, training, records. Can you imagine, on one inspection we had even been written up for not having a retention program or a 5BX[21] program! What can you tell an airman sitting here about the benefits of re-enlisting? About all you can promise him is another tour if he sticks around! I don't know. Guess I'm just getting too old for this kind of business anymore. For about a week now I've just been moping around mostly. Oh, I keep busy, but there's really not too much being done. Gots to get moving again.

Time to say good night and here I've been thinking again how I'd like to hold you and hug you and kiss you good night. If I did, though, I'm afraid neither one of us would get to sleep soon. So, I'll just close my eyes and dream about it, and only one of us will have to stay awake. Be sweet, my beloved. Be good now and take good care of yourself and all the little ones for me. I love you so.

Your Leo

6 Apr 66

My Darling,

How nice it was to hear from you again today. I was looking forward to it. Also received a letter from Bob Bishop at the same time, so got the double-barrel information about he and Dorrough both making Senior. As of that writing, they hadn't turned loose any of their assignments, but he said he believed they were going to put them out 1 April and that he'd drop me a quick note to let me know whether or not to find a bunk for him.

I hardly know what to say about the girls acting up again. It's discouraging for me to hear about it, so I can imagine what it's like for you to put up with it. It sounds like Karen will have to be stomped on the toes with the outbursts for things like not be able to spend a week with Nancy at her grandparents. As for Stephanie, I hadn't heard any more from you on the subject, so I thought maybe she had gotten over that bit with getting money for goodies.

The more I hear from you about old grandma, the more I'm expecting you to say it's all over with. Of course it's been like that before but obviously

---

21 5BX 5 Basic eXercises – a fitness program developed by the Canadian Air Force and adopted by the USAF in the 1960s.

never this bad. I can't see how she can go much longer at the rate that her condition has been deteriorating this past month or so.

It's been a bad couple days so far this week, as far as work is concerned. There are so many problems coming up every few minutes – and sometimes a bunch of them at once – that it's a job keeping up with them, much less getting much done. I'll consider myself fortunate indeed to get out of here without an ulcer!

Lots of activity hereabouts, of course, with the current political crisis, The whole base is sealed off and nobody comes or goes for anything, As a matter of fact, there's even no going to the docks for food. They're using what they had on hand, and then I imagine we'll be on c-rations for awhile. Just about every usable inch of ground is now occupied by Ky's troops who have come in and parked here. Tents and lean-to's are up all over the place. We've got a big Air Force tractor trailer parked outside and some of them have even strung their hammocks from the underside to take advantage of the shade. These are all Vietnamese Marines and paratroopers loyal to the Saigon government. No big explosion yet, but we're waiting to see if there'll be any activity between them and the local forces backing ousted General Thi. There are fortifications, barbed wire, gun emplacements and tanks crammed in here. The U.S. military is keeping strictly hands off, waiting to see what develops.

Things have been relatively quite tonight. Yesterday evening we were sitting out watching the air activity. Being in back of the barracks, we could only see part of the sky, but in that one part I counted 29 aircraft – some ours and some Vietnamese. Our jets were way up and just kept circling the whole area round and round. Pretty soon they'd come in but more would have gone up to take over the watch. Light aircraft (like that Jacksboro Captain flies) were all over scouting the area, as were a number if choppers. The outer perimeters were constantly being lit up by flares once darkness set in. Since martial law had been declared, I guess things calmed down a bit in town. One can go boo-boo trying to figure these people out, but that's their way of life.

Good night, my love. Give all the kids a hug and sugar for me. (I'm saving those for you for personal delivery.) I hope Lynn is calming down and letting you get a bit of rest. I love you ever so much and I'll repeat for the umpteenth time that I miss you terribly.

Your Leo

Clerihew Knows Enemy Below When Viet Cong Start Shooting

It's sometimes hard to see the Viet Cong in the underbrush but..."When they start shooting at me I know they're down there," Star-Telegram war correspondent Bob Schieffer quoted Capt. Walter Clerihew of Jack County last week.

Clerihew, whose parents, Mr. and Mrs. Arthur Clerihew who live at Jermyn and whose wife, Pat Sloan Clerihew, and children, Arthur, 10, Susan, 7, and Tex, 21 months, live at 618 W. Pine, is an Air Force forward air controller, or FAC, and his job is guiding the jet bombers onto their targets.

He flies an A-1 bird dog which he said he can get up to a hundred miles an hour in a dive. His job is to spot targets and dive close enough to frop smoke bombs to help the jets place their bombs properly.

A graduate of A&M, Capt. Clerihew was an Air Force weather forecaster and jet pilot himself before assigned to what Schieffer describes as one of the most dangerous jobs in Viet Nam. He has 15 1/2 years to his credit in the Air Force.

He racked up missions 276 and 277 the day Schieffer made the run with him and expects to double that number before leaving Viet Nam in another six months.

ABC Breakfast Set for Monday

The Jack County Agriculture and Business Council will have its regular breakfast meeting Monday, March 14, 7 a.m. at the Green Frog, according to Aldon Nash, president.

Bob Gordon, new work unit supervisor, will explain the functions of our local Soil Conservation Service, said Glynn Boykin, program chairman.

Everyone is invited to attend.

"That Jacksboro Captain", Walter Clerihew, appeared in March in the Jacksboro (Texas) Gazette-News. Used with permission.

Friday, 8 Apr 66

My Dearest,

It was real nice getting another letter and some pictures from you today. It's 8:30 P.M. now and I'm at the shop, but figured I'd scribble a bit to change the routine. Don't know if I'll get to finish this here, however, still have quite a bit to do.

There was one cute picture of Lynn in those you sent. She looks like a little butter ball. I particularly got a charge out of your description of Paul's actions. When you mention things like him running or trotting with his arms bent at the elbows, I can almost see him from the looks of these pictures. He has the appearance of a real cut-up.

It's really been surprising (pleasantly) to hear Bryan was so good at the dentist. I know his old daddy was as guilty as anyone for giving him goodies at all times of the day. I checked in here last month to get checked and have my teeth cleaned, but all I could get was an appointment – for 18 July! There's a trailer set up, and that's the dental cleanic – check that spelling – clinic. They've brought over a number if trailers, mostly to serve as quarters for some crews and commanders.

Yes, I remember Mother's uncle Ben and his son stopping by for a few minutes. I'll call locator tomorrow if I get the time – and find out where he works. Guess most of the day I'll be busy getting sandbags put up around RAPCON[22] units. The ones they had up got a bit weak and tumbled all over the place.

You asked about the laundry facilities, well they're something else. You bring clothes in; they mark it on a slip and give you your half. Then the bundle is tossed to a bunch of women sitting on the floor with magic markers. Everything that's unmarked gets your mark put on it (Initial and last four – so for me it's D-6769). Of course the 7's get the old European treatment of (seven with a line through it) which they picked up from the French. They then get washed in electric washers – Japanese, I guess. Getting everything back is something else again. Anyone doing a tour here and not losing 10-20 items would probably get investigated. The Vietnamese are among the greatest slicky-slicky artists. If anything's not nailed down, log it out 'cause it'll be gone in short order.

Still nothing yet on whether I'll stay here or get shipped out. As a matter of fact we haven't even received the promotion orders yet. All they had gotten was the message saying we'd been promoted. They expect the orders around the 15th or so.

---

[22] RAPCON Radar Approach Control, an aircraft navigation aid.

Things have still been fairly quiet hereabouts – on base, anyhow. I can imagine all that must be printed in the papers stateside about this business around Hue and Da Nang. Sgt Rodrigues, one of my controllers, came back from R+R to Bangkok today and he said that's all he read about. Even thought he wouldn't be able to get back – but it was only wishful thinking! He hitched a ride on a C-123 cargo flight out of Pleiku, but we've got 3 others who were due back today and I understand they're stuck down at Nha Frang so there's no telling when they'll get back. Rod was saying how he enjoyed his R+R – no lines, no jets, no mortars, no cannons, sleep late, air conditioned hotel, hotel swimming pool, food—all kinds. One day I feel like going somewhere and the next I say to heck with it. I'll probably take one somewhere pretty soon, however, just to get a change from all this.

Everyone's getting to look pretty raunchy hereabouts. No Vietnamese, so no haircuts. I've got a washing to do tomorrow also. Nothing like scrubbing fatigues in a bucket!

Ky's troops are still all over the place. Don't know what they'll decide about this whole mess. Was going around getting stuff today and saw the rest of their force down the other end – tanks, etc. You all probably know more about what's going on than we do right here. I have seen some of the papers from back stateside, however, so don't believe everything you read as Gospel truth either. Got a call from our troops on Monkey Mountain wanting to know what to do if they have to evacuate. Right now they're stuck there as nobody goes anywhere. If they leave, it'll be by chopper. Those on top of the mountain were just about to log it out last night, so our troops, who are half way up wanted to know what to do. Told them what to do, and then "come home – all is forgiven".

There's 200 days even until DEROS, so I figure about 185 till I get out of here. I still rather think of it as only 6 more paydays! Looking at those pictures again, you can imagine how much I want to be with you all soon. God willing, it'll be here before too awfully long. I love you, my Don Leta, with all my heart. Be sweet, my darling.

Your Leo

Sunday, 10 Apr 66

My Darling,

This is going to be short and sweet 'cause I'm beat – more than I've been yet. Did want at least to get a quick note off. It's Easter here now, but a lot of people don't know it yet since it's somewhere around 2 A.M. and I'm just about to hit the sack.

We've been going all day. This afternoon I had a crew of about 20 out sandbagging our RAPCON unit. We worked till supper time and there was still so much to do I called the shop and told my Senior Controller to get all available men for 6:30 P.M. So that's where we've been all night and what a mess we were. The Lt, 2 SMS, 2 MSgt's, Techs, everybody was shoveling.

Just took my 2nd shower since supper time. No mail today, but some did come in tonight so we all got our mail around 1 A.M. Got one from my girl and one from Mom. Sat out front and read it under the street light. Green and Grenier were still sitting out there when I called it quits.

Will write more tonight on your letter and Mom's, and the situation here. Things were touch and go here for a couple days, and I'm not sure where we stand right now.

Excuse the scribbling as I'm sitting in the latrine! Didn't want to disturb the "day workers".

Love you just loads, Don Leta. You must realize that by now. I can hardly wait to be with you again. Be sweet, my love.

Your Leo

Sunday, 10 Apr 66

My Honeybunch,

Got another sweet letter from my girl today. That's actually two today since I had received the other at about one in the morning.

Today was a pretty quite day, and I slept a good part of it. I'm sore all over from yesterday, as these old muscles haven't had such a workout in ages. Right now it looks like things are quieting down a bit. Most of Ky's marines were boarding aircraft heading back Saigon way, and the Vietnamese Air Force types who had headed for town at the outbreak of these demonstrations started filtering back. Patience is supposed to be necessary to deal with these people, and I can see why. Their actions sometimes make you wonder if it's worth it. So many are like wheat – bending with the wind. They'll go with whoever holds the upper hand at the time.

The last couple days Army "Ducks" and "Beavers", big vehicles that travel on both land and sea, have been bringing chow on the base. They load up from the ships in the harbor and then come overland to the base the back way, thereby skirting the city. Maybe now that things are quieting down a bit some of the VN will return and I'll be able to get a haircut. The PX has been closed lately also since it was mostly staffed by local people. They did open a little annex in the Airmen's Club for things like cigarettes, soap and shaving gear.

I was glad to get your second letter since it sounded that you were a bit happier over the girls' deportment than in the first – especially with Karen's acting up. I hardly know what to say in that direction. First it was Steph's behavior, with her stealing etc, and now Karen with her moods. I don't know how serious it is, but it seems that 9 out of 10 kids at one time or another hit the "you don't love me" stage. I can even remember myself sitting around moping and crying 'cause there "wasn't anything to do". Of course, I couldn't do anything in the work area – that wasn't pleasant enough.

I was just re-reading one of your letters where you said you didn't like the news coming from Da Nang "a rebel city controlled by communists". I'm led to believe there's quite a bit of fact in what's said about Da Nang, not that it's controlled by communists, necessarily, but that they have some sort of "agreement". There's little in the line of armed conflict Vietnamese vs. VC in this area. The only ones you hear about are Marines vs. VC, or mortar attacks on installations by the VC. It's said that the local people in town pay two taxes – to the government and to the VC. I wouldn't doubt that this is true because you never hear of assassinations or bombings or threats to the local populace in Da Nang. That's one of the big contentions between Saigon and the I Corps area that we're in. They don't do everything Saigon tells them to do. I'll tell you, it's a crazy system!

I'm glad to hear that Lynn has been good so far – at least as of your last letter. I know how much that will help, not only in giving you more time to get things done, but in letting you get a bit of rest occasionally. I hope she keeps on that way.

You don't have to worry too much about my bringing home any Dai's for you all to wear. I guess Stephanie would be the only one able to wear one. It is amazing what they do with beer cans, however. You can buy a big footlocker for $2-$3, with your choice of Falstaff, Schlitz, Pepsi, or combinations, all over it.

Never did hear about that proposed TDY to Hawaii – so guess they don't need my services there. A more probable reason is that someone with more influence got in on it. The last cycle, our Personnel Officer (another Schmo!) went. He had his wife fly there to meet him. And here I was planning on you and the kids all coming over for a few days – yuk, yuk.

I guess Mom said the same to you as she did to me in her letter. She did sound sort of depressed. She talked about Vivian's moodiness. Viv's always been like that, tho. Of course, from Viv's angle too I realize it's not always the easiest thing in the world to have the mother around. Personally, I feel it's often the children's responsibility to take care of their parents when they can. Too many of them get shuffled off somewhere just because it's an inconvenience to have them around.

Well, back to the pits tomorrow. Only got called once today, which was a rather pleasant respite. All that physical labor, though rather exerting, was nevertheless a good change from the normal routine. Plus it gave all of us old folks something in common to talk about today – our aches and bruises!

Good night, my sweetness. I love you terribly. I'm not going to go into too much detail 'cause in your last letter you said you wished I wouldn't write letters all about love because it bothered you. So I'm just gonna say that I think you're just yummy!

Your Leo

Thur, 14 Apr 66

My Honeybunch,

What do you mean, every time I write it seems like I've still got the same number of days to go? Today is shot, so as of now there's 193 more days left, and that's maximum, counting up to 26 Oct. Actually, I hope to be out of here a few days before that – how much depends on when my replacement gets here. Right now, my next goal is the 25th of this month – we'll be half way through, and starting downhill. After that it'll be the latter part of July, when assignments should be in for October returnees. You know, I keep telling myself I'm going to quit counting days because it just seems to make time drag all the more, and the next thing I know I'm figuring how long to go yet. It's just that I'm so anxious to be back home with you and the kids.

Got a letter from you tonight and was surprised to hear about them sending flowers. I can't imagine who was behind that as no one had said anything. I'll have to find out tomorrow.

We underwent another organizational change today. It was getting to big and unwieldy since we've assumed responsibility for six other places besides Da Nang. I've now got the Base Comm Branch, which takes in Crypto, Teletype, Inside plant (central office and switchboard) Outside Plant (telephone, wire, cable and antennas). Our present Chief of Maintenance leaves in 76 days and we're due in a Captain and a Lt.

Finally got my promotion orders today, direct from Randolph. Was wondering when they'd get here as they're needed for pay. They're here in time so an MPO has been submitted for me to get my raise.

Grenier and I decided to go ahead and put in for R+R, so we both submitted at the same time to go to Hong Kong in June. I don't know that I'll get much of anything there, and I'm really not all hopped up about seeing Hong Kong; all I want is the change – no getting called at all hours, no jets in your ears – no lines – no sweating out anything. If I can't get to Hong Kong, I may give Thailand or Taiwan (Formosa) a try.

You know, I've started a letter twice to Steph's class and never did get very far. I will definitely get one off by this weekend. I wanted to send along a couple little things about Vietnam. I got one thing at the PX (it re-opened today), a magazine on Vietnam. That way the teacher can probably tell the kids something about the country.

You'll not have to worry too much about sewing on stripes. I did two sets of fatigues by hand and had the other fatigues and my 1505's done at the laundry. Still need some on my summer blues, but that can wait a while yet. It's a long way around an E-8's chevrons!

You mentioned being shaky after having killed a mouse. You'd probably pass out here then. We sometimes sit out and watch rats moving around. Or in the barracks they run up and down the rafters over our heads. I don't remember if I told you a while back about the 2 or 3 that Grenier had in his locker. He said they were making a heck of a racket in there – like they were fighting.

A couple of our troops got their Purple Hearts on their way home. They got caught in that mortar attack on Tan Son Nhut a couple days ago while waiting for their flight home. Nothing serious for them, fortunately. They both caught a bit of shrapnel, one in the arm and the other (blush!) in the butt.

Gotta shower, sweet. Haven't had one since yesterday! Love you just loads and gobs. I'll be so glad to end this letter writing, but only because we'll be together. Give all the kids a hug and kiss for me and tell them all I'll write to them soon—and promise this time not to do too much lecturing. Love you, darling.

Your Leo

16 Apr 66

My Darling,

How nice it was to receive another of your wonderful letters today. I sure look forward to them, especially when a couple days go by without any. I'm hoping Lynn Marie keeps up her good behavior so that mommy doesn't get worn out too often.

That was really a surprise about the Bertone's heading for California. Since it's only for three months, I'm surprised Angie is not going alone. I wouldn't of figured they'd pull the kids out of school with less than two months to go. It will be nice that they can swing by, however, and I'm sorry I won't be able to be there – my schedule is full.

Sunday, 17 Apr 66

Ended up going to bed earlier than I had planned last night. There was another of our occasional power failures and this one lasted longer than usual.

I laid down for a while and the next thing I knew it was Sunday morning. I spent the day doing little more than moping and staying in bed. It was just too hot for anything. Yesterday it was only 97°, but the humidity was 94%. I'd sit at the desk for about 15 minutes and get soaked, so I'd go into the relay room and cool off. Kept doing that and the next thing I knew I started sniffling – that figures, so I changed that routine quick like.

Everything's been fairly quiet hereabouts. All the extra-curricular activities, that is. We still have all our daily crisis at work. For a while, though, things were somewhat in a state of flux due to the local political situation – what with Ky's troops here on base pointing things towards town and the local troops in town pointing right back. They're all gone now, however, and the others have come back. They had blown this place when those troops came in. Crazy, man! Other than that, we seem to be back on routine. Flares in the distance and outgoing mortars/cannon rounds. You get pretty well used to them after a while, but if it's broken by a particularly close noise everyone stops and listens for the next one.

The city of Da Nang is still off limits, even thought we do go out in the daytime when there's work to be done at Monkey Mountain, Da Nang East or at I Corps. Most of the local help has returned, even though I heard a number of them had moved out of the area when all the trouble was brewing. If things stay relatively calm, it should go back on limits before long. No one is looking for it to happen until next month at the earliest. I finally got out and got a haircut at the PX this week. It wasn't too bad when I got there in late afternoon – only 57 people in front of me!

I'm afeered that's all there is honeybunch. Real exciting, huh? Oh by the way – in case you didn't know yet, I did get the letters you had written in the hospital, so I assume others you wrote to go theirs also.

Good night, my love. I'm still missing you something awful and counting each one of these slow stinking days. Be sweet, my darling, and take good care of yourself for me.

Your Leo

18 Apr 66

Hi Sugarbun,

I can see already that this is going to be a shorty letter. There's just not been very much happening the past 24 hours, at least as far as I'm concerned. As a matter of fact, about the only thing of significance I can think of is that I got another letter from my girl.

Sgt. Chisum went to Clark for check-ups. I mentioned him to you before—his family is at Waco and that's where he hopes to go back. About a month or so ago he had a stiff neck, could hardly turn around. Since then he's been coming down with dizzy spells. He said the doctors here thought he had some kind of inner ear trouble which was affecting his sense of balance. Since they have no way of checking here, they sent him to the Philippines. He's due to go home in June or July.

It's still kind of hot every day, but it's the humidity which has been murder the past week or so. Here it is, 10:30 PM and I'm all sticky just sitting here. My next task will be to hit the shower.

Lost a couple more troops over the weekend. MSgt Smith, my teletype honcho, left for Okinawa. That was his first choice since his wife's from there. The problem is that he had to go directly from here, so it'll be about 3 months before his wife can get there as she's in the states. It's the same for a couple other guys who are going to Japan. They'll have to go directly from here, so there'll be additional delays for their wives to join them—the wait for port call, etc. I don't much know if I'd care too much for that extra time. (Now guys going to Europe who can get concurrent travel, or even those who don't have concurrent travel, are better off since the normal route is through the U.S.)

The BX has been kind of skimpy as a result of all the local turmoil, but things are starting to get re-stocked slowly but surely. I guess the supplies kept coming all the time but just sat out in the bay since little was off-loaded except for necessities—food, beer, etc!

I'm glad I already excused myself—no news. I can now tell you how much I miss you and love you, but I should hope that's not news by now. There's now 188 days to go maximum. In effect, it's just about half over with and I pray the second half doesn't seem as long as the first. I know it will, however, since the closer it gets to departure time, the more eagerly I'll be awaiting each passing day. Goodnight, my happiness. I'll see you in my dreams.

Your Leo

19 Apr 66

My Dearest,

What was just another routine day around here was made a little better by another letter from my sweetheart. When I got my writing stuff out tonight, what was right on top—the letter I wrote last night. So this time you should be receiving two letters. Though I mostly write at night, they don't get mailed until I'm on my way to chow in the morning. Don't know how I missed it this A.M.

Looks like I'm going to have to do like in the other letter and plead nothing happening. Things have remained relatively calm all told, outside of work. Even that wasn't too bad this morning, and only a small flap in the P.M.

The kids' grades didn't seem too bad. Even though Steph dropped a bit, it's still quite respectable overall. Looks like Karen still has her problems with history (Texas, that is!), but outside of that it's not bad. I suppose now they're on the last six weeks and you'll be able to rejoice with all of them home! Do they have any type of summer program in Jacksboro, do you know? Maybe that would soak up a bit of the time anyhow. I suppose they still have their pool in operation.

Well, it doesn't look like we'll be going to Hong Kong unless we want to put it off until August or September. Right now I don't feel like I want to go past June before taking a break. May put in for Bangkok, or maybe Singapore, if I can find out from anyone what it's like. There are times when it doesn't make any difference if I get to go on R&R while I'm here, and at other times I wish I was going right away. Depends on what experiences I've had the past 24 hours, I guess.

It's getting so that wearing any item of clothing more than one day is almost impossible. It still hasn't been too bad, heat wise, but that mugginess is something else. Usually, when I go to lunch I hit the barracks afterwards, strip to my underclothes and stretch out under a fan. More often than not I have to change at least my shorts and T-shirt. And here I am working indoors most of the time. I really feel sorry for our wire people, or those on the flight line, outside all the time.

Another quiet day comes to a close, my sweet and you know what? I love you. I love you with all of me and I know it'll always be so. Six more months of this I can do easily enough because I know that at the end of it all will be waiting my wonderful wife and children. Sleep good, my love.

Your Leo

22 Apr 66

My Dearest,

Even though it's almost midnight now, I'm in the shop and figured I'd best get a letter off to you before you think I've gone and defected! Just got back from a couple days TDY checking some new activities. Had them check mail when I got back, but no letter from my girl. Did get one from Mom, however.

I imagine Mom writes you just about the same she does me, so I shouldn't think there would be much of anything new to you. She told me of the call you made when Angie told you of their coming your way. She said Florence thought she would go there, but she had decided to go to Theresa's. I would think that's better as, like she said, there would be more chance of her getting out.

This new job I've got now is good, mostly because it's a bit of a change. I have more time to get things done and more opportunity to get out to the shops and other working locations. Also, I can now sneak out for coffee occasionally without everybody wondering where I've gone!

I guess things have loosened up quite a bit around Da Nang, at least temporarily. The town is still off limits to the military for other than official business, but they've allowed the civilians to move back in. They had all been evacuated to the base by boat and chopper at the height of the demonstrations a couple weeks ago. They all had to live in tents and makeshift quarters, poor souls. We go off base on telephone or cable jobs, or to go from and to Monkey Mountain and Da Nang East, but

Leo's sister Theresa, nephews Gary and Steve and mother Blanche

only during daylight hours. We are still holding off after dark. The beach has opened up and Grenier and I are planning on sneaking out there Sunday. China Beach is part of the South China Sea and fronts on the Marine Facility at Da Nang East. Actually, it's part of the military reservation. They've got a bus shuttle set up to travel back and forth. I'll have to watch out that I don't burn myself up. My arms and face are no sweat, but I'm afraid the rest of me is pretty white and "tender" yet.

You know, I'm still sitting on my R&R application. Grenier also. Since Hong Kong is booked up for some time yet, I was trying to figure out where else to go and, I don't know, my heart just doesn't seem to be in it. As I said before, some days I want to make it and other days it doesn't make much difference whether I go or not. It must be another mark of old age!

Well, six months done now, and we can start on the other half, but I'm afraid it's not really going to be downhill like we like to think it is. The last month or so may be considered downhill, but six months is still about seven months too long for me. My next goal is 90 days away, in July about this time, when I hope the October assignments will be coming in. It may only be the consecutive tour assignments, since they usually come in first, but at least mine won't be too far behind.

I just had to stop for a bit and go through all the pictures again. Looking at them, I don't think I've ever spent such a long year—and here it's only half over. How wonderful it'll be to fuss at you all again! Isn't it strange how you take everything for granted when it's around you all the time? Believe me, I miss it now. I love you so very much, Don Leta. You'd be surprised, at least I am, at how many of my waking hours are taken up with thoughts of you— wondering how you are, or what you're doing, trying to figure what time it is back home (it's after midnight on Friday here, so it's after 10A.M. Thursday in Jacksboro). Mostly, I guess, I try to see our first day together again. You are my happiness.

Your Leo

24 Apr 66

My Beloved,

I took advantage of another lazy Sunday and did not do much of anything. As a matter of fact, only got one phone call, but got that resolved fairly quick. No mail today, but did get one yesterday evening.

It was nice to just hang around today, but I don't know if it's really worth it. There's too much time to think when there's nothing to do and I get more lonesome than ever at those times. I want so much to be with you again.

Hearing about old grandma I keep wondering how she keeps going on. For a while, from your letters she seems to have recouped her strength and in the next one she seems just about done. I can't possible see how she can go on much longer.

I hope Lynn doesn't get too much more colic trouble. I can remember what it was like trying to get the others to sleep when they got like that. I'd sure like to be able to see her now when she's starting to perk up some. At least this time I'll have an excuse for not giving her baths until she's old enough to hold herself up a bit! I'd just as soon be back as have the excuse for not doing it— even though you know I still wouldn't do it.

I got hold of a piece of plexiglass for my desk (that's where I am now—and Grenier, Larkin and Henkel are gabbing about Korea—Henkel's wife is Korean). Anyhow, I put some of the pictures you sent under this glass. Again, I don't know for sure that I did right. Every time I look at them now I get to thinking and wishing again.

We had originally planned on going to China Beach today, but none of us ever made it. It was real hot and sultry again—the sun out in the morning but loaded with clouds and hardly a breeze. No matter where we went it was so uncomfortable. That's why we ended up here. Last night we ended up having a three hour meeting of the NCO Advisory Council, so that just about shot the night. The night before last when I wrote my last letter I finally got to bed at 3:30A.M., and was back up at 6:30 to go to work, but wasn't tired or anything.

Well, my love, I'm afraid this was another of those inconsequential letters—but at least "no news is good news". About the only thing that happens to me of any consequence are those things which make me think of my family or that bring me a bit closer to them. In that case, the only thing that has happened which counts is that since last I wrote we've two days closer together.

Leo at the desk, photographs under the plexiglass top.

Good night, my wonderful girl. I love you with all of me.

Your Leo

25 Apr 66

My Darling Don Leta,

Just had a coke at the club—it's so hot and muggy yet—and headed for the movie. It was so crowded with people waiting to get in that I just kept right on going to the shop. Now I'll be able to get my letter out earlier than planned, and still try to make the last show at 9:30.

Another fairly routine day today. Did get out for a little while to check on progress at our new Comm Center. The building is finished and equipment installation is now going on, to be finished in about another three weeks. Already it's too small and a request is at Saigon to expand it some 1500 sq. ft. It seems everything is done that way around here. You plan for something and by the time it's approved and built your requirements have increased so that all plans are outdated.

They better place the town on limits pretty soon. We all had a good laugh tonight as Carter was telling of being approached in the mess hall by some "sweetie", telling him they'd have to get together some night and "really let their hair down". He took quite a ribbing about it.

Some 60 people of this squadron, mostly in maintenance, are being reported as surplus and available for reassignment—according to our authorized manning document. It includes Grenier and me. Of course, we'll go nowhere though, because along with it will go a request for waiver. It's just that the book says if you don't have a slot on the manning document of an individual, he's to be reported available for reassignment. That should have been done in my case within 5 days of my making E-8, but they never did it.

No mail from anyone today, so nothing to comment on in that area. Today is the official half way point of my tour, however, so that's worth mentioning. Not too awfully long ago it seemed quite far away. Actually, it's a little better than half since I'll be leaving here at least a couple days prior to the 26th. Three of my people, all telephone types, are leaving within the next 3 weeks.

That's about the extent of the excitement, sugarbun. Have to get out for another haircut tomorrow or Wednesday. My hair is just starting to get where it looks like heck as I try to let it grow back in. Be sweet, my love. I love you loads and loads and miss you as ever.

Your Leo

26 Apr 66

My Dear Lanis,

To start with, you can tell Mommy I won't be writing to her tonight since there hasn't been much of anything happening since I last wrote.

Your mother sent me all your grades from your last six weeks tests and I was very pleased to see that you're still doing so well. Keep up the good work. It won't be long now, just one more round of six weeks tests, and all you kids will be on your summer vacation. After vacations, when you start back to school again, it will be pretty close for me to come back home.

I guess by the time you receive this, your cousins will already have visited you while on their way to California. I hope you all enjoyed their visit. When daddy gets back next fall we will probably go visit all the folks in Rhode Island if we get stationed up that way. In about another 90 days or so I should find out where we'll be going.

You'll have to write me again pretty soon and let me know how you've been doing and what you think of your baby sister. You be sweet now and remember that your daddy loves you great big bunches and misses you loads. Give everyone a big hug and sugar for me.

Your loving Daddy

27 Apr 66

My Darling Wife,

When I left here on my way to the barracks after writing to Lanis last night, I received a pleasant surprise—a letter from my girl. Some mail had come in pretty late and Larkin had picked mine up for me.

It's a good thing I did get that letter as there still isn't much new to report from here. It was real hot and muggy, as usual, and that just adds to a slow day. I did spend the afternoon, or at least a good part of it, pulling an inspection of the Comm Center. You should see our Comm Center here—a real cracker box, and yet there's about 10 people in there all the time. We've just had a new one built—should be in around 15 May—and it's already too small for the additional equipment coming in.

Oh yes, there was one change in the routine. Sgts. Green, Larkin and myself were out this morning checking the squadron barracks and tents. This is done by different branches every Wednesday. We were about a third of the way through when in walks Lt. Sawyer and Sgt. Hawley to inspect. Goofed up. Our turn isn't until next Wednesday.

Even though I've been thinking I probably wouldn't be letting you get too much sleep when I first get back, I do think I'd see that you get more than you seem to get now. I do hope Lynn settles down, particularly at night, so you can at least stay up with everything to be done. It's a good thing mother has been able to spell you at times so you can get some rest.

I've been meaning to ask since I got Mom's letter and she told me that Angie was leaving his car with Chippy, how did they travel? Since they were going to Jacksboro, I had naturally assumed that they were coming by car. I imagine they will have come and gone by the time you get this. I do hope they stopped long enough to make the detour worth while.

Boy, we're getting old. It's enough that we have six of our own, but you telling me that Pat had written and mentioned her newest one, and that the second girl is now four, really makes it seem like time is rushing by. I can say that she particularly sends me with those names though—Bon, Dot & Bea—ugh.

Yes, the rats here are carriers of disease, particularly typhoid fever. Or rather, not the rats themselves but the fleas and lice they carry. That's why the idea is not to kill them, but to catch them. Wire cages with bait in them are all around the place. If the rat is killed, the bugs will leave it, so they try to catch the rat and kill both it and its parasites by gassing. I've not heard of anyone being bitten by one yet.

Sgt. Chisum came back from Clark tonight. I had told you he was sent there for some dizziness trouble. He did have an inner ear infection that they got cleared up. Right now in our squadron alone we've got: MSgt. Demaree on crutches with his foot in a cast—broke his foot while turning hurriedly in the barracks (half-looped, I believe); SSgt. Trexler with his arm in a cast, broken playing softball; and yesterday A2C Woronecki with left arm in a sling and right arm in a cast after being a hit-and-run victim—some Vietnamese in a truck. That's where the danger is around this place, not from the enemy, but from (we) ourselves.

What's the matter—can't stand that extra $81.94 (I think) a month already. Here you are telling me about the new station wagons. Really, I would like something with more get up and go than a six cylinder, especially in a vehicle as heavy as a station wagon, and I don't particularly think I'd care for another Ford. What was it the Ford cost us, about $3,000? Of course, going to an 8 cylinder engine, and the power items you mentioned would bring the price up quite a bit, particularly if it's also got an automatic shift—and at the prices you mentioned I would imagine they would have. I wish we could get a decent price on ours. Keep shopping around. When you see someone is about to break down and let it go at a big loss just for the sake of good customer relations; or because in a burst of deep patriotism they want to do something for a woman whose hero husband is off fighting the bad guys . . . grab it!

Guess that's all for now, honeybunch. I do wish I were back to help you with the kids. I'd just love to be tucking you in bed so you could get your sleep!! I love you, Don Leta, with all my heart.

Your Leo

27 Apr 66

Hi Pal,

It's been a long time since I wrote to you, and also since you wrote to me.

I'll bet you and Paul are both getting to be big boys now, and I hope you still take care of your brother so he doesn't get hurt or in too much trouble.

Mommy told me about how good you were at the dentist and how the dentist thought you were a real man about it. I guess you're still being like a soldier, just like when you get your shots.

I hope you like your new baby sister Lynn Marie. You take good care of her now, because that's the last one we can afford!

Be a good little man and write to me again pretty soon.

Daddy

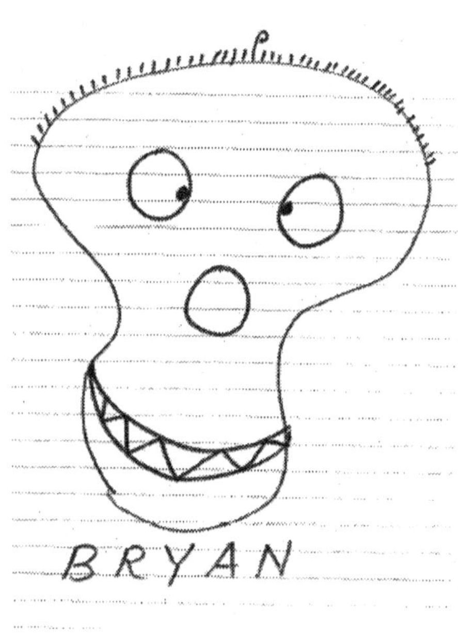

28 Apr 66

My Sweetness,

Ah, the day is complete when I get a letter from my girl. I'm at the shop again. Come here almost every night now since it's cool. The place isn't air conditioned yet, but Larkin and I moved into the room beyond Radio Relay (same building) and they do have window-type air conditioners. We just leave the doors between us open and keep cool. Here it is, past 9 P.M. and I'm just soaked from perspiration.

I see again where Lynn Marie has more colic trouble. I do hope the change of bottles helps. It's bad enough for her, but I can imagine what it must be for you having little enough time to rest as it is.

You mentioned getting a letter from the Kirchgasler's and their going to Japan on a second honeymoon. Heck, some people I know haven't even had a first honeymoon yet!!!! Oh well, we can say it's all been one long honeymoon—yuck. Did they say what they were going to do with the kids? I also got a bit lost when you mentioned that Joanne said, "Don't volunteer for Okinawa." I thought they were on Guam, or did they get transferred, or did they hear about it from someone—or am I all wet?

Still haven't turned my papers in for Hong Kong. I'm always going to do it tomorrow. It's still the same; sometimes I can't wait to go and at other times I don't much care. I sort of hate to spend the money too, I guess. Its five days, so we lose about 15 dollars rations and subsistence. Then of course, everything there costs the individual—hotel, etc. They do have an R&R hotel, but the only difference is that it's one where they make reservations for you. It's still civilian in every respect.

I hope you don't keep having too much trouble with the car. I'd dread the thought of you going off someplace with the kids and getting stuck somewhere, especially at night. If it was the carburetor, I hope the parts were replaced and not just fixed temporarily as before. I figured it was fixed but I guess it was worn parts—if that's what the problem was this time.

Another big hardship of war was temporarily alleviated today—the club received its first shipment of beer in 16 days! Went to chow after getting off work and the place was mobbed. It's been sparsely settled lately but I guess it didn't take long for word to get out that beer was available. What they did get won't last long at that rate.

I used to sneak a little siesta at lunch time but I've given up on that now. Can't find a place to stretch out where it's not roasting, fan or no fan. It's not even any use any more in trying to get to sleep too much before midnight.

Went to the BX this afternoon for a few things. They didn't have much of anything in stock. Finally had some Crest toothpaste. All they've ever had before was Colgate and Ipana. Did get some more shorts and T-shirts. Those wear out quicker than anything else here. Another thing I've got to get is about another dozen pair of heavy wool sox. They're better than cotton in absorbing sweat. Before leaving here I also want to get either a B-4 bag or a suitcase (they have some Samsonite here) rather than lug that cruddy duffle bag around. You can't even pick it up without getting filthy. When I head back I'll probably send as much as I can as hold baggage directly to my new base anyhow.

Good night, sweet girl. I love you so deeply and it makes me feel so bad that we'll still be apart for almost six months more. I don't want to get back only to be with you, but to help you carry the load you've been bearing by yourself for so long. Be sweet, my love.

Your Leo

29 Apr 66

My Dearest,

This will be a shorty for sure tonight. Not much to report, plus there was no mail in the Squadron today. It's been hot and sultry again all day, then we got about a 15 minute rain at 6 P.M. or so. It cooled this off—for about an hour, but I think it's worse now because of it.

About the only news was that we had a bit of a reunion today. We had a SMSgt Currier, wire maintenance, report in today. Come to find out, TSgt Davies here worked for him about 12 years ago. Then when I met him I thought he was familiar and he reminded me we were at the NCO Academy together. He used to be stationed at Malmstrom (Montana). Then I noted on his locator card that he was from Rochester, New Hampshire—Grenier's home town. Called Grenier in and found out that Currier and Grenier's dads used to play pool together. So they got off discussing the old home town. He's been in about 22 or 23 years, I guess. He originally was going to Thailand, but while on leave they changed it to Vietnam (1882 Comm. Sq.). He was down at Phong Rong for a week before they sent him up here.

Well, tomorrow's pay day and after this one there are only five more pay days before I ship out. I'm gonna hate to see them go by! I remember when I was looking forward to 11 of them. They can't go by fast enough for me since I want so much to get back to my wonderful family. Love you, honey bunch.

Your Leo

30 Apr 66

My Dearest,

Another "quicky" type note so I can get this in the mail as soon as possible. No mail today, so far (haven't checked this evening yet). It's about 4 P.M. now and I just returned to the shop from purchasing the enclosed money orders.

Today has really been a scorcher. I don't know how hot it got but it seemed to be the worst so far.

I did get some mail, come to think of it. It came from Tacoma, Washington so we figure Airman Tapscott, our former clerk had a hand in it. Besides me, Lt. Carol, Sgts Larkin, Henkel and Grenier all got some. I got 3 books (pocketbooks), all dealing with anti-communism, as did the others. Supposed to get us all motivated, I guess.

I love you, Don Leta—just in case you forgot! Love you, love you, love you.

Your Leo

Sunday, 1 May 66

My Darling,

I didn't get to have an exactly restful Sunday today where I could hang around doing nothing. It was another work day, as will probably be all Sundays from now on, from the outlook. Had a meeting this afternoon with the Marines concerning a system we're installing and will be maintaining for them until their people are trained to handle it, so that did take up part of the day.

It's just as well there was work to do, because I probably would have spent a good part of the day here anyhow. It was just too hot anywhere else. You can just sit quietly in the shade somewhere, not moving a muscle, and in no time you're all wet. I don't think today was quite as bad as yesterday, when the temp was 112.

Went to the 7:30 show last night and saw "Bus Riley's Back in Town." Not too bad. It was 9:30 when I got out and went to the club. Larkin, Grenier and Currier were there and we had a couple beers. After leaving at the 11 P.M. quitting time we just sat in front of the barracks and gabbed for a while. By then Green and Davies joined us. Larkin heard some late mail come in so he got the key and checked for all of us. I had one from my honeybunch. By then it was almost midnight so we all decided to go have some midnight chow. Finally got to bed around 1 A.M. or so. By that time at night it's fairly comfortable.

Signed off a couple more of my troops going home. One left this morning and the other tomorrow. Lucky dogs! Have a couple more leaving within the next week or so. Some of the July assignments came in; 8 of them. One got 1st choice, two 2nd choice and 1, state of choice. The others didn't make out as well. July is supposed to be a poorer month for getting your choice since that was a big build-up here, comm. wise, so there are quite a few going home—about 50 in this squadron.

I was glad to hear of the small expense involved in getting that darn carburetor fixed. I hope that takes care of the problem, 'cause like I mentioned previously, I'd hate to think of the thing cutting out on you when you're out in the middle of nowhere.

Been thinking again about R&R. The more I think about it, the less I'm sure that I'll go. Might just put it off for awhile yet. To be honest, I hate to blow the money! It'll probably cost around $100 just for hotel & food, plus what I'll lose for being out of restful Vietnam. Think I'll wait a while yet and see if I'm getting combat fatigue! What I wanted to do was maybe get in a bit of shopping for things you can get at a pretty good price. A tailor made suit of the finest materials costs $35-45. What I need is some good, comfortable pants. Maybe by having them tailored so that they'll sag below my tummy naturally, without my having to wait until they get old and you want to throw them out, I'll be ahead of the game.

Sgt. Grenier was talking to Group last week and they said he and I were no longer authorized here so we'd probably be reassigned to Tan Son Nhut. Green asked if they had any vacancies and they said no, but they'd probably bring us there TDY while they figure where to put us. That sounds like a stupid Saigon move. I still think they'll leave us here, at least me since I'm better than half done my tour, and carry us as surplus. I've been suggesting that they declare me surplus to Southeast Asia and send me home, but nobody will listen!

Well, not much news again, love, as you can see. I'll be glad when I can give you such news as where we'll be going and when I'll be getting on that plane for the Land of the Big BX. I can't get away from this counting each day—it makes it seem so slow. I love you all dearly, my sweet. I don't know how often I look at these pictures of you and the children on my desk, and how it hurts not to be able to be near you all. I love you.

Your Leo

Monday, 2 May 66

My Darling,

I received your newsy letter relating the happenings of the Bertone/Dubois gathering. It really sounds like things were jumping around there for awhile.

Your description of everyone conking out seems that they all had a full day, even up to Stephanie falling asleep with Lynn on her lap. Must be something she picked up from her father! I particularly got a charge out of Bryan telling Angie to throw him up high like his daddy does. It was nice that Gale and Judy got to go to school with the girls. I was surprised they allowed them to do so. It'll be nice if they get to stop by on the way back also.

You mentioned about waiting now for the Bishops to stop by. Did you hear about their assignment? I wrote to Bob after his last letter, in which he told me of making E-8, and he was expecting to get his assignment in another week or ten days. I told him I was anxious to hear where he was going (jokingly saying I hoped it was here) and to let me know soon, if only by postcard. Haven't heard anything yet. That will be a pleasant break also if they get to stop over.

Uncle Angie and Auntie Vivian (Leo's sister), Judy, Gale and Joyce in our Texas house.

I have one vivid memory of their Jacksboro visit. The Bertone girls, my sisters and Paul and I were outside on a crisp, cloud-filled day. The clouds took such shapes that they begged a child to imagine the animal or object they resembled. One cloud looked like a skull. My sisters had us all kneeling on the ground and praying, for they convinced us this dreadful skull-cloud was a sign that Jesus was coming back that very day!

I was noting a statistical breakdown of E-8 and E-9 promotions in a later issue of the Air Force Times. In 306's the ratio was 1 out of every 8.1 promoted, for 304's like Bob is was 1 out of every 3.1. Dorrough's field was the one that had it made. They had a ratio of 1:1; there were 20 eligibles in the Air Force and they made 20. Another field made 72 out of 72 eligibles! My old field of administration had a ratio of 1 to 287.9!! Four out of 1199 or so made it.

Today was a bit of a rat-race—work wise. There were a million things to do to start with and other problems kept popping up. Then we had about 20 people running around who are not usually here. Some were working putting air ducts in the ceilings, another crew was using air hammers knocking out a cable vault, six more were putting in a new track shot. On top of all that there was a 1st MOB team (1st Mobile Comm. Group out of Clark) here to sign over to us the equipment they had been maintaining at Hue, Dong Hu and Marble Mountain. That's one of two outfits I want to stay away from as far as possible—MOBs or GEEIA[23]. That kind of outfit has a home base which is just some place to go between jobs. Most people dread getting assigned to them. They spend little time at home and it's back out on some job or another.

Not much news again, honeybunch. Just knocked off another day. Really giving it hell! Only a little less than a million to go—it seems. I miss you and love you with all of me.

Your Leo

3 May 66

My Darling,

I just want to write a few words quick-like before calling it a day, so I can get something off to you anyhow.

It's 12:20 P.M now – the end of a long day. And a rat race it's been too. Seems like everything was going off at once – new projects, installation teams, visitors, equipment troubles, etc. Fortunately, today remained overcast just about all day, with a real brisk wind. It was a relief from the heat and humidity that we've had.

Four new people came in for me today, all teletype repairman. One was TSgt Taylor, who will be the section chief replacing MSgt Smith who rotated about 3 weeks ago. Also got a staff and two A1C's. I needed a few more people since we've got 14 different places to service.

` Nothing else is new, honeybunch, except that tonight's meal was fit for a king – almost. Sauerkraut, hot dogs and french fries – but the beans were missing. Now I'm getting hungry again. Think I'll make midnight chow before hitting the pad.

Love you loads, sweetheart. Slowly it's going by – 173 more to go. Sgt Taylor told me a MSgt Smith, 306 type, was coming to Vietnam in July but he didn't know where yet. He's SSIR cleared, which means he'll go to one of 3 places: Saigon, Bien Hoa or Da Nang. I guess it would be too much to hope

---

[23] GEEIA Ground Electronics Engineering Installation Agency

he would come here. Since he'd be my replacement I'd greet him with open arms, hug him, buy him candy, etc., and then dump it in his lap!

Be sweet, my love. Hope to hear from you tomorrow. It's so good getting your letters. Smack, smack – smooch, smooch.

Leo

Wed. 4 May 66

My Dearest,

We had a relatively quiet day today, after yesterday's hectic runaround. As a matter of fact, didn't really get a whole lot accomplished. I did get to take a break and made the scene at the BX, but didn't end up getting very much. First off, it was still too soon after payday and I was about number 60 or 70 in line waiting to get in.   This in the middle of the afternoon. By the time I got in, and also after I came out, there were easily 200 in line. Looked like the Marines were coming in by the truck loads. The BX didn't have much of anything, but I did get some foot powder, which they hadn't had before.

Mentioning foot powder makes me think that it, heat powder and ointments are the current rage here. Since the temperature has been rising steadily (except for yesterday and today) more and more people are coming down with rashes, athlete's foot, jungle rot, etc. I wouldn't be far from wrong by saying a good 50% are down with something or other in this area right now.

The First Sgt has it all over his legs, stomach and backside. Sgt Currier, who just got here, has both arms so splotchy that he looks like he had a king size case of measles there. I've been holding out so far, though I was having foot trouble a while back. That seems to be cleared up now.

We have two sessions of Commander's Call here. Had one yesterday and there'll be one Friday. I didn't go yesterday but the guys were talking of the latest word to come down from Group relative to people getting sent home a month or two early because an outfit was over strength in certain specialties. That's now pretty well out the window. Group said that if anyone has too many people that they can send them home early, they'll have them go to some other base for that month or two to help out wherever they need them — digging, filling sandbags, anything. Guess I'll figure on staying a full tour. Wasn't planning otherwise anyhow, but it was always nice to have that faint glimmer of hope in the distance.

Nothing else is new around here, honeybunch. Did have to pull barracks and tent inspection today. What excitement! No mail today, so nothing to comment on in that area.

I've been thinking so much of you lately, even more so than usual, it seems. It's probably that I've sometimes got a bit more time to myself to sit quietly and not to get so many calls at night. Time is still what bothers me. Not the time that's past so much, but all the time there is to go yet.

I love you very much, my sweet.

Your Leo

5 May 66, Thurs.

Hi Honeybunch,

Another day gone by and I'm back at the shop now. It's about 9:15 PM and I was going to go to see Jack Lemmon in "How to Murder Your Wife" but there was too much of a line for me. It's still on tomorrow so I'll probably make it then.

After chow tonight I stretched out on the sack and conked out. Didn't make it up until 8:30. Went to the club and had a couple of cups of real potent coffee so I'm wide awake now. I'll probably play heck trying to get to sleep tonight. Oh, I was talking about the movies before, so I thought of sending you an excerpt from the daily bulletin. Every day there's some comment about the theatre and the movie that's playing. The guy who writes it must be a frustrated comic. Some of his descriptions are cute though, especially when he's describing some ridiculous movie of the type like "Monster from Outer Space" or one of those "A La Go-Go" things.

We had about a one hour respite in my office just before quitting time. This construction man from RMK, the civilian construction company working here for the government, was in putting a hole in our ceiling to duct the air conditioning. We were gabbing while his 4 Vietnamese workers were cutting the hole and he asked if any of us spoke French. Currier and I both do, so he told us to ask this one Vietnamese if the thing looked OK to him and how much of a job it was going to be. That's all we needed. We ended up talking with him for an hour, and he wouldn't much quit. One of the other Vietnamese also talked French and by then Grenier came in so we really had a session. He had been in the French army for 10 years, was 44 years old and

had 7 kids. He'd been to France, Italy and Germany. I showed him the pictures on my desk and the set of them in my drawer. Just like these people too, the go ape over that stuff. The two who didn't speak French kept asking the other two who was this one and who was that one. They said I had a "jolie" (handsome/pretty) family and that I must be "malheureux" (sad) to be separated from them. They thought my wife was "tres jolie" – very pretty. They all started jabbering and pointing when they saw Bryan's picture near the sign of Da Nang. They thought there was

Bryan with helmet and toy rifle,
in "Da Nang", Texas.

a Da Nang in the U.S. and I had to explain what it was. You asked again if I had received those pictures. As you can see I did, but thought I had mentioned it before.

There was another letter from my girl (you!) today. Actually, I haven't been expecting as many letters as you've written, figuring you'd be pretty well tied up with all you have to keep up with now. You mention having received but two letters last week — I know there was a stretch where I skipped quite a few days, like when I went up to Dang Ha. I've written every day the past week or so, however.

I enjoyed your relating Bryan's comments on what he was going to be when he grows up and forgetting Lorenda's name. I guess I'll let him be a doctor since that's where the money is, but if things keep up the way they're going he'll probably be another G.I. in Southeast Asia.

Nothing more new today. Everything was pretty routine, as a matter of fact. I got quite a bit done since not too many problems popped up. My biggest accomplishment was getting rid of another day, leaving me with 171 days and a wake up. Today we had our first commercial freight flight direct to and out of Da Nang. On one June they're supposed to start passenger service directly out of here to the states. Right now we have to go to Saigon to catch our flights. So I guess when I'm ready, I'll get right on here, go to Japan and then on to Texas.

Good night, my sweet. I love you loads and miss you tremendously. You're my own sweet honeybunch.

Your Leo

Re-Discovering Da Nang, Texas

I recall a trip from Jacksboro to the hospital at Fort Wolters in Mineral Wells. Mom stopped and took this picture of me standing by a sign, wearing a plastic helmet and holding a toy rifle. I was tickled to discover my father's reference:

> "They all started jabbering and pointing when they saw Bryan's picture near the sign of Da Nang. They thought there was a Da Nang in the U.S. and I had to explain what it was."

What was "Da Nang" doing in the middle of Texas? I had a notion, but I wanted to find out the whole story.

Internet research revealed that Fort Wolters was an Army helicopter school during the war. The fort has been closed for years, but at the time there were about 1,500 helicopters in use there. (The property is now a business park with some of the facilities put to commercial use. Many abandoned buildings remain, including the hospital where Lynn was born. It makes an interesting auto tour. The Wolters Industrial Park is on the eastern end of Mineral Wells.)

Fort Wolters, proper, had several large landing fields. To give the pilots cross-country flight practice, about 25 small landing strips were constructed in the surrounding counties. The landing strips were given names of Vietnamese towns and geographic landmarks and were laid out on compass bearings approximating the actual points in Vietnam.

Research in the Gladys Johnson Library in Jacksboro turned up a 1966 Jacksboro Gazette-News article about the helicopter school. *"Jacksboro is along two of the cross-country flight routes and one of the staging areas. Da Nang is about three miles south of Perrin"* Armed with this clue, I turned to Google maps and aerial photos. You can see the remnant of the landing site from the air - go to Google Maps www.maps.google.com and enter "Perrin, TX". Follow US-281 south for about 2 miles. The landing strips can be seen in the Google "satellite" imagery. Look for three, parallel features running north-to-south, located southwest of the intersection of US-281 and Rambling Road. They can be viewed from the ground, though with some difficulty, by driving slowly along Rambling Road and gazing across the field while the landing strips come into north-south alignment.

1972 Comm Sq. Div. 20
APO San Francisco 96337
7 May 1966

My Darling,

The new heading on this letter is in deference to our eldest daughter who, in writing her latest letter to me informed me that she had the correct form throughout the letter since that's what they had just covered in school. She did such a good job that I won't mention to her that one doesn't put "NEXT PAGE" when going to a continuation sheet!

I think she does increasingly well in her letter writing. They are quite interesting and most of all I'm surprised at the length. Stephanie did quite well in hers also. I think both of them have quite a good handwriting.

Those letters came yesterday with one from my honeybunch. I took a night off Friday and went to see that Jack Lemmon movie. It was kind of crazy, but good for a few laughs.

We've been getting some of that Texas rain for the past day and a half. Though it's sloppy (practically no drainage and beaucoup mud) it's not too bad until it lets up a bit. Then the air is so heavy you get uncomfortable just breathing it. To add to it all, this has not been one of my better days. Seems like 8 zillion projects and problems popped up, none of them very good. It's day like this that I take a recount on the calendar to see if I maybe made an error and have less time to go than I thought! No luck, there's still a maximum of 171 days!! Around here, though, everybody cuts off a day wherever they can, so it's 170 days and a wake-up (not counting the last day), or 5 paydays, or 25 Sundays, etc.

Things continue to be quieter around here than they were the first four or five months. There is still some pounding going on at night, but it doesn't seem to be as heavy as previously. Just as long as it keeps up that way it'll be OK with me. There are light skirmishes every day, anywhere from 5 to 25 miles from here however. Also, they've tightened up considerably on river security, which cut one of their favorite avenues. The last time they hit Da Nang it was by coming down the river in sampans and setting up their mortars on the riverbank.

A belated Happy Mother's Day! Tomorrow is the day and how I wish I could be spending it with the wonderful mother of our children. I'm afraid there may be a bit of selfish desire in that wish, but I'd like to be there anyhow. Well, like the losers always say, "Wait till next year."

Good night, my sweet. Take good care of yourself and give all the children a hug and kiss for me. I love you all so much.

Your Leo

9 May 66

My dear Don Leta,

It's still so nice to be able to stop by on my way to chow and find that there's another letter here from my girl. There was one today which contained news of the Bishops' and Wojciak's assignments, also of returning the Kirchgasler's to Guam from where you had put them on Okinawa!

So Bob is going to Tinker and Vern to Myrtle Beach. Tinker is HQ for Central Comm Region (as Westover is for Eastern Comm Region), but it also has a big GEEIA outfit there (HQ, I believe) and I'd be afraid to get stuck in there. They're among the "traveling" outfits.

Boy, how time flies (except unaccompanied overseas tours). Here you are mentioning Dick Wojciak graduating next month and it seems such a short while ago that we were at their house and he was just a kid, playing out back with the little ones. The Wojciaks gobble up that sunshine don't they? But I don't know that I'd care to retire someplace like good old hot, humid Orlando.

NAME OF PUPIL	DATE TESTED NO. / YR.	SRA ACHIEVEMENT SERIES — MULTILEVEL EDITION — PCTLE SCORES – PRESSCORE ®
DUBOIS STEPHANIE	0366	
45 79 90 83 83 87 52 87 82 76 50 63 53 76 70 52 65		
SOC. STUD.	SQL.	C.& P. / Gr. Us. / Sp. / Total — LANGUAGE ARTS	Rea. / Conc. / Con. / Total — ARITHMETIC	Comp. / Voc. / Total — READING	COMP. / Wkt / Charts / Total — WORK-STUDY SKILLS

I'm returning Stephanie's achievement test scores. In any percentile system, 50 is the mean – or average. The score always shows relative standing, not individual accomplishment and reflects the number of people taking the test that you did as well or better than, in percentage. Thus a score of 75 would mean that you did as well or better than 75% of the total taking the test. A low score doesn't necessarily mean a dunce, unless all scores are consistently low. For example, ten kids take a ten question test and eight get all ten correct answers, one misses one answer and the other misses two answers. The eight would all show scores of 80, one missed would show 20 and two missed would show 10. She did fairly well – no record breaking performance, however – except in social studies and reading. I would have expected her to do better in reading, but in typical Stephanie fashion she probably hurries through her reading to get it over with rather than to understand it. As best I can make out, the areas covered were:

1. SOCIAL STUDIES
2. SCIENCE
3. LANGUAGE:
    A. Capitalization + Punctuation
    B. Grammar Usage
    C. Spelling
    D. Total (Totals here are not average of a, b and c, but an overall standing. Thus her 87 means she did as well or better than 87% of those taking all the language tests, putting her in the top 13% in that area.
4. ARITHMETIC:
    A. Reasoning
    B. Conclusion
    C. Comprehension
    D. Total
5. READING:
    A. Comprehension
    B. Vocabulary
    C. Total
    D. Comprehension
6. WORK-STUDY SKILLS:
    A. References
    B. CHARTS
    C. Totals

We're living today! The air conditioning project was finished and the unit turned on. Two of the guys went home tonight with the sniffles!

I splurged on another six pairs of black woolen sox today. That gives me 16 pairs and I need them. Got to change around noon since this weather sure makes my feet sweat and I want to keep away from all the rashes that are going around. With laundry the way it is, ten pairs wouldn't quite hack it. The way it looks I guess I'll make it through this tour without having to get any more fatigues. I do need shoes however, and I know more shorts + T shirts will be required.

I know you'll be overjoyed to hear that the club has beer again! Another big crisis has hit, however, which may have serious effect on the whole war effort. NCOs' ration of hard liquor has been reduced from 6 bottles to 3 a month.   That may sound like a lot, but let me tell you, six wasn't enough for some people. (Airman can't get hard liquor.) I had bought a bottle of I.W. Harper in December or so and still have quite a bit left. For a while I used to have a snort before hitting the sack. I imagine this one will last me the rest of the tour. The First Shirt buys and drinks his 6 fifths each and every month – brrrr. He leaves in July.

Some more of the guys got their assignments, those going on consecutives, they just about all got their 1st or 2nd choice – 2 to England, 4 to Germany and 1 to France. Sgt Rodriquez, who used to work for me in SMC is going to France. I was surprised that he got it in view of plans to vacate all French bases by 1 April 67. That would only give him about 6 months there. He use to be assigned in France and speaks and writes it a bit. In the next 90 days, until the end of July or so, just about everyone who was here when I came will have rotated. It'll be encouraging to know that I'll be one of the old troops + one of those next to go.

Had another one of our young troops get into trouble last night. Drunk for one thing, but this is not a first incident here, plus which he came here with a record to start with. Immaturity I think is his problem. I think they should chuck him out. A while back he had heard that his wife would need a caesarian (their first child). He got all shook up over it, so what did he do? Got himself drunked up, went down to one of the whorehouses and got in a brawl. That didn't do much to resolve his problems. Last night he got soused again and started breaking things and was going to fight with the First Sgt.

Some of our NCOs are not doing much better. We've got a Ch. MSgt and a TSgt who have had their security clearances pulled for some shenanigans. Quite a few others have had their share of Article 15 and reprimands. As a matter of fact, I've got one of mine on the Control Roster now. Before you get the wrong idea – there are some good troops too!

Not too much new here, honeybunch. It rained a good part of the day yesterday. Today was scattered clouds, but they bunched up after supper and we had about an hour or so of rain. It's supposed to be like that for about a month – late afternoon showers or thundershowers about 80% of the time. Makes it all the muggier the rest of the time, but it does cool it off for sleeping.

Sleep was slow in coming again last night. I just kept laying there and thinking of you again. Gosh how I long to put my arms around you and hold you close. I love you, my darling, and I know it will always be so. Be sweet, my happiness.

Your Leo

9 A.M – 11 May 66

My Dearest,

Just a little note this morning. Hope to get to write more tonight. I intended to drop you a line last night, but once I took a shower and stretched out on the sack, that's all she wrote.   Didn't blink an eye until six this morning. I shouldn't even be telling you this, what with the little opportunity you've had for rest since Lynn came home.

No mail yesterday. Grenier got two letters. I mention this because we've got a running joke going. His wife writes just about every day, but it's seldom more than one sheet this size (with bigger writing), so I tell him heck, it's because she only writes once every ten days – all at once – but only mails them one at a time! Then, when I get a letter I tell him to wait for me before going to chow since my letters are so long and so full of information that it takes quite a while to read them!

Getting hotter than a firecracker again. I laid down last night and it felt like the sheets and mattress had just been taken out of a hot dryer. At 6:45 this morning I was sweating while having my toast and coffee – and glass of ice water.

Bye-bye, honeybunch. See ya a bit later today. Love you great big bunches.

Your Leo

11 May 66

Hi Sweet Girl,

Back again the same day. Thought I would be at this letter writing a bit earlier tonight, but a few problems popped up that had to get squared away first. It's just about 10:30 now.

I really enjoyed the letter from you today – the one where you describe your "sex education program" with the girls. The guys who saw me reading the letter and laughing must of thought I was joining those who cracked up here. It sounded real interesting – you'll have to tell me about it when I get back! I can just picture them taking it all in. You never did mention what you told Stephanie when she asked if it was fun – you must have forgotten that part! I wonder how much talking they did when they got back to school – if none, I imagine it must have been killing them.

Well, I guess it's a good thing I finally got that letter off to Steph's class. Can you imagine that Gomez girl pulling a trick like bringing her father home so she can show him off! If he was a Green Beret here he earned his way home. Those guys spend their time right out in the middle of nowhere. There's an I Corps Captain (Army) who's a Green Beret and I see him every now and then – usually when he's looking for something! He's usually got some other officer with him and he always introduces me as "his Air Force Sgt Major". I had gotten him fixed up with some phones and a couple of hot lines and a few other odds and ends. I guess a good part of what they get is what they can scrounge. He's a young guy, probably around 28-29, and you'd picture him as some All-American or something – over 6 feet and around 200 lbs, real good looking and he always has a big grin. He had just come back from a forward camp and he thought it was like being on R+R around here! And here I thought it was bad. Now when he comes in I just say, "Hell – I'm not going to get any work done again today!" – and he proceeds to talk for another hour.

Lt. Carol is down to 50 something days and I'm still wondering if he'll make it. A nail-chewer like him you've never seen in your life. After some of the words we've had (once Larkin ran over and closed the door 'cause we were both getting a bit loud). I didn't figure he'd do it, but he's putting me in for another commendation medal. I must remember to get into another hassle with him soon!

Our lawn mower used to spit out a bit of oil, but that was due to the filter being broken. It doesn't have an oil leak or anything. The only parts needed are those for the filter. I don't remember if I still had the old one around anywhere. If there's a repair shop around, I'd bring it in and have them tune it up and put on a new filter. Also, we may need a new blade. Why don't you have daddy check it and see what he thinks. I think it might be better to just trade it in on a new one. I think that's what I had in mind before you sent me here!

The monsoon season up here is not until around the 1st of October. Once it's over in the Saigon area, it's just about to start up here. The predominant winds blow in a certain direction and that's what brings the rains. Later in the year they switch and then it's our turn.

If you go out and buy some pants for me, just make darn sure the legs are not tapered. With my delicate calves those things just don't hack it! The BX here occasionally gets some hang-around-in type pants, but I'll be darned if they're not all slim legged. I guess they figure there are so many women wearing the pants nowadays that that's what in demand. I've got a couple of cheap pairs that I wear around here, but I don't figure they'll be fit to take home after being through our modern laundry a few more times. Besides, these old things make me gray and balding and short and fat! I want to get some that will make me look tall and dashing – so you'll remember me when I come home!

Not much else happening here – abouts, honeybunch, except that it's still hot. Somewhere in the hundreds again today. They've got half of the air conditioning going, which does some good in this building. They can only turn half of it on, however, because the base power plant can't handle all of it yet. No telling when they'll be able to take it.

I'm going to have to be knocking it off for now, my sweet. My gosh, how I miss you. I know I keep saying it over and over again, but I never in a million years thought it would be this bad being apart. Oh, I knew I'd miss you and think of you a lot, but not to the point where it would go on and on without lessening. The days are passing, but ever so slow. With today shot, there are 165 more – which is 166 too many. As soon as we get settled again, we're going to start our retirement planning, I'm telling you. No more of our being separated for me. I love you, Don Leta, with all my heart.

Your Leo

12 May 66

My Beloved,

Absolutely, positively and definitely, there's nothing new to tell you about tonight. I could tell you of the letter I sent to SSO on circuit monitoring or what's been decided about Talk Quick or the polar modifications, but I think I'll just skip it. Hope you're not disappointed!

Today was another scorcher. It's getting that I'm seeing less and less of the outside of this building. I used to stretch out a bit a lunch time, but that's just about impossible in this weather, so I head back here. After supper it's the same thing since most of the time it doesn't cool off until quite late, and then only barely. These two guys were up here from Tan San Nhut today, on their way to Dong Ha, and I asked them how the weather was there now. They said it was quite a bit cooler there, but the rains were with them – just about every day for the past two weeks. If they think it's hot here, wait 'till they get up north.

Honeybunch, you don't know how hard it is for me sometimes not to go into a big old mushy letter, even though I'd just be saying the same things over and over. It's especially true at times like this when I keep stopping to look at pictures of you and the kids. I want to be with you so much. I think I'll write Uncle Sugar about using one of his old Titan missile silos where we can lock ourselves in the first day I'm back. (Maybe he'll let me return 30 days early so I can get it ready!)

Good night, my darling. I'm going back to the barracks now where you'll be the last thought in my mind as I go to sleep. I love you so.

Your Leo

Fri, 13 May 66

My Honeybunch,

This has been a pretty full day, capped by a wonderful letter and pictures from my girl. Lynn looks real cute – and so chubby with that bonnet on. Oh well, I guess she's just another one of those attractive Dubois children. As for her mother, the pictures of her are delicious!

Spent part of the day down at the Marine area – just about missed lunch, too. Since last December GEEIA has been supposed to be putting this new system in and it's still dragging. Yesterday we were told that GEEIA was out and we were tasked to bring it up. So, went down there with 3 of my crypto people and Grenier, who is our maintenance quality control inspector. We wrote up all the discrepancies and then my troops got the units working but the lines were bad. I had a couple guys going back out at 5 o'clock, but just before then I was in with CWO Robinson, our Operations Officer,

Don Leta, Paul, baby Lynn and Lanis

trying to get the phone number of the Western Electric Co. representative in Saigon. He called Saigon to find out and while doing so was told to drop everything on the system, that GEEIA was sending engineers out to check it all and get it running. So we're right back where we started.

Another project we're in the middle of now is moving to the new comm center. 2/3 of the circuits have be switched, so it should be only 2 or 3 more days before that's wrapped up.

Hot, hot, hot! I don't know what it got to today, but it was one of the hottest yet. Couldn't go outside more than a few minutes and the sweat would start pouring. Grenier and Currier just walked in so I know we're in for some hearts games tonight. My office is getting to be like a day room after duty hours. I wonder if the air conditioning could have anything to do with it?

Good Lord, what did you do around that place with 27 people? I should think the noise alone would have been nerve wracking. Of course, getting everyone fed probably wasn't that much overall with people like mother, Loma and Ruth around.

That MSgt Smith (crypto) isn't coming to Da Nang. He's probably going to Tan Son Nhut or Bien Hoa. I really hadn't been entertaining any great hope that he was to be my replacement – that early, anyhow. I planned on a full year anyhow, so just as long as I get out on time it doesn't make much difference to me if they get anyone in here in time or not.

That's about it for now, sweetheart. Am enclosing a picture and clipping of some of the local "color". Love you loads,

Your Leo

Saturday
14 May 66

My Dearest,

It hasn't been too bad at work today. Got a reasonable amount done without too many interruptions. Got a short visit also from the new Wing Commander, Col. Rankin, who came around with Major Perry.

Some more of the troops got their assignments today. MSgt Whitten in Comm Center Operations is going to Eglin – had asked for Keesler as he's from Mississippi. Sgt Hodgson, the FSgt got his choice of Fairchild, Wash. TSgt Chisum, who I had mentioned to you before as being from Waco, is going back there. He had come from there (HQ 12th Air Force), and that's where his home and family are. He was tickled pink and had to call me about it this morning. That guy has got more things done for us than anyone. Almost automatically, if you need a date some new equipment is due in or a crane to move a tower, Chisum knows where to get it. I wouldn't be surprised at all if they did pop up to see you all once they're settled again.

Nothing else is new honeybunch, except that this date brings the magic number down to 162. I figure my next step is about 72 days away when it'll be down to 90 and pretty close to assignment time.

Good night, my beloved. Give every one of the kids a big hug and kiss for me. I'm still stocking up and saving those for you for personal delivery. I love you and miss you so.

Your Leo

15 May 66

My Darling,

Not very much to write about, workwise, as things have been kind of slow in that area today. I did afford myself the luxury of staying in bed late this morning, not coming to work until 9:30. Being Sunday, not too many projects were in the mill

It's past midnight now, and things have cooled off considerably after some late showers. It's still awfully muggy though, but I guess that never leaves.

There was another sweet note from my love today, including more pictures and the prose from Stephanie's class and her note to you that she stuck on the mirror. I think her last sentence is a classic: "I am praying for you but I guess it doesn't work." The picture of Paul laying on the couch "reading" the comic book was cute. Almost like he knew what he was doing.

Well, the Viets are at it again, as you undoubtedly know. Overnight in comes Ky's troops again and early in the morning they go out and take over I Corps Headquarters. It's located in a compound just about one mile off base. They caught them all by surprise I guess, as they also went into town and took over the radio station. At times today there was quite a bit of small arms and machine gun fire close by, so it's unquestionable that there was some resistance. With the relatively small force that came up this time (about 1000 men), I don't see how they can make it stick. It'll spread to here for sure, so I figure we're in for considerable unrest. The U.S. is still maintaining a strictly hands off policy, so we shouldn't become involved except in defense. The troops didn't set up camp here like the last time. Some went in this morning and then I watched a stream of them, full field packs and all, walking in this afternoon. Until the rains came tonight, the whole sky was lit by flares for some time.

I don't want to get pessimistic, but sometimes you can't help wondering what you're doing here. Helping someone who wants to lead their own peaceful life is one thing, but to get somewhere like this where the country is split while trying to fight an outside enemy is another thing. It's like being in the states and the north fighting the south while someone else is waging guerilla warfare all over the states. Ridiculous!

Another week gone by and now we're half way through May. Each day by itself seems to go by pretty fast, even the weeks with this seven day work schedule, but it still seems so long until October. Well, May will soon be over and we'll cross off another payday – that'll leave only 4 more paydays. I've gone through 203 days in Vietnam now, so that leaves a maximum of 162 to go. I like to say maximum, that way there's always that slight ray of hope that it may be a few days less. If I get half a chance, I'll be trying to get a 15 day rollback, which the Commander can grant if manning permits. Depends on whether I have a replacement here or not by that time. Guess I'd better write to Randolph and make sure they're looking for somebody to come take my place! – and then get him here in plenty of time.

I've been staying up to see if anything comes off tonight, but it's almost 2 A.M. now and everything's quiet so guess I'll call it a day (night). Six A.M. comes awfully early. Sgt Grenier came in around midnight to write also, so he's ready to go too.

You know what? I love you. I love you more than I can ever write about. I've so often thought of our many year's together – before and since our marriage – and must have relived so many of these instances over and over again in my mind. Even our first days together, after all these years, mean so much to me, as do all those since. You're my life, my happiness, Don Leta.

Your Leo

16 May 66

Hi Sweet One,

Just another one of my shorty notes tonight I guess, honeybunch, as it's been a pretty routine day overall. Things have been fairly quiet so far — didn't know if it would be with the local situation the way it is. Of course, we're all quarantined to the base and Da Nang is off limits. We don't hear anything of what's going on either — just rumors — nothing on the radio, no newspaper deliveries, etc. I don't know if they're unaware of what the situation is, or if they just want to keep everyone in the dark.

Did get a surprise this afternoon. This call came in for me from Don Muang, Thailand. He said "Is this Leo — Leo Dubois?" Sure enough, I recognized the voice. It was Don Williams from Ellsworth. I was surprised to hear he was there since when he left Ellsworth he was headed for West Pakistan — same as Sgt Lewis. We didn't get to talk very long as a priority call cut us off. He did say Sgt Spencer was down there with him. He's due to go back in September, so he obviously never did go to Pakistan, but must have been switched enroute. He said he had about 115 days to go, so he'll be leaving the early part of September. Bangkok is an 18 month tour, but places like Ubon, Udorn, Don Muang and Korat are out in the boondocks and the tour is 12 months.

Good night for now, my love. Miss you something awful. You're my very own wonderful, sweet girl.

Your Leo

17 May 66

"161"

Hi Honeybunch,

Got a new secret lazy man's plan now. When there's not much to write about, like today, I'll just find some clippings and stick them in an envelope to make it look like a fair size letter!

That's the way it's been, with nothing much new other than a couple medium size work crisis. Did get a letter from Bishop about his assignment. He's going to the 3rd Mobile Comm Gp. They're a traveling bunch, though I don't know if he'll do much traveling as an E-8. Most of our MOB support comes from the 1st MOB, out of the Philippines, but some 3rd MOB people have been this way also. We've got about 20 1st MOB types around now.

Listening to Bob, he sounds like the Schooley's felt he should have turned it down so Vern could grab it. He said they weren't friendly for a few days. He has to attend a short (5 days) course on CCTV (closed circuit TV) before leaving Keesler, so that allows Cliff to finish school. He said the packers pack the 26th and pick up the 27th, with their clearance inspection scheduled for 1 June.

They traded cars last week. A Ford Ranch Wagon with power steering, automatic shift, air conditioning, etc. The only bad thing, he says, is that it makes the pickup hot and bumpy!

I told you this was going to be a shorty. Think I'll take in the movies tonight, "Harper" with Paul Newman. Haven't been in some time lately. Love you, sweetheart, with all of me, and I miss you terribly.

Your Leo

18 May 66

My Dearest Don Leta,

You're getting gypped out of a letter of any length tonight due to the heavy demands made upon me as a noted author and lecturer specializing in Vietnamese customs, culture and philosophy! In other words, I tried to comply with your other two daughters' requests that I write to their class at this late date. If I was going to do it at all, I had to get right with it in order to get the letters there before school lets out.

I know you're probably nervous hearing news of happenings around here, but don't worry too much about it. We're keeping our noses out of it and are just as safe right here as anywhere. Innocent bystanders, that's all we are.

Your Leo

Clippings to make it look like long letter! Oh yes, "wake-up" means the last day doesn't count, that we'll just "wake-up" and get out of here. With today shot, it's 159 and a wake up.

19 May 66

My Darling,

I don't think there will be too much to this letter tonight, even though I received a long missive from you today. I'm pooped. Got to bed rather late last night (this morning) and had to get shaken out of the sack this morning. On top of that, this has been quite a hectic day, so I'm about ready to call it quits.

It took some doing to get those letters out to Karen's and Lanis' classes. Their late requests forced me into some fast and furious research so that I'd have something different to tell them about Vietnam. I wrote Karen's first, so by the time I got to Lannie's, my subjects had just about been exhausted. I did find a few pictures in a Vietnamese magazine, so I sent them along to supplement the letters.

We're still going on from day to day here, not really aware at any time of just what's going on. The base is sealed to the point where we can't even get to the BX just outside the gate — not that it would do any good since they've locked it up. There have been a number of brief clashes off base, but it's pretty well restricted to Vietnamese vs. Vietnamese. What a crazy war! Can't tell the enemy without a score card. It must be quite frustrating to an American military commander to have to fight what actually is a political war. I'm waiting for the time when you'll have to get permission from Washington before you can shoot back at anyone trying to get you. That may not be such a joke after all.

Your letter from Ann sounded like she didn't have any good news at all. We all get so concerned with our own problems, a natural reaction since they affect us directly, but then you hear of all these problems people you know have and it makes one stop a minute and count our blessings.

It was truly a sad reunion for Ron and Carolyn[24]. Especially their boy having come back safe from Vietnam and have something like that happen to him. It is hoped their daughter comes out of it alright.

Things really must have been pressing on Carolyn's mind for her to break down like that. It's fortunate indeed that their guest was a medic and took charge of the situation. The first thing to be done in resuscitation is to make sure the patient's air passage is clear, but in the excitement and what not you don't use a checklist I guess to make sure you're going step-by-step. The dual dejection over the uncertainty of retirement plans and Becky bringing all her problems with her could cause it, I guess. I don't know, it seemed to me that Ron was smarter than that — to be getting out without knowing where he was going to go or what he was going to do. We're going to have to talk this business over at some length, because I don't intend to get caught that way.

---

[24] Not their real names

Even if it's to sweep the streets, I want that laid out for me before retirement. I think this business you hear from so many that they're going to take it easy and look around for awhile first when they get out is ridiculous. I'll want a job while I'm doing my looking around. So, put that on the list of things for us to discuss – after we're done discussing how much I love you. On second thought, maybe we'd better not wait quite that long!

You asked about Bob's assignment to the 3rd MOB (you said 1st, but they're at Clark) and whether that was the same as GEEIA. GEEIA is the Ground Electronics Engineering Installation Agency, and they're concerned with putting in new systems or installations. Like our new Comm Center here – it was installed by GEEIA people. So, you can see it's a traveling outfit. MOB (for Mobile, as in 3rd Mobile Comm Group) is also a traveling bunch. They install non-permanent facilities and also at times operate and maintain them to augment an organization or until such time as the organization has the people to take it over. Our track shots at Hue and Dong Ha, for example, were run and maintained by MOB personnel until we took them over last month. This gear is not in a permanent installation. It's all located in vans that can be moved when we're ready. Now that we've taken them over, the MOB people who were here TDY for 90 days have returned to their home base.

Here I've gone on more than I thought I would, but it looks like my second wind is giving out also. So on that, my love, I'll leave you for now – in this letter but not in my thoughts. I love you dearly.

Your Leo

21 May 66
Saturday – 8 P.M.

My Darling,

Here I go making excuses right at the start, but this will definitely be another shorty. I'm just sitting here yawning at the start of each line. No mail from anyone the last couple days, so there's not too much to comment on in that area.

Everything is still OK here, though we did receive a few rounds of mortar fire and some stray shots on base. It's been a bit different between Ky's troops and the rebels in town, however. On and off all day there was rifle and machine gun fire, as well as grenade and mortar blasts. For a while we could just sit outside and watch the VNAF planes strafe and rocket rebel positions. All of a sudden the action seems to reach a high pitch, and then things are either quiet or sporadic until later when it gets heavy again. Ridiculous! On our part, we just try to go on about our business – but you can't hardly make like nothing is happening.

They've opened a little BX again in the Airman's Club where we can get soap, toothpaste, razor blades, etc. As you might guess, since we can't get haircuts, I need one. Another problem is clean clothes. I put a big batch in the laundry and before I could get it out the laundry shut down. So, not wanting to wear the same thing <u>every</u> day, it's back to the washboard.

Goodnight, my sweet. Don't worry too much about much of what will undoubtedly be broadcast stateside. We're still sitting relatively good here on the base itself, though the eyes are on the fighting which is going on in the city of Da Nang itself. I'm so very much in love with you, and I miss you terribly.

Your Leo

22 May 66

"156"

My Dearest,

It was so nice hearing from you again today. Even though it was a short letter, any word from you is precious and looked forward to eagerly.

Things remained fairly calm overnight, though we were prepared for anything. The clubs all closed at 7:30, as did the movie, so there wasn't much more to do but sit and wait. Flares glowed around the perimeter all night and planes kept circling overhead, but nothing developed. There's been some light firing going on in town, but no heavy stuff that I could tell. It looks like somebody, Ky's forces or the rebels would be making some major move soon.

Other than that, life goes on as it usually does. Every day brings its new crisis, or reawakening of old ones. I've had my share of them and it doesn't much look like it'll be letting up much. The next couple months brings in a couple new "crash" projects, as they all are it seems, so we'll be busy humping on that. If they make time go by faster, I'll be thankful for that anyhow. Sometimes I wonder, though, 'cause it doesn't seem to be moving at all. Still some 5 months to go, and that looks like ages yet.

Thought there would be more to say, but guess there isn't. A combination of being fenced in like this and getting very little news of what's going on in your own back yard keeps one pretty much in the dark. What news we usually do get can normally be classed in one of two categories – old news or rumors.

Bye-bye for now, my love. Miss you loads and loads.

Your Leo

24 May 66

"154"

My Honeybunch,

Skipped writing last night as I waited around to see if anything would develop. However, things stayed pretty quiet as the rebels threw in the towel. They had been given until 1800 last night to either quit or they would be wiped out. Sunday, Ky had sent in more troops and tanks, and that night Vietnamese planes circled the city, broadcasting this ultimatum. In addition, they dropped leaflets advising them of this deadline. A copy is enclosed.

CÙNG ĐỒNG-BÀO ĐÀ-NẴNG,

Cuộc hành quân ĐÀ-NẴNG do lực-lượng tổng trừ bị Nhảy-Dù, Thủy-Quân Lục-Chiến và Biệt-Động-Quân đảm trách chỉ nhằm hai mục đích sau đây:

— thứ nhứt kêu gọi một số quân nhân ly khai trở về hàng ngũ tiếp tục chiến đấu chống Cộng.

— thứ hai ổn định tình hình để đồng bào được trở lại cuộc sống bình thường, buôn bán làm ăn hầu tạo điều kiện thuận tiện cho cuộc bầu cử sắp tới.

Đã ở ngày qua, từ 15-5-66 đến 20-5-66 Quân-đội chỉ kêu gọi bọn đồng đội cùng dân chúng trở về nếp sống bình thường. Mặc dầu súng và lựu đạn của nhóm chống đối nổ vào họ nhưng họ chỉ phản ứng bằng cách bắn chỉ thiên. Sự kiện đó đã chứng tỏ thiện chí của các lực lượng đảm trách việc tái lập an ninh trật tự.

lực-lượng chánh-phủ không đàn áp Phật Giáo. Lực-lượng chánh-phủ không nổ súng vào các chiến hữu dù những người đó có tư tưởng, chính kiến khác biệt.

lực-lượng chánh-phủ chỉ kêu gọi họ trở về với cương vị của họ, chấm dứt những hành động gây rối phạm pháp.

Sở dĩ có vụ chạm súng ngày 20 tháng 5 là vì nhóm quân nhân ly khai nổ súng trước, gây chết và bị thương cho một số quân nhân thuộc lực-lượng chánh-phủ, bắt buộc các quân nhân nhảy dù và Thủy-Quân Lục-Chiến phải phản ứng ngoài ý muốn.

Hiện nay hơn 400 quân nhân đã ra trình diện, một số lớn là những người ý thức được việc làm sai lầm của mình nên đã chấm dứt hành động vô kỷ luật. Một số khác đã rời bỏ các ngôi chùa, mang vũ khí trở về đơn vị.

250 vũ khí đã được thu hồi.

400 quân nhân này đều được bảo đảm tính mạng, đối đãi tử tế và trở về phục vụ quân đội.

Bộ Tư lệnh Quân Đoàn I xin đồng bào yên tâm, tuân hành triệt để lệnh giới nghiêm, giúp lực lượng chánh phủ tái lập mau chóng an ninh trật tự tại thị xã Đà-Nẵng.

Đồng bào nào có bà con là quân nhân theo phe chống đối, hãy yêu cầu họ về trình diện gấp. Họ sẽ được hưởng mọi sự khoan hồng của chánh phủ nếu sớm nhận thức là phải. Trái lại nếu họ không về trình diện trước 18 giờ ngày thứ hai 23-05-1966 thì sẽ bị coi như đào ngũ.

Có như vậy, tiềm lực chống Cộng mới không bị suy giảm, an ninh trật tự mới chóng vãn hồi để bà con được tiếp tục buôn bán làm ăn, và cuộc bầu cử Quốc-Hội sắp tới mới được tiến hành một cách thuận lợi.

Thân ái chào toàn thể đồng bào.

Unsure of what would happen, many planes were evacuated from here Saturday and Sunday. They started coming back in early this morning. During the day the Vietnamese hired help started filtering back to work, as if nothing happened. All this turmoil seems to be a natural way of life for them, and I guess it is since many of them have not known anything else.

No mail from my girl today, so no comments in that area. Did get a letter from Mom yesterday, but she didn't have too much news either. I guess she's finding it quite different with Theresa, able to relax more and at the same time get out shopping and visiting when she wishes. She said Aunt Nellie wasn't doing too well, which I think is the condition she was in when I entered the service. I don't expect she has too much longer, however, but you can never tell – like Grandma Mary.

The rotation is starting to pick up now. A couple troops left this week and three new ones came in. Next month and July will be quite heavy. Chisum, whom I mentioned to you as going back to Waco, has his replacement, a TSgt Smith, due in the next 2-3 weeks, so he was able to get a rollback of 3 weeks. That means he'll leave here 3 weeks before his normal return date.

I hope my shoes come in pretty soon. I ordered some as mine are slowly giving out. I still have two pairs – high tops and low quarters, but they'll never last 5 more months. As a matter of fact, I'm sweating out one of them lasting 5 weeks.

Nothing else from here, sweet girl. Did run across a small article on the 3rd MOB that explains a bit of what they do. An airman I got in yesterday just left that outfit.

You know, ever since I've left you back there you've been in my thoughts – but I actually think it's getting worse, if that's possible. I think of you and miss you so very much, my darling. I do hope it doesn't get any more intense than it is right now. Your so sweet and I want so much to be with you again. Goodnight, my love.

Your Leo

25 May 66

Hi Sweetheart,

The mailman was good to me today and brought me a letter from my girl. It's about 5:30 now so I won't get this finished until late since I'm waiting for a meeting at 6 o'clock – NCO council.

Many of the people got some encouraging news – promotion-wise. The next cycle to every grade up to Master was due 1 June, however, USAF held up to review what the increase in AF strength would do to the promotion picture. When they had it all tabulated, they came out with new quotas to all grades which just about doubles the promotions. It's the largest quota since the Korean action. So now, promotions won't be made until around 15 June, with the people getting a date of rank of 1 June and drawing pay for it as of 21 June. Another surprising part was that they'll make 238 more E-8's and 400+ E-9's. For E-9's, the quota will be larger than the original batch they made on 1 April. All in all, many troops have their hopes up – hope too many don't get disappointed.

Well, things seemed pretty calm today. Just about all the hired help has returned to work. I was even able to get my laundry out and another batch in. Guess it's Saigon's turn again. Larkin was talking to this CMS down there on the phone today while the chief was sitting <u>under</u> his desk. Guess they had some stray lead flying around also. I think I'm about ready to pack my bags and tell them all my mommy wants me home!

The weather hasn't been bad at all the last couple days. Cooler – and there's been a good breeze. This is the time of late afternoon and evening showers, so the winds are pretty good. Much better sleeping, also. Monday, however, was a full day of steady rain and even with raincoats or ponchos you'd get soaked – plus not being able to walk anywhere without going through water up to your ankles.

I don't even remember if I told you in last night's letter – it's been so long ago, but we got some people jumping yesterday A.M. About 6 A.M. yesterday we got a boom, then another, louder one. Everybody hit the deck and crawled under their sacks. Then nothing else. Thought at first 120's were incoming. Come to find out it was the F-4C's coming home after they had been evacuated, and a pair broke the sonic barrier. Those jaspers cruise at about 1400 MPH. They're the ones who have shot down most of the MIGs up north.

Well, back again. It's almost 9 P.M. now and we're done with our sewing circle and gab session. Made all sorts of major world–shattering decisions!

I got a charge out of your description of the Vietnam Widows' Club. It is nice that there are people close by with something in common – even if it must be Vietnam. It also seems odd to me that there is a group of that size in a place the size of Jacksboro. (I don't mean a formal "club", but 4 wives with husbands in VN.) Anyhow, you mention that Sgt Payne is on Oki and his tour doesn't begin until he gets "south." I'm sure this will be found to be in error. They use adjusted tours to determine the length of stay. For Okinawa, the tour unaccompanied is probably 18 months, while here it's 12 months. That means 1 ½ months there gains him the same credit as 1 month here. If he spends 3 months on Oki and then came here, he would be credited with 2 months and would spend 10 more months in Vietnam. Likewise, if the unaccompanied tour on Oki is 24 months, he would have to do 2 months to get credit for 1 month VN time. It works the same going from here anywhere else on the same tour (not consecutive assignments.) You also mentioned facilities weren't ready for him yet, so I'd have no idea where's he's going. It could be some place like Phan Rang or Can Tho, in IV Corps, the southern part of Vietnam.

The BX opened its doors again today, so went on a shopping expedition. Splurged on some Vienna sausage, canned apricots and corned beef hash! What I really wanted – and needed – was a haircut, but they were mobbed. I'll just hold it back with a ribbon until the initial mad rush is over, I guess!

Guess that's about it for this time, my sweet. Maybe tomorrow I'll get that notice I've been waiting on telling me that their sending me here was all a big mistake and that I should hurry back to the states! What the heck – if I'm gonna dream I might just as well do it big. Be sweet, my love.

Your Leo

26 May 66

Hi Honeybunch,

Here it is 10:30 and I just came back to the shop. I'll knock off a quicky here and then I have to get a report written up, so no telling when I'll get out of here.

This was one of those days. I must have spent half the day either on the phone to Saigon or trying to get a line to them. When it wasn't that, it was 16 other things, including another of my troops getting an appointment with the medics. I guess they'll probably send him somewhere for a psychiatric check-up. I don't know, it's a vicious cycle I guess.

There's not much going on here right now that's particularly newsworthy. Things are pretty quiet, at least from our end, though nobody seems to know for sure what's going on in town. Heavy demonstrations in Hue, however, report our troops up there. This all seemed to be just the noise type, however, with no violence involved.

Looks like the heat is returning to us. It's been warming up the last couple days, but the nights are still fairly comfortable. Now see, I'm reverting to weather reports, which proves there's little to write about.

We're now down to 151 days. You know, it won't be awfully long before we get below that magic 100 mark. Any amount of time that keeps us apart is too long, however. Miss you and the children so very much, my darling. I love you, love you, love you – loads and loads.

Your Leo

27 May 66

My dearest Don Leta,

Well, we made it through another day, this one highlighted by another sweet letter from my favorite wife.

I don't feel quite as pooped tonight, but I had trouble staying awake early this morning. It was somewhere around 2 A.M. before I hit the sack, mostly because I wasn't tired 'till then. Worked until around midnight but after that, it was just sitting and reading. I think of it now and that's probably why I've been getting headaches in the evening. I do enough reading and writing during the day without taking any more on at those hours. There's not a heck of a lot else to do though – as a matter of fact, there's nothing else to do.

Finally got a haircut today. It was still crowded – and hot – but I just sat it out and got it over with. When I got there they were up to number 4 – and I had 37. It really wasn't too bad though, about 2 hours.

Had some IBM people here from Japan this afternoon, so I spent awhile with them at the Comm. Center. I had called for maintenance assistance last Tuesday, but they got stranded in Okinawa awaiting transportation. This gear is on its way out. We're shortly to have installed a new and bigger IBM data processing system. Also, Base Supply is getting a Univac computer. What is war coming to??? Wish they'd invent something to replace me!

You keep mentioning of sometimes thinking that I won't come back and worrying about what's going on here. I'm not kidding you, even though I know it won't prevent your worrying, but I'm as safe here as any place I can be in Vietnam. What shelling we do receive is short-lived and we have all sorts of shelter. The building I'm in is brick and it would take considerably more than a mortar hit to put us out of business. The guys here are forever receiving stateside newspaper clippings and the way some of it has been played up really gives us a laugh. I guess it makes good reading, though.

That's about it for now, sugar. Had gotten about halfway through this letter when Currier, Grenier, and TSgt Taylor, my new Teletype chief came in with a challenge to play hearts. Naturally, not being a coward, I had to take up this challenge. Night, night for now, my sweet. I love you and miss you more than every.

Your Leo

29 May 66
Sunday

My Darling

Didn't get to check my mail until this evening, when there was a letter from my girl. We were up to Monkey Mountain for a while today – had to check on some equipment.   Also received a couple more books from Tapscott, who used to be our clerk. I had mentioned his sending books before. He's a fanatic for all right wing causes. Everything's a plot to overthrow the government.

Boy, it would be murder for the Cross's if everyone came down with mumps – especially since Mary and Bill have not had them earlier. I guess there's always the good side to look at too. The boys won't miss a bunch of school over it. It would be good if our boys got them now also, 
especially Bryan. That much less to worry about in later years.

From all your descriptions of Paul, I sure do miss seeing him. I'll bet it's really comical to see him imitating his big brother. I know that when I look at these pictures of him he right away gives me the impression of being full of life and a character. I guess it's just his being a chip off the old block, at least as far as the character bit goes!

When I went to get my mail this evening they had the payroll posted. They always get the payroll a couple days before payday. Anyhow, they've got me down to draw $502 this payday – as compared to the $353 I drew last month. I'll have to strut down to Finance tomorrow to find out what gives. Either they've goofed on this one or a review indicates I was shorted sometimes in the past. I'd like to accept it without question, but I fear they'd then come to get it back when I couldn't afford it – the Indian givers! Anyhow, I'll find out what gives tomorrow.

If I ever get to Hong Kong, I'd like to pick up a few things, so I'm trying to get from people who have been there some idea of what they have to offer. I'll probably make a list to send you and perhaps there would be some item you'd like. One of the big things I know the guys have gobbled when someone brought a batch back were beetle watches. I though maybe of getting one for each of the girls. They're about the size on the right and are real colorful. They're worn on a long chain around the neck and when you press the antennas together the back or shell opens, displaying the watch. They sell for $30 + stateside, I understand. In Hong Kong they're $6.50 each.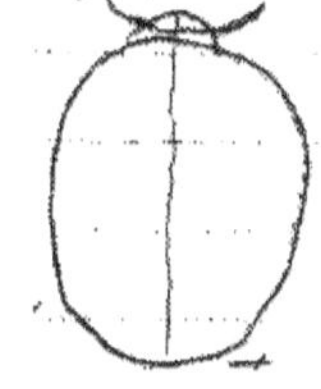

Was surprised and happy to hear that the Zimmermans got their assignment to Alaska and that it's the long tour rather than remote. It seems to me he's been trying for that ever since I've known him – while at the same time sweating those out here. I can remember particularly how she worried about his getting sent to Vietnam. He may see Grenier up there if he gets his choice, since he has asked for Alaska – or Australia.

I'm gonna have to quit here. Need to get my beauty sleep! – plus which it's shower time.

It's slow but it's moving, honeybunch. Less than 150 to go now. A couple months from now and assignments will be coming in. Then I can really feel that it will be downhill. It seems that ever since I got here all I've been looking forward to is being back with you. I love you so deeply, my dearest. Never has anything been so discouraging as not being able to be near you. Be sweet, my love, and take good care of yourself for me.

<u>Your</u> Leo

Tuesday, 31 May 66

Hi Sweetheart,

The letter I started last night got waylaid, and I never got much beyond this point. We had us another one of our periodic hullabaloos – a cut cable. When that happens, we loose a bunch of circuits and everybody and his uncle gets into the act. At times it actually gets so bad that you have to hold up coordination and restoral actions to answer phone calls wanting to know all about it. Honest, they bug us about when it'll be restore, what happened, who's working on it, what color eyes did the guy who cut it have, etc.—even before our troops can get to the site of the damage. Oh well, 147 more days!

There was also some celebration last night. Some was caused by the publishing of the promotion list and the rest in observance of Passover— Passover in promotions, that is. It was a surprise, in as much as promotions weren't expected until around the 15th of June. Even though they'll have a date of rank of 1 June, they don't get to sew them on or start drawing pay for it until 21 June.

This squadron did exceptionally well – a total of 35 new stripes, 21 of which were in maintenance. Grenier made Master and was he ever tickled – only had 4 year in grade. There were two MSgt's made, both in maintenance. I got four Staffs and one A1C in crypto, but didn't make any in Teletype where I was hoping to get a Tech Stripe.

Not too much else is new, honeybunch. No mail yesterday or today, so nothing in that area. I did get the pay bit squared away. In re-tabulating my records they found that they had added my regular rations and quarters twice, hence the overpayment. No delay in getting paid, however, since they just added my name to the supplemental payroll and I drew my money right there at Finance.

Tomorrow it's off on another month. As I look back on May, it seems—now at least—that it went by fairly fast. It sure didn't look it on 1 May, however, just as it looks like a lot time through June. Before awfully long it also will be history and we'll be starting on what I hope will prove to be assignment month. You know, it even looks like I might make it through the next 140 days or so, though there were (and will be) times when it still seems like ages away. Often I think how easy Korea was in comparison—but then, I didn't realize the full value of what I had like I do now.

Good night, my sweet. I'll see you in my dreams. Love you loads.

Your Leo

Too much of a mob getting Money Orders today. Will send them in next letter.

Wednesday, 1 Jun 66

My Dearest,

What otherwise would have been a bad day all around was enlightened by another nice long letter from you and Karen both. Karen amazes me with her letter writing and I would never have guessed that she could sit down and write so much. It's not just rambling on, either, but proved quite interesting.

It's back to the hot days again, making it uncomfortable to just sit still. Then on top of all that, it seemed like the problems were coming from every which direction today. It doesn't seem like anyone escaped getting their share.

Another one of my troops got himself into some trouble and on top of that I think they're going to have him sent out to have a psychiatric check-up. Three of my other people rotate this month also, so that won't help too much. Somehow, I don't think I'd be able to talk them into extending for few more months!

We're supposed to get two captains in Maintenance. Capt Kimbell, presently at Tan Son Nhut should be here in another week or 10 days. I've talked to him on the phone a few times. Around the middle of July, a Captain Rayfield is due in. Lt Carol will be leaving the end of this month, as is our personal officer. Then, Major Perry leaves in August. By then I should really be one of the old troops.

Towards the latter part to this month we're gong to have a get together, officers and key NCOs, for a steak dinner. Doesn't know for sure yet where it's going to be. We may have it at the Take-Ten Club. That's an NCO club for all services, located in a secure area in town. I guess it just opened up again and Major Perry got the Base Commander's O.K. for us to have it. A lot of the guys here had joined—$2 a month—but I've never been. I use to hear them say mostly it was because they had good steaks, as well as floor shows every Saturday. At least they did 3 months ago when the town was on limits. Now it's used mostly by the Army and Navy troops, and civilians, still living in the compound in town. The town itself is still off limits to all except on official business. I really don't look for it to go back on while I'm here.

I guess it's a good thing school came to an end when it did, what with that torrid romance Stephanie was involved in. Just like her mother! If it had gone too much longer at the rate they were going I might have made it home just in time for the wedding. It must really have been getting to be something if even teasing from her sisters didn't chase her.

I know this gets monotonous, sweet girl, but there's just nothing else to report. Could probably arrange for Charlie to pull a raid so I'd have more to write home about, but think I'll just stick to dull notes until something else happens. I love you so much, my sweet, even though I went another full 7 hours not thinking about you—until I woke up this morning. Miss you so much, sweetheart. Oh, how wonderful it will be to hold you close again. Good night, my love.

<u>Your</u> Leo

Friday, 3 Jun 66

My Dearest Don Leta,

Skipped writing last night and ended up getting 12 hours sleep. Maybe I shouldn't even mention it, with the lack of sleep you've had these past months. I know that yesterday I couldn't hardly keep my eyes open all afternoon. It was probably building up on all of us because we all got a good laugh out of what happened the night before. You know when I last wrote I mentioned that we had all had problems. Well, anyhow, Grenier came in on us in the office and I was asleep in my chair, with feet up on the desk; Sgt Currier was asleep with his head on another desk, and Laskin was curled up sleeping on a third desk!

I received Bentley Page's address in today's letter from you. I never could find out what outfit he was in before. I called the Air Police Squadron today and he was off and they couldn't reach him. He's supposed to go on days tomorrow (they work shift, so I should be able to contact him tomorrow morning). There are about 66 men in the AP's here, so it's a ball trying to get hold of one. They pull all the guard duty—a thankless and sometimes ticklish task. The first one I can remember getting it here was an AP, last January during a mortar attack. They've been considerably strengthened since then.

I've been wanting to see Sgt Nelson—his baby boy was born 23 March—to ask him how many teeth his baby had! We keep kidding each other about whether one or the other is walking yet or talking, etc. I just called Airman Sayed in the other office to ask about his daughter, born 23 March – their first. Told him that when he has acquired my experience, his children will progress much faster!

The First Sergeant went up to Hue and Dong Ha on the 1st to pay the troops. I had thought of going up with him this past month, but now I'm glad I didn't have the chance. They've been acting up quite a bit up there and I guess rides back are pretty slim right now. He's usually back the next day, but today I talked to him on the hot line and he wasn't sure when he'd be able to get a hop. The way many of these Buddhists have been acting, I'm thinking maybe we should include a gallon of gasoline apiece for them in our foreign aid. It would probably save us all a bunch of trouble.

I sure do wish I could see both Lynn and Paul, what with your description of them. Boy, to think Paul will be two years old and Lynn over seven months by the time I see them. (Their mommy will be as young as ever, though.)

It was good to hear that all the girls were promoted. Lanis did exceptionally well, and Stephanie did quite good. I was particularly glad to see that Karen pulled out after the trouble she had at the start. I'm sorry for all the "what can I do's" you'll now have to put up with by yourself the next couple months.

Boy, we've got a bunch of people going around every day sounding off numbers. It seems every "old timer" in the Squadron say "15", "29", "47" or some other such number every time you pass him. Of course, that's the number of days they have left before DEROS. During June and July there are 79 people rotating out of this Squadron out of our 250 or so.

Gonna try to make the movies tonight. Haven't been in quite some time—but again it'll depend on the mob waiting to rush in.

Good night, sweet girl. I'll chalk another day off the calendar, bringing me that much closer to the one I miss and love so much.

<u>Your</u> Leo

5 Jun 66

My Beloved,

Wednesday or Sunday, I don't think I've known the difference between any of them all week. They just seemed to mesh one into the other. After a hectic week, activity came almost to a standstill this weekend, comparatively speaking. It enabled me to catch up on my paperwork, particularly APR's and medal recommendations. I was also able to get some of my backlogged letter writing done.

Speaking of letter writing, I've been amazed at Karen's proficiency in this area. I remember how she used to fuss about writing. Two from her in one week is what really stunned me. They were quite lengthy and interesting also. Have you read her letters?

The heat is still with us, and I guess we'll be stuck with it for a while yet. For about an hour this afternoon it quickly turned cool as wind and dark clouds came in out of nowhere, it seems. It blew up so much dust you could barely open your eyes and everything over 50 feet away was blocked out. It rained a bit, much less than I expected, and then moved out just as quickly as it had appeared. Everything cleared up real good then and brother sun came back stronger than ever to resume his cooking.

This morning report on our squadron came down from Hawaii yesterday and I was carried in a separate section to indicate I was mis-assigned, that there was no authorized place for me in Vietnam. Naturally, exceptions are made for Southeast Asia in view of the short tour, so waiver is granted to keep me here until my tour is completed. The dogs!

Brace yourself for a shock now. I've got some film packaged and ready for mailing in the morning!!! It's undeveloped so you'll have to send it out yourself. I'll air mail them so they should be there shortly after this letter.

There's a bunch of new people coming into the base now for the big June-July turnover and I ran into a couple more troops I knew, including a TSgt in the AP's who was at the academy with Currier and I. SSgt Sutek from back at Orlando is now out of missiles and working on the flight line. There's also an airman who was in our outfit at Orlando, but I don't remember his name. Haven't seen him yet. I imagine there'll be a few more before the big cycle is completed. Silvey was up here on TDY from Bien Hoa again so had some coffee with him. Also had let this MOB TSgt in to modify some equipment and he said he had seen Spencer at Don Muang, Thailand. With talks of ever greater troop buildups here, I guess they'll all be through here at one time or another, at least people in fields like communications and aircraft maintenance.

I guess Lt Carol[25] will make it out of here after all, though I've often wondered about him. Boy, that guy makes everybody nervous. He just paces back and forth, back and forth, chewing his fingers. I say fingers because his nails have been chewed away for a long time. He's supposed to leave by 1 July and I'll be glad to see it – it'll mean I'm only 117 days behind.

We're getting more gear all the time and now I'm busy trying to get the manning document increased. I'm afraid that for a while many of the troops are going to find themselves with very little spare time. In a way that's a blessing around here since there's nothing to do with spare time anyway. It's not all that we've got so much equipment, but it's so darn scattered—a bit like back at the missile sites, except that you can't just get up and go any time you feel like it. Like at times we need to get a bunch of stuff to Hue or Dong Ha and there's no aircraft space, so we call the Marines and stick one of our trucks in their convoys that go up every week or so.

Guess I'll be heading for midnight chow shortly. I've been going quite often lately as I never get to bed much before 12 or 1. Good night for now, my sweet. How I long for this waiting and separation to come to an end. I get so lonesome for you and the children at times. And you've been so good through it all. I know it's no picnic having to take care of those six and still try to get the everyday items taken care of. I love you so much, Don Leta, and I want desperately to be with you again so we can do all these things together. Not too awfully long now and we'll see that day together –

Your Leo

---

[25] Some names have been changed to protect privacy.

6 Jun 66

My Dearest,

It's always so nice when one of those days comes around that brings a letter from my honeybunch. I'm back at the shop now, and it's almost 10 P.M. There are so many people here tonight as there are during the daytime. Some are working, but most are writing, reading or listening to tape recorders. I laid down after supper again and fell right to sleep. Stayed there until 8:30. Now tonight I'll probably never get to sleep. Had a miserable night last night! I went to bed shortly after midnight and didn't get to sleep until near 4 A.M. I got up around 3 and went to sit outside for a while. Looked around and there was Grenier in front of his barracks with the same problem so we ended up gabbing for a bit before trying it again. I was surprised I didn't feel shot when I got up again at 6:30.

All the guys sitting around waiting for port calls to come in from Saigon get an answer today. They said they'd not be leaving from Saigon any longer—that they'd finally be starting the runs right in and out of Da Nang. I think I had mentioned that they were going to start that shortly. Cargo trips by commercial airlines started last month, and some of the R&R trips are by commercial fare, but now they'll be starting passenger runs directly from and to the states. I'll see if I can get on one going straight to Jacksboro International!

Looks like we'll finally get our mailroom situation squared away. It's been, and is, a mess. The present mailroom is in the barracks and mail call is something else, with lines 16 miles long! We're just nearing completion of a day room building between wings of the barracks, the only space not occupied by tents, and that's where our mailroom will be. Chisum had his friends at RMK, the civilian contracting firm, build us 300 individual mail boxes, something like they have in Post Offices. Each one has his own box and lock, so we'll be able to check our mail at any time of day or night.

I've just about logged out the movies here anymore. It gets so crowded it's hardly worth the long wait and struggle to get in, even though there may be some picture I'd like to see. For instance, the line for the 5:30 show starts forming between 3 and 3:30. You can imagine, with some 5,000 + Air Force types, plus swabbies, Marines and Army troops all restricted to base, a theater holding about 300 people is not quite going to hack it.

Boy, your definitions of Paul sure make him sound like a big one—now getting E or EE width shoes, and the other day wearing a pair of size 6 shorts when you tried to get him in the pool. And now you mention that you had to get a new potty chair since he won't fit in the other one. I sure am missing a big year with both him and Lynn. Now Lynn must be something else if she's all as sweet as your say—or is that just the mother talking? I think they were all cute—up to a point—but then they started to walk & talk! I'm glad that she's being as good as she is, though. It's bad enough as it is, I can well imagine what it would be like if she was a fussy one. When she first sees me,

I'll probably be the boogieman to her. Her mother will have to make her understand that I'm really harmless.

Another day chalked off the calendar as I close this letter, my sweet. Slowly, but regularly, they're moving by and it won't be too awfully long before all this waiting is history and we're together again—a moment I long for so much. Be sweet, my darling, and remember that I love you with all my heart.

<u>Your</u> Leo

7 Jun 66

My Darling,

This has been one of those sluggish days that almost makes one say "I should of stayed in bed". At least, that's the way it was as far as the work accomplished today was concerned. It was routine enough until lunchtime, but after that I'm afraid it would have taken an attack to make me move very fast.

I'm afraid that's what this letter will probably seem like also. What can you write about a day like this? No mail today, so there's nothing to cover in that area either.

I did get a visit this afternoon from A1C Linn, who was in the 4504th at Orlando and later at Ellsworth. He worked for Sgt Savery at Ellsworth. He's over here TDY from Tucson with SAC and is supposed to go to Bien Hoa later this month and then back to his home station in July after 120 days TDY here. Mostly, I heard about how everything is so fouled up and how the Air Force is going to be the loser 'cause he's going to get out—then what are we going to do. After Eight years service he's still an A1C and it's all politics etc. If I remember correctly, at Orlando he was more of a talker than producer also.

I must admit I didn't much feel like a retention NCO today! There was one thing we had today—our own version of music. Larkin had his tape recorders plugged in and we had music, stereo of course, all day long. He's got a couple of pretty good units – about a $500 investment, I would guess. There are a lot of guys who have bought stereos, tape recorders, amplifiers, etc. while here (or on R&R TDY to Japan, Hong Kong, etc.) and have spent quite a bit, but still much less than what it would cost them stateside. Quite a few of the young airmen, especially, have done this. Fortunately, Larkin plays good music – Roger Miller, the New Christy Minstrels, calypsos, etc., but sometimes these airmen have them on here during the night shift on in the barracks and that "yeah –yeah – yeah" type rock-n-roll or whatever it is will drive you batty. Plus which they can play it only one way – loud!

We got a couple new troops in again today. Walked by the theater around 3 P.M. and there was a whole mob of brand spankin new troops there for the newcomers briefing. Though many of them outrank you and probably have more service, you still feel like a "veteran" who's been through it all and is waiting to leave while they're nothing but recruits.

I think I've just about decided not to go on R&R. With less than 140 days to go I think I'll just stick it out. That way I'll be able to send a few extra dollars home as back-up for whatever move and leave we get when I get back. I'll send some here shortly—the next time I get down by the P.O. and starting next pay day I'll send $300 a month. At least most of our bills will be taken care of even though I know there are always new one, especially with six kids. Heck, you almost need just one paycheck just for shoes + clothes. Have you been able to set aside any in reserve? I know at one time you mentioned having around a hundred in the bank.

I ended up writing more than I thought when I started. It's about 1 A.M. now and I'm not sleepy yet—besides, Al Hirt and his trumpet is now keeping me alert. I imagine it'll be somewhere around 2 before I get to bed. I've been looking at all the pictures of you and the kids again. They're probably the most looked at snaps I've ever had. Gee, how I miss you all honeybunch. I know there'll never be another time like this year. I just seem to want so much to just reach out and touch you. It gets particularly bad some of those nights when I can't get to sleep for one reason or another. It might be hours that I just lay there and think of you—us. I love you, my sweet, so very, very much. Good night, my love.

Your Leo

DaNang, RVN
8 June 66

My dearest Lanis,

I received your letter today and I was very happy indeed to see the fine grades you received on your final report card. I very proud of your doing so well.

Now I guess it's relaxing time after that long school year. That will go by fairly fast and the next thing you know you'll be in the 4th grade, but not at Jacksboro Elementary for too long. It should be some time around your first six weeks test that I'll be returning home. Right now I have about 138 more days to go.

There's not too much new to report from out here, sugar. We have to stay on the base all the time, except for the few times when we have some work to do at Monkey Mountain or Marble Mountain, or sometimes some of us to to Hue or Dong Ha.

You keep doing as well as you are for the rest of the summer, sweetheart, and remember to give mommy any help you can. Loads of love and kisses.

Your Loving
Daddy

9 Jun 66

My Darling,

I know it must get monotonous to hear it from me so often, but I'm afraid that once again there's not very much going on—or at least, anything that would interest you. Heaven knows there's enough going on work wise, but I'm sure that would make even duller reading.

There are a couple daily rituals which we go through that I can tell you about. Every morning between 9 + 9:30 is coffee break. So we up and head for the club to drink a hot cup of coffee—sweat—and come back to our air-conditioned shop. In the afternoon is cake break time. We leave our cool building and head for the club. The sweat is rolling off by the time we sit in that hotbox for a cool cake. The cake does nothing, and we continue to perspire. We chug back to the building and by the time we get there our shirts more likely than not are wet clear through. Invariably we then say how nice it is to get back where it's cool. Craziest war I ever fought!

As I was writing this, there was considerable booming towards the south end of the field. We checked outside and Robinson was sticking his head out the other door checking also.   It was all outgoing. They don't take too many chances. Any time there's any movement at all in certain areas it's away we go. They might only get some cow or water buffalo, but at least they're not letting anything else in.

I've been wanting to send you some more money but haven't had the opportunity to get down to the P.O. yet. May get to do so tomorrow. I've mailed some film, so those will probably already have gotten to you by the time you get this.

Hope there's more to write about tomorrow, honeybunch, short of a VC visit. I love you loads and loads and need you so much.

Your Leo

10 Jun 66

My Honeybunch,

Today must have been the hottest of them yet. Not only was the sun real hot, but there was a rather brisk wind all day and it was just about as hot as the sun's rays. To top it off, when a gust blew up it would just spray you with hot sand. Went to the P.O. and it was bad enough going down but coming back we were facing into it.

Firing lasted well into the night last night, really nothing unusual, even though the firing earlier had been a bit heavier than usual. As usual, we got all the latest today—from some stray dog setting off a trip flare to Ho Chi Minh approaching on a peace march. Alas, history will never record what happened.

This has been a fairly steady day, but not one where I exactly strained myself, except for the long hours. They just about finished our day room and we made first use of our mail boxes tonight. They all have individual locks which we have to buy for 55¢ or Piastres. When we leave we can either take the lock or leave it and get our money back. This makes it pretty good since we can check mail 24 hours a day. That's much easier than trying to get there during certain hours, not always possible around here. Also, mail comes in at all hours, daytime or midnight as well.

Have to make another trip to Monkey Mountain this weekend. Guess I'll probably go Sunday afternoon since that's usually the slackest around here. Besides, the breeze usually blows up there and it'll be a bit better than here on the field. Larkin, Henkel and myself are going. I don't know for sure if Grenier is going up.

Good night for now, sweetheart. I sure do miss you – and I could go on saying that forever I guess. You mean so very, very much to me honeybunch. Take good care of yourself for me.

<u>Your</u> Leo

11 Jun 66

My dearest, darling, sweet honeybun,

I've just about decided on one of the primary prerequisites of any retirement site. They must have a completely paid for church and school, built with such foresight that no expansion will be required for at least 50 years, and endowed with 50 million dollars by some old millionaire who passed away!

Needless to say, I received your letter today telling me of what Father would like, and what he has already done for the church. I guess we can help him out a bit, but I don't know about $79. Thinking again, if he would charge "rent" we'd probably end up needing two pews for our family, so maybe it'd be cheaper to cough up. It is nice to see that he's taking such an interest, though, since it doesn't seem like anyone got that concerned before.

Had a rather busy day today. What with everything else going on here, had a quick notice to chug down to the Marines for a meeting. So I grabbed Airman Letka, my Talk Quick expert and we went down to discuss moving that system from its present location to their new command post across the river. It's one of the things we take care of for the Marines, and as it ended up, Col Hill, the Marine Comm officer for I Corps was impressed. It so happened that when we went into the Major's office, Major Kyle received a call from Col Hill saying there was some trouble with the system. We went over and in 3 minutes it was cleared so they thought that was just great. As communicators, they make good fighters!

Well, I'll be knocking off for now, honeybunch. Want to try to get to bed early tonight (before 12) and have to take a shower yet. Love you loads & loads, sweetheart. Oh, looking at these pictures again I want so much to take you in my arms and hug you close. Good night, my happiness.

<u>Your</u> Leo

13 Jun 66

My sweetgirl,

I've just been sitting here spooning a bit again while thinking of you. I miss you so much and 134 days still seems like such a long time to go yet. With three billion people on earth, how come I miss one woman so? I'm just in such a hurry for all this to be over with and for me to be going back home that now it just seems to be dragging all the more. Well, this month is just about half over, so I guess time is still moving on after all.

Yesterday was miserable here. It must have been the hottest day yet. It was hot again today, but not nearly as uncomfortable as yesterday. I was going to go to Monkey Mountain but put it off 'cause I dreaded the hot, dusty drive.

There was a letter for me from my honeybunch today. Sweet, that's another reason I want to be back – to help with the kids. You mentioned Karen again, and her tantrums and going into a rage. I hope the doctor can tell you something when you take her tomorrow, even though none of them have seemed too encouraging so far. She surely hasn't been getting any better. Was she quite that bad before the last time they changed her medicine? I'm surprised the teacher hadn't reported her conduct as being rebellious or anything, even though I remember you mentioned she said Karen had seemed depressed. Do you suppose she just does her fussing and feuding at home? I can't help but worry about it, knowing you have five others to keep up with, and here I am unable to help at all. Make sure you get the word to the Red Cross if anything goes wrong, and keep me advised of what develops. Don't just skip it over 'cause you don't want me to worry. That will just make me worry all the more. A little mortar fire around here doesn't bother me nearly as much as the uncertainty of wondering how you're going to take care of everything back home all by yourself.

About 6-7 more guys got their assignments this weekend – some happy, some not so happy. One guy wanted California and got Lackland. Another wanted the southeast and got Kansas. One guy wanted overseas and ended up in the Midwest. The others all got their first or second choices.

There's just nothing new here. We're still restricted to the base, the movies are too crowed, the BX still doesn't have too much to offer, the NCO Club is too hot, and the bowling alleys, golf course, race track and swimming pool haven't been built yet! It's just the routine of up around 6:30 and back to the barracks somewhere in the vicinity of midnight. I'm afraid that routine will be pretty much the same for another 130 days or so.

So, good night for now, sweet girl. You've just been so wonderful to me and for me all these years. I'll be thinking of you again well into the night, and how my heart and all of me can feel the longing pains of wanting you. I love you so.

Your Leo

Karen

    Karen, 13, was the oldest in our family. She was artistic and witty, always creative. I smiled earlier when I read my father's mention of the letters she wrote him. On this day, though, Leo worries about her moodiness and depression.

    From ten thousand miles away, does he have the power to help Karen? We fear that even if he were miraculously transported home, he would bring not a cure, only companionship. We fear the unspoken in his instruction, "Get the word to the Red Cross if anything goes wrong".

14 Jun 66

Hi Honeybunch,

Busy, busy, busy day today. Got going bright and early this morning and kept quite active until about five minutes ago. It's around 8 P.M. now and we just finished with our Airman of the Month board and monthly meeting of the Squadron NCO Council. I like days like this because they don't allow me much time to think or dream of what was or could be. The only negative part was that there was no mail.

Grenier came in about 30-40 minutes after work started this morning and we went down to the old comm center to update our plant-in-place records (drawings) on that facility. That's where our new Autodin (punch card system) is going to be located. We already have all the equipment and are waiting for an installation team. Then, at 10 o'clock I had to go to the other side to confer with the Marines. After a 30 minute lunch break I came back to my desk, signed a couple things and initialed a bunch of others and then took off for the mountain. By the time I got back there was some part I had to see about. Off to another 30 minute chow break and then back to the board and meeting.

We had a pleasant surprise last night – a cool front came in. It got hot enough today though, but it sure felt good for awhile to sleep under a sheet.

Outside of all this "hot poop", everything here is about normal, or if anything, a little more quiet than usual. No hearts tonight. Think I'll quit early and get me some sack time. Wish there was more to tell you, honeybunch – like our assignment is in or I've got my flight number – but guess that kind of stuff will have to wait a couple months yet. Good night, my sweet. I love you.

<u>Your</u> Leo

15 Jun 66

Hi Pal

How are you and Paul and your new baby sister doing? I didn't write a letter to mommy today since there's not anything to tell her.

Boy, you must be getting pretty big now. I'll bet when I come home I won't even be able to throw you up high 3 times! I'm gonna try, though. Maybe I'll throw Paul up too, since he's not as big as you.

One time, when mommy wrote to me, she told me about you helping Steph and Lanis wash the car. I bet you did a good job. She also told me about you having a good time at the pool.

I didn't draw a picture this time since there's already a picture of one funny soldier on this letter. You keep being a good boy now, and daddy will be back home with you in about 133 days.

Loads of love,
Daddy

16 Jun 66

My Sugarbun,

Enclosed is a picture of me faithfully writing home. One of the airmen in Radio Relay was taking pictures one night and snapped this one. He just got

them developed today (locally, just outside the gate) and gave it to me to send home.

No mail today. Haven't heard from you since Monday – hope everything is alright. Did get one piece of mail yesterday – a form from Sears in St. Davids, Pa., requesting a character reference for Mr. Peter Donovan who was seeking employment there. So guess Pete was one of the bunch who decided to go make his fortune on the outside. I've wondered what happened to all those kids back in 465L since they were all due for discharge within 3 or 4 months of each other. I know a couple of them had already committed themselves to extend or reenlist before we left.

We had to go through the cleaning routine here again as we were expecting VIP's – and for once they came when they said they would. It was Major General Gould, Comm-Elec Officer from HQ USAF and Col Hennessay, Southeast Asia Comm Region Commander from Clark. As is usual, it was more or less a walk-through affair and then off they went again.

Everything else seems to be about the same here. As a matter of fact, it's even getting a bit routine-ish, which isn't so hot for making time go by. Still haven't been to a movie in some time, but I'm thinking of fighting the mob tomorrow night. Today & tomorrow "Cat Ballou" is on. It's the picture for which Lee Marvin got the Academy Award – sort of a western comedy. It'll be a change in the routine, anyhow.

Also have to make a big formal party Saturday – formal, that is – clean fatigues. Received a formal invitation today, in a sealed envelope and delivered by a messenger who awaited my reply. It's a Grand Opening Ball at the new comm center. Steaks & beer will be served and our wives are also invited if we can find a baby sitter. Music will be by Victor Charlie and his Strung Band, if he can break his engagement for an attack somewhere else that night. The invitation was sent by MSgt Whitten, the Comm Center NCOIC, who rotates in another couple weeks.

That's all the news what am, my sweet. We can chop off another day and bring it down to 130 now. Slow but sure. I can stand the "slow" as long as it's "sure." Hope there's some mail for me tomorrow. Will check again before going to bed as they sometimes get night deliveries. Love you loads & loads, my darling.

Your Leo

17 Jun 66

My Dearest,

How good it was to get a nice long letter from you today. It seems to me they take longer to get here than they used to at first. It must be that they've got a lot more since the build up of forces. This one was written the 11th and postmarked in Fort Worth the 12th. Since you're a day ahead of us, that means it took 6 days. Think I'll mention this to my congressman in my next letter to him. Regardless, it's still nice to hear from you, even if it does take an extra day now.

Nope, I've just about made up my mind now – I won't be going on R&R, unless things get so bad that I just want to take a break to get away from here for 5 days. In that case I'd take the R&R anywhere and wouldn't be figuring on spending much outside of food & lodging. There are a couple things I still want to get, but I'll just try to get those through the BX. I'll still be keeping enough for that type expense even if I do send a minimum of $300 to you each month. By the time I leave here I should have a few dollars and, depending on where we get assigned, I should be able to figure fairly well what we'll need for expenses. Right now I am holding back a few dollars – originally for R&R and now for "sales" or hot items the BX might get in, plus more underclothing and shoes – which I'm still waiting for, by the way. I also want to get a B-4 bag or piece of luggage of some sort instead of fighting that cruddy duffel bag on the way home. Here I am, already planning my trip and I still have over 4 months (129 days) to go!

I figured the brown chair would need covering fairly soon – actually, it needed it before I left. Go ahead and have Mr. McRoberts do the covering. He could probably do them (though I've wondered about the brown chair because of the type back it has) but I'm afraid it would be too long before we could settle down to doing it. When I get home we'll be making mad, passionate love all the time, then traveling, except to stop nights for the kids to rest and for us to make mad, passionate love; visiting and then settling down somewhere, after a suitable time spent in mad, passionate love! Yep, I think you'd better go ahead and have it done so I can take care to spend my time on necessities of life. I'd like to see the kids too, if I have the chance maybe while you're resting. Come back – don't leave home. I was exaggerating a bit!

Sounds like we've been blessed with a child who will probably need special fittings for shoes the way you describe Paul's feet. How much does he weigh now? The pictures I have of him make him look like a block and he appears to be quite heavy.

I still go to midnight chow about every other night. As a matter of fact, Grenier is reading now while I write and we'll be going over in about 30 minutes. I don't think it's bothered my waistline too much. I'm probably about the same weight I was when I got here. Many are the people who have lost weight here though – some up to 50 lbs.

I believe the film I had written a commentary for is one of those I mailed to you. It had never been developed. I had gotten film here with mailers enclosed in the box, but I couldn't use it because it was a different roll – different type, that is. Only the type sold with the mailer could be sent in that mailer.

I had some time ago delivered a dissertation on conception preventive measures. You asked that I think long and hard on this subject, and believe me this I've done – then, and since. I am still of the same conviction. I could not possibly subject you to the trials of childbearing again, and to this end, as I had told you, I would abstain completely if this were the only possible way. I just love my girl too much to ask more. Likewise, I also feel that the use of birth control pills would be proper. I don't feel any more could be asked than what has already been given. You mention seeing the Chaplain at Wolters, and here is another thing to consider. More harm could possibly be done if you used the pills and yet felt that you were doing wrong. I do not, but we don't all think or feel the same. I definitely would not want you doing anything on my account, the children's or anyone else's, if it were contrary to your convictions. So, perhaps we had better both stop again and think long and hard about this. I will likewise speak to the Chaplain on this subject. Whichever course is chosen, it must be because we <u>both</u> feel this is what must be done. It doesn't seem that there's much of anything that comes easy any more as we're being, and increasingly will be as the children grow, asked to make more and more difficult decisions. I'm sure we'll do what has to be done, because we mean so much to each other.

Good night, my happiness.

<u>Your</u> Leo

18 Jun 66

My Beloved,

It was nice getting another letter from you after what had been a so-so day. Believe I had mentioned to you before that they had an open house scheduled for the new comm. center this morning. It really wasn't an open house, cause only a few had been invited. Big ceremony – the Base Commander cut the ribbon (with the usual photographer being in tow) and then we had coffee & cake. It's 8:30 P.M. now and I've just come back from the "Comm Center Ball," held in the old, vacated comm. center. We had beer/coke, barbecued chicken and beans. Really lived it up!

I just don't know what to think about Karen and the way she's acting. I'm afraid there's no easy answer to that problem. I feel so bad that I'm not there to help and that you must bear all of this by yourself. I hope that cutting down on the medicine brings about some improvement. There's no telling what must go through her mind, and it does seem strange about her crying when Paul went over to love her without coaxing. You never know what psychologists/psychiatrists will say – I think 50% of them are all wet anyhow – but maybe even all the attention (smooching type) I've paid you in front of the kids may have some bearing since I didn't pay similar attention to Karen, particularly as the younger ones were around. I just don't know. Hope she gets no worse and that I can get home soon to help.

There's not been much change around here. Tomorrow's Sunday and it's just another work day. Depending on how things go, and if I feel up to it by then, I may knock off around 3 or so and go to China Beach – if I can get hold of a truck, that is.

Another big batch of people have come on base the last couple days, four in our squadron. All June-July replacements. Quite a few were E-8/E-9 also; I've never seen such a concentration of rank in one place before. Don't know what the heck they're going to use them all for. Seems to me that the chiefs will soon be outnumbering the Indians. Sgt Rodrigues, who used to work for me in SMC and is now back in Radio Relay, is going home next month having been assigned to Chateaureux Air Base, France. Approval had already been procured for concurrent travel of his dependents and he got his orders with this authority indicated on them. Now, McNamara indicated last week that movement of dependents to France would be suspended since U.S. military bases in France would be discontinued as of July of next year. He doesn't know what's going on now, and I feel he has an especially legitimate gripe. His last three overseas tours have been unaccompanied. He was in Turkey and Morocco, both remote, before this. They sent out a wire trying to get a reading on his present status. Lt Carol leaves in another 9 days and we're thinking of having a party for him – the day after he leaves!

That's all for now, my love. Be sweet, and remember that you mean more to me than anything in this world.   <u>Your</u> Leo

20 Jun 66

My Dearest,

There's not very much to report today, even though I didn't write last night. I had planned on going to China Beach yesterday afternoon but got off on a survey of the old comm center as a site to install our new data processing plant and didn't finish with that until quite late in the day. After supper I took a shower and changed clothes then laid on the sack for a few minutes. At 10 P.M. I got up! Couldn't sleep by then so I came down to the shop. It was past midnight when we left here and they had picked up some mail and were putting it up. So, at about 1 A.M. I got a letter from you and sat under the street lamp to read it.

Today was a fairly active day. Until shortly before quitting time I stayed pretty busy, and right now it looks like I'll keep going for the next 2-3 weeks while we get this installation squared away.

A bunch of assignments for October returnees, including Grenier's, came in today. It was sooner than we expected them. These were all overseas assignments on personnel who had requested consecutive o/s tours. They usually come out a month or so before stateside assignments. Grenier got Elmendorf, his first choice. I think there were 10 in all — nine of whom got their first choice and one second choice. Pretty good average; but I'm afraid the average is not as high on stateside assignments. Two of my NCOICs leave soon. Sgt Hooper, who had the SSO comm. center crypto, is going to an AF station in up-state New York. Sgt Williams, the base comm. center crypto boss, is going consecutive to England. One leaves in 5 days and the other in 3 weeks.

I've called a number of times to the Air Police trying to get hold of Bentley Page but still haven't contacted him. I had left my number but haven't heard from him, unless he called while I was out and didn't leave his name. I'll be trying again tomorrow.

It seems to take me forever to write to you sometimes. I stop so often after writing a few words and get to thinking about you — and us. Sometimes minutes go by before I get to the next line. I miss you so much, honeybunch. Like now, Larkin has his tape recorder on and the Christie Minstrels are singing "Your Kisses are Sweeter than Wine" and I'm thinking how I could go for a jug full of yours right now. Another 10 days and we'll start on July — that much closer to our reunion. How I look forward to being with my family again. Good night, my sweet.

<u>Your</u> Leo

22 Jun 66

My Darling,

Yesterday was another skipped writing day in as much as there was nothing much to relate, nor was there any mail. I didn't get to bed 'till around one or one thirty. There was considerable activity to the south until well into the morning, with mortar and artillery fire all night. Flare ships kept the sky pretty well lit up out there, but never did hear what, if anything, happened. Someone did say there had been a hostile force spotted some five miles from the base – but you soon learn to give that kind of statement as much credence as one which would have reported that it was LBJ out stumping for votes!

Tell you what I've been in the mood for lately – some of your banana bread and apple cake—hint, hint. Maybe you could send me one more batch, say between now and the end of July. That should hold me. I was just drinking a cup of instant coffee (burp) and was thinking how good some banana bread or cake would be. Our desserts here usually consist of canned peaches, canned pineapple, canned pears, and sometimes bread pudding – dry and without sauce. I think that if I had some by the end of July, I could probably make it the rest of the way – but otherwise I have my doubts!

Would you believe it – I worked yesterday!! I mean work, where I had tools in my hands and got filthy dirty. Got a couple of my boys and we went to the old comm. center where we tore out a bunch of old electrical power and signal lines, cleared cable racks, dismantled equipment cabinets, etc. We're trying to get things squared away for installation of our new Autodin (data processing – punched cards) set-up. I was real good at it; but then, I've always been pretty fair at taking things apart. It's putting things together so that they'll work which gives me so much trouble. The best part of it all was that there was no telephone down there!

We got three more late promotions in yesterday – guys who've been here a couple months, but who were considered at their old bases. This gave us another Tech, Staff and A1C. All told, there have been 43 stripes passed out to people in this squadron – a pretty good haul. I've been waiting to see if the AF Times showed anyone we knew back at EAFB making it. Ed Rossley surely must have gotten it this time.

I wish I could stop counting days. It just seems to go so slow. I would rather look up every now and then and see that another 10 or 20 days have passed. No such luck, though. I'm so anxious to head back home that I can't help but count – sometimes 10 times a day!

There's one thing, however. Thinking of you, especially at night when I go to bed, isn't quite as bad as it was. Perhaps it's just that it's been that way for so long now that, like many other things, it becomes somewhat of a routine. Not that I don't think of you as often, or miss you any less. Heavens knows that's not the case. I think it's more that I hurried to that dream world, closing my eyes and imagining we were still together by re-living many past incidences.

Instead, I'm now resolved that all that is passed and gone, and instead I'm thinking of the future. What I wouldn't do to really be holding you now. I love you so much, my darling, and I can never miss you any more than I have and do. Be sweet, my love.

Your Leo

Fri, 24 Jun 66

My Dearest,

How nice to hear from you again after missing your letters for a couple days. I hadn't much of anything to say yesterday and had skipped writing last night. It's now about 7:30 and I'm just pooped. Right after I write to you I'm going to wash and hit the sack. I'm bound and determined to get some sleep tonight. I worked up a bit of a sweat today and my old weary bones are feeling it.

I feel so sorry, my sweet, that you're without any free time or anything to relax, or at least get your proper rest. You've seemed so depressed of late in your letters, particularly over Karen's deportment. Of course, when that happens then every other little thing that doesn't go right takes on added significance. I don't know how we'll work it, honeybunch, but when we're together again we'll manage in some way or other to get ourselves some time out of the house by ourselves. I know that my coming home and our being together again won't solve all our problems, but at least there'll be two of us to carry what you must now shoulder alone. I know that just being able to hold your hand during the few quiet evening hours alone will help ease many of the pains. I love you so much, Don Leta.

I also received a letter from Mom today, though she didn't have too awfully much news. She was telling me of the Della Posta's pool – and I just can't see how they put a pool on that little, uneven plot of land they have. Sounds like a bit too much for me. Guess I just can't get too used to swimming pools in that part of the country. Once again she started her letter by saying that every time she hears from you she also gets a letter from me.

Well, the kids should have the bulk of their teeth work done by the start of the school year. Guess it's a good thing they're all being taken care of now while we can. I can't say that I ever paid any attention as to who did or did not have their permanent eye teeth. I can just picture Stephanie with two teeth pulled! Hope her boy friend doesn't see her!!

Say, have you heard from anyone at all who enjoyed and found their niche in retirement? It seems to me that just about everyone we've known who had or were contemplating retirement didn't know where to turn next. I'm convinced that, unless you want to accept any unskilled labor type employment, you have to get into something where there's a demand, and then sell yourself.

I was surprised over Ann saying Bob failed the Civil Service Exam and had nothing waiting for him when he got out. I think he's a real good troop. I wonder what type positions he was looking for – probably something in hospital administration. Well, I've given Uncle Sugar over 18 years now and, between us, the rest of my time in will be for me. The service is going to have to be my part-time job while I prepare for the hard cruel world. I expect it will probably be a busy time for us also, depending on what will be required in preparation for this change. I'll still be a "young" man of 39 – for about 7 more months, so I see no future in waiting until I pass that magic point into the "old" forties!

Grenier has a camera something like Daddy has and the marker where it tells how many feet of film you have left needs to be recalibrated. That's probably why there was so much blank space on the first roll. He has some film in his camera now which he said he would shoot Sunday and then let me use it. I promise it won't take me as long to get these shot and mailed! I also made another purchase and I'll be mailing a package when I come into some money – like payday. I've already got it all wrapped and addressed, but I can't quite swing the postage price right now. Big John and I saw these things at the BX and we both splurged. He's a good natured sort. I keep riding him about making Chief – telling him he made me put his name on top of the sign-out board over mine, threatening to move Larkin & me out of the office 'cause we're only MSgt & SMSgt, etc. He just laughs and keeps sucking on his pipe. Big John weighs 260 lbs and is about 44 years old and yet there he was, earlier tonight, fixing the track antenna atop the 90' pole outside. I'd never get up there. 90 feet is way the heck up – when you consider that the normal street pole is from 30 to 45 feet.

I was remarking today that here we are nearing the end of June and it doesn't seem awfully long ago that it was only the 2nd or 3rd and I was thinking how long it would be 'till the end of the month. Six more days and we'll be starting on July – and I'll say again that it'll be a long time to the end of the month. Today is just about finished and we're down to a maximum of 122 days – just about 123 days too many.

I've been thinking of you so much more the last couple days, it seems. It must be full moon time or something. We're so close in many ways and yet I look forward to being with you again with mixed emotions – like it was getting to know someone all over again. You know what I'd like to be doing right now? Nothing – just laying on the couch with my head in your lap. Oh, my sweet wonderful Don Leta. I miss you so.

Your Leo

25 Jun 66

Hi Honeybunch,

Received another letter from my favorite wife today. That's always the highlight of my day, getting a letter from you. It'll be so nice to do away with this letter business. Less than 4 months now and we will be able to forget about them.

They came out with a schedule today covering returnee flights to the states. They will attempt, within space limitations, booking all people out during two periods of the month. All those whose DEROS is from the 1st to 14th of the month would leave between the 14th and 15th. All others would leave during the second period, between the 15th and 19th. With my DEROS of 26 October, I'd be with the second bunch.

The new marine PX opened yesterday. It's located on the Marine side near Hill 327, about 6 miles from here. Larkin went down today and he said it was huge—some 32,000 sq ft spread over six large Butler buildings. Obviously they were stroked too—separate departments for radios and tape recorders, projectors and cameras, jewelry, luggage, etc. They even have representatives from one of Hong Kong's larger tailors, and sample materials. They take all measurements and send to Hong Kong to have the suit made. When it gets here another tailor goes over it and makes any necessary alterations. Opening that PX should really ease things at the AF BX, where things were really getting rough, mostly because it was so crowded. It was nothing to go down and stand about 200th in line just waiting to go in.

 I'll probably take a couple days trip in another week or so. We're getting some new facilities at Kham Duc, southwest of here. Sgt Grenier and I are supposed to catch a chopper down sometimes soon. We're picking up that site and another one up north.

Right now it doesn't much look like I'll be able to take that swim at China Beach as I've been threatening for so long. Tomorrow's Sunday and that's the only chance I'd get, but right now it looks like a full day in the making, especially with the AUTODIN installation.

Grenier was telling me today that he had received a clipping from his wife, I guess out of the Air Force Times, which was telling about some people having to retrain again. He couldn't find the article but he said 30690's were included. Isn't that ridiculous? It won't do then any good as far as I'm concerned since they're not going to get that much use out of me with what little time I have left. For that reason, I shouldn't think they'd retrain me. By the time I'd finish any schooling I'd still have less time than before to do them any good and, lets face it, at my mark I wouldn't be touching any of the gear anyhow. I'm waiting to see what the article said exactly, but we don't get the Times here 'till a couple weeks late. It's usually available in what we call the library.

I didn't get to bed as early as I would have liked last night and right now I'm exhausted. I'm going to try to make it a bit sooner tonight.

Hope everybody has straightened out health wise. I know it's more than enough for you when they don't have the sinus, asthmas, etc., without adding all these other illnesses. Daddy will come back from the wars and it'll be mommy who will have to be cared for after all she's put up with. But that's what I want to do – take care of my honeybunch from now on. It's still a while, sweetheart, but we're getting there and one wonderful day we'll look up and find that day has finally arrived. Good night, my love, Sleep good.

<u>Your</u> Leo

26 Jun 66
Sunday

My Dearest Don Leta,

A fairly quiet day thus far, I'm taking advantage of the afternoon calm to do a little writing – without guarantee that it'll be finished at this time.

I played lazy this morning, staying in bed until eight o'clock. It was almost nine before I got in to work. Didn't get to go to mass this morning, so will have to make the 5 o'clock one. That takes care of any plans to make it down to China Beach. This would have been a pretty good day for it since things are fairly quiet right now. Tonight I've got a conference to attend, so that will take care of the evening hours.

Capt Kimbrell joined us this week, so Lt Carol has quietly slipped out of the picture. The Lt. finally got booking on a flight – he'll leave here 1 July on a Boeing 707 jet from Northwest Orient Airlines. A couple of our other troops will be on the same flight. Those 707's are nice. That's what I came over on – 600+ miles per hour. I guess they're all anxious to get a look at the "round eyed" airline hostesses!

Big John Currier has been getting a good indoctrination of what he's got to put up with here. He's only been here a month and his cables have been cut or damaged five times. He's already shaking his head and this is still the good part of the year for his people. Wait 'till the monsoon rains come. That's when the cable troops really get into it – up to their ears, literally. Larkin right now is the one who has his hands full with radio and radio relay. There are times when he gets hit so hard and so often that he ends up going around in circles. He's going around muttering something like "55 days to go"! Fortunately, my end with crypto and Teletype seems to have settled quite a bit – at least as far as big problems popping up are concerned. We've still got quite a bit keeping up with it and at the same time putting in new facilities, but at least the big circuit restoration projects are not constantly with us—right now, that is. Fortunately, I've got 3 good NCOs handling my major sections so they keep things pretty well in hand. I just pat them on the back and tell them to keep hanging on—for whatever number of days I have left! I'm losing one of my good troops on that 1 July plane—SSgt Hooper in Crypto. He's going to a detachment in upstate New York. He's one of those guys with 10 years in grade and 16 years service who can't seem to get promoted. Not the brightest guy in the world, but he more than makes up for it in effort and determination. I was hoping to see him make it this last cycle. He handled my section out of Security Service. The Lt out there and I were gabbing one day and I talked him into getting his CO to write a letter of commendation on Hooper. I just wrote him an outstanding rating APR and put him in for the AF Commendation Medal. I also wrote a letter nominating him as Squadron NCO of the Quarter and he made it. He has now been submitted as Base NCO of the Quarter. Hope all this together helps him get that stripe next go-round.

We got a new E-8 in on the Operations side of the house—a Sgt Weikhorst, here from Andrews. The Squadron now has three E-9s and four E-8s. The other one in operations (there are also two in Flight Facilities) just made E-9 the last go-round. He's Sgt Thelsthorster and a pretty good type—I call him Sgt Tail Busters 'cause he got paged at the club one lunchtime and I hear that's the way it sounded on the P.A. System.

A few of us are a bit irritated of late. Sgt Green has a chance to hitch a ride to Okinawa with the Marines Friday, returning Sunday, but the Lt wouldn't let him go. It was different when he had a couple trips himself to Saigon, Bangkok and Clark, however. The Commander is a pilot and is always going here and there, but he never takes any of the squadron troops along. He went to Bangkok a couple days last week and took three guys from supply Sq with him, but none of our own people. Same thing when he goes to Clark, Oki or Taipei. Heck, I wouldn't mind a day or so at any of the places, both for the break and the opportunity to pick up a few things. The CO leaves in August, so by then we'll have had a complete turnover of officers since I came here.

How much does Lynn weigh now, or have you had the opportunity to weigh her? I wish I could see the little pumpkin. Just think, by the time I get to see her she'll probably be crawling all over, trying her hand at getting into trouble. Speaking of weight, how are you making it? I've been meaning to stop by the dispensary and weight in but never seem to make it. Oh well, July is shot moth for me again (3, I think) so guess I'll check it then. I imagine I'm still pretty close to what I've always been.

Just had a short interruption as one of my NCOs brought me a traffic ticket he just got for illegal parking. Guilty! He got one a couple weeks ago that we got squashed. They're on one of their ridiculous drives now. Before, they used to do nothing and now they'll give you a ticket for parking if they can reach you between the time you get in the truck and the time the motor is started! All this while the Vietnamese and Marines are zipping by every which way.

Well, my sweet, I've just about run down again. I'd like to just make us some toast and coffee and relax together for a while like we used to. Do you think things will ever be the same again? Somehow I don't think they will be. Things will have to change after such a separation—but I'm still going to want my coffee and toast! It's just that I feel I can appreciate you and what you mean to me so much more now, rather than taking such a large part of it for granted. Oh, I love my sweet girl so very much. All I feel like is not doing anything or saying anything, but only holding you real close to me. I know how hard these past months, and the next four, have been and will be for you honeybunch, and I love you all the more for it. I know that's not too much help in getting a diaper changed, correcting the kids, cleaning the house, etc., but it's still there and increasingly will be. It's really a bit frustrating for me to try to tell you this in a letter. It seems so inadequate. Even when I'm back home, I probably won't be able to say it just right. But I know that if you can read into my just holding you close as I mentioned, it will all be there for you to see.

Even though there's nothing else to write about, I don't feel like closing this letter. In some small way, while I'm writing to you, it makes me feel a little bit closer to you. How wonderful it would be to reach out and touch you. I had to stop here and thing how it must have been for the troops during the Second World War, when they went for 3 and 4 years, not knowing when or if they'd return. Or those people who choose to go somewhere unaccompanied, so they'll do 18 months instead of taking their families there for 3 years. There just has to be something missing in their lives. Don Leta, I'm so happy with you and grateful that we were brought together. I'm especially grateful that you put up with so many of my silly actions before we were married. Imagine getting looped on our first date! And not knowing your name until I don't remember when! I will say you were a glutton for punishment. You know, I don't remember exactly when I first realized that I love you. All I know is that the more I was with you, the more I wanted to be with you. There have been so many attempts to define love, that it would be presumptuous of me to add my definition. The simplest way for me to say it is that I wanted my life to be yours, and your life to be mine. That's how I feel it is now—our lives are one—and that's how I hope it will always be. Thank you so much for everything, my darling, especially for being mine.

Your Leo

26 Jun 66

Hi Pal,

I got a letter from mommy yesterday and she told me that you wanted me to write you another letter and to send you a funny picture. Well, I don't know how to make funny pictures, only nice good looking pictures, so this time I'll send you one of my friend Sgt Ima Picklepuss.

You take care of yourself now. Be a good boy and help around the house in taking good care of Paul and Lynn. I'll be seeing you again pretty soon.

Hugs & kisses,
Daddy

Ridiculous!

Military life is famous for the nonsense it imposes. Rules are rules. The rule on parking has no exception for war zones. Is there a rule against common sense?

Notice a sudden up-tick in Leo's scorn. The word "ridiculous" will now appear frequently. Previously monthly, but now weekly, he finds a ridiculous practice to skewer.

27 Jun 66

My Dearest Don Leta,

It's much more comfortable now that I've taken a shower and come back to the shop. It's 9:15 P.M. now and I was going to hit the sack but had to come back to write my girl since I got another letter from her today.

We got wrapped up moving the IBM equipment into the old comm. center and it was just after 8 P.M. before we finished. The last piece was the worse – 3,600 lbs of it. The others were 234, 800, and 1,140 lbs. Big John gave us a hand and it took 8 of us to uncrate and move that last piece in. Civil Engineer personnel had come down with their jackhammers and put a hole in the wall for us to get it in. Couldn't get it in otherwise due to the angles of the walls and this unit being about 7 feet long.

You were right. If I mentioned in one of my letters that you were a day ahead of us, I meant it the other way around. You're a day behind. Today is the 27th here and 26th at home.

Poor Steph. I hope she got to camp out and came thru it all right. Imagine she'll really find this bedwetting a handicap as she wants to spend more nights out. I'd like to see what Linda's father looks like. Does he wear stick collar, bowler hat and vest? Sounds to me like he's living in the past somewhere if he doesn't even let his daughter go swimming or camping with a bunch of girl scouts.

I was going around showing everybody a copy of orders on my replacement today. We received orders on a MSgt Lester Williams, 30670, coming here in August. He's stationed at Barksdale, so he's another "SAC trained killer"! All his orders show is an EDCSA of 16 August, so he must awaiting port call. We should get a copy of the amendment to his orders showing his shipping date, or at least his reporting date to Hamilton. Think I'll drop him a few clues tonight or tomorrow so he won't come here cold. His leave address is in Bossier City, La., but I notice he's originally from California, since his serial number starts with 19. Now, if he ever gets here and we're adequately manned, perhaps I can finagle my way out of here a couple weeks earlier. I'm not packing my bags yet, though!

Lt Carol caught a plane out of here at 1500 today. He was at Base Operations at 10 A.M. and they said they had a plane going to Okinawa and he could catch the C-141 there for the states so he check out right quick like. I hated to see him go (yeah!). He didn't even say good-bye to anyone! Real pleasant sort. Now if we can get rid of a few more of these old tiers who feel that they're the only ones making this place run, we'll all be better off. In another 30 days or so they'll all be gone.

Well, honeybunch, that about does it for tonight. Not much else is new. Everything remains pretty quiet, hostility-wise, and steady, work-wise. Each day runs its course. Since today passed also, I can now cross it off and look forward to being with my sweet wife and wonderful family in a maximum of 119 days. Good night, my love, Sweet dreams.

Your Leo

28 Jun 66

Hi Sweet One,

This won't be too much of a letter tonight, as there's nothing new from this end. I did start the day off with a bang, however. I woke up, slowly opened my big limpid brown eyes, looked at the clock – and noticed it was almost nine! Grenier and Big John have been riding me all day about it.

It's almost 11 P.M. now and I just finished writing a letter to that Sgt Williams at Barksdale. Thought I would bring him a few words of wisdom on what he should bring and what to expect when get go here. For instance, the thing for off duty wear now is shorts. The BX got some in and quite a few people wear them after duty hours. Just the thing in this climate, except for mosquitoes.

It's sure nice to be able to go around now saying I'm down as low as 118 days. Next goal—88, followed by assignment and then the ultimate— orders and departure. Nobody seems to know for sure around here when assignments for October stateside will be in. I've heard everything from mid-July to late August. It's really immaterial. There's nothing I can do anyhow, but it's just the idea of getting the word and ending the suspense.

Grenier was telling me today that the business about training of 30690's was dealing with imbalance skills—those are the ones, like 306's, who are in greater demand overseas than stateside. What they want to do is train them additionally in something else in addition to crypto. That way, they'd use them overseas in crypto and back in the states in either crypto or this additional skill. Those open to 30690's are airborne radio and closed circuit television. I'm not too worried about it, however. I've still got the additional AFSC in administration that I can be used in, plus which I'm getting too short to train.

That about does it for this time, honeybunch. Not much, but I did want to drop a note by anyway. I did want to say something I'm been holding back all these years – I love you deeply and miss you loads!

Your Leo

29 Jun 66

My Dearest,

This being Wednesday, I wanted to go ahead and write even though there's not much new to relate. However, since this won't go out until Thursday's mail, it'll probably reach you Saturday and you'll at least have a letter for over the weekend and know for a couple more days at least that I haven't as yet defect to the VC!

Had a fairly busy day today, even working up a bit of a sweat. We were out all over the place trying to locate a last modem for our AUTODIN Center. Down at the far south end of the field they've got an open storage area where they've just thrown a bunch of stuff (box upon box) and where we've got some big cable reels and GEEIA material. Never did find the modem, but you should see the stuff going to waste out there—imagine toilet paper, envelopes, office supplies, electrical equipment, etc., just stacked in cardboard boxes and being ruined in the heavy rains and sun. Realistically, it's not too uncommon in a situation like this, I guess, since there's always so much stuff moving about all the time. They're starting to square things away now. Right across from us is a big field. The Vietnamese would not allow the Air Force to build or store anything on it—it's their soccer field. I have yet to see anyone playing soccer there. Consequently, stuff was stored all along the street, so that only a narrow traffic lane was available.

No mail yesterday or today. As a matter of fact, very little came in for anyone. I did get a letter out last night to Sgt Williams, my replacement—I hope, from Barksdale.

That's it for now, sweet girl. I think you're just luscious and I love you loads and loads.

<u>Your</u> Leo

30 Jun 66

My Darling,

How wonderful today to get a nice long letter from my favorite wife. It had been a couple days since I received any mail, but this really made up for it. I'm sorry you hadn't gotten more yourself. This letter was written Saturday and you mentioned not getting a letter since Wednesday. It must be the mail delivery itself since I know I haven't skipped more than one day at a time for some time now. If it doesn't straighten up in the next 3 ½ months or so, I think we'll just have to stop writing each other

Everybody got paid but your old daddy today. I got a call from Sgt Duckworth early this morning saying, "Sarge, you're not gong to be very happy with me today." Duckworth was my Senior Controller when I was running SMC. In getting paid, his name was after mine on the payroll. He signed in my block rather than his. Of course, afterwards he signed in the right place and drew his own pay. Now I must wait until the payroll is turned in, which won't be until Monday since they've got to go up north and out to the mountain to pay our troops. Old Duckworth felt so bad too, I had to keep telling him not to worry about it, that it would only delay my pay 4-5 days and that no harm was done. Anyhow, he only has a short time left here and said he wasn't sending money orders as usual this month, so he insisted I take $300 of his money so I could go ahead and get it off to you. I was kidding him that now they would probably extend him through a couple paydays just to make sure that my pay wasn't fouled up! Of course, this incident was all that was needed by many of the troops – SSgt Duckworth goofed up so SMSgt Dubois couldn't get paid! The poor guy has been taking a ribbing all day.

Big John just came in before I started this letter and got me up. This has been a real hot, humid day, and by the time it ended I was pooped. I came back to the shop to finish some paperwork and to write you about 6 P.M. Anyhow, it's going on 10 P.M. now and there I was, lights out and asleep on the desk! Now I probably won't get to bed until all hours—but I sure do feel better. John said Grenier laid down after supper—oops, he just walked in! John himself went back inside the plant and took a snooze. What a bunch of warriors!

You mentioned talking with Homer Van Zandt and that he had been stationed at Dong Ha. That's one of the places we have up north that I've mentioned to you a few times. It's about 11 miles this side of the border (41 miles from Da Nang). There's some heavy fighting going on in that general area now. Somebody mentioned that we got a call from our troops that right now they were on double red alert. That's just one stop away from abandoning site. I imagine things will pick up in tempo a bit now that they've decided to hit places like oil storage areas at Hanoi and Haiphong. I see where they no sooner struck there than we started hearing from all the righteous people of the world—who have been sitting on their hands all this time.

I was glad to hear that the girls had such a good time at camp, but it sure did sound like a messy affair, but then they don't have the best area in the world out there for outdoor living. I'm particularly glad that Stephanie got by without embarrassment from her wetting and that Karen found herself a friend. The way Karen was relying on Linda for companionship would seem to indicate that she's not too hip on going out on her own to make new friends. It's too bad about

Jacksboro Officer on TV Interview

Capt. H. R. Van Zandt of Jacksboro was interviewed on a taped TV program shown over NBC on the Today program, noon news, and Huntley-Brinkley report Wednesday. The interview was on channel 3 and 5 in this area.

Capt. Van Zandt, a member of the Military Intelligence Detachment attached to the 173d Airborne Brigade, told of interviewing Viet Cong prisoners while the film showed movies of the prisoners. Information of value is obtained from only one of ten prisoners, he reported.

Capt. Van Zandt has been serving in the U.S. Army since graduation from Sam Houston State. Initially he was commissioned in the Artillery. He has been in Viet Nam since July and returned from a three year tour of duty in Germany in 1964.

He is a son of Mr. and Mrs. R. L. Henderson.

Mrs. Van Zandt and their two children, Kenneth, 7, and Cynthia, 3, are living in Mineral Wells while their husband and father is overseas. Mrs. Van Zandt is the former Marilyn Logan, daughter of Mrs. Leola Logan of Jacksboro.

Courtesy, Jacksboro Gazette-News.

the way Linda's father acts in so many of these things. Over the long run Linda will miss out on quite a few experiences.

It sounds encouraging that Karen seems a bit better as far as getting into tantrums is concerned. A certain amount of fussiness and sulking I know we'll keep getting from all of them (can't understand it, I've always had such sweet disposition!), but at least maybe you won't have put up with the prolonged outbursts. I hope that the medication is what was causing it, and nothing more serious.

Happily, June is now shot and I can start complaining to myself about how long it is until the end of July since tomorrow is only the 1st. Then, I hope by the end of the month I can say it went by pretty fast.

That's it for now, sweet girl. We're getting there, honeybunch, and I can hardly wait to hold you again, I love you so very much.

<u>Your</u> Leo

1 Jul 66

Hi Honeybunch,

There won't be an awful lot to tell you again in this letter, but there's one thing I did want to ask you. Does this month seem to be dragging by to you??

No letter from my sweet one today, though I admit I didn't expect one after yesterday's long missive. There was a letter from Mother, however. Poor Mother, I can almost tell so often what she's going to say—"we want you to come home, even though we know it'll only be for a short time, and you will probably be going so far" and "we will try to make the best of it." She was telling me about Paul bending over for daddy to spank. That must make a cute picture. Reading her letter it really sounds like she wouldn't mind quite so much our leaving there if it wasn't that we were going to take her little "sugar doll" Lynn with us. She must really be taken with her.

Green and I are planning on going to Kai Son Sunday, leaving at 6:30 AM and returning at 6:30 PM. We'll be going by Marine Chopper. It's a Special Forces camp west of Dong Ha. We've got a beacon going up there.

A new list of flight reservations went up on the board today – some 30 or so leaving this month. With another 15-20 in August, that will just about take care of the bulk of those until the next big batch in October. Very few arrived here or will be deporting in September. The magic number is now 115. I still keep counting the full term, but secretly keep hoping that my manning is up to snuff by then so that maybe I can sneak off "like a thief in the night" a bit early. Really, I don't know why. At least here there are no dishes to do – or diapers to change!

I snuck off to the BX today and got a few goodies – fruit cocktail, peaches, crackers, pork and beans and potted meat. Now I can feast when I like it! Noticed they had gotten some new items in that they haven't had before, for instance, small and large carved chests, small round carved-top tables with glass tops over the carving, oriental carvings, jewelry broaches, step tables, chests of drawers, even carved and inlaid Chinese screens (only $210 for the one on display). Anyhow, I just looked at them, and went on with my potted meat!

The big rumor today was that the town was going back on limits. I can't see it myself but all the big lovers, those in the know, said they knew of sure signs. All the bars supposedly opened up again last night. That would be about right – they'd (the bars) be the first ones to know. Anyhow, if the town does go back on limits this weekend, then I'm out $0.60. I bet Sgt Rodrigues an ice cream a day, Monday thru next Saturday, that it wouldn't go on limits. They got an ice cream machine and opened an "ice cream parlor" out of an annex to the Airmen's Club. Thriving business for which I'd like the concession. Tastes like cold condensed milk, but it's something different.

Will cut for now, my sweet. It's getting pretty late and I want to get my shower in yet. Take good care of yourself for us, my love. I miss you so,

<u>Your</u> Leo

2 Jul 66

My Dearest,

It's getting quite late but I did want to get a letter off to you tonight, especially after having heard from you today. I don't know, maybe I should plead fatigue or no news or some other such excuse and just not write tonight. Yet, I've been thinking so very, very much of you tonight – even more so than ever – and I've just got to write. As little as it is, at least when I'm writing to you it makes me feel a little closer. There's so much I want to say to you Don Leta, and yet there are so many words that just won't do the job. About all I can do is repeat, time after time, that I love you with all my heart and miss you more than I can ever say. You're my whole life darling, and if it wasn't for the children you've brought forth, it just wouldn't matter when I returned if you were not there. Oh, how wonderful it would be to just be able to hold you close right now. Though there's only 114 more days until we're together, the one thing which does bother me is not so much anything happening to me, but the fear that we may not see each other until beyond that time. I guess that's kind of selfish, thinking of what I want rather then worrying about all of you, but that's the way I feel right now. Of course I'm concerned about you and the children, and always will be, but the thought that keeps returning is that concerning me and my wonderful wife. My God, Don Leta, I never knew it would get this bad. How did I ever come to depend on you so much? Maybe I should even use discretion and not say anything since it would probably reveal a weakness, but I think part of the reason that I even logged out any plans for an R&R was because of the way I felt. I need you so—and I don't want anyone but you. I guess in a way I wouldn't trust myself away somewhere. I've been thinking, or dreaming, so much again these past few days. I'm afraid that, instead of slacking off in my "old age", I'm desiring you all the more. I long for the softness of your sweet breasts and the warmth of your embracing thighs. You probably think I'm awful mentioning such delicate subjects in a letter, and perhaps you're right. But then, I've never felt quite this way before. And it's not just any female body, because, even with the town off limits, there are ways of satisfying that craving. But you, to me, are something special, and you always will be. I cannot think of another woman regardless of her enticements, as ever moving me as you do. That's because, besides flesh and bones, you're contentment, warmth, satisfaction, security, love, companionship, enjoyment and happiness, all contained in your daily life. I love you so much, my Don Leta.

I started and wrote this letter in a vein I had not originally intended, so I'll not switch now and move to other things. Rather, I'll write tomorrow in reply to your last letter. I expect we'll be pretty busy tomorrow, but someway or other I'll get something off to you. A bit of activity has been generated here as a result of recent bombings up north.

Good night, my love. I'd like to have something to remind me of our closeness, but I guess it'll have to be memories since I brought nothing else with me. Please be kind, my dearest, and forgive me my small moment of weakness. It's just that I miss you and love you so. Could you possibly think of something intimate, known only to us that you could send to remind me of you? I would dearly love to have such remembrance, though I have no suggestions right now as to what it might be. Just so it's something I can say is from "my Don Leta".

Your Leo

3 Jul 66

My Beloved,

It seems so often now that I start my letters by saying it's going to be a short one, but I'm afraid I'll have to do it again tonight. It's 9:30 now and I'm about dead after finally quitting at 8 P.M. That shower sure felt good, but now I have a terrific headache. I had a crew of 6 people and a truck and we handled PSP (pierced steel planking), 2x10 lumber and sand bags. Afterwards, we were tearing down the old bunkers and putting up new ones. It's a big crash project right now, particularly as a result of our recent bombing raids at Hanoi and

Haiphong. Down go all the mortar shelters and in their stead we're putting up bomb shelters. The project will probably be going on all week.

Because of this latest development, I had to cancel out my trip to Kai Son. Green and Grenier went up, however, and said they were thankful that they were here at Da Nang. Kai Son is manned by about 38 Americans and a bunch of Montagnard Tribesmen. It sits on a plateau between the mountains, about 4 miles from the Laotian border. It is completely surrounded by jungle and elephant grass. Everything is underground, and they move about the place in trenches about six feet deep. Even the planes (small observation types) are brought underground at night.

Well, they burst my balloon over the weekend also. There was a blurb in the Daily Bulletin about there being no more rollbacks (leaving early) except for hardship or humanitarian reasons and that they'd have to be approved by the Base Commander. So guess I'll be here for the next 113 days. At least they could have let me hope a little while longer.

I did have one of my troops go on emergency leave today. His little boy had to undergo surgery and supposedly it was nothing major, but the Red Cross report said his wife was all shook up and the doctor recommended he come home on emergency leave. I guess that's the way it is when you have two kids. I guess this is a legitimate case, but I'll tell you there's no doubt about some of them popping up here which are no more than mommy wanting daddy home. I actually feel sorry for some of these guys, because they shortly become wrecks themselves, to the point where they're of little use to anybody. Of course, some of them are not beyond trying every which way to finagle their way out either. There's always a certain number of "operators" and "string pullers". They ought to send all that type to places like Kai Son.

Wonderful wife, this will be it for tonight. If an attack comes, I hope it's tonight 'cause I know I'll sleep right through it! I love you, my sweet, with all my heart.

<u>Your</u> Leo

5 Jul 66

My Darling,

It's just as well there was no mail yesterday, as I couldn't have done much in the line of answering. There was one today, however, and now that I've had my beauty sleep, maybe I can write a bit and maintain some degree of logic in my writings.

After getting off today at 5 o'clock, I went right to the sack. It's quarter to 10 now and I feel much better – still sore, but at least I can keep my eyes open. After putting in a full day outdoors Sunday, I slept like a log that night. Then, yesterday I worked in the shop until 4:30, ate chow, and then went out to the sand pit with a crew of 14 to fill sandbags. We quit at about 9 o'clock. This morning they finished the shelter. You can imagine how much there was to it when an average of 40 people worked on it for a total of 35 hours. It's nothing like the little bunkers we've been using. This one is about 9 feet high and the ceiling (roof) is two feet thick. The walls, including a center bracing wall are four feet thick, and the shelter will accommodate 300 people. It took around 6,000 sandbags, each weighing 40-50 lbs, a complete covering of pierced steel planking. This one should at least last until 26 October!

Things are getting a bit tight around here right now, manning wise. The inputs are just not keeping up with the outputs. They're kind of slow coming in – I guess mostly due to transportation delays. Ground radio is short-handed and I'm now hurting for crypto people. Besides losing people and replacements being slow in coming in, new programs are being added all the time. Right now I had to put them all on 12 hour shifts with no day off until at least 31 August. Besides that Master due in next month, I have two 5-levels due in this month.

I see the poor farmers are still living from hand-to-mouth. I guess that's why they'll send Tamara to Europe—one less mouth to feed. Hoppy engaged!! Good gosh, he can't even see over the dashboard.

Well now, thanks for all those Christmas and Father's day presents you bought me. The way you've had to keep going, it'll probably be that we'll both be hearing that record album together for the first time.

Hope there's not too much wrong with Karen's teeth, but if there is I guess it's better we see about it now than let it drag on and get worse. It is funny that the dentist in Rapid City had never suggested anything in that area. If you talk to the doctor at Wolters about it, maybe it would even be possible that they might be able to check her in their dental clinic. I've heard tales of dental bills, and I guess we'll be getting first hand knowledge at this rate. What will the four extractions cost for the other girls—about $8 each? I think you had mentioned it before, but I don't remember. It's a good thing I'm getting a little extra money here while these bills are coming up.

I sure hope that assignments come in latter part of this month. I'm kind of anxious to find out where we'll be setting down for the next year and a half or so. It's now 111 and counting—slowly. Just thought, that's only three more paydays. It's going, my sweet, and before too long it'll be behind us. We'll still have our problems, for sure, but at least we'll be together to face them. And maybe once again you'll have a bit of time to relax—if I let you. I love you so much, my honeybunch.

<u>Your</u> Leo

6 Jul 66

My Dearest,

The opportunities seem to get more and more frequent where I have the chance to give thanks for what I have. The comparison was made once again today as I received a letter from my wonderful wife and some real nice pictures of you and the kids. I miss you all so much. On the other side of the coin, I was trying to help one of my NCOs who has more family problems, and I ended getting pretty well disgusted with things.

I may have mentioned a while back that this guy had approached me in the club one night, crying and saying he had to talk to somebody. Anyhow, he had pretty well taken to drink at that time but has since straightened up. Anyhow, on 28 June he got a message through the Red Cross saying his wife had an automobile accident on 25 June and was in the hospital – and that his sister-in-law would advise him of the details. He never did hear from the sister-in-law, but today he got a letter from his wife. Most of her injuries where around the head and face and she had quite a few stitches taken. The doctor didn't know yet whether she'd need plastic surgery. They have two kids. She was hit broadside while on her way to work, about five miles from home – some other G.I.'s wife, the husband being in Europe. The car was completely demolished and she doesn't even know if the other car had insurance. It must have had, though, since it had a base sticker. Well, this guy has a DEROS of 3 August, so he only has a maximum of 27 days to go. He's been probably the best teletype man we've had and it's not a question of an emergency leave, but of just releasing him a bit early. I've gone to everybody and his uncle and now I'm waiting to see what happens tomorrow – whether they say he can go or not. After hearing of another case today, if they don't let him go, I'll be in to see the Old Man. This other NCO, also one of our better workers, got a letter from his wife. She left home and left the kids with in-laws. He's only got 29 days to go and these big-hearted souls were going to let him go seven whole days early. I think I'd of just thrown the 7 days in their face and stayed the extra week – and let my congressman handle the repercussions. This right on top of both our illustrious Chief of Maintenance and Operations Officer bugging it out early. I'm just about

Kneeling on the floor, Lanis (left) and Stephanie. On the chair, Karen, Paul, Don Leta, baby Lynn and Bryan

fed up with this business.

Well, to more pleasant subjects. I really enjoyed the pictures. You look especially good in one where you're sitting with the kids. It looks like your face is fuller. It might just be that you are so full of smooches that haven't been delivered yet!

Mary was real fortunate about Don's accident. Boy, I don't know, how can they let the kids ride on the hood like that? I hope that cures that foolishness. It wouldn't have taken very much for that to have been a quite serious matter. It also would have been a bit difficult to explain what happened to the authorities.

While I think of it, the enclosed picture was taken outside the shop here by one of the troops. He just bought himself one of those new small Polaroid cameras ($23) and was eager to use up his first roll of film.

Most of the heavy work has been done around here for a while, so today I just rested my weary bones. We sure had a sore bunch of troops. Even the Major had been tamping sandbags.

The FSgt left this morning, two more leave tomorrow and 6 more this weekend. They're moving out – but I'm still waiting for them to come in. Got a message today saying I've got 4 crypto types coming in this month. Those I'm eagerly awaiting.

This is it for now, my love. I miss you as ever, but knowing it's all going by and we'll soon be together keeps things in perspective. Be sweet, my wonderful wife.

<u>Your</u> Leo

8 Jul 66

My Darling,

This has been mostly a paperwork day, sprinkled with meetings. Besides Commander's Call this afternoon, I had one meeting with my troops this morning and two staff-type meetings this afternoon. I swear, this place is getting more and more like stateside with the requirements they're coming out with and with their reports and other paperwork. I'm waiting for them to start standby inspections & parades next!

That troop I told you about a couple letters ago (or was it yesterday??) is going to be allowed to take off though his normal DEROS is in August. He's processing and running his clearance now. I had a good talk with him when this came up about not hitting the bottle again like he did the last time he had troubles and he seems to be OK, so I guess he'll get out of here in one piece.

I guess we've got us "one of those" base commanders now. The drive is on to get things cleaned up, etc. Grass has to be cut and there's one lawnmower on the whole base, so "idiot sticks," shears and scissors are getting a workout. Another thing put out today was that AF people will have to wear AF clothing. Let me tell you that's a blow to many of them. You've never seen such a mixture of uniforms in your life. Fatigue caps or unit baseball caps only can be worn with fatigues – no more camouflaged hats, Aussie style "go-to-hell" hats, Marine fatigue hats, etc. Also out are camouflaged fatigues, Army baggy fatigues, Vietnamese rank insignia, and I don't know what else you see around here. That I'm glad to see because it was really getting out of hand. You couldn't hardly tell what some people were.

It hasn't been too bad hereabouts lately, except during the heat of midday. As a matter of fact, a couple nights I woke up and put a sheet over me. It's still plenty hot enough, but the humidity must have dropped a bit. The nights haven't been too bad, and everything there seems to be fairly calm also. No more than normal on the flares or outgoing mail.

We've still got people goofing up and then spoiling things for the rest of the troops. Once people have their flights out scheduled, and if they're released by the Squadron, they've been allowing some to grab another plane out, as long as the original booking is cancelled 7 days in advance. Well, we had one hitch to Japan without canceling his original reservation. When he got there, he found he couldn't get a hop out to the states, so he grabbed another plane back to Tan Son Nhut. He had missed his original booking so now they put him in leave status and it'll be a while before he gets out—all the time using up that leave. When old Leo leaves it'll be on a scheduled flight. To heck with this business of trying your luck in getting lifts half way round the world. Also, going that way it's often island hopping and you can take 5 or 6 days getting stateside.

There was no mail today, sweet girl, and there's not much more to relate. I've been looking at all the pictures again and I don't know how I could miss you all any more than I do. If only time wasn't passing so slowly. July will be a third over this weekend, so that's something. Before long we'll be in the magic month of August – birthday and anniversary time – and that much closer to October. I try so much to picture you near me, my love, but a strong imagination is just not enough. Good night, my darling.

Your Leo

10 Jul 66

My Dearest,

What a nice welcome back gift today – two letters from my favorite wife and a box of goodies. Seventeen people had banana bread and apple cake this morning. That took care of two breads and four pieces of apple cake. One little problem. Now I can't eat lunch! When I saw in your letter where Stephanie and Lanis had baked this, I told the others and they were amazed. A couple of the young troops especially kidded about how old my daughters were and whether they were attached.

Also had a letter from Mom here. She said she was going to babysit at Chippy's for a couple weeks while he worked days. That way Florence would be able to take off later this month when Chip has his two week vacation.

I received the rest of the pictures you sent and, let me tell you, though I know it can't be so, the more I look at all these pictures, the more I want to be with you and the children again. I miss you all so much.

Leo's mother, Blanche Dubois

To answer a couple questions: I know Sgt Williams is my replacement because we're authorized only one MSgt, AFSC 30670, which I'm now filling even though I'm now surplus since I'm SMS, AFSC 30690. I'm sure he'll be on leave before coming here, and his orders will have to be amended, like mine were, to indicate a reporting date. His EDCSA (estimated date carried strength accountable) is the date his old outfit drops him from their roles and the new outfit picks him up. It's strictly an accounting date, and he could be anywhere on that date. Actually, he could arrive here any time in July, August, or September. I wrote to him, so I may get a letter in return. Otherwise, we should be getting a copy of the amendment showing his reporting date.

I'm sure I had mentioned "Big John" Currier in my letter as having been at the academy with me. He's got five kids and his wife is German. They're presently staying in Rochester, N.H. He was stationed at Malmstrom before coming here—in the same field as Rossley—cable.

Had another surprise the other day when SSgt John Zimmerman walked into the shop. He was one of my data troops at EAFB. Had gone from there to Offutt. They pulled him back into his old field of radio relay and he's assigned to the 1st MOB out of Clark. The last four month's he was at Bien Hoa. He came through here on his way to Phu Bai, near Hue, to set up a new track shot. He's now working out of the team we have here and was getting briefed. He'll be up there about 5 months. Goes back home in January. For the first couple minutes I was calling him George, before I realized that was the wrong name.

Do you remember if it was Elmendorf that George Z was going to? Grenier was asking me and I couldn't remember if it was there or Fairbanks. I know those two will get along since Grenier is a bug on going into the mountains hunting.

This is a pretty quiet Sunday afternoon, so hope to get a couple more letters written.

Just got another call bringing more troubles. I'm afraid after this go-round there'll be a few people hereabouts who are not going to like ole Leo. I had mentioned to you before about his one man we were trying to get out early. Well, yesterday, new developments. The Group Commander (1964th, Saigon) got wind of some officers cutting out early so now down comes the word that nobody gets out early hereafter. So they told this guy that now he couldn't go, that they had to write a letter to Group, etc. Heck, he's already cleared, closed out his pay records, been debriefed, etc. Halfway through this paragraph I went down to talk to the Commander and Lt Sawyer. They've already got the letter written and it's going down by courier tomorrow. Additionally, the old man is going to call Group tomorrow, letting them know the letter is coming, etc. So he may still get out of here on schedule.

Here I am counting days 'till I get home and you've got a more immediate goal—counting days for the start of school! That's still some 55 days away, so I'll still have around 50 more days by then. With today shot, it's now at 106. Next week I'll be below the hundred mark. I can see why you're anxious though, with the six around both day & night, day in and day out. Heaven's, it'll be bad enough with three little ones once school starts. Maybe you'll at least have a chance to catch your breath during the school day.

Grenier had just come in to write and I mentioned to him that you received 4 letters at once. He said that's what his wife said in her letter. Of course, it was the 4th of July weekend, but it still must have been held up somewhere.

No more news, except that it's hotter than blazes again. It's been nowhere near any hot records we've heard so much about, however. It got cool for a few nights—when I say cool I mean not as hot as usual—but that seems to have passed. Everything else is pretty much the same, including my almost constant thoughts of you. I swear, Don Leta, I can't get you out of my mind—not, I'll admit, that I try very hard. I just want so much to hold you close. I do believe I need you more with each passing day. This positively has been the longest year of my life—probably because it really hasn't been my life, at least not without you. Be sweet, my love, and take care of yourself real good for me.

Your Leo

11 Jul 66

Dear Sweetest Girl What Am,

One of the primary rules of letter writing is not to open up with excuses, but once again I'm going to violate that rule. This will be another shorty. Just isn't that much going on which leaves me only one interesting subject, and you know how I hate to talk about myself!

I was writing to Mom last night when a call came in that another one of my "children" was acting up, so had to log out any more writing after that. Just as I expected, this guy was bombed out, so I had to get after him bright and early this morning. That's always a nice start of a day. This is the NCO who just came back from 3 weeks of psychiatric evaluation. Been back one day. You've got your kids to keep after and I've got mine – 30 year old ones!

Three October assignments came in today. They were marked "Special Category Assignments," whatever that is. Two of the guys are in operations and one, MSgt Demaree, is maintenance. He got his 1st choice of L.G. Hanscom and was tickled pink. He's a bachelor – looks like the old comic Joe E. Brown. He's been in hot correspondence with this girl in Massachusetts and had asked for Hanscom so he could go back there. The guys have been kidding him that he's dead now – won't have a chance once she gets hold of him. He's a good natured sort – about 35 years old. Made Master when he first got here. I don't have any idea how far behind the rest of the October assignments will be. Of the other two, one got his 1st choice and one his 2nd choice.

Five more troops got on the plane for home – via Saigon – tonight. With that load, that makes just about a clean sweep of the Orderly Room. The new FSgt hasn't arrived yet. He's due around the middle of this month.

You'll notice how I slyly skipped writing on both sides of the sheet. Makes it look like a longer letter. Just another little trick I've picked up after 15 years of marriage!

Good night for now, sweet girl. Love you loads and loads, and I'll be storing it up for about another 105 days. Be sweet, my love.

<u>Your</u> Leo

12 Jul 66

My Beloved,

What has been a trying day, running from technical problems to personnel problems and just plain running around was suddenly changed into a bright and fruitful day. I received from my wonderful wife what was undoubtedly the sweetest and nicest letter I've ever read. You're so very, very dear to me, Don Leta. You'll never know how wonderful you made me feel and how so much more I'm thankful that you're my very own sweet girl. There's so much that I'm thankful for – our years together, and the opportunity of one day soon coming home to you. I'm going to quit tying to say anymore right now because I know I'll just be going around in circles.

They returned one of my troops who had been under psychiatric evaluation with the report that he was suffering from "mild depression." I know where he caught that too – in the bottom of a bottle of gin. As if there wasn't enough to do and put up with around here, they give you someone like this. Then you end up with two problems – the original job that has to be done, and taking care of this guy.

There's really nothing to write about, news-wise, even though this has been a hectic day. It's only 8 P.M. now and already my eyes are getting heavy. Our new Chief of Maintenance, Capt Rayfield, did check in today but I haven't met him yet. Really doesn't matter – nobody could be so bad that I couldn't put up with him for a hundred days or so. 104 to be exact!

I've been wanting to pick up something for each of the kids while I'm here but as time gets shorter I keep wondering if I'll have the opportunity at any time. Even in town it would be quite a project since I really haven't seen where they have much of anything. Saigon I guess is the only place where there would be local goods of any variety.

Well, my sweet, I guess it'll be off to hug my pillow once again. The poor thing has been catching heck since I've been here. Someday, though, I'll be able to give it up for the real thing. Until then I'll have to content myself with reliving our moments together and hope that those times will be back soon. I love you so much, my dearest.

<u>Your</u> Leo

13 Jul 66

Dear darling,

After a 3 ½ hour meeting we finally broke up. Finished work at 5:15 tonight and had to come back for a six o'clock meeting of the Advisory Council. In addition to our regular business we selected an Airman of the Month and an Airman of the Half Year. Since seven airmen had to appear before the council, this ran into some time. Got a couple of these young troops shook for a minute. When they said they were single I'd mention that I had four daughters. For a few seconds they'd be lost for a reply. All but the last one who said, "I know, but I'm not ready yet"! I guess they were exchanging experiences outside!!

No correspondence today – very little mail came in. Some of the guys were talking about Da Nang going back on limits; however, I heard to the contrary tonight. Sgt Mathews, the Comm Center honcho, is also on the NCO council and he said a message had come in saying that Da Nang was not going back on limits – that facilities had been expanded on the base, etc. It specifically mentioned enlargement of the library. It used to sit six people, now it has room for about 16 to sit down. Big deal! The only other recreation we have is the movie (seats 300 – used by about 7000), one softball game a night and a few weights that can be used by 4 or 5 people at the time. Of course, there's also the club if you just want to sit and drink. The NCO Club has 2100 members with no other place to go, so you can imagine how nice and comfortable that can be. If things don't straighten up here in the next 103 days I'm gonna leave!

Looked outside during a coffee break in the middle of tonight's meeting and there were 200-300 Vietnamese Marines in battle dress unloading from trucks in the field across the street. Don't know that there's anything coming off. They may be replacements for those still in town, or they may be coming back from or going up to Hue. We'll see if they're still around in the morning. It was only infantry – didn't see any more armor around and I know those in town have tanks. Of course, they could only be relieving the troops but leaving the armor here.

Though I didn't hear from you today, I still had your last wonderful letter to hold me over, and I read it once again – for the umpteenth time. It was just a couple weeks ago that we started into this month and I mentioned then how long it would be; yet, here we are half way through (by the time you get this). Now it's the second half of the month which seems long, especially when I get to thinking of how much I want to be with you. Gosh, how I miss my honeybunch. You know, not to belittle our days or nights together, probably the best feeling of contentment I've known are those moments just prior to sleep; half the time during which you had probably gone to sleep yourself, and where I could touch you – even if it was only our legs or feet that were in contact. It just felt so nice to have you close by.   I guess that, with everything else, added its little contribution to this difficulty of our being separated.

I'm going to start another tape tomorrow night, so perhaps I can get it out by the first of next week. Larkin gave me a brand new 7 ½ inch reel which I transferred to six smaller reels that Joe Drusbowski, our tech rep, brought up from Saigon. He got hold of a bunch of small empties for Big John & I. I've now got 9 reels of blank tape.

Good night, my love. I'm going to read that letter once more tonight before going to bed, and then dream of the day when I'm once again with my happiness.

<u>Your</u> Leo

14 Jul 66

My Dearest,

Two letters today – one from my sugar girl and another from John Hill. I'll hold on to his letter and send it to you if it happens that we go to Westover. He says there's plenty of housing. He applied before getting there and had a house waiting for him. However, he says they've since discontinued that practice and now you have to be there before you can apply.

Our troops came in from Khe San this evening. All but combat types were evacuated as action picked up. They came in looking like veterans with grenades hanging from their belts, etc., and full field packs on their backs. I guess the Viets who came in here last night were headed up there. They cut out before daybreak this morning. Our boys at Can Tho also got a couple rounds of mortar fire this morning. Everything remains quiet at Da Nang, however.

At five o'clock this evening, the Marine 1st Division Band played for about an hour in the cantonment area. Actually, it wasn't the band but their orchestra section. They were quite good and it was something different. They also had a singer and a couple of musical soloists, plus this young Marine who did the limbo. He was something else. He went under the bar at about 12 inches! I could picture Henderson and me trying it!!

Don't you be worrying about my health, honeybunch. Physically I'm still my same old dumpy self at 170 lbs and feeling pretty good. Mentally, I must modestly admit that I'm in excellent shape. When the time comes where I can't laugh at some of this business, or crack some witticisms to the other troops, I'll know I'm in bad shape. The only time I get a bit morose or melancholy is when I start pitying myself for being so far from you. That's why perhaps some of my letters may have given you the impression that I was down in the dumps. Outside of that, my mood is usually pretty good. On second thought, I think I'm in pretty rough shape – good for only about 102 more days and the only way I'll be brought back to health is to get tender loving care and to be fussed over when I get home! But seriously, don't worry about me, sweetheart. There are a number of people hereabouts who have asked me how the heck I can still laugh at some of these things instead of getting excited. When it's time to get excited I'll be there, but there's no use crying over everything that comes along just to keep in practice. There's really more to it than that – I can't expect my people to stay calm during these periods if I'm running around in circles.

One of our telephone men, Sgt Schneider, got a letter from a friend of his at Randolph telling him that he was being assigned there – his first choice. So, I guess the assignments for October have been made up since that's when Schneider leaves also. I still figure it'll be 3-4 weeks before it filters down to this level.

From what you mention of the tape recorder, it all sounds primarily like a power problem. The 9 volt battery runs the amplifier – for the sound.

The other six penlight batteries operate the turntable. Make sure the copper contacts at each end are firmly against the batteries. Also, when the batteries are changed it's better to change them all. If there are still weak ones in there, they'll put a drain on the others. I had tried that recorder before sending it to make sure it worked. Outside of that, it hasn't been used. See if you can have it repaired somewhere locally. The one I have here still works fine. Guess I mailed you the troubles.

Saw Silvey for just a few minutes at chow tonight. His flight out of Saigon for stateside is scheduled for 31 July. He's been running both the Qui Nhon and Can Tho aerial ports – both Detachments of the 15th Aerial Port Sq. here at Da Nang. His DEROS is 31 July and that's the day he leaves. I kiddingly told him it was too bad he didn't know anyone who could have scheduled him out sooner – since Aerial Port Squadrons are the ones who make the flight bookings.

I just found your secret note on a blank check.

Good night, my dearest. This is always the hardest part of letter writing. There's so much I feel and want to say, and no matter how I jumble it around it comes out – I love you.

Your Leo

15 Jul 66

Hi Honeybunch,

Just a little itty bitty one tonight, as there's just nothing to relate. There were no mail deliveries at all today, so there's nothing from that end.

We got a pretty good rain this evening, lasting about an hour or so just at quitting time. It came down so heavy, though, that you can't go very far without sloshing through it. Waiting for it to stop, I didn't make it to chow until almost seven. It's about nine now and though I've got a bunch of work to do, I think I'll knock off, get my shower and hit the sack.

This one guy I told you about having troubles at home (wife in accident, etc.) caught a hop out of here this morning going back to the states. He caught one of the National Guard planes that come here occasionally. I don't know where this one was based. Now I got a call this morning on one of my crypto people. Seems a Congressional Inquiry came in – something about a possible humanitarian reassignment. Losing another man would hurt about now. There are four due in this month, but that's no guarantee they'll all make it here on time.

Good night, sweet girl. I keep thinking of you and the kids all the time as I slowly mark the days off. By the time this reaches you we'll be into double figures and on that long road toward zero. I love you so.

Your Leo

16 Jul 66

My dearest,

There's nothing like topping off a Saturday night with a 7 o'clock meeting. That's what we had tonight as our new Chief of Maintenance, Captain Rayfield, took over. He just gave us a little pep talk and brought us up to date on the latest happenings at the staff meeting, a procedure Lt. Carol seldom used. His philosophy (Carol's) had been "the less the enlisted men know, the better." Capt Rayfield has been here for 4 or 5 days, and seems to be a half decent sort. Just as long as he behaves for the next 100 days, I'll be satisfied. Capt Kimbrell, who's been here the last couple weeks, will move over to replace CWO Robinson, who leaves in another week. It had looked like we were going to have two maintenance officers, but the operations officer scheduled to come here never made it, so therefore the switch.

We did get four new people in today, but none of them were mine. Three went to ground radio and radio relay, while the other was a TSgt, our new Material Control (supply) NCOIC.

Boy, you really came in with a bunch at a time when going through the latest dental episodes. I hope Lanis & Steph are both feeling up to par. That was too bad about Lanny getting stung on the face at a time like that.

As for Karen – ouch! Dependent on whether any encouragement is offered at the Wolters hospital, I definitely think you should see a specialist. Since this is no little thing, we should get a complete and thorough evaluation. As for which course of action to take from the alternatives you've stated, here again I feel I would give considerable weight to what the doctor said. It's difficult enough just being a girl and going through the gap in the mouth period, much more so I would imagine with Karen in her present condition and changing moods. Since there is that trouble with the mouth taking on a V shape, you might find out if one could be removed and the other, which is coming is straight but doesn't have room, could be left in while pulling the one to the outside of it – like so:

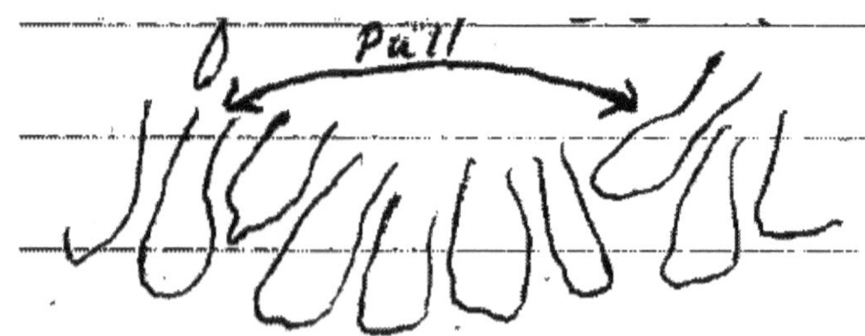

I wonder if that would lessen the V possibility.

It does seem more logical, at this time, to pull the four offending teeth, even though I know the cost of surgical removal will still be quite high. However, it still would be better to get some other opinion (medical) before deciding. Then, if the consensus is that the straightening process would be definitely warranted, that's the route we should go. I know it'll be expensive, but health is one area we won't scrimp on. It'll mean a few more sacrifices but that's something we're fast growing accustomed to. If her teeth look good enough in front and no trouble would result, it may be that the original idea of surgical removal would be best.

Well, I'm glad you broke down about the air cooler/conditioner. There's no telling where we'll be going, so we may even be able to use an evaporative type. If I remember Texas summers, it'll be used! I should think the little ones – Lynn & Paul – especially need it at nap time. Where were you planning on putting it?

I sure do miss the kids when you start telling me some of their actions, especially the boys and Lynn. She must really be getting cuddly about now. I can just see Paul and Bryan with their displays of affection, and Paul going around imitating his big brother, like the car bit on the picnic table.

Gonna cut this shorter than planned, honeybunch. One of our troops went out on a job at quitting time and both he and the truck can't be found. The stupid jerk went out after dark unarmed and alone and if he's not located skosh he'll be carried missing in action. Will write again tomorrow. Love you with all of me.

<u>Your</u> Leo

Gross Malocclusion

A couple of the letters include drawings of teeth. Leo was disposed to take aggressive action in the dental health of the children, even though it put stress on the thin financial resources of the family. "It will mean a few more sacrifices. . ."

In high school, Leo won a nomination to West Point Military Academy from his Rhode Island congressman. But he failed the physical exam on account of his teeth: Gross Malocclusion. He had to look up the definition of this frightening term: Crooked Teeth.

Why did crooked teeth exclude a person from the academy? Leo cooked up this story to explain the military rationale: There was a battle on a jungle island that ended in fierce hand-to-hand combat. The following day, the general toured the battlefield. The bodies of the enemy dead were stacked in two piles. He inspected the first pile. All the casualties bore neat, clean bites. He proudly reflected on the fine work of the officers he led. Then he looked over the second pile of bodies. Shredded. Chewed. Gnawed. The general sneered with contempt, "Enlisted men!"

"100"

17 Jul 66

My Darling,

A day like this could really spoil a guy if it happened very often. I didn't get out of bed this morning until 10:30. After coffee, I came to work and have just been going at a leisurely pace.

Big John and his antenna man caught a chopper for a trip up north this afternoon. They're going at a nice time since the VC hit there last night. It was an isolated attack causing but minor damage, so things are not too bad. I imagine they'll be there for 2 or 3 days anyhow. It was John's man who was missing last night, and they finally found him with some Marine out celebrating the 16th of July – which only comes once a year! Needless to say, some ass-chewing took place. Likewise a couple of radio troops who had their truck stolen a couple nights ago. They had left the keys in the cab. The truck was recovered last night, and both those troops were figuring they'd have to be paying for it. There's been a rash of stolen vehicles lately and the Base CO had just put out the word that if someone was found negligent they'd be liable for the cost. The AP's recovered it on the flightline.

Got a laugh this afternoon. Sgt Shirley in outside plant showed me a clipping sent to him written by Jim Lucas, a nationally syndicated columnist, and which was printed in some Midwestern paper. It tells about one of the many unheralded people fighting this war – an A1C in Comm Sq. This guys a switchboard operator and it tells how he installed switchboards all over the place (an operator installing???), how he works around the clock, etc, etc. It surprised us because we obviously didn't know half the things this guy did! I can just imagine some of the hair-raising war stories which must make the rounds back stateside. Those who have been in some of these actions probably say very little.

Think I'll try to make the movie tonight – Burt Lancaster in "The Train." I haven't been to a show in ages, after going to quite a few when it wasn't nearly as crowded. The George Jessel show is on tonight also, at 7:30, on the soccer field right across the street from here. He's supposed to have an accordionist and a girl singer with him. It's 5:40 now and I just looked out and notice they're setting up the stage on a flatbed trailer. There are already a number of guys getting their choice front row seats. I might go out if it doesn't get too crowded. Don't care to fight the mob – unless it's the one to board the plane for the flight home.

Speaking of flights home, things seem to be in a bit of a mess in that area. They were supposed to start flights out of Da Nang, but now I understand that's been put off until around November – too late to do me any good. Seems the airlines wanted some kind of guarantee that this was a secure base. Anyhow, everyone still has to go to Saigon and fly out of there. We've still got a number of people scheduled to leave between now and the end of the month who still haven't received a flight reservation. So, now they're starting to send people to Saigon seven days prior to DEROS and they've got to hang around there trying to get out on space available. What a rat race. I guess before long they'll be starting to run troopships here again to relieve this flying backlog. I'd sure hate to look forward to a two week or so boat ride home, though I don't figure there's any sweat in my case.

Took a quick run down to the Marine PX yesterday so I could stock up on a few goodies – sardines, crackers, ginger snaps, etc. They'd gotten a few more things in that you used to see but little of, like civilian clothes and oriental pieces – trunks, bars, tables, bronzeware, etc. They also had quite a shipment of luggage – much of it impractical for a GI, naturally. I still want to pick up a B-4 bag to lug my stuff home with instead of that scroungy duffel bag, but I don't want to get it until I'm about ready to leave. No storage space. They also had a bunch of those coffee and end tables, both carved with the glass tops, and the ones made of etched bronze plates. They seem quite reasonable. Those with bronze plates have separate legs that come apart. If I get any of that stuff what I'll probably do is ship it as hold baggage to my next base. Speaking of hold baggage, it all used to be flown to the states and then shipped overland to its destination. Now we have to turn it in to the Naval Support Activity here, and they send it back by ship as hold cargo. Takes quite a bit longer, understandably.

Came back to finish now. Just went to watch Jessel's show, which wasn't bad. The old coot keeps rolling along. He's in his early 70's, I guess. It sure was short, however – only 35 minutes. Guess I won't make it to the movies after all tonight. I've lost the "mood."

These evenings are the worst of all when I can't find something to do. It's not too bad when I've got some work, or we play hearts (which has died down some now), or the few times when I'm just too pooped and hit the sack. Sometimes, though, the night seems to be six days long! I'm just so anxious to be back with you. I miss you so very, very much, my love.

Your Leo

18 Jul 66

My dearest, darling, sweet honeybunch,

Since today is shot, for all intents and purposes, I'm crossing it off the calendar and that leaves us with 98 to go.

No mail today, though I did get your short letter about midnight last night, in which you broke the news to me that you were leaving home – to go to Fort Worth and Kay's for the night. And here I thought my worries were all over! Coming home to you was all that was keeping me from extending my tour so that I could spend more time in this lush, semi-tropical paradise! Oh well, with my next wife, things will be different. I wonder if some little oriental girl would fully appreciate me!!

19 Jul 66

I never did get any further last night. I put my feet up on the desk and fell asleep. When I woke it was 8 P.M. and when Larkin and Buck left they had put out the light and locked the door. So, I went to the barracks, took a shower and went to bed – and then couldn't get to sleep 'till quite late!

Got another sweet letter from my girl at noontime, in which she told of her "wild" shopping spree and parties in the big city. You must have hit town at the right time for all the bargains you latched on to. You've never bought so many dresses for yourself before at one time. Hope you don't expect to get to do this every 15 years, now that you've had the taste of it. Guess I shouldn't complain – you didn't buy one of those $80 bathing suits. In that case, you can go again in 10 years. One thing that did surprise me was that you made no mention of having to take too long in shopping for slacks. I remember the last time – with all the kids – and it took about 16 hours!

I hope you charmed Mr. Big and his wife from General Dynamics. I'll be needing a job some day! I'm really glad you enjoyed yourself – heaven knows you had a little break coming. I know you enjoy going shopping with someone without the kids hanging on, but it was particularly nice that you were able to spend some time at a moonlit lake with all those men – and their wives & kids!

Once again, there's nothing much new here, unless you count work. There's always plenty of that, it seems. Of course, there are problems with my "children," on and off. Had to call one in today and talk to him – this one on letters of indebtedness. I don't know how some of these single kids run up some of the bills they do. Supposedly, this one sends $200 to his sister each month and she's supposed to pay all his bills. If that's true, she must be having a ball 'cause that's the second lien on this guy.

Here's what I call time flying by. From the start of this letter to the end, the time remaining dropped from 98 to 97. If that were true, I'd load up on coffee and keep writing the whole night through. Three months, or two paydays, or 97 days – all still seem like such a long time to wait before I'm able to see my honeybunch again. Gosh how I miss you and want to hold you tight – never to let go. Good night, my darling wife.

Your Leo

21 Jul 66

My Sugarbunch,

I had just taken a shower and was sitting on the edge of the bed at about 1:30 last night (this morning) when "Boom-boom," twice in succession rocked the building. I knew for sure that wasn't outgoing mail and thought "Here comes Charlie!" Nothing else happened, however, so we realized it was one of our hotracks breaking the barrier again. You get kind of used to the noises around here, but every now and then, especially when things are quiet, there comes one along that jars your teeth.

No mail either yesterday or today. I didn't write last night but I didn't want to let two days go by without at least a little "love note," even though there's not too much happening, at least not that's reportable.

One of my boys had him an experience last night. Sgt Taylor, who runs my teletype shop, was awakened about 2 o'clock. Something had bitten him. He reached over and got his flashlight. Turning it on, he saw this big rat in bed with him. He said it was about the size of a cat and he chased it away. The rat had bitten him on the finger and he had a couple pretty good teeth marks. He sleeps out in one of the tents. Sgt Mathews, the Comm Center NCOIC, woke up also but they never caught the rat. Taylor chugged over to the dispensary where they cleaned it out and gave him a shot of tetanus, telling him to come back in the morning to start rabies shots. When he went back, the doctor checked it and said he wouldn't need the shots – that the rats around here are not rabid – and it didn't look like it was infected. Anyhow, he checked again later with the flight surgeon and got the green light. The one thing rats are feared for here is the plague – for which we get shots. As a matter of fact, I got a plague shot and smallpox vaccination just yesterday. It's not the rats themselves that carry the plague, (also known as the black death), but their fleas. That's why they don't want you to kill rats. If they're killed, the fleas will leave the body. They catch them in baited wire traps and afterwards drown them, fleas and all, in DDT. You've never seen rodents like these. They'll just walk right up to you if you're relatively quiet or still. You can sit out any night and watch two or three of them roam around in search of food. The doctor told Taylor he's had guys come in with the end of a finger chewed off. They'd gotten drunk and passed out outside somewhere. Glad I don't have that trouble on the second floor where I'm at.

Had a man come in today on 90 days TDY from Tan Son Nhut. He's to give us some training on a new piece of equipment we're getting. He's a former instructor at the Crypto school at Lackland and has only been in Saigon since early this month. I asked him if he knew Jerry Cromer down there. He's the one that used to be such a clown in school, and who I met at Clark while we were both coming this way. He said he did, and that Cromer had made Master this last go-round. I hadn't known as I'd only seen partial lists of promotions.

September assignments came in the first part of this week. If that's the schedule, then the October assignments should be in around the same time next month. We've only got four people going stateside in September (plus seven going on consecutive overseas tours) so it's a small rotation month. Of the four stateside returnees, three got their 1st base of choice and the other got his 2nd base of choice. Everyone has done so well thus far, I just know I'll get Podunk Air Force Patch in the state of Confusion!

Big John has been up at Hue four days now and what he figured was a two day job increasing the height of antennas. Talked to him last night and all he could do was cuss and fuss about the trouble he was having. Says he should have retired! Grenier went up this morning for some QC inspection work at Hue, Phu Bai and Dong Ha, so don't expect to see him until Sunday or Monday. I'm just as glad I don't have too much gear that way.

It seems that when everything goes smooth, you find yourself with time on your hands. But when something goes bad, it really goes, and before you can get it squared away there are seventy or eighty other problems. We're going through another of those cycles now. HAS ANYBODY SEEN MY REPLACEMENT!!

Speaking of replacements, there was a load and a half came in either overnight or early this morning. I went on coffee break at about 9:15 this A.M. and saw 30-40 brand new ones in front of the base theater, waiting for the incoming briefing. Then, as I turned the corner, here comes about 50 more – coming from personnel & headed for the theater. The Squadron got 5 or 6 out of that bunch. We also got us a nice new Lt. – Nelsen by name – who will be our Maintenance Control Officer. I also understand there's a new Lt. in to replace our Personnel Officer. Maj Perry's replacement should be in before too long, as he rotates in August. He got here the day before I did but has an adjusted tour since they sent him here from Korea.

That about wraps it up for now, my delicious mommy-bunch. Miss you loads and loads, and I'll be saving up about another 95 days worth of loving for you. Be sweet, my dearest.

Your Leo

22 Jul 66

My dearest Don Leta,

A hectic and somewhat discouraging day was brightened somewhat by another sweet letter from you. I was pooped by quitting time and went right to the barracks, took a shower and stretched out on the sack "for just a minute." Finally got up at nine o'clock and made it to chow before the serving line closed down. It's 10 P.M. now and we're having a pretty good rain. I'll probably be here until 1 or 2 o'clock since there are some APRs[26] I've got to go over and get on their way. I've been tasked to monitor all maintenance APRs and with as many people as we have coming and going right now there's quite a backlog.

There's been a series of technical and planning problems giving us a headache right now. When it gets like this there's not much breathing space. Sgt Mathews from the other Comm Center was here a while ago and he's got nothing but problems. All his people are on steady 12 hours a day, 7 days a week. Replacements are slow coming in. I'm hurting here also. While losing people on schedule, replacements come in two or three months behind schedule. Puts quite a bind on those that are here. Right now, none of my crypto people get a day off, plus which a good part of the time when they're not working they're on standby and get called in.

I wondered about the Bishops since we hadn't heard any more from them. It's funny that you had a letter from Marie the day after you called. If Bob's category H holds out, I imagine he can expect an overseas assignment as soon as it expires. Larkin and Grenier were both in that 9-level school at Keesler, even though in different classes a few weeks apart, and they're always running back and forth to each other when they hear of another of their classmates coming to Vietnam.

Yes, that's Bob Hackley coming to Vietnam, so he must have made tech. He's not an AP though; if you remember, he retrained into a Command Post Controller. The other one you mentioned, Richard O. Baldwin, is not the one I know. That was Jerry Baldwin and he either has or is just about to retire. He was planning on retiring somewhere around Fort Worth. The last couple weeks the AF Times has been getting here much earlier. We had the July 20 issue here on the 21st, yesterday. I noticed another Ellsworth (821st Comm) type on the list – TSgt Vance – for assignment to Greece. Do you remember him – a big roly-poly type? He'd been there as a Comm Center operator for six or seven months. For a while he was acting FSgt while we were without.

You're mentioning that the church is crowded now that it's fixed up and new pews are in made me think of the folks in Orlando trying all the different churches until they found a comfortable one.

There's one good by-product of all this activity – you're too busy to think of time. You can see why any isolated or remote area is fertile rumor country. You can make people believe anything they <u>want</u> to hear, so they'll grasp at anything they're wishing for. This afternoon I told three guys next door in Radio Relay that the October stateside assignments had just come in and that I was going to Westover. They all wanted to believe me, and yet they had these silly grins on their face because they know I tell some stories with a straight face. Well, I came into my office and sat down. I no sooner got to

---

[26] APR Annual Performance Review

work when Sgt Shirley, who's telephone exchange is at the other end of the building, called me on the phone and said, "I hear the October assignments are in. Is that right?" I've been conditioned to this before and I don't believe a thing I can't see with my own eyes!

We shipped a couple people off to the hospital at Cam Ranh Bay today. Sgt Demaree, who I told you had his October assignment to Hanscom, had broken a bone in his foot about four months ago. They put a cast on, and he was on crutches for some time afterwards. It still bothered him a couple weeks after the cast was removed and they found it hadn't healed right – so another cast was put on. It's now been off for about 10 days, he's still on crutches and it still bothers him. They checked and it still hasn't healed right so they shipped him off to the hospital. Then, last night, CMS Thelsthorster, who heads the Operations Section, went on emergency sick call. Off he went to the hospital also for treatment of either gall stones or ulcers – and they think it ulcers. That's all I'd need is to come down with peptic ulcers again.

I've about run out of "exciting" news, honeybunch. One thing I do want to bring to your attention, however, is that I'm using both sides of each sheet! Also, please note that I leave very little in the line of margins – so each missive is chock-full of choice, juicy comments!

I'll tell you one thing you might do when you have the chance. Get hold of a Texas driver's manual so that I can go through if when I return and get me a driver's license. Do you know where you have to take a driver's test? Do they give it in Jacksboro or do you have to go to one of the "big" cities? I'd like to get that taken care of relatively soon after returning.

Then only other thing I have to add you've already heard a zillion times – I love you. I'll tell you, it must be that cycle again (just checked, but there's no full moon!) but there are times when it seems to get more intense that at other times. I guess you've just been too good to me and for me, all these years. When I think of all those nights I've wasted in front of the boob tube instead of talking to you, I think I'll have to chuck that thing out. Here I haven't seen it for a long time and I don't even miss it. We're just going to have to do a few things together – like go to wrestling matches, or skiing, or the fights – things we both like! But seriously, there's so much time that I wasted at home. During that time I could have told you at least another million times how much I love you. My intentions are good, now at least, to remedy that in the future. Just to be near you now would mean so much to me. I've looked at your pictures so often that at times I've almost got myself hypnotized into believing you're about to come out of one of them and come into my arms. Gosh, how I want you, my beloved. Being so far away when I want you so much is awful. I think sometimes that you'll probably think there's something the matter with me, from the tone of some of my letters. It's just that I'm still the dreamer I've always been, in many ways, and I've such wonderful memories of you to fall back on. I'll probably be so excited to see you and be with you again that I won't be much good to anyone! – for awhile! I miss both your spiritual and physical tenderness. You know, my daring, though I often selfishly took advantage of my position to possess you, throughout it all, my wish was also to make you happy. I know it didn't always work out that way, but that was always my first desire – and will always be. Oh, there's so much I need and want to talk to you about, honeybunch. All I can think of right now is crushing you to me. I want so much to once again feel and know the loveliness of you body and the love of your heart. There's no question whatsoever, my happiness, that I'll always be

Your Leo

23 Jul 66

My Darling,

No news is good news, and no news is what I've plenty of tonight. Things have been quite hectic, what with the big action going on up north, so things don't exactly stay in the routine stage very long. Air traffic has been exceedingly heavy – the busiest I've seen it yet. Things being pretty well centered on this activity, very little routine flying is being done. Even our mail plane didn't make it today, so no new word from my honeybunch.

Really had some fancy supper tonight – Vienna sausage and sauerkraut. The first 100 or so also got canned beans, but I was too late. Seems they've only got enough chow until Monday, after which we'll have to go to C rations again. Seems none of the ships unloading have food, so I guess rations will be our diet for a while.

Six new NCOs checked in to the Sq. today, including the new First Sergeant, MSgt Dale. I haven't seen him yet. Only one maintenance man was in this group, a SSgt in Power Production.

Just got a call on one of our circuits from the Marines at Da Nang East (Marble Mtn.). They said not to call them on the order wire, that they were under mortar attack. Took a check outdoors and noticed that there are quite a few flares up that way. No activity out here, however. They usually get the brunt of any attack as the VC try to get the gunships (armed choppers) congregated at the Marine heliport.

We ended up with an informal meeting last night, and by the time I finally got to bed it was after 3. Got up again at 7, so now I'm about ready to quit.

I know this is but a shorty again, my sweet, but there just isn't very much more right now. I love you dearly and miss you, as ever.

Your Leo

24 Jul 66

My Dearest Don Leta,

I hope tomorrow night I'll be able to write a longer letter, but I'm really pressed tonight and I'm afraid it's going to end up into the wee hours again. No mail from my sugarbunch again, but did get a letter from Mom. Mail has been slow and unsteady, I guess as a result of the airlines strike. There was only a handful in today.

Leo won the NCO Academy
Public Speaking Trophy

This morning I was sitting at the club reading yesterday's paper and having coffee and this guy came up and grabbed my hand. It was Sgt Salmons, who had won the Commandant's Trophy at the NCO Academy. He was in Charlie Battery with me. He's made Master and was here TDY from Headquarters USAF. I didn't get to talk to him but a few minutes. He told me that Sgt Ferguson, the medic that was across the hall from me at school, had been killed in an automobile accident while going from Vandenberg to March a short while after we got out. I know I had mentioned him in my letters while there. He was just a little guy, and I used to hang around with him more than anyone else.

Mom didn't have any news, other than she has a new friend—Lou Lou—a parakeet uncle Charlie gave her. Theresa also has one—Mimie—so they're all set!

Gotta go, sweet. More meetings and work, I'm afraid. Love you, love you, love you – loads and bunches.

<u>Your</u> Leo

25 Jul 66

My Beloved,

The dam must have broken on the mail barricade because a bunch of it came through today, much to everyone's joy. Mail's about the only thing there is to look forward to – next to leaving. I received three letters – yours, Stephanie's, and one from Mrs. Houle. It's still slowed down however, these letters being postmarked 18th and 20th.

I got a charge out of Steph's efforts at poetry. As a poet, I think she'll make a good tap dancer! She seems to think the last word of every line has to rhyme, whether her poem is 4 or 14 lines long. At least she's trying and seems proud of her achievements. I thought I would answer in some poetic fashion. She'll probably get a charge out of that.

I'm sorry to hear that Karen has still been acting up. Let's hope the change in medicine helps some in tempering her disposition at least. I just don't know what to think about her if things don't level off before too long. I hope she can get squared away after I return. The doctors sure haven't been making much progress, it seems, as we've never really had a clear diagnosis or prognosis. All it looks like now is a matter of control rather than of cure. Did Dr. Knoop give you any idea of when that consultation with the Carswell orthodontist would be? Is he supposed to notify you or are you to check with him?

I was going to write last night about talking to Chaplain Woerdeman about our situation, but ended up having but little time in scratching out the few words that I did manage. We finally got out of here after 2 A.M., by the way. Anyhow, I called him yesterday and asked when it would be convenient to see me. He said that since he had already cancelled his golf date (a local joke, hereabouts), that anytime an hour before or after evening mass would be O.K. First thing he said to me when I started talking to him was, "Why are you embarrassed?" He said this was hardly anything new, that I was the fourth one just this week that he had discussed this subject with. Then he said he wasn't going to say any more until I had told him everything – how I felt, how you felt, why we shouldn't have any more children, etc. After I finally finished he asked a few questions and then related the church stand, why it came about, etc. He said he didn't give everyone who came to him with this problem the same answer, that each case was different and required different resolutions. He felt that, of paramount importance, was the husband and wife's mutual agreement and belief on what was best, and that these reasons not be based on purely selfish reasons. He also thought the pill would be approved later this year, again primarily for these reasons, and that further steps would probably be taken but not for a generation or so. He said it is sanctioned by priests in many parts of the world now. The fact that we already have six children shows that we have in the past given full consideration to our obligations. He further mentioned that another problem which arises is the very fact that we are a military family and this is cause for further consideration in sanctioning preventive measures. I mentioned you're talking to the Chaplain and he said he thought in closely the same lines, though he knew the same is not voiced by many of the older clerics, steeped in their ways. He didn't particularly feel it was a necessity to see a Catholic doctor for the same reason, unless it was entirely a matter of health. In that case, he felt a more objective view in the hazards involved could be given in light of the Church's beliefs, where another doctor might just want to do it as an easy way out, where the health aspect wasn't definite. Finally, he said that he couldn't "yes, do it" or "no, don't do it," that that would have to be our decision – not mine, or yours, but ours. He said we would seem to be justified, but only we knew for sure.

You asked if I felt that regardless of what measures we might or might not take, if God intended us to have another child, we'd have it. Of course, I believe this. For one thing, it's fact that conception has occurred when prophylactics, diaphragms or other devices were used. It's often been said that abstention is the only true preventive, but He even proved He could overcome that by the Immaculate Conception. The rhythm method notwithstanding, it was God's will that we had our latest, as we had all the others, though we both couldn't understand how it happened – at least according to the calendar. So, if we resort to the pill and the Lord decides we should have three more children, then we will have to prepare ourselves for triplets. By the same token, if God feels that we have what we need, any measures we take will probably be successful. As fruitful a woman as you have been, it's a wonder you did not conceive during the first months of our marriage, prior to my going to Korea. Perhaps it was God's will and He did not think us truly ready for such responsibility. He has sure made up for it, however.

You said that in re-reading parts of my letters you think I must be living in some kind of dream world because I think so much of you. You're right! You do have quite a few faults – like you don't pamper me enough, you throw away my comfortable pants, you wake me up when I'm watching the off-the-air TV at 2 in the morning. But I try to overlook major faults in my kindness and understanding. Instead I concentrate on your virtues – like you're a wonderful wife and mother, you chose me to be your husband, you're sweet and lovable, you're wonderful in bed – and in the living room – and in the kitchen – and on the stairs – and all over. I just love you, that's all. To prove it, here it is midnight and the guys have all gone to midnight chow while I'm still writing to you. Now if that's not true love, I don't know what is!

Well, my honeybunch, I'll be heading back to the barracks now and dream myself to sleep. Still 91 more days before I can hold you again. Thinking so much of the time, I hope it doesn't drag any more. My lips ache for you – you're just so yummy!

<u>Your</u> Leo

27 Jul 66

My Dearest,

Back to writing after having played lazy and skipping last night. There wasn't very much to write about anyway, not that there's much more tonight, even though today I did get a letter from you.

I've been feeling all pooped out lately. Besides that, I came down with other troubles and went on sick call this afternoon. The doctor checked me over and gave me medication. When he gave it to me I had the feeling he wanted to say "Shove it up your—!" It was ointment and suppositories. I've got hemorrhoids – just what I need in this heat and humidity. He said to try that first and if it didn't resolve the problem he'd have me sit in a tub of hot water 3 or 4 times a day. He doesn't want to cut except as a last resort because of the great risk of infection. I sort of suggested that maybe the thing would be for them to send me back to the states to have it done! With less than three months to go, I wouldn't have to come back!

Speaking of the states, we're now down to 89 days. One of our maintenance men left this morning and TSgt Rodrigues (the one who's France bound) leaves tomorrow morning. He's still not sure of his status, even though a bunch of messages have gone out. They also posted the list of flight schedules for August. Eighteen of our people will leave that month, including the CO and personnel officer. Someone said the new Commander was a Major Groves, also due in next month. Sgt Weikhorst, an E-8 in Operations, was just in with a CMS Collier who just came in this afternoon. Sgt Collier comes here after 3 years at Westover. He wasn't expected, as Group told the Sqdn a while back that he would be diverted to Cam Ranh Bay. Today, however, Group told him he was definitely coming to the 1972nd and sent him on up. The assignment business sometimes gets really goofed up around here. Now they sit with authorization for one E-8, 29190, and they've got one E-8 and two E-9s filling that position. On the other hand, they're so short of airmen that every one of them is on 12 hour days, with no days off.

I don't know yet, but I might go to Hong Kong after all if I get a chance next month. For one thing, I don't know anyone who'll be going and I did want to get those beetle watches for the girls, plus maybe a few souvenirs. Of course, an air conditioned room, fresh vegetables & fruits, and no regular 14-16 hour days, 7 days a week, has some bearing also. Oh well, next week I'll probably feel different again.

The house the Wojciaks were buying, was that directly across the street from the one in our former back yard? Maybe if we ever get down there, we can get some fruit off "our" trees. I wondered if those things would ever put out. I'm glad to see that the place hasn't run down. I guess people who buy a place because it has a well kept yard can reasonably be expected to like such an area and take the pains necessary for its upkeep.

Everything keeps going about the same here, my sweet. Right now we've got a few technical problems that have just about everyone going around in circles. It gets frustrating, to say the least, after a while; especially when others not having to solve the trouble are forever bugging you for information. Makes you feel like wrapping it all up and giving it to them to resolve.

It's about 1:30 A.M. now, my love, and I'm going to call it quits. I still (yet) miss you terribly and love you with all of me. Be sweet, my darling.

<u>Your</u> Leo

28 Jul 66

My Dearest,

This is really getting to be a merry-go-round. Right now we're in the midst of a pack of problems and projects. I'm really off lighter than some people. Larkin laid down on the floor in back of the equipment racks somewhere around 3 P.M., his first nap since getting up yesterday morning. Sgt Buck had been laying there for about 4 hours. It's going on 11 P.M. now and I've been working on a report while they're still trying to resolve circuit troubles. At least I got about 5 ½ hours sack time last night. It's not that the physical work has been so hard, like sandbags & bunkers, but you sure feel exhausted by the time that sack comes around.

Big John is still up-country. He had gone on what he figured would be a two or three day job – eight days ago. I don't know when he'll get back now. Get to talk to him on the phone every now and then. Grenier was up with him for 4 days and then came back. He's supposed to go up to another up-country site for a day or two tomorrow.

Yesterday I mentioned to you that we had gotten a new CMS in Operations. Well today they squared that business away and he will leave for Cam Rahn Bay this weekend. Confusion. It does look like Operations will get some help by the middle of next month, however, as they've now got about 18 operators programmed in. The only trouble is that a bunch of them will be brand new 3-levels to be trained. Sgt Collier (that E-9) says it's getting pretty tight back stateside with so many people going overseas, and that all bases are feeling the pinch for qualified people. More and more new troops have to be trained. On top of all this business, they keep trying to go more and more stateside all the time with their paperwork, reports, PEP program (AFCS's version of SAC's old MCS "brownie point" system.) Then, more and more, we get inspectors in – from Group, Clark, Hawaii. Some times they almost convince you they're more interested in whether the paperwork is all nice and straight than if the equipment is working. I think I must be getting too "old" for these young man's wars.

I know these must be pretty dull letters here lately. Since there's nothing new to report, all I do is moan about our little petty problems. All I'm trying to do is to get you in condition to listen to my gripes again so it won't be so hard for you to adjust to it once I'm back!

Not much, my sweet, but that's all there is for now. I'll be so glad to get this letter writing over with and be with you again. I love you and miss you so very much.

Your Leo

29 Jul 66
30 Jul 66

My Sweetness,

Since I'm starting this just at midnight, I thought I'd cover both dates in case I don't get around to it again by next midnight. It was after 3:30 this morning when I left here, and got back up at 7. For the first couple hours this morning everything was blurry. I had a hard time focusing on the headlines, so didn't even try to read the paper. Cleared up around nine or so, though. Sgt Buck and Green went to bed early tonight, but Larkin is still out on a separate problem. Capt Rayfield had to finally quit around ten o'clock. He looked like he'd been on a three day drunk.

Didn't get any mail today. Noticed a clipping in the paper today about mail (enclosed). Also another article about the Church & birth control. It's probably old news as far as stateside papers are concerned. I imagine there'll be all kinds of pronouncements and speculations on that subject until some word is finally given by the Pope.

I've already interrupted this letter three times for business. As if this war didn't know there are times (4) reserved for writing to honeybunches. That (4) is because I got another interruption – telephone calls, one in and one out. I sent one of my teletype people and one crypto man up north to assist the outfit at the other end of this circuit we're trying to get in. They've been working since early this morning and it's going on 1 A.M. now. A while ago they called for parts – found many things wrong with their equipment up there. Got an airman set up to take it up tonight. Larkin came in so he's running him out to the Marines. I got him a flight with them as they're going up there at all hours. He'll just drop the parts off and chug right back. It's a great life!

I should be able to knock off here pretty soon. I can get to go to Hong Kong and I think I'll take them up on it, if things calm down long enough. I can see what you have to put up with not getting enough sleep at times. It would be nice to have an air conditioned room and just sleep 'till noon. Just like being home again!

Good night, my wonderful girl. I love you with all my heart and am so anxious to be with you again. That's all I want right now – just to be with you and the children. Goodnight, my happiness.

Your Leo

30 Jul 66

My Honeybunch,

I'm starting this during my lunch hour, having just finished reading a letter which just came in from you. Maybe this way I can get it finished at a reasonable hour tonight and hit the sack earlier. Of course, that depends on things holding off. We still have problems, but at least the pace has slowed a bit. Green and I made it in by 8 this morning. I don't know when he quit, as he didn't come back in until after midnight, but I was in the sack by 2 A.M. It's almost noon and Sgt Larkin just came in – no one's even seen Buck, who was here when I left.

Opening my drawer, I see where I did it again – mentioned sending clippings but didn't put them in the envelope. Gonna do it right now. Speaking of envelopes, I'll be glad when you're done your present batch. It's got a bad flap – too much glue. When you seal it, it also sticks to the letter as well as the envelope. I'm complaining because every word from you is so precious, and today I tore off 1 ½ letters from one word and a letter from the next word. For all I know, I may even have lost a comma in between!

Well, we've just about made it through this one. After tomorrow we'll have but two paydays to go. I'm kind of in a hurry for Monday morning to come around so I can start my monthly rounds. On the first of every month I've been going around asking everyone if it was me or did they also think the month was dragging by!

I'm sorry this is so short again; my sweet, but there's just not much to report. I love you great big bunches and am so anxious to be with all of you again. Be sweet, my darling.

<u>Your</u> Leo

31 Jul 66

My Dearest,

We've finally made it through another month and tomorrow I can start saying I've only got a couple months to go—even though 85 days is a long "couple months".

This has been another full work day, but nothing particularly exciting happened. Big John finally made it back from up north. He's been moaning and groaning today about how he wants to get out of this place—and there he is with about ¼ of his tour done. There are a number of guys around here who have been kicking themselves for some time. Back in the days when they could run off into town I guess they were having a pretty good time for themselves. Thinking they'd take advantage of it, and the extra money, etc., they extended from anywhere up to a year. Now there's nowhere they can go and nothing they can do and yet they're stuck to do that extra time. Good luck to 'em, or as they say around here, "sorry 'bout that"!

No mail today. I don't even know if any came in to the squadron as it didn't seem like anyone had any.

Saw an article and pictures of an old buddy, General McKee (real close friend!) of mine in yesterday's (delivered today) Stars & Stripes. Seems like old Seth (I always used to call him Seth) is moving right along. Heck, I knew him when he was nothing but a Major General!

Major Perry received his flight number and is supposed to leave next Sunday, the 7th. His replacement, Major Groves, is due in on the 5th, so it'll be a quick switchover. As irregular as these incoming people get here, it's quite possible they won't even get to see each other.

No more big news for now, sweetheart. It's almost 10 PM now and if things hold off here for the next hour or so I'll be able to hit the sack at a decent hour. Goodnight, my darling. I love you and miss you so.

Your Leo

2 Aug 66

My Dearest,

Maybe, before too long, things will slow up again hereabouts long enough for us to sit back and enjoy a few minutes of absolutely nothing. For the past couple weeks I've just about forgotten what it's like. It's only nine P.M. now and things are not too bad, so maybe I'll get to hit the sack at a decent hour. Even now, my eyes feel so heavy I don't think I could write very long, even though I didn't write last night. I did get a letter from you yesterday evening, but none today.

I'm going to go ahead on R&R the 10th of this month. That way, the day I come back will also be the day the Group QC inspectors are due up here again. We need them so bad! Grenier and I were going to go together but couldn't make it. We could go to Japan, Taiwan or the Philippines at the same time, but Hong Kong or Bangkok seats are fewer and further between. The Air Force here was allotted seven seats on the 10th and five on the 20th. The rest on these 82 passenger flights are mostly Marines, with a sprinkling of Army and Navy Types. At least, that's on those leaving out of Da Nang. There are weekly flights out of Saigon in addition. The flights are by Northwest Orient and Pan Am, under contract.

I haven't had the chance to get down to the Post Office yet to get money orders; hope to do so tomorrow. I'm going to be short-changing you for the last time because of this trip. I don't want to go short-changed, so I'll send what I have excess on to you upon my return.

Hope the little pumpkin has gotten squared away on her spitting up. It's a good thing she's been healthy and fairly well behaved otherwise. That's probably all you'd need with everything else to take care of. You keep doing your job, honeybunch, and your old daddy will be back to give you some help before you know it—well, maybe not quite that early.

Yesterday saw rain all day long. At times it would cut down to a light drizzle, but then it would pick up again. It kept on all night long. Until around 3 this afternoon it was still overcast, with occasional light rain or drizzle. The sun then broke out and now it's getting hot and sticky again. When I hit the sack around 1:30 or so this morning, it was actually chilly—had to use covering for one of those few times.

Quite a bit of pounding up in the hills, but things have been staying pretty quiet around the base. Still quite a bit of activity up north and our troops report hearing the B-52's dumping their loads. Talked to one of the troops on the phone today and he said they just had another incident. A convoy making a BX run got hit by machine gun fire on the main highway. Lost a couple of men and a few wounded, including one of the 1st MOB boys. One of them received wounds last week also when a grenade was thrown into his jeep.

I was thinking of getting the Texas driver's license primarily for the trip to wherever we'll be going when next we move. I'm deathly afeared that if I don't have it you'll do all the driving and I'll be the one with the job of keeping the kids in line! It'll really seem like something driving back there after chugging around on the beautiful boulevards hereabouts in trucks. Top speed here is 25 mph, and that's only on the open road. Mostly it's 15/20 mph. That's O.K., 'cause some of these vehicles we've got won't go much faster.

A couple more of our maintenance people are leaving this week. Larkin has about 20 days to go. Lt Sawyer has already left and the old man leaves in 3 or 4 days. For the bunch of us, we're anxiously awaiting the passage of another two weeks or so to see if the October assignments get here. After that, I guess I'll get busy and start packing—yuk, yuk.

Boy, I though I was bad about being away and ready to go home. You should hear Big John. Originally it wasn't too bad, but now all he keeps harping on is how he shouldn't be here—that he's not authorized, etc. etc. I'm afraid John is a typical wire man. He's not happy unless he's climbing a pole or stringing cable. This desk work is definitely not his cup of tea—but I'm afraid he's stuck with it for the rest of this tour.

Good night for now, my beloved. It's a long, slow and hard road, but before too long it'll all be behind us. I love you so much, Don Leta, and you mean so much to me that there's no question the hardest part of all this is not being together.

Your Leo

DA NANG, RVN
"4 AUG 66"

Happy Anniversary, My Darling.

It's a belated one, I know, but not because I'd forgotten. Things had been such a rat race these past few days that I haven't seemed to get anything straight. Tonight I've got to take time out to write, especially after not having written yesterday. There was no mail yesterday, but I did hear from you today—dated the 29th—and since you wished me a happy anniversary in it, it arrived on the right day.

Yesterday was another one of those pass-out times. I took a shower at 6:30 P.M. and then stretched out for a few minutes before putting my fatigues on and coming to work. Well, I never made it. Did wake up at 4 am. to go to the bathroom and then went back to sleep until 7:10, almost late for work.

The way things are going now, I'm still unsure if I'll be able to make that Hong Kong trip. Unless things straighten out, it'll definitely be off. As it is, it looks like Grenier will have to cancel out because his falls right in the middle of the Group QC Inspection. I don't know whether I'm getting too short or what, but things seem to be getting worse instead of better—workwise, that is.

I was talking to TSgt Griner today. He came over when I did—runs the air conditioning shop in Civil Engineers. He said they received their assignments the other day—he was going to Maxwell—and that later they cancelled them all and said they had to go back through the computer at Randolph. Sounds kind of silly. Now he says he probably won't get what he wants. The base (35th Tactical Fighter Wing) put out a policy that personnel may be granted up to 29 days early release if their replacements are aboard and they're not needed. At Commander Call yesterday, we were told that, of course, that didn't apply to us since we were only tenants—that we went by Group's policy. Group, full of kindness and consideration for its personnel, will allow up to a

The Pawtucket Times

AUG 20 1961

City Man Wed In Texas

Sergt. Leo Dubois, Don Leta Hughes Are Married

MRS. LEO E. DUBOIS

Staff Sergt. and Mrs. Leo E. Dubois are residing in Fort Worth, Texas, following their marriage Aug. 4 in the garden at the home of the bride's parents in Jacksboro, Texas. Rev. James Pucek conducted the double-ring ceremony.

The bride is the former Don Leta Hughes, a daughter of Mr. and Mrs. Lanis Hughes, and the bridegroom, stationed at the Carswell Air Force Base, is a son of Warrant Officer and Mrs. Aldor Dubois of 84 Benefit street. Andy Kimes of Enid, Okla., was soloist and Miss Ruth Whitaker played the wedding music.

The bride was given in marriage by her father. She was attired in a ballerina-length gown of white organdy. Her fingertip veil fell from a band of white carnations and she carried a bouquet of white carnations. Mrs. Bill Cross of Jacksboro was matron of honor for her sister. Her dress was of green organdy and her flowers were yellow chrysanthemums. Nancy Privet was flower girl. Sergt. John Linehan of Fort Wayne, Ind., was best man. Sammy Akins of Jacksboro ushered.

The reception followed. The bride was graduated from Jacksboro High School and attended Texas Wesleyan College, Fort Worth. The bridegroom was graduated from St. Raphael Academy.

maximum of five whole days! Heck, I don't look to get even that much, so I'm counting every single one of those 81 to go.

I had written to Sgt Williams, my replacement from Barksdale, but never heard from him so don't figure he had any further questions. We're giving some equipment training to some airborne type and this TSgt knew Sgt Williams, being stationed at Barksdale before coming here. He received a letter from him the 2nd of August which indicated he was supposed to leave the states yesterday. He should be here any time now, depending on how long he gets held up at Saigon. If they try to keep him too long, by gosh I'll go down after him!

So Jim Moensen is going to March. I don't figure there's too awfully much demand for his type of people overseas, except in the bigger organizations since he's in the eyewash business—graphic arts & drafting.

My base pay as a MSgt would have given me a retirement of about $232 a month. As a SMSgt, I should get somewhere around $250. Actually it comes to a little more than a flat 50%. I'll be getting out with 20 years 4 months. If I got out at 20 years 6 months I would get 2 1/2% more. The next increment wouldn't come until 22-6. Even getting that extra 2 1/2% for two months wouldn't be worth it since I'd have to re-enlist. Rots of ruck!

Don't bother sending anything special with the package you're preparing—unless there's room for some of you! Maybe there will be since you said you lost one inch in the hips! I'm glad to see that Karen has lost some, but she's still got quite a way to go. Maybe this loss will give her a bit of encouragement to work on some more.

There's still so much work to be done here that it's odd now that I get a day like yesterday—only 11 hours. Usually it's been from 7:30 until midnight or later. At least it keeps me out of trouble off duty—even though there's no place to get into trouble. One good thing, each day runs into the other so you're always trying to figure out whether it's Sunday, or Wednesday, or what.

Well, my sweet wife, we come to the end again. You know, I've kidded a lot about our "long" married life and yet the 15 years we've had seem like such a short time. It does seem like quite a while ago that we were married, but the time we've been together seems so short. I love you so much, Don Leta. And don't you worry about me putting you on a pedestal. I know you have your faults, just like I have one or two little ones, but they're more than balanced by your many good qualities. You've brought me so much happiness and you're so good for all of us. I hope we can sit together sometime and reminisce about our years together—as we babysit our great-grandchildren.

Your Leo

5 Aug 66

My Dearest,

While it's still been hot but bearable during the days, it's getting to be routine now that every afternoon about 4 o'clock the clouds move in and we get varying degrees of rain. At least it makes the nights a bit better for sleeping. It's going on 9 o'clock now, and there's just a light sprinkle out.

Things haven't been too bad around here tonight, after another fairly busy day. Right now I think the biggest problem is just staying abreast of things and keeping everything straight. I should have a bit of help in that area pretty soon since Sgt Williams checked in today. Went by to see if he was around the barracks around chow time, but couldn't find him. I haven't met him yet. Guess I'll swing by and pick him up in the morning.

Got a shorty note from my sweet honeybunch this evening, as well as an anniversary card from the Della Postas. Nothing else much transpired, except that you can see I finally did make it to the Post Office today—both Grenier & I.

Big Bad John tied one on last night. Boy, he's going to make this an extra long tour for himself. He came in just as I was about to quit last night, about 11:30, feeling loud and happy. Said he was going to write a long letter to his wife. I came in at 7:30 this morning and there he was, sleeping on the desk with a GI. blanket over his head. It's going to be a long war!

No more to say, my love. As each day passes—ever so slowly—I wish more and more that the time had come for me to at least start on the trip home. I want and need to be with you so very, very much. Good night, my darling. Sleep good.

Your Leo

6 Aug 66

My dearest Don Leta,

Now's a good time to write since I'm full of balony—I mean salami. Green got a couple hunks of kosher salami in the mail today, plus a couple of pizzas. Now we've got to find a skillet for the pizzas. Had some sardines I threw away tonight, as did Larkin. Notices were posted all over the place saying not to eat sardines bought in the BX in the past week—they could be deadly. Guess somebody must have gotten hold of a bad batch, either here or in the states and the word on that shipment was passed on.

Picked up Sgt Williams this morning and got him started on his duties. I'll be leaving him in the Comm Center for a month or so to let him get familiar with our local operation. He's a former ciphony man (secure voice, 30670B instead of C like I was), so he's never had our type of equipment. At Barksdale, he's been running the MARS radio station for the past 15 months. He's about my age, having come in the service only 3 months after me—in March '48. He has four kids and his family is still in Shreveport.

Captain Rayfield was in just a bit ago. He was a bit blurry-eyed, having just come from the Officers' Club where they'd had a little get-together for Maj. Perry, who leaves tomorrow. We did have a small bit of excitement tonight. An Army truck hit our diesel generator just outside here and knocked it over. The truck ended up against the power pole and got banged up a bit. One of the army types got his head banged against the windshield since it was broken, but no one was hurt. It happened right outside the door here so I went right out. When I saw no one was hurt, I ran back in to call power production and get them out here. That generator furnished our back-up power and if we lost our other power we'd be out of business without any back-up. Best I could make out, this Army truck (weapons carrier) tried to pass a Marine flatbed and turn left at the same time. He sideswiped the flatbed and ended up against the generator and pole.

We keep having our little problems here, and with that Group inspection coming up and all the work to be done, I don't know if I'll get to take that R&R. I don't expect I'll know either until the last minute.

I'll tell you, every day it's getting more and more stateside. All the uniform mixtures are now taboo—something they've needed, really. No more wearing all sorts of hats. They're now giving tickets out for that and such things as not having the name tapes on your fatigues. The latest is washing vehicles. You get a notice, like a ticket, saying your vehicle is dirty and that the Base Commander wants clean vehicles. You have to answer what action you've taken within five days. Green and I both answered today—he got one and I answered the one my teletype people got. Ridiculous. To top it off, you have to wash it out at a water hole—go fill up your bucket and out of this stagnant pond and wash with that. Next thing you know we'll be having the old SAC type vehicle parades.

Enough griping for this time. I'm getting too short for that kind of worrying, being in the seventy's now—79 to be exact. Just a little more and it'll be an even two months before I back with my wonderful girl. Good night, my beloved. Sweet dreams. Mine will be because they'll be of you.

Your Leo

7 Aug 66

My dear Stephanie, I was most happy
To read your poems, so bright and snappy.
They were quite good for your first try
And with practice will be better by and by.

There are so many beauties to put in rhyme,
Of God's green earth—of space—of time.
But most of all it helps us make others
Feel in their hearts a love for their brothers.

A simple thing like lines that match
Gives many people a moment to catch
A little feeling of peace and joy,
Or maybe a laugh to a girl or boy.

And when people are happy, and calm and free
They'll love each other—and you and me.
We'll use this love to show our neighbor
We're all children of Jesus—our God and Savior.

Please write again when you have time,
Even if it's only a few short lines.
That's what I look for in this long year,
Letters from those who I hold dear.

Be a sweet girl, my little Stephanie,
Help your mother, with Karen and Lannie,
To take care of Bryan, Paul and Lynn.
'Till daddy comes home to help you again.

Pretty soon we'll arrive at the month of September
At school, at work or play, always remember:
Just doing your best when things get harder
Will make me proud to be,
Your loving Father

8 Aug 66

My dearest Don Leta,

Having spent a mail-less day yesterday, other than an anniversary card from Mom, it was doubly nice today to get a real sweet letter from two of my girls—you and Karen.

I was very pleased to hear that Karen seemed to be a bit better, especially her saying she was sorry and kissing you.   However, we mustn't get overly optimistic at one incident and assume it will happen all the time. I'm sure things like that will take time, with quite possibly a number of relapses to her former ways. We must trust in God and accept His will being done.

This time I won't have to make this a shorty letter since there is some news to report. The assignments came in for us, and they were the worst ever as far as people getting their base of choice. There's one thing anyhow, Mother will be happy over it. It wasn't my first base of choice—or second base of choice—or state of choice—or first geographical area of choice—but, it was my second area. So, I guess your folks will be able to visit a number of relatives when they go to Oklahoma—Altus, that is.

I was quite disturbed at first. I thought sure it was going to be the 4th MOB, which just moved up there from Hunter AFB, Georgia. Isn't that where the Schooley's went? Three airmen are going to Altus—all the 4th MOB—but mine is with the 11th Strategic Aerospace Wg—SAC. I guess it's the old 11th Bomb Wing of Carswell fame. I wanted nothing to do with those traveling MOB outfits. I could just picture myself getting there and having them say: "Don't unpack. You're going on 90 days TYD to Da Nang. The guy who left there left such a mess behind that they need someone to straighten it out!"

In forecasting, you list 2 bases, 1 state and 2 general areas. Of 15 of us who just received assignments they broke down as follows:

> 2 got 1st base of choice
> 1 got 1st state of choice
> 7 got 1st area
> 2 got 2nd area
> 3 got neither of their choices

You remember my mentioning Carter—he's from East Texas somewhere. Anyhow, he got his 2nd area—Turner AFB, Georgia. That wasn't too bad, except that he couldn't figure out what kind of outfit he was going to since it wasn't comm. It was the 1374th MCH Squadron. He found out in short order what that stood for and what the outfit was like. It's a mapping & charting squadron. One of our recent arrivals came from there and he told Carter that everyone below the rank of MSgt spends from 6 to 9 months TDY overseas. His buddy was TDY to South America, along the Amazon River, while he spent six months on a mountain top in Ethiopia! Carter's fit to be tied. He'll only have 8 months to retire when he goes back. He went to see about it at the Orderly Room and in effect they told him "Sorry about that." So he said by gosh he was going to write his congressman. Anyhow, now they told him they would get a message off about it. He came to see me about helping him write to his congressman if he gets no results. I don't remember if I told you about Sgt Mayes, who also goes back in October. He had asked for and received a consecutive overseas tour. He got his first choice, Italy, and immediately put in for concurrent travel. They disapproved his concurrent travel, telling him that this was going to be a 12 month remote tour on some mountain! Needless to say, they went out right quick to cancel that and try to get him assigned to Germany.

Start the pills! I have no qualms about doing something about this at this point in the game. I'm sure we're all right as far as these steps go, and there'll be no repercussions.   It'll be difficult enough getting by with the three girls growing up and the others so young yet, especially during the reorganization and resettlement we'll be undergoing with retirement. Heavens knows we'll have enough on our minds without worrying about another little one—either started or with us. Lynn will just have to learn to play with the bigger kids. The only thing is, I hope taking those pills don't bother you too much at first, as I believe you mentioned the doctor said they probably would.

One thing, definitely and positively, we'll have to do something about—and that's you being in the middle of your period when I'm due home! What a catastrophe!! Maybe I'll just have to stay here about five days longer. Or maybe I'll get home about three days before the start and then you'll have a rest "period". It'll be my luck to get there on schedule—for once. Oh well, it's said that "everything good comes to him who waits"—and it is good! I just want to be with you, that's all. But since I will be with you, I'll want you all the more. I'll go boo-boo if I spend too much time thinking about it again, but memories of our wonderful moments of love just don't fade very fast. I know I'll want six hands so I can feel all of you at once.

There's not much use guessing at just when I'll be leaving here—it could be anytime in the next 77 days. I shouldn't say anytime, really, since it'll be somewhere near 77, but I don't know if it'll be 73, 74 or what. Regardless, it's coming and it'll take forever for me. Be sweet, my darling. I love you with all of me.

Your Leo

9 Aug 66

My Darling,

Today is anticlimactic after having received the assignment news yesterday. No mail or any other exciting happenings today, so there's not very much to relate

There was a bit of moaning, groaning and gnashing of teeth from some today who were just getting over the initial shock of not getting anywhere near what they asked for. My shaky disposition didn't last too long, cleaning up as soon as I found out it wasn't a MOB outfit. Three—no, four—of the guys here were at Altus, two of them just prior to coming here. They all seemed to like it. I haven't found out about base housing yet, but they've all said housing off base is real good and cheap. One kid, an A1C, said he paid $90 for a house that was fully carpeted except for the kitchen; 3 bedrooms, 2 baths, two car garage—and it used to rent for $140. Of course, that's probably the exception. Have you ever been to Altus? I know you have, or had, relatives there at one time. SAC doesn't have a Comm Sq there as such, like they had at Ellsworth. Rather, communicators are part of the HQ Squadron. No missiles! They used to have the Atlas before they phased out. So, all communications should be on base. About how far from Jacksboro is Altus—around 250 miles? Well, maybe we'll be able to get some company some times. All I'm really happy about is that we'll be together, without the constant threat of taking us apart again.

That's all for this shorty, honeybunch. Down to 76 now and 1/3 of this month just about gone. Good night, my sweet. I love you loads and bunches and miss you terribly.

Your Leo

15 Aug 66

My Darling,

I do hope you haven't worried too much over not hearing from me the past four days. I went out for what was originally going to be a day or two and ended up being unable to get out of there until Sunday night. That was real nice, 'cause I was supposed to leave for Hong Kong Saturday noon. Now Grenier is supposed to go this Saturday and he probably won't make it either. The inspection team delayed three days and that will be right in the middle of his R&R. My next chance to go now is not until 17 September, so I doubt that I'll ever make it there.

There were two sweet letters from my honeybunch, as well as the package and a letter from Mom. The package came thru in good shape, but the banana bread was all moldy from sitting out in this heat. Oh well, I can wait a couple months or so.

Your letters were particularly welcomed, for I don't think I've ever thought of you so much as in these past four days. It was a particularly lonesome place, and just sitting waiting to get out made it all the worse. At Da Nang at least I can get embroiled in something or other and the time will pass a bit quicker, but where I was it's more of a sit and wait type operation with absolutely no diversion. The last couple days were spent just about all thinking of you, 25 hours a day.

Gosh, I love you and miss you so terribly, terribly much Don Leta. Even without exaggeration or putting you on a pedestal, you mean so much to me and I'm so happy and proud to be your husband. All I want to do now is spend all of my days trying to make you happy. God but I love you.

Seventy more days! That sure sounds nice when compared to the hundreds I used to mention. Your many comments about the kids, especially the little ones, make me all the more anxious also, especially Paul's antics and little Lynn coming along so fast. For those two especially it'll probably seem strange to have me around all the time. I'll probably catch the crying bit also when you first leave them with me to go to the store or anything. I think I can put up with it, though!

Good night, my beloved. At first this month started fast, but it seems this past week has just dragged and the month is only half over. I think as time gets closer I get more and more impatient with the passage of time. I long to hold you close once again, my happiness.

Your Leo

16 Aug 66

My dearest Don Leta,

I've hungered all day for another letter from you and was rewarded with one tonight. This missive took six days to get here—longer than usual. It seems that, as time goes on, but particularly of late, my thoughts of you are so strong. After all the letters I have and will have written during this long year, I still feel it will have been such an inadequate, frustrating and totally unsatisfactory way for me to even begin to let you know all you mean to me, my lovely Don Leta. I love you and miss you so, my darling.

So you're exercising. You had best keep it up and get in the best possible shape because you're liable to have quite a few wrestling matches on your hands once I get to you! I don't know why you felt funny about doing them when I was home just because you couldn't do them as well as I. Heck, I didn't expect you to do them as well. After all, I don't remember you as playing too much football or refereeing too many basketball games. I wish I was home to put you through your drills right now—and then follow it up with a good massage (after the kids are in bed, of course)!

I was suppose to hit another one of the sites this week but that's been put off indefinitely now. It'll be OK with me if I don't have to go at all. Sgt Williams seems to be a pretty good technician and is working out well. Since I've a while to go yet, I had put him down in the Comm Center so he could become familiar with that. While I was up north we had a new crypto man report in. Didn't even know this one was coming so we had no advance word on him. He's TSgt Judy and comes from McClellan. Isn't that an odd last name. Don't ever remember hearing it before. We're due in one more this month, though I don't know his name or rank. All I do know is that we're supposed to get a KY-8 trained troop, something we sorely need and have been sweating out. With Sgt Judy here now, I can bring Sgt Williams up sooner to take my place and let Sgt Judy run the Comm Center. Then I can slowly ease out of the picture. If, after a while, nobody notices my absence from the activity, maybe I'll just pack my bags and skip off—joke! It won't be that easy, 'cause I know if I do slip out of this desk I'll end up taking care of administration 'till I leave. Like every other place I've been, there haven't been too many very sharp in admin. Like now, one of my additional duties is to process all APR's on maintenance personnel. Many days that takes 50% of my time.

Our new Commander, Major Groves, also checked in during my absence. I haven't met him yet, but I can see what's coming. He seems to be one of those shiny floor, dusted shop types. They've already had a G.I. party in the barracks. I hope he's not one of those who doesn't know anything else so he spends all his time having you paint and grow grass. Maybe he just wanted to make his presence felt right off.

They've had another crisis this past week also. I guess a bunch of the troops had to put in about 42 hours straight. This wasn't in my area, though, but involved radio and radar. Never a dull moment.

Larkin finagled himself a two day trip to Bangkok. He goes home in another eight days—then on to Germany. Five or six others will be leaving this month also. Outside of two guys in Flight Facilities who came in September, that will make all us October arrivals the "old timers" here. I'll be happy to relinquish the title to the November troops.

Had about a two hour interruption to my letter writing just now. Sgt Williams had come up here tonight to write a couple letters and we got to jabbering about everything in general and nothing in particular. Then there was a bit of a problem at the Autodin terminal, so we went there. So now, at 11:15, I can finally get back to my writing. The only trouble is…..there's no other news.

With this day gone, we now passed to 69 as the magic number. Though there's no doubt they'll pass as well, even two or three more days without you seems to be too long to wait. When I first see you again, I feel that it'll be a monumental display of self-control not to crush you then and there.

How often, like right now, I close my eyes and picture myself snuggled up to you. I know it really isn't, but is seems so much stronger than it was six months, or three months, or even three days ago. I know there are some things I've repeated so many times in my letters, but that's because I feel them so often and so strongly. You mean so much to me, honeybunch, and I do love you so dearly—and in so many, many ways. It's funny, in a way, but with so many stronger examples I could give, I'd say that even being in the same house with you, without even seeing you, would be so wonderful. I love you just for being the lovely, wonderful and understanding person you've been with me all these priceless years we've been one together. Oh God, these last days had better hurry by. There seems to be a burning and restless feeling deep within me that I can't seem to describe, or quite understand. It seems to be a constantly churning desire to see you, to talk with you, to be near you and to possess you—mentally, socially, spiritually, physically—just every which way. I'm not cracking up, my darling. I'm only trying to say what can't be said—trying to make you feel what only I can feel—trying to write things for which there are no words known to man, only to the soul.

When I start writing like this I often have to stop, and this is when I must face how selfish I am about all this. Saying how much I love you and all you mean to me, telling you how much I want to make you happy—all of this is really for myself. Only this way can I assure my own happiness. I could never be truly happy until I knew that you first experienced happiness.

Though I want and try to act hard and unsentimental about many things, when I think of our separation is when I turn softest. How could one possibly have come to love another so much in what is the relatively short period of 15 years? I could never again feel about another woman as I feel about you. All these things I should have said to you time and again; but I didn't and even when I return I probably won't be able to say them. But they're in my heart, my dearest, and they always will be.

Mingled and interwound with all this is that ever-present dream of sleeping with you again. I get so angry with myself when I think of the many times when you were tired or not "in the mood" and I still persisted. Not the least of this seeming animalistic desire was the wish also to give you a measure of the tenderness and pleasure which you brought me. I relish the memories of these closest of moments, and not few are the times that I've relived them. There is something extra special in realizing that here also was a gift that was exclusive and would be known by no other. I long to once again know the feel, the taste and the loving comfort of your body. I've felt so close to you at those times, not only physically but in all other ways, but I don't think any closer than I do now while 10,000 miles apart.

I know I could expand and go on and on, my dearest, and I do feel like writing so much more. But once I reach the end of this epic, I could still sum it up in but a very few short words. And these would say all I could ever say about you—Don Leta, you are my whole life.

Your Leo

17 Aug 66

My Beloved,

That short stay in the hills and not being able to write to you must have done something to me. Now I find myself wanting to write at all hours. It

took me until 1:30 to finish my letter to you last night and then, this morning, I was wanting to write to you almost as soon as I had gotten to work.

I'm on my lunch break now, and after checking mail and finding TWO letters from you, I just had to skip lunch and come back to at least start this letter. How wonderful was that first packet of pictures. As much as I look forward to getting them, it

hurts so to see you all and not be able to be with you. The one of the girls with Bryan wearing granny glasses was cute. I took a double take at Stephanie on that one. She reminds me so much of Vivian when she was a child. Most of all I treasure the one of you standing with Lynn and the one of you and all the children. I know it's not that long since we've parted that it's my imagination—but, by golly, you're getting prettier in your "old" age. You look so good in those two pictures that I can't even put them down. A matter of fact, both are spread out in my left hand even as I write. They're going to go in the best space on my desk, where I can look, drool and dream to my heart's content.

It's now 6:30, honeybunch, and this has been a go-go day, what with the arrival of the Group inspection team. At least, by 5:30 tonight I was composed enough to go for supper. Those pictures of you still bother me, though. It's even worse since you said there'd be more in the next letter. Now I'm wishing another mail delivery would come in today.

I was speaking to Major Linkenfelter, the Weather Sq. Commander, and he said he was going to Hong Kong shortly and if I could go he'd take me along, providing there was room. I might just do that instead of going on R&R. That way I could still get a few things without the added expense. Guess it'll depend quite a bit on how we get though this inspection. I spent the afternoon at the comm. center with the crypto inspector and got through that part of it

O.K.   Sgt Williams has been getting things in fine shape in that area. Tomorrow we'll check the Autodin and Talk Quick terminals and also start on teletype and telautograph[27]. Oh yes,—you asked about 30670B and C. The "B" was for ciphony, that is, voice encryption, while "C" was for teletype, data and facsimile encryption. They've now done away with the letter prefixes and we're all 30670's.

Received a clearance verification on another 306 due in here. I don't have anything on when he's due, however. This one's a TSgt Albert Frechette and from his serial number I see he's from Maine. That's all I have on him thus far, except that he's one month younger than I am—for what that's worth! There'll be rank in crypto, if nothing else. Before this, the highest ranking crypto people I had were Staffs.

Got a hold of the 10 Aug issue of the AF Times today but didn't notice any earth shattering news, unless you want to consider that article which stated "chances for SEA returnees will be sharply reduced beginning with October forecasts." I could have told them that much!

I was just doing some quick rough figuring on the amount of travel pay I'll get on that move to Altus. The total travel pay will only be around $125. If we had gotten Westover it would have been around $500. That won't be a heck of a lot, even though from Jacksboro it's just a hop and a skip and wouldn't be very expensive. I had been hoping Uncle Sugar would foot part of the bill to visit back east if we were stationed there. It wouldn't be worth it too much now with retirement and resettlement only some 18 months away.

There's just no more news tonight, my sweet—except that another long, slow day has passed leaving us with 68. In about another month or so I should have my flight reservation and then we'll know for fairly certain just how many days will be between us. Sometimes I figure I'll work out some plan to not have you meet me until at night, just so we'd be able to spend that first night together without driving back to Jacksboro. The only thing is that I don't think I'd have the patience to wait any longer once we were that close. I love you so, my wonderful, sweet, darling Don Leta. Take extra good care of yourself for me, my beloved.

Your Leo

18 Aug 66

My darling Don Leta,

Things have been especially nice for me so far these past three days, what with all these letters and pictures from you. Received another letter and more

---

[27] telautograph: a forerunner to the modern fax machine, the telautograph was used to transmit handwritten weather reports and charts since weather symbols were not available on keyboards.

pictures today. I could go on and write a couple pages about these pictures again, but will skip that—for now.

Today's letter was the one in which you mentioned just having received word of our assignment. There was only one thing that surprised me. You didn't mention Mother's reaction. After seeing yours, perhaps she didn't dare say too much.

No, I wasn't particularly overjoyed myself, wanting to get somewhere around Massachusetts, Connecticut or New Hampshire, somewhere where I could branch out a bit and make contacts and more definite plans for retirement. I also want to take the opportunity of getting some training and education in the business field so I can step right into a vice-presidency somewhere. As I mentioned briefly before, I intend to spend some time on this and coast through the last 16 months or so of my commitment to Uncle Sugar.

If at the time I had forecasted I had put in for Altus, I probably would have been laughed at. Even now, I can't hardly imagine why the 11th Wing would need an E-8 in my field. When I'd tell anyone that I had requested Westover they'd all say, "Heck, you've got no sweat. After all, they have about a 1,000 man communications outfit and there should be room there."

Maybe you'll be able to find out a bit of advance information about the housing. Sgt Buck, who came here from there, says it isn't too bad. If it's not so hot, or too small, I think I'd probably like just as well to live off base, provided we're still close enough to get things easily. Besides, being off post, maybe they wouldn't be quite as prone to yell after me if they needed something! If you don't make it up there before I get back, we'll be able to go by ourselves some day anyhow. Being only 143 miles, it would only be about a three hour ride.

Definitely, I think we'll skip any further thought of taking leave to go east. It would mean too much loss of school for the girls, not to mention the expense. Besides, we wouldn't use so much leave time, which means money in the bank when I get out. Just cashing in 30 days leave at retirement time means around $650.00 extra, and I'm sure we'll be able to use that.

All in all, I guess we should look at the advantages and make the best of the rest. I can think of a whole batch of bases I would have liked less. At least there some of your relatives will be able to come up and we can likewise take a quick run down. But, like you mention, all that really matters in the end is that we'll all be together again.

I can see the big grin on Paul's face as he's bending over for his paddling from grandpa in today's pictures. All of these have been so good and I just can't get over how nice you look. Especially good are those of you and the kids. Looking at them over and over again, I got to feeling so proud. I've shown them to everyone who has even looked like they were approaching me.

Nothing much new today, honeybunch. It's been mostly a day with inspectors, both crypto and teletype. There'll be here a couple more days and so far we're not doing too bad.

Good night for now, my love. I'll chalk off another day, bringing us to 67 day's away from each other now. Two more days and it'll be 300 days done here. I love you and miss you one day's more than I did yesterday. Be sweet, my dearest Don Leta and take good care of yourself for me.

Your Leo

19 Aug 66

My Darling,

There's just about nothing to report tonight, so this will no doubt be one of my patented shorties. There was no major happening hereabouts, even though I did get a letter from Aunt Jeannette. She didn't have much news. She mentioned Marie's oldest boy being 16 years old and preferring to go to work rather than school. That sounds about right! Every time I hear of one of those kids being that old I take another look at myself. I can feel those years coming faster and faster! Here I am getting older and grayer (balder) with each passing year (day) while I look at your pictures and you seem to be getting younger and prettier.

Looks like I'll be taking another short trip either tomorrow or Sunday. If I get out early enough in the morning I should be able to get back the same night. That should take care of things until I get out of here.

I was at the BX this afternoon—seems like the first time in ages. I went ahead and ordered some clothes made. They've got three tailor companies from Hong Kong here. They had a bunch of sample suits and materials. It takes about three weeks to have them back. You're measured here and the clothes are made in Hong Kong. Then, when it gets here you have as many fittings as required to fit properly. There was a Marine there getting refitted. He ordered a suit over two months ago and then went out in the field. He had just gotten back to Da Nang and came to pick up his suit. There was just one small problem. He had lost 23 lbs!

They also had a whole new bunch of sports shirts, shorts and slacks, as well as a batch of Hush Puppies. The shoes were $6.50. Isn't that kind of low for that brand name? They must be figuring on everybody going civilian around here. The other thing they set up was a mail order outfit run by the China Fleet Club. This is a branch of the Navy PX that procures goods from some 40 or so Hong Kong shops. It was too crowded to even get near the counter. I wanted to check to see if I could get beetle watches that way. Speaking of Hong Kong and all, Grenier is supposed to go tomorrow and it looks now like he'll have to cancel out. I haven't seen him tonight so don't know if he's going to try to go later. We can get Tokyo or Kuala Lumpur (Malaysia) just about any time, but other places are a bit harder to come by.

So far we're all doing fairly well on the inspection. They've written up a bunch of discrepancies, but it's all minor stuff.   If I get off tomorrow, a couple of the inspectors are supposed to come with me. Whether or not we make it, they're scheduled to leave Sunday.   One of the inspectors, TSgt Lovelady (teletype), has been here before and was making his last inspection round. We came over on the same plane together—he got an assignment to Florida (his first area of choice.)

I feel bushed tonight and think I'll try to get to bed before 11. I don't seem to get so tired physically, but it's still few nights that I ever get over 5 or 6 hours sack time. Good night, my love. Sixty-six days now between us and then I'll be able to hold you in my arms again. I miss you and love you so.

Your Leo

20 Aug 66

My Beloved,

Luck was with me this morning and I caught an early Marine chopper out of here at 6:45. By lunch time we were done and ready to head back but had to wait around until almost 4 o'clock for a ride. For the first time in what seems to be ages I took a shower right after supper and went to bed. Wouldn't you know it, at 7:20 I got a call that I was wanted down at the office for a 7:30 meeting. I had already been snoring up a storm.

It's now almost 9 P.M. and I'm wide awake. Anyhow, we received a debriefing on the Group inspection and I guess we came out of it o.k. They said there was no doubt that we were the best comm squadron in Vietnam. We already knew that! That being so, I'd sure hate to see the shape of some of these other outfits.

Grenier didn't get off on his R&R flight, so tonight we had a ceremony of burning his R&R orders. He's going to try to go also if Major Linkenfelter still goes and has room. He had just received money from his wife to spend on R&R, so now he says he'll see what my clothes look like and will probably buy some here. Sgt Demaree bought some at the same time from a different tailor, so he wants to see what both of them look like first.

There was a letter from you waiting for me when I returned. (By the way, please note the change in my address from Drawer 20 to Box 54.) From your brief description of the house Marie Payne lived in it, does sound like the rentals were fairly reasonable.   I've been unable to solicit any further information relative to base housing from this end. You should be able to get a pretty good look, however, if you and Marie get to go after school starts. If base quarters are air conditioned that sure would be nice next summer. I'll shortly be writing to the Wing Comm Office (they don't seem to have a comm. Squadron as such in the Wing) to see if I can find out a few of the particulars.

It's been blistering hot again here lately and the late evening cloudiness and showers which we were getting for a while seem to have quit. The guys on the inspection team said they were still getting quite a bit of rain down south. Another thirty days or so and we should be starting into the monsoon season up here. I don't much look forward to it, even though it does make it a lot nicer sleeping at night. The ones I really feel sorry for are the troops who must work mids and sleep in the daytime. It's just about impossible the way the heat builds up in the tents and barracks. I use to take a quick catnap every noontime, but that's been out for some time because of the heat.

They finally got the transformers in and installed and so air conditioning was brought to the base theater. You think it was hard to get in before—when you'd sit in there wringing wet—then you should see the lines now.

Gren, Larkin and I were just sitting here gabbing and eating some of your delicious jam (peach—I didn't care too much for the tomato) on some saltines I got at the mess hall. Green's trying to dig up a pan—he's got a pizza. Anyhow, in comes Sgt Francis and Airman Shannon, just back from one of the outlying sites. They'd been gone three days and hadn't had a bath or shave, working on power generators. What a mess they were. You can imagine, no change of clothing and sleeping in bunkers at night.

Halfway through this last paragraph I stopped again. We've been outside. There's a lot of small arms and heavy automatic weapon fire from the south end of the field and the sky's lit up with flares. There must be some attempts of infiltration going on. It's the same area that got hit with mortars Tuesday night, but I don't hear any of those tonight. Larkin was yelling— "Knock that stuff off. I leave in four days!" It's 10:30 now and there's still an engagement.

I'm gonna go ahead and knock off for now, my sweet. I've been looking at the pictures again and, oh how I'm anxious to be with you. I just can't get over how wonderful you look. Good night, sweet girl.

Your Leo

20 Aug 66

My Honeybunch,

Got a quick request. Please go through the military papers I've kept and see if you can find a Form 398, Statement of Personal History.

Mail it to me as soon as possible as I need to get some of the information into records prior to my leaving here.

Love you, love you, love!

Your Leo

21 Aug 66

My Dearest,

This has been a pretty short day, as most days go. Didn't get up until noon after having gone to bed at 4:30 a.m. As I wrote last night, there was some activity at the south end, but that ended after a couple hours. Also, the "Take 10" Club in town was the scene of a hit and run grenade attack. Ever since I've been here I could never understand why guys would go there. It's an NCO Club for all services and is supposed to be pretty nice and have good food. Right now, it's supposed to be open only to those living in town or in the compound there, mostly Army types, even though there are always a certain few who go from the base even though the city is off limits.

Everything has been pretty quiet today, and I must confess I haven't gotten much of anything done. No mail, so there's nothing in that area. Gren, Larkin and I ended up having pizza and spam last night, chased by Ritz crackers and homemade jam. Then, a water main broke just outside the central office, shorting out one of our cables, so we helped the outside plant types a bit in getting set up to splice in a new section.

Carter was in to see me this afternoon to get some help in writing a letter to his Congressman. They came back from HQ AFCS and said his assignment to that outfit in Georgia was firm. Our new Commander, Major Groves, was writing to the Commander of that outfit to see what could be done. In the meantime, Carter is getting the necessary documents together to put in for a humanitarian reassignment. I hardly think he'll have much trouble in getting another assignment for humanitarian reasons.

It's bedtime again, honeybunch, and as usual I dread going. Even those nights when I don' have to be up so late I'll stay up and write, or read, or just gab with the others. It's nothing unusual to be in the shop at two or three in the morning and find others here, just hanging around. It would be so much nicer just to be able to "hang around" you. Time is moving ever so slowly, though we're down to 64 now and the month of August is 2/3 over. With the present trend, I'm figuring my flight will be out of Saigon on about the 22nd, which would mean my finishing work on the 16th and leaving Da Nang on the 20th. If that's about right, we'd be down to about 61 days. That's still ever so long the way I've been longing for you. I don't have myself hypnotized that it's going to be paradise forever afterwards. I'm a little more realistic than that. But I do know that one big difference is that we'll all be together. I'll hold you again tonight in my thoughts, my love, making it seem as real as I possibly can. This will hold me, as it has thus far, until it's possible to stop pretending. There always has been and always will be but one sweet, wonderful girl for me—My Don Leta.

Your Leo

22 Aug 66

My Honeybunch,

Lots of work but not much news to report, my sweet. There was no mail today but I'm taking advantage of a fairly quiet night in getting some letter writing myself. Just finished a letter to Mom and one to John Hill, telling him I'll have to take a rain check on looking him up when I get to Westover!

We got 18 new people in the squadron today—12 for operations and 6 for maintenance. I don't know yet if any of them are my people. We have a few including Larkin leaving this week. Larkin got a rollback and he's leaving early—one day before his DEROS! Big deal.

I'm going to try to get a letter off to Altus within the next couple days to see if I can get any information at all. Carter received a letter from the First Sergeant of the outfit he's scheduled to go to at Turner and it was one of the best and most complete welcoming and introductory letters I've seen. They must have a rarity—a First Shirt who knows what he's doing. He told Carter how much people of that unit go TDY. He mentioned, however, that if Carter was a 304X4 (which he is) he would be working on Turner itself and not going on TDY. At least that's the way I read it.

It's a quiet night around here right now. I don't know where everyone is. Grenier's doing some work out at the radio site and Green's in his office. I imagine we'll join up again in an hour or so for some midnight chow, or at least coffee.

Guys have told me things would get worst and time drag all the more once I had my assignment and I believe them. I hadn't paid much attention to them before but they were right. This is doubly so knowing that my replacement is here. Now that my replacement is here, I know when I'm going and my time is getting shorter, it's kind of hard getting motivated to be active in much of anything. I want Sgt Williams to start taking over some of this work, but at the same time I don't want to run myself out of anything to do. Time would surely stand still then.

I wish things were back to the way it was during my first few months here when the policy was that if your replacement was aboard you could get out up to 30 days early. Even after that we could get released 14 days early, but now the absolute maximum is 5 days. That's for us communicators. The base units can still get up to 29 days rollback.

All this makes it so much harder just waiting and looking forward to being with you again. I imagine you've already gotten that impression from this and my other "sad" notes! It must get awfully repetitious to you after a while, but of the many thoughts that go thru my mind, the dominant one by far is the one dealing with our being together again. This has been such a long year already, and yet the next 63 days seem longer yet. I know they'll also pass, but at their own time.

Good night, my beloved. Once again I'll be kissing you and holding you in my thoughts until sleep overtakes me. Oh, how terribly I miss you and want you, Don Leta. I ache for you as I dream of our many wonderful moments together. I just keep on pressing towards the time when we can live those moments anew. I love you so, my sweet Don Leta.

Your Leo

23 Aug 66

My dearest Don Leta,

Nothing will make a man miss home more than eating hot G.I. corned beef hash on a hot day. Ugh! That's going to be with me the rest of the night, I'm afraid.

No mail today—3 days now, As a matter of fact, no mail of any sort was delivered. I did get my orders, however, as you can see.

Now don't go packing and moving to Altus right away. I would rather you wait for me. Besides, there's a hitch in my orders that I spotted right away and it may be that we'll get some other assignment. The squadron will be sending out a message tomorrow to get a reading on it. I doubt very much that a SAC Wing would be authorized an E-8 in my field. The orders show me shipping as a 30670 (CAFSC means Control Air Force Specialty Code). Since I made Senior I'm no longer a 7-level, but a 9-level (30690). What I think may have happened is that I forecasted as a MSgt, 30670, in March. When I made the promotion, I checked with the Orderly Room to see if they should go in with a change to 30690. They assured me that PACOM would change it when they annotated the records. Now we'll have to wait a while more to find out what they're going to do. I hope it doesn't take them too long to give me the word. We may very well still be going to Altus.

PERMANENT CHANGE OF STATION ORDER — MILITARY

(Items preceded by an asterisk for overseas only.) (If more space is required, continue on reverse.)

1. INDIVIDUAL WP ON PCS AS SHOWN BELOW	

2. GRADE, LAST NAME, FIRST, MIDDLE INITIAL, AFSN

SMSGT DUBOIS, LEO E.

3. SHIPPING AFSC (Officer)

4. (circled) 30670

5. ☐ OVER 4 YEARS SERVICE (A1C Only)

6. UNIT, MAJOR AIR COMMAND AND ADDRESS OF UNIT FROM WHICH RELIEVED

1972 Comm Sq (AFCS)
APO San Francisco, 96337

7. UNIT, MAJOR AIR COMMAND AND ADDRESS OF UNIT TO WHICH ASSIGNED AND DUTY STATION IF APPROPRIATE

11 Strat Aero Wg (SAC)
Altus AFB, Okla., 73521

8. PURPOSE OF REASSIGNMENT IF OTHER THAN DUTY

9. REPORT TO CMDR., NEW ASSIGNMENT NLT

10. *(Reassignment from overseas units to CONUS unit only.)*
REPORT AT NEW ASSIGNMENT NLT ___35___ DAYS
AFTER DEPARTURE FROM CONUS PORT OF ENTRY UNIT

11. DALVP — Yes

12. ESUEA — 20 Oct 66

13. TDY EN ROUTE (Indicate Location or unit and address.)

14. PURPOSE OF TDY

15. SECURITY CLEARANCE FOR PERIOD OF TDY OR COURSE OF INSTRUCTION

16. TDY REPORTING DATE

17. APPROXIMATE NO. OF DAYS

*18. LEAVE ADDRESS

Rt 1, Box 134C
Jacksboro, Texas

*19. NEW MAILING ADDRESS (Use upon completion of TDY, if appropriate.) GRADE, NAME, AFSN

20. DURATION OF COURSE (If reassignment is to attend course of instruction) ___ WEEKS

*21. ☐ CONCURRENT TRAVEL OF DEPENDENTS IS NOT AUTHORIZED

*22. ☐ TRAVEL OF DEPENDENTS IS PROHIBITED

*23. TRAVEL OF DEPENDENTS TO A DESIGNATED POINT ☐ IS ☐ IS NOT AUTHORIZED

*24. ☐ TRANSPORTATION OF DEPENDENTS AND SHIPMENT OF HHG TO TDY STATION IS NOT AUTHORIZED

*25. CONCURRENT TRAVEL OF DEPENDENTS IS AUTHORIZED (List names of dependents and DOB of children.)

*26. AUTHORITY FOR CONCURRENT TRAVEL

27. TRAVEL TIME WILL BE COMPUTED PER CHAPTER 36, PART 1, AFM 35-11.
TPA WITH ___5___ DAYS TRAVEL TIME

28. ___66___ POUNDS BAGGAGE, INCLUDING EXCESS IS AUTHORIZED

29. DISLOCATION ALLOWANCE CATEGORY

Other

*30. MODES OF TRANSPORTATION AUTHORIZED FOR OVERSEAS TRAVEL

A. ☒ MILITARY AIRCRAFT   B. ☐ COMMERCIAL AIRCRAFT (Category Z)   C. ☐ MILITARY AND COMMERCIAL VESSEL   D. ☒ COMMERCIAL AIRCRAFT OR VESSEL (Also foreign registry if US registry is not available) RAIL OR BUS WITHIN OVERSEAS AREAS

*31. REPORT AT MATS PASSENGER SERVICE COUNTER
☐ McGUIRE AFB   ☐ TRAVIS AFB   ☐ McCHORD AFB   ☐ CHARLESTON AFB

*32. FLIGHT NO. OR NAME OF VESSEL

*33. PIER NO. AND ADDRESS

*34. REPORTING TIME AND DATE FOR SCHEDULED DEPARTURE
NET
NLT

35. *A. PRIOR TO TRAVEL COMPLY WITH AFM 75-4. *B. WHILE ON LEAVE OVERSEAS COMPLY WITH AFM 35-22, AND CHAPTER 1, AFM 35-10.
C. In the event of limited war or mobilization and individual is traveling: PCS UNACCOMPANIED-proceed as scheduled. PCS ACCOMPANIED-contact your last commander immediately for instructions before reporting to port. In the event of general war or if the CONUS is attacked report to the nearest active Air Force Installation as soon as possible.

36. REMARKS

This is a Hq USAF directed move. DEROS: 25 Oct 66.

37. AUTHORITY, AFM ~~XXXXXXXX~~ 39-11 and Hq USAF

Line Number JZ0060, Oct 66, returnee.

38. DATE

12 August 1966

39. SPECIAL ORDER NO.

A-4976

40. DESIGNATION AND LOCATION OF HEADQUARTERS

DEPARTMENT OF THE AIR FORCE
HQ PACIFIC COMMUNICATIONS AREA (AFCS)
APO SAN FRANCISCO 96515

41. PCS EXPENSE CHARGEABLE TO

F927 F748 5773500 327 P577.02
1290 2121 2141 2161 2293 8503725

42. DISTRIBUTION

```
70 - Indiv concerned
30 - CBPO-ADM
 5 - Losing Unit
 5 - Gaining Unit
 1 - Postal Officer, Gaining Unit
 1 - AFCS (CSDASD)
 1 - PCA (DA)
```

43. CUSTOMER IDENTIFICATION CODE

4 5 748 5776 503725

44. TDY EXPENSE CHARGEABLE TO

45. TDN

46. SIGNATURE ELEMENT OF ORDERS AUTHENTICATING OFFICIAL

FOR THE COMMANDER

Jack O. Hall

JACK O. HALL, CMSgt., USAF
Administrative Officer

APCS-W AFB, Hawaii

AF FORM 899 (AUG. 62)

☆ U. S. GOVERNMENT PRINTING OFFICE — 1963-699-837

Not much else is new, honeybunch. We've had a drizzling rain most of the afternoon and this evening. I'm writing now but don't know when this will be finished as we have a meeting at 7:30. Ritual now—7:30 every Tuesday. This new Commander has his weekly staff meeting at 4:30 every Tuesday, so Captain Rayfield has his at night.

Well, Tonight's meeting was rather quick—just 30 minutes. Not too awfully much was passed on—words on late reports, APR's, uniforms, etc. The only hat authorized now is the regulation fatigue cap, excepted of course the flight or garrison caps with 1505's or blues. They had knocked off all the odd headgear all the cool cats were displaying. Actually, with other uniform violations, at times you could hardly tell what service a man was in. Latest victim to the new ruling are the squadron hats—baseball style caps with the squadron designation that maybe 1/3 of the people wore.

Larkin was just in and I started telling him something about line distortion but he shut me off real quick—telling me he didn't have but 14 hours to go here. He leaves for Saigon at 11 tomorrow and departs Saigon on the 26th. The lucky stiff!

A week from tomorrow is payday. Better than that, it means the end of August and into September. Then I can start saying "next month I go home". It also means school and I'm wondering how much, if any, of a break that will be for you. There'll still be 3 little ones at home, plus the hustle of getting them off every day. Maybe, if you can get them all to act at once, it might even be possible for you to get a few moments rests in the afternoons. I know you didn't get too much of that when you only had one or two at home.

I leave you for now, sweet girl, with 62 days or so to go. I'm still thinking of you so much all the time. It seems that about 10 times a day I just feel like stopping what I'm doing and want to write to you. It seems a bit ridiculous when there's no news, but that's not even in my mind. All I'd be able to write is "I love you so," over and over again. Until then, I'll have to make do with these wonderful pictures of you and the children, and our memories. Good night, my beloved.

Your Leo

24 Aug 66

Happy Birthday, My Love,

I've just been talking to our MARS[28] operator, hoping to get a phone patch through to you. We had the states but there was too much interference so they're going to keep trying and call back. I didn't figure they'd get through until around 9 P.M., our time, so I went to chow. When I got back they told me MARS had called ten minutes earlier. They said they had a good clear shot at that time.

There was no mail today for the fourth day and I was wondering if anything was wrong. That wasn't my primary reason for trying to get this call though since I had been planning it originally for our anniversary. However, at that time the station was down. It's supposed to be better in a week or so, once we replaced the antenna. The one that's on now had toppled and got badly bent, but usable.

It's 8:40 P.M. now and I just got a call from Sgt Buenavitas at MARS saying they were just now getting up with the states and he would call me first as soon as they got through. I've been holding off writing any more until I see if I get to talk to you.   Oh, I miss you so much, my sweet, that I even feel wobbly sitting here thinking that I may get to hear your voice in a few minutes.

We've reached the 11 P.M. mark now and still no contact. Lt Nelson was just in the shop and we've been talking business for the past hour. I'll be waiting up as long as MARS is still trying to make contact. They've been making contact with Sacramento and San Diego but can't seem to hold a steady receive signal at this end.

Well! Finally got through around 12:30 A.M. our time and it's too bad we had such a bad phone patch. Most of the time I could make out your voice but couldn't tell what you were saying because of the static. I understand I was coming through to you fairly well. Isn't it funny though; I had so many things running through my head while waiting—things to ask, sweet words, etc.—but come time to talk they had all deserted me. Then of course there's always that psychological barrier when knowing there are people at both ends monitoring the call. A couple of your replies were picked up by the operator and relayed to me.

I don't guess I'll be going to Hong Kong unless Maj Linkenfelter gets me a hop when he goes. He said he'd be flying either there or Bangkok before very long. If so I'll go with him if he has room. Otherwise, I'll skip it entirely. I've ordered a couple of things through the BX already and I'm getting short enough over here now that staying these next couple months won't bother me.

I had also asked about Karen—how she was doing. Last letter I had from you said you were going for the appointment at Carswell. I was glad to

---

hear she seemed to be doing well. Green just told me that he talked to the mail clerk tonight and he said the mail must be pigeonholed somewhere since he's gotten very little air mail delivery the past 3 days.

Buck, Green and Grenier were all here when MARS called me. We were all eating some of your preserves—on graham crackers—with coffee. When the phone rang, they all got on the extension right quick, just to tease me. But then they hung up and left the room.

Even though it was a poor quality circuit, it was so nice hearing the sound of your voice. I don't know why I should have expected it to sound any differently, but it's just been so long since I heard it. Gosh but I miss you, sweetheart. It's 61 days until DEROS, so it should be less than 60 before I leave here, and believe me that can't move fast enough. Just thinking of hearing your voice again now almost makes me shake. Oh, if only I could be holding you close this minute.   Then, on top of that, looking at the latest pictures of you right now only makes the ache in my heart and in my body more intense. Golly, how could I ever miss anyone so much and have these strong feelings continuously increasing. I keep telling myself to calm down now, that I'll just have to be patient and pretty soon it'll come to an end. Then right afterwards it starts all over again. I love you, my dearest Don Leta, from the very depths of my heart. Be sweet, my happiness, and take extra good care of yourself for me. When I return I'll grasp you and never let you go! Then there'll be no part of you that will not know my kisses—and as soon as I'm finished, I intend to start all over again. Right now I'd be happy just to hold your hand, and press it gently, knowing that you were near me.
Good night, my beloved.

Your Leo

As I folded this letter, I looked
at the heading and remembered:
The first thing I had planned on
saying to you was "happy birthday",
See what you do to me—even
from 10,000 miles?

25 Aug 66

My Darling,

How can I tell you that I love you in some new way that hasn't been tried some hundred times before? It was so nice to walk up and get three letters from you at once. I don't know where they've been, as they bore postmarks of 18, 20 and 21 August.

One letter made me feel so awful because you hadn't heard from me in some time and were worried. I hope that doesn't happen again, honeybunch.

I've got two more trips to make, taking Sgt Williams with me, and that should be it for the rest of my tour. However, prior to going on these outings I'll make sure to let you know. Neither one should be over two days unless we run into transportation difficulties. I know it doesn't do any good to say don't worry.... but, don't worry. If something would have happened to me, I'm sure you would have been notified.

I had almost forgotten about having the chairs covered. It's good though that you found someone who would do it for about 20% less. I was afraid that might be the way I'd have to occupy myself when I first got home—especially if it's the wrong time of the month!

It's too bad you didn't get to see the orthodontist yet. I don't know, the more I think about it, however, the more I feel that it would be better to go ahead and have done whatever the orthodontist recommends. Especially in Karen's case, with her other problems it would probably be better. I've heard others comment on it and I know the cost would be astronomical, but I don't think that should carry too much weight in our final decision.   We'll see what develops.

I haven't been feeling too bad. I have had some periods when I haven't felt too good, but mostly it was just a sluggish feeling. I'd been to the medics once about it and got some pills. The doc said to try and get some rest and he also recommended I take some supplemental vitamins while here.   So now I religiously take my One-A-Day pill. This is not the same kind of pill you're taking!

One of our troops pulled a lulu last night. I've seen them over here. This guy just made Tech last cycle and was booked out for home tomorrow. Last night he got drunk and in a knife fight with a guy who just made SSgt last go-around (a GEEIA troop). The Staff needed 17 stitches on his chest and the Tech a bunch in his left arm where tendons and an artery were cut. Now the Wing Commander cancelled the Tech's flight and I'm sure there'll be a few stripes available. Imagine that, letting yourself get in that condition on the eve of going home. Probably the most ridiculous part of it all was what they fought over—interpretation of a maintenance document (Tech Order).

I'll also be glad to sit close to you on the couch and listen to "our" song about you—My Happiness. I think I'd be content to just sit there with you all night listening to those good songs of 15-20 years ago. I miss you so, Don Leta. Well, maybe within another two months we won't have to go through this any longer. I'm so anxious and look forward daily to that time. Good night, my happiness.

Your Leo

27 Aug 66

My dearest Don Leta,

"How much do I love you; let me count the ways." That's in a poem somewhere and I think of that so often when I'm about to write to you.

There was no mail yesterday, but I intended to write anyhow. I came to the office after supper and started looking through a TRUE magazine I had picked up at the BX a couple of days before. To shorten my story, it was 8 o'clock when I woke up. So, I locked up and went to bed by 8:30. I was awakened around 11 or so by some booming noises. As soon as I got oriented and realized it was thunder and lightning, I went back to sleep. When I said no mail, I meant no mail from my favorite girl. I did get a letter from Mom, however.

Today I did get a letter from my sweet girl, as well as one from mother. You must have told mother what I wrote about her, at least, being happy over the Altus assignment. She started off by telling me I must think she's gloating over the assignment and that she's not near as selfish as I must think she is— that one of these days, when the children get scattered everywhere, I will understand. Again, she brags about her little doll Lynn!

Of course, best of all was another letter from my luscious honeybun. Gosh how I love you, Don Leta. You mentioned the birthday card I sent you. Had you noticed it had been opened and re-sealed? I've had it for about two months, signed it then forgot whether it was birthday or anniversary! I knew the BX had been out of one of them. Anyhow, repeated trips to the BX didn't do any good. All they had were greetings to other couples on their anniversary, or cards for silver/golden anniversaries.

I'm sorry Karen was disappointed over my deciding not to take leave back east at this time. I'll have to try to get a letter off to her shortly. As I mentioned, it's not firm yet that we'll be going to Altus, so we may still have the opportunity. As for going around next June, that's a possibility which I feel better wait a while for final decision. No telling what shape we'll be in by then. I'm not sure if I'll have caught up with my smoochin' & lovin'! As for the assignment bit, it may be a while yet before we hear unless it's definite. Otherwise, they'll have to go back stateside and get me a new assignment. I believe I told you what happened. I forecasted in March as a MSgt—30670. Promotion made be me a SMS—30690. I fear they never corrected the forecast, so the computer looked for a place that needed a 30670. The problem now is that if I went there and they weren't authorized a SMS—30690, I'd be reported as surplus and available for reassignment. Another move I don't think we'd need. As far as leave when I get home, I don't imagine I'll use too much of it resting up. As a matter of fact, I'll probably be in a hurry to get to the base so I can rest up days! I would, however, like to try and save as much leave time as possible and practical.

There's not much news, sweetheart. I expect to be out a day or two the early part of next week with Sgt Williams. Otherwise, things have been relatively quiet. Still an occasional crisis, but I've pretty well managed to keep out of those.

Good night and sweet dreams, my beloved. I've just been looking at the last few pictures you sent and I still can't get over how good you look. Delicious!! I just can't wait to get my arms around you! I miss you terribly and it's so hard now as the time gets shorter and shorter. Five more days and we'll be able to say "next month". I'll be so happy when I can say "last month" to you personally. You're the sweetest and most loveable girl in the whole wide world and I ever so happy to be able to call you mine.

Your Leo

28 Aug 66

My Darling,

Received your quicky note today, enclosing the 643A, Personal History Statement. I thought I had a 398 but I guess not. I've filled those things out so often in these past 18 years that I guess I don't remember just what was on file. The trouble is that the 398 now requires the darndest information and I'll have to be writing off everywhere for that. There'll be a lot of things I'll need from you (or your memory). I'll let you know as soon as I get everything together.

I was a bit disappointed of course that there wasn't a long letter from you, but I know you wanted to get it off without delay. You briefly mentioned our radio-telephone conversation. We now have our new antenna installed and they said it improves the system. I plan on giving you a call, if I can get through, when I hear the final word on our assignment, as well as when I'm given a definite date to leave Vietnam.

Things have been relatively quiet work-wise today, so I'm taking advantage by writing during duty hours. They put up a notice on the bulletin board that starting this payday personnel will have to report for pay at certain times, be in clean uniform, shaved & hair cut, etc. I'm expecting the next thing they'll be coming up with around here will be retreat ceremonies and Saturday morning inspections and parades. Damnedest war I ever fought!

Back to my letter again, only now it's almost 8 P.M. I'm ready for the sack too, having been up last night until after midnight again. I keep telling myself I'm going to get more sleep, but I never seem to get there. I am going, however, right after this letter.

There really isn't much more to write, sweetheart. I don't remember if I told you or not, but Sgt Carter's assignment was squared away. Our new Commander, Major Groves, spoke to Carter and agreed that he had a legitimate complaint and he was justified in writing to his congressman. However, he asked Carter to let him try to do something first. He sent a message to Turner AFB, explaining the situation to Carter's new Sq Commander. They received a reply saying that in view of what Maj Groves had written, Carter was being reassigned to the Field Maintenance Sq at Turner instead of the Mapping & Charting Sq. That way he'll stay on base. Needless to say, Carter is happy.

No decision has been made yet on what to do about the two NCOs who got into that knife fight. I guess they're waiting for all the reports to be in. The TSgt who was supposed to be going home had his flight cancelled so now there's no telling when he'll get out of here. From scattered reports, he was so drunk when all this took place that he was completely incoherent. This guy was one who everyone would have stood up for. He was a working fool who did a tremendous job for a year and was rewarded with a promotion last June. I had the paperwork to process a recommendation for the Commendation Medal on him. Now, he'll probably be lucky to go back with more than one or two stripes. I've seen this place do strange things to people—or people behave strangely in this place—during these past months. At first I tried to reason some of them out, but no more. It's beyond me.

One consolation—we're down to 57. Even if I stay the limit, that means only about 50 more duty days, then I'll be processing, clearing, etc. I sure would like for them to decide to start flying directly out of here instead of our having to go to Saigon. They were supposed to have started a while back but I understand they (the airlines) reneged when General Walt wouldn't guarantee them that this was a secure base. Heck, I don't know what they want. The air strip here is a safe as Saigon and they're in and out of there all the time.

I'm wondering if some of my underclothes & sox are going to last these 8 weeks. They're getting kinda holy. One thing I'm planning on is that they'll cut down my laundry enroute since I can just throw them away! I've already put some aside for that purpose since I don't think they'd make it through another Vietnamese washday.

I've got to go, honeybunch—off to bed by myself (I should hope!) again. I never hate to hit the sack, however 'cause besides being tired I know I'll be closing my eyes and thinking of our many wonderful moments together, and dreaming of the future. It'll be so nice to hold you close, my sweet. I try to think of it now but it's so elusive—just keeps slipping away. I need you so much it hurts. Good night my sweet, wonderful Don Leta.

Your Leo

29 Aug 66

My Darling,

There's really not a thing to write about tonight, but I did want to send off a short note anyhow. No mail today. I had expected a little 'cause yesterday I received a short note with that form and figured you would write that night. Some times I get to expecting a little too much.

This has been a fairly busy day. Not too much chance for goofing off. I did make it to bed relatively early last night, but then I couldn't get to sleep. Then, about eleven or so, a fighter hit in the other side of the strip so I was up again. Couldn't see much with buildings in the way, but it did burn for quite some time. They couldn't get too close I guess because there must still have been rockets aboard. You asked once how close we were to the runway. Well, lookee:

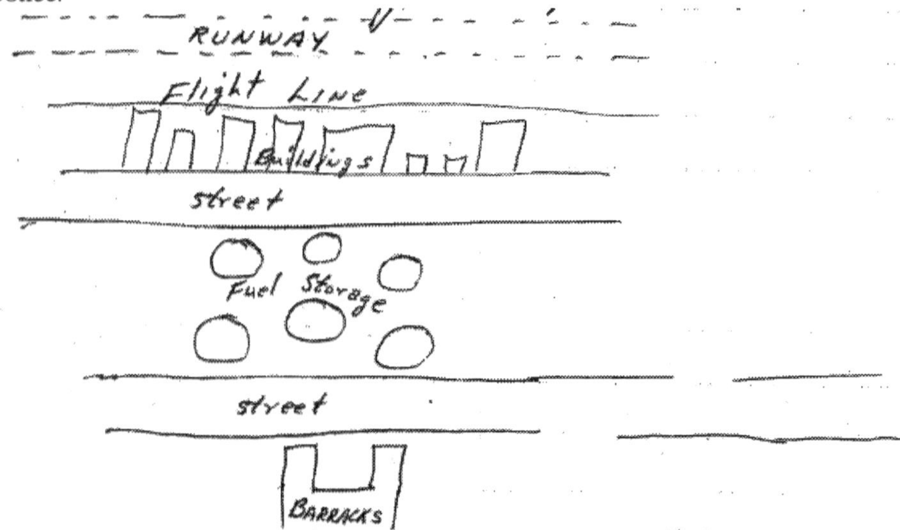

I'm glad I remembered you asking about that. It enabled me to use up about a dozen lines!

That's all there is, sweet wife. Except that we're past another of those big long days and we're down to 56. Gosh how they're dragging. I'm sure the shorter the time gets the more I think of it—and the longer it makes it seem. I wish that as every day ended we jumped right into the next day, because it's the nights that are especially hard. I love you so very much, Don Leta, but I wish I wouldn't think so much about it. It just makes being apart that much harder. Good night, my wonderful girl—my happiness.

Your Leo

30 Aug 66

My dearest Don Leta,

There's been a bit of a wait, but it was nice again today to receive two letters from you. Mail is still goofed up. It looks like a bunch of mail had been delayed somewhere: At noon time I picked up a letter from you written the 25th and tonight I received the one written the day before. You were expecting the Bertone's at any time, so I'm already resolved to no mail tomorrow. With the bunch you'll have, it'll be something just to get your talking done, much less writing.

Also received a letter from Karen today, letting me know of many of her "big" problems. I must answer it real soon, even though I just wrote to her. So many of these big trials I remember having myself as a kid. I was one, you know! I wondered if you had read it. Probably not.

One of my troops who also leaves in October got his post call today. He has a DEROS of 4 October and his call is for 28 September out of Saigon (26 September out of Da Nang.) A few of the other early October returnees got theirs also. While I think of it, and you mentioned it in one of your letters today, the reason we leave Da Nang 2 days before the flight out of Saigon is not due to processing at TSN. Rather, there's no processing involved, other than checking in at the terminal. The reason we start out two days early is that transportation in country sometimes gets a bit slim.   Plus it's base hopping— Hue to Nha Trang to Pleiku to Tan Son Nhut—and you're liable to get stuck at any of them. The others who got post calls had from 4 to 6 days before their DEROS also. I hope I do as well, even though any time prior to DEROS is time gained. Any amount I can subtract from our present 55 is fine with me.

It's a good thing you mentioned not to forget the money order for Bryan's birthday. You know, I had completely forgotten about getting that. I'll have to pick one up tomorrow. If I didn't send it, I'd probably have to forget about going home!

I had checked again on Hushpuppies at the BX but they didn't have any my size. They're supposed to have more coming as this was ¼ of their order. Also checked on the suit I ordered (brown, Italian silk and something else I can't remember right now) and they expect them in towards the end of the week.

Now, see. It wasn't only me that said you were getting prettier all the time. This year away from me must be doing some good! I'll have to plan on doing it more regularly. The kids will probably have twice as much trouble as before with cavities now, as I imagine you'll be making quite a few trips to Clay's Drive-In for candy. I still think you look so delicious in these pictures.

I've been rather busy today, mostly writing studies and programs. With more systems being planned all the time it requires constant re-evaluations to determine how much more equipment, parts, personnel, etc, are going to be required. After the 1st of the month I'm going to try to pass the shops over to

Williams and let him run them all. Then I can spend my time getting all this stuff worked out in final form.

Tomorrow is payday and after that we've only got one payday to go. A bunch of us are also waiting for Thursday to come around, 'cause then we can say "next month I go home." It'll still be some 50+ days for me, but at least it'll sound good. It seemed to me for a while that this month wasn't moving at all, but here it is just about over with. I know September will seem to be dragging by to me!

I guess the whole thing is just that I'm so anxious to be with you again. Too anxious, probably, insofar as thinking about it all the time while knowing I've still got a definite time to do. I couldn't help it anyhow, no matter how hard I tried. You just mean too much to me, honeybunch. Though I've thought of you constantly, it's been a while since I've been thinking of our first being together again, and it now seems to be starting all over. I know that if I had to leave you like this again I just couldn't do it, unless it was a question of national survival. I never want to be away from you more than the normal short periods that people have every now and then, like a day or two. I just want to be selfish and keep you with me all the time.

My life just isn't the same without you, Don Leta, and I don't like it this way at all. There's no purpose or reason for so many things like there is at home. I don't know what I'd do without my sweet girl to come home to. Gosh, but I love you and miss you. You know, even so many of the routine things we've done, the menial tasks and the projects alike, were all so much a part of our life together. You washing clothes or me doing dishes, though we don 't think of it as such at the time and may occasionally lead us to gripe, are still part of our helping each other go forward together. I miss everything we've ever done together or apart for each other and the children. Oh, Don Leta, there's so, so very much I want to say to you. How awful it is that we're so far apart at times like these when I want so much to hold you close and tell you how much you mean to me. Really, I don't think I'll ever be able to adequately tell you, at least not with words alone. I know I'll be so proud to have you and the children around me again. I want everyone to see my wonderful family.

It's really discouraging to sit here and try to describe feelings. How does one describe hurt, or happiness, or joy, or desire? It's just impossible. These things are so abstract they can mean a hundred different things to a hundred different people. How can I let you know how I feel inside of me when I say it hurts not to be able to hold you? Who else knows what I'm speaking about when I say it's a mixture of hollowness, throbs, heart beats and many other mysterious sensations? I can't begin to tell you what it's like because we have no known thing to compare it with. If I knew how you felt at certain times, perhaps it would be possible to compare, but I'm certain you, like any other human, would be incapable of fully and adequately transcribing it to language we'd both understand. That must be why they coined words like "frustration"! It is so frustrating because I'm feeling all these things right now, and there's no way to satisfy them. It must have to do with the other mysterious word people are always trying to describe—love. It must at least be part of it.

I used to feel like this and I'd say, "255 days", then "155 days", and now "55 days" and each in turn would seem like an eternity. When I can say "5 days" the feeling will still be there, except that the hollowness will be a little deeper, the throbs a little heavier, the heartbeats a little faster. I need you, Don Leta. I want to slowly, very slowly, undress you and take you to bed. Then I want to caress you and to forget this long year in those caresses. I want to feast on the softness of your breasts, to gently feel the rise and fall of your tummy and the inviting warmth of your gradually opening thighs. Then we will be one in body, just as we are in all other ways. Please don't feel offended of my descriptive prose, my sweet and wonderful wife.   Granted, it does make me feel better just to write it. But, really, what I'm trying to do, in a way that's so totally inadequate , is to have you understand, if only the smallest degree more than previously, how very, very much you mean to me—and how, without reservation, qualification or other attachment, I always wish to remain your husband, your admirer, your servant, your lover, and

Your Leo

DaNang, RVN
31 Aug 66

My Honeybunch,

Great and exciting news to announce tonight. We had strawberry shortcake at suppertime, or at least plain cake with frozen strawberries on it. That makes three times for cake and twice for pie since I've been here. With only 54 days to go, I don't look to see any more before I leave.

Absolutely nothing else to relate, my love. This has been a pretty routine day, with enough new paperwork to keep me busy. It seems that every day brings a bit more statistical ridiculous reports or projects. We've got a couple to do now that are doozies — and of absolutely no value that I can see.

Good night, my sweet girl. I love you, love you, love you.

Your Leo

31 Aug 66

Hi Pal,

I'm sorry it took so long for this money order to get to you since your birthday will already be gone by. Boy, you're getting so old and big now, I'm sure I won't even be able to throw you up real high one time!

It won't be very long now until daddy comes back home, then I'll be able to play a bit with you and Paul, and give you a ride on my "pony boy". I'll have to play with baby Lynn too, 'cause I haven't even seen her yet. I hope you're helping take good care of her.

You keep being a good boy now, and watch after your brother.

Lots of love,
Daddy

1 Sep 66

My dearest, darling, beloved, sweet girl,

How wonderful it was to receive two letters from you today. The mail situation is still not the most regular thing going, these missives having been postmarked two days apart.

I really don't think there'll be any big need for "re-considering" bringing the kids along to pick me up. I expected that would be done all along, at least with those big enough to go, depending on what time I get in. I had figured being alone with you as just another part of my dream. I don't think things will be <u>quite</u> that bad that I can't wait to be alone with you. It's odd that Bryan had mentioned running to me "as fast as he can", because I had even imagined that. It'll be so nice being with every one of you again.

You mentioned going to Uncle Robert's for dinner last Sunday after church and you made my mouth water.

The new post office opened in Jacksboro. Postmaster Mixon Stamper prepares to send Bryan to his dad in Vietnam.

Photo courtesy, Fort Worth Star-Telegram.

The chow is pretty good here, considering, but there's not an awfully variable menu. The meat is almost all canned to start with and fresh vegetables (and fruits) are practically non-existent. We do get lettuce and some small, hard tomatoes from somewhere out of country, but by the time it's served the tomatoes don't have too much taste and the lettuce is quite wilted. A few (very few) times we had oranges or apples and they kept better so they were usually pretty good. The club has some new TSgt who has recently taken over their kitchen and things have improved 100%, in appearance if nothing else.

I stayed up last night, finally getting to bed at 4 a.m. this morning. Grenier & I went to midnight chow and then returned to the shop where we planned on listening to the Clay-Millerberger fight which was supposed to be aired by shortwave radio at 11:30 a.m. There was some difficultly, and they didn't get it on until almost 3. So, we sat and played checkers until then (cheer, cheer—I won, 4 games to 2). This being Sunday, I played it loose and didn't come in until 10:30.

I was sorry and concerned to hear that both mother and daddy were not well. It's bad enough for one of them to be ill at a time. Hope mother's troubles are from some passing virus or something rather than complications from her recent surgery.

At first I thought it was nice that Bill was able to get a vacation with the new baby home, but now I'm not so sure. I can't quite figure his strategy—or Mary's—that he takes a vacation and then spends most of the time away. When does Mary get her vacation?? As for the boys at the plant forever calling when he's home, I should think clueing them in would straighten that out. Besides, I wouldn't have the gall to be off somewhere while the neighbors helped hang my washing. Remind me to hang around for the next one, since I was off enjoying myself when Lynn came!

I'm getting increasingly anxious about getting word, firm word that is, on our assignment. I had mentioned to you about one man, Sgt Torres, our personnel man who takes care of assignments, being the only one who leaves in October and who hasn't received his assignment. Well, he finally got it and he's none too happy. Asked for Spain and Italy—got San Antonio! He wasn't as lucky as I—at least I got the country I asked for!

That's about the extent of the latest local gossip and excitement, my honeybunch. Charlie was a good boy and didn't throw anything at us last night, election eve. The skies around us were kept well lit up with flares all night long, making sure no one tried to sneak in under cover of darkness. They'll be on extra alert for a couple or three more nights until things have settled back to normal after the elections.

Gonna try and make the movies tonight. It's suppose to be pretty good—"Nevada Smith", a western with Steve McQueen. A couple of the guys have seen it and said it was a pretty good show. Last night I missed ANOTHER rock'n'roll movie that was on.

This is about it for now, sweet girl. Gots to take a shower now and get ready to write off another day. I love you bunches & bottlefuls, and miss you as ever.

Your Leo

2 Sep 66

My Beloved,

Next month I go home! Does this month seem to be dragging by to you??   I've been waiting all of August for the chance of saying that to everyone around here.

No letter mail today, but did receive the tape letter, which was even better since I could hear your voice and that of all the kids. I really enjoyed it— the kids sounding so hopped up and all. I had to play it on John's recorder inasmuch as mine needs a battery (the 9V jasper). I'll tell you; if it's not one thing it's another. I've been three months getting the little penlight batteries, and they still haven't gotten the others. John said tonight he believed they had some now. If so, I'll make a tape tomorrow night and rush it off.

The girls sounded real good relating their experiences at Six Flags, and Karen with her telling of the "date" with Angie in payoff of her bet—especially that part of his opening the door for her; she never had that done for her before (her father's sterling example!) .

As the tape wound closer to the end it went faster and faster, making your voice higher and higher in pitch. I could control it fairly well by holding my fingers against the reel and slowing it down. That's the big problem with battery operated portables. It just about has to be played at the same speed as recorded, so if one set records with fresh power and the other plays back with weak batteries, it throws it out of kilter. Same if you record weak and play back strong. John got hold of a converter but I haven't been able to find one yet. You use house power by plugging in the front of the set where it says "external power".   That only runs your turntable (the job done by the 6 penlight batteries). The amplifier (sound) still runs off the 9 Volt battery. The turntable is the one that causes the trouble.

I've only heard the tape once so far—too many people around—but I intend to turn it on again in a bit. I didn't hear Paul in the background, but now that you mentioned he called out I'll listen for it. I was trying too much to hear what was being said by the others.

There's not been too much new around here. Grenier took a quick run to a couple of the sites this morning, but he was back by 4 P.M. I'll not be going now until after the Vietnamese elections on 11 September, if at all. Right now I doubt that I'll go any more since it looks like Williams is taking pretty good charge of things. Maybe in another week he can have all of it. Then I'll get on a few of the other things hereabouts that need to get done and play it sort of loose.

Of course, the feeling here as well as all other places in Vietnam is to play things pretty close to the vest from now to elections. There's always the possibility of the VC trying something to cause confusion or try to gain publicity to influence the voters. So extra precautions are being taken in all areas.

Still no word on my assignment. They must have gone back to Randolph or Offutt to get a reading on this, as long as it's been already. So, there's still no telling when I'll get word. The original message query went from here to Hawaii (Wheeler), and they would have answered by now if they knew, I'm sure. Heck, we could end up just about anywhere now—though all those places I mentioned when I first forecasted are still the best bets.

I started writing last night and had almost half a page done but never finished it. There just wasn't a thing to relate. It had rained just about all day long, looking a bit like the rainy season. They're predicting a much wetter monsoon season than last year. More like the year before when one five day stretch brought 31 inches of rain. At least this cooler weather is better for sleeping, especially for those troops who have to work mids. I don't see how they sleep at all during the day time.

Well, my love, I'm gonna quit again for a while (until tomorrow night). It's just about midnight again. After hearing all of you on tape, I seem to miss you just that extra little bit more. How very wonderful it'll be to be together again. That's all that's in my mind. You really and truly are and always will be my happiness.

Your Leo

3 Sep 66

My dearest Don Leta,

A broken record is what it must be sounding like by now, but nothing very exciting happened today except that we were able to scratch off another day.

It's pretty well assured that I won't be venturing from Da Nang anymore to go out to the sites. Monday crypto and teletype officially will belong to Sgt Williams.   I'll be spending most of my time from now on in administrative matters, re-writing maintenance operating instructions and re-working the maintenance manning documents to justify more people.

One other guy leaving in October (the 5th) received his flight reservation today. He'll fly out of Saigon 8 days prior to his DEROS. I don't know why I keep telling you about all these people going home. Wishful thinking, I guess.

I was talking to this guy in Saigon today (on the phone). He's flying up here tomorrow with some parts, so I asked him if they had any 9V batteries in the BX there and he said he was sure there was. So, he's supposed to pick up a couple for me. I'll probably have a chance to make that tape tomorrow night. Big John checked at the BX here for me and they still don't have any.

No mail today, honeybunch, so nothing to relate in that area either. John received a box of cookies from his wife today. They were mailed 27 July so they must have come book mail. We all stood solemnly by as he walked to the trash with them. They were packed in a metal can but it wasn't air proof.

This is it for now, my love. I've been listening to the tape again and closing my eyes making believe I'm with you. I miss you so much, my wonderful Don Leta.

Your Leo

5 Sep 66

Hi Honeybunch,

You're probably going to be wondering what happened to me again since I imagine there's been no letters for a couple days. I didn't write Saturday as there wasn't much of anything new and I had no mail either. Then, last night I made a "tape letter" instead of writing. I'll have to mail it tomorrow, however, as I didn't get it off today. I went down to the Post Office and there was such a mob that it would have taken me a good half hour just to get stamps so I turned around, figuring on going back later in the day. I should have known better. Other things came up and I couldn't get away.

Though I've turned over supervision of BASECOMM to Sgt Williams, I still spent almost all day on it with him getting a couple of projects squared away. There's still a bit more to do on it after which he should be able to pretty well carry it himself.

I was down to the BX this morning after receiving a call that my clothes were in and went do to try them on. The trousers fit just perfectly but the coat needs some more tailoring. I'm supposed to go try it on again tomorrow. I had also gotten two white shirts made to my size—imagine me with tailored shirts—but at $2.50 each I figured I couldn't lose. In all I'm spending $84 on clothes. That's extravagant for me but I'll probably not have the opportunity (or money) to do it again. I'll have a brown suit ($40) and a gray suit ($35), tailor made, to wear at the kid's weddings! I couldn't remember before what the material was—it's Italian silk and wool.

Received a letter from Mom today. She didn't have too much news. Said she'd been over to see Marie's latest—looked like the rest of her clan—and commented that Marie was still the same big kid herself. She was excited over the Bertone's coming home, but it seemed to be mostly because the other kids (the neighbors & Chippy's) were excited.

Also received a letter from my honeybunch. I'm not sure I understand the registration procedure for school in Jacksboro. If Karen was pre-registered, why weren't Steph and Lanis? Is it just that they start doing it at certain grades? That is quite a novel way of assigning kids to classes (and teachers also), by having to draw numbers for it. Sounds like a lottery! I also got a charge out of your description of the "lottery" for the 5th grade assignments, where James Jonas didn't get in Stephanie's group. I'd imagine it would be better for the teacher. Has Steph commented any on it yet?

It's just as I anticipated. The comment made about Bryan being the only model child at Bible School only confirms what I suspected all along. He's just like his father!

It's been real hot here again the last couple days, while at night we either catch some rain or it's so close to it that you can just feel the heaviness and wetness of the air. Last night, as I mentioned on the tape, I thought Charlie was throwing them in, even though it was kind of early for him. It was confirmed, however, that a couple rockets were set off while they were loading a marine jet. It hit in the VC stockade over towards the main gate.

Well, sweetheart, it's down in the forties bracket now, and before long it'll be in the thirties. I'm still hoping I'll be able to chop a few days off the total when my flight reservation comes in. Still no word on assignment. If by the end of the week there's still nothing, I'll see if they'll go out with a tracer to find out what's being done. I've seen too many people sitting here waiting until the last minute to get either an assignment or a flight reservation. Also, I'll want to ship some hold baggage and it would be nice to know where to ship it to.

I'm going to sneak off now, my lovely girl, tho it's only 9:15. I'm going to try to make the 9:30 movie, though I can't even remember what's playing. Good night for now, my sweet. I miss you terribly and love you loads and loads.

Your Leo

"48"

6 Sep 66

My dearest Don Leta,

A rather busy day today but I'm just about pooped out now and think I'll hit the sack early tonight. Very little mail came today – none for old daddy.

We did get off on another of our crisis binges this afternoon when we received word that the Group Commander was going to be down tomorrow. Of course everything has to be washed, polished, painted, etc. He's supposed to be here for 24 hours, though I don't know the purpose of his visit. It might be an advanced tour in preparation for next month's visit by General Klocko, the AFCS Commander, and General Shtogren, PACOM area Commander. Excitement, excitement!

They did get smart on base and added another showing at the movies each day, this one at 11 A.M. As I mentioned before, they don't have much of anything else to keep the troops occupied and anytime there was a half decent movie it was almost impossible to get in unless you spent at least an hour in line. Now they have shows at 11 a.m., 1, 5:30, 7:30 and 9:30 P.M. They wouldn't have too much trouble filling any of them. Even all the rock n roll, cartoon features and monster pictures are sellouts here.

Checked again, a daily routine now, on any word of my assignment but nothing yet. Everyone leaving in October has his orders, including my uncertain ones, except one person—our personnel clerk! I guess he hasn't any pull.

I'm sorry this is such a shorty again, my sweet. Perhaps tomorrow there'll be a bit more for me to relate. I miss you tremendously and love you enormously.

Your Leo

7 Sep 66

My Beloved,

I thought there would be a letter from you today but no luck. Should have one for sure tomorrow. We were told today that a C-130 with mail aboard from here went down off Formosa Monday, so anyone who had mail aboard lost it. I don't even remember if I wrote that night or not. That may have been the night I made a tape recording instead of writing.

Again there's not very much news, honeybunch, though I did manage to keep fairly busy all day and a good part of the night. The Group Commander, Colonel Schultz came in about 3:15 this afternoon. It was almost six by the time he left this office and Capt. Rayfield followed it up with his weekly meeting, so we got off to supper a bit later than usual.

We've again started getting more rain in the late afternoon and evening. Though it wasn't bad at all in the month of August, we did manage to accumulate about 15 inches in that 30 days. Most of the wet weather lately has been fairly light, with only a few heavy showers.

They're clamping down again on people spending money. The G.I. is the one who always gets restrictions on this stuff, while the civilians go about their business. The latest thing is that people going on R&R can't charge any more money than they were paid over the board the last payday. So, if you drew $50 last payday, that's all you can take with you. Otherwise, you have to have a letter from the Squadron Commander stating that you've saved the money, received some from the states, etc. I don't know what they'll come up with next.

It's already going on midnight—dream time again my love. These crawling days are taking their ever-loving time in getting us together. All my thoughts have been filled with visions of our holding each other. I miss you so very much, my sweet Don Leta. Take good care of yourself for me, my beloved.

Your Leo

"46"

8 Sep 66

My Darling,

The famine was broken today by the receipt of letters from you and Karen. I'm cheating a bit by starting this letter during lunch break, though I don't figure on getting too far with it right now.

Karen really sounded elated over all the "exciting" things that happened to her all at once—powder, lipstick, shoes, leg shaving and the prospect of matching shoes as well as skirts and sweaters. I'm getting old, mommybunch (you're not, though)! She did sound happy. Pretty soon she'll be tapping us for high heels and her first formal—by then you can join me in feeling ancient.

Nothing new so far this morning. It's hot and muggy, especially with the sun following last night's rain.

I knew I wouldn't get much of a start on this. It's now almost eight. After supper tonight the clouds came in again—but no rain so far. A real good breeze came up and it was quite comfortable. We sat out in the field for a while and watched the softball game. A couple of crumb bum teams were playing. Very little softball, but lots of laughs.

My left arm is little sore right now. Grenier and I paid immunization a visit. Got typhus, typhoid and cholera. Now all I need next month before going home is a plague shot and tine test. I'd hate to be getting all these shots just before leaving. Even here, where so many of the diseases are prevalent, you'd be surprised at the number of people who either put off their shots or write them off rather than take them. I counted them up tonight—got 18 of them since this assignment.

A week from now and we'll break into the thirties on days left. It's still too long, but there's really not too awfully much time between us anymore, honeybunch. If I had to stay here much longer I'm afraid I'd soon be starting my letters "Dear Friend". Well, maybe not quite that bad!

Good night, my sweetness. You and the children are seldom out of my thoughts. For the umpteenth time I say that I miss you so very much, my darling. It'll be such a wonderful day when I'm winging my way home to you. Good night, my love.

Your Leo

9 Sep 66

My Honeybunch,

Broken record…broken record…broken record. No news today…no news today…no news today. I'm afraid that's what some of my letters are getting to sound like of late. Very little mail came in today, so there's nothing from that angle either.

Did meet a couple people today. The FSgt of the 441st Mortar Battery (USMC), stationed on our south flank was around on a scrounging mission. His name's Dubois and he's from upstate New York. He said there was also a Navy Chief here with that name, but he was outcast—from Louisiana. Then, as I left the club after chow tonight, this MSgt Buck, no relation to the one in our outfit, called me. He said "weren't you stationed at Carswell and didn't you play football?" He said he was in the 492nd and used to work with Sonny Hale. Just got here.

TOUCHDOWN…(Leo Dubois.) Carswell fullback, starts on a 30-yard scoring run against San Marcos Sunday at Farrington Field. Brian Mullenick (11) is ready to lend assistance, while G. F. Hageman, San Marcos tackle, trails the play.

Carswell Tramples San Marcos, 71-7

Saturday's High Scores

Photo courtesy, Fort Worth Star-Telegram

It's been pretty nice today, gloomy but cool. Didn't get to see much of the sun and there was a fair breeze just about all day long. I could tell it was nice sleeping weather when I got up this morning—half an hour late! I sure was tempted to just turn over and catch a few more winks.

We've had about 15 new people come in to the Squadron so far this week. We're due in another 28 before the end of the month, mostly radio relay types for new shots we're setting up. Only a few people, about 10 or 12, are due to ship out in September. After that, the October rush will start. If things follow the current trend, I should only have between 30 and 35 duty days left. Right now it's 45 'till DEROS.

I wish they'd hurry up with some word on my assignment.   I'd like to do some packing and get hold baggage out of the way. Sometimes that stuff takes so long to get to its destination that I'd like to get it off as soon as possible.

Good night for now, my honeybunch. Be a sweet girl and remember that I love you with all my heart.

Your Leo

"44"

10 Sep 66

My dearest Don Leta,

It was cloudy again just about all day today. At lunch time I went early and it was only 12 o'clock by the time I got back to the shop. By then everyone else was taking off for chow, so things got pretty quiet. That's all I needed as my head started nodding and my eyes got heavy. I got up and went to the barracks since it was relatively cool. It was 3:30 by the time I woke up! When I got back to work I found out that Grenier had gotten back at 1:45 and Green at 2:30, both having slept during their lunch break also.

So, there was some exciting news to pass on to you after all! Everything else has been about the same hereabouts. The Vietnamese elections are tomorrow, so everything hereabouts is buttoned up tight. Security precautions have been doubled but things have been fairly quiet. It'll be o.k. with me if they stay like that for the next 40 days or so. The BX and other facilities employing Vietnamese are all closed until after the elections.

Thought sure there would be a letter from you today but no such luck. I know in the last one I received, you were all tuckered out so you must still have been recuperating—plus which I guess it was school starting time. One good thing, we get Sunday mail deliveries here so there may be something for me tomorrow.

Grenier got his replacement today—a TSgt Donald Webb from McClellan AFB, Calif. He was there was only three months, having gone there from the 9-level school at Keesler. He was with Bishop & Schooley and knew them both, Schooley a bit better because he (Webb) bowled a bit. I guess Schooley still spent a good deal of his time on the alleys. If you write to Marie again, you can tell her to tell Bob not to get too comfortable—that the one year on station bit doesn't seem to be working too well. Grenier himself had 3 months at March after 9-level school before getting shipped here.

Well, sweetheart, gonna say goodnight again. I love you so very much, Don Leta, and how happy I'll be just to be with you again. It'd be so nice about this time at night for one of us to make some toast & coffee or hot chocolate, and just relax together. Be sweet, my love, and remember that you'll always be the only one for me.

Your Leo

"40"

14 Sep 66

My Darling,

Last night was supposed to be a writing night, especially after getting a letter from you yesterday, but I never made it back up after stretching out on that sack. After supper, Grenier & I set out front of the barracks for a few minutes, and already I could feel my eyes getting heavy. I told him I hated to go up and hit the sack, 'cause if I did I'd sleep and then wake up around 10 and not be able to get back to sleep 'till all hours. I was wrong. I laid on the bed with my sox still on, figuring on taking a shower in a few minutes. It was 5:30—this morning—when I woke up and got to that shower.

Today has been a fairly long day. Besides being rather busy, tonight we had our Airman of the Month board and NCO Advisory Council meeting. We just got out of that and it's almost 9 o'clock.   Grenier and I are both on this and it was our last session, CMS Tindell and MSgt Williams taking over for us.

As you can see from the attached, word has arrived on our assignment. Never did get a reply to the message we sent, but did get these amended orders. I was holding off but plan on getting a letter off to the 11th Wing tonight to see if I can get any general info since that seems to be where we'll end up. If things go accordingly to schedule (and they never seem to around here) we should be getting definite word on flight reservations in about another 10 days. Just think, tomorrow we'll be in the thirties—39 at the most.

I was sorry to hear things have been so hectic for you lately. Just hold on. Like you say, all problems will be solved when I get home!! I guess it's wishing too much, but I did hope the girls would settle down a bit once school got going again. But from your description of their activities, both fussing and raiding the ice box, it doesn't sound much like they have. I do hope whatever is troubling mother now can be resolved with rest and medication and that they don't have to resort to surgery again. As for old Grandma, she'll still probably go on and outlast many of us.

They've gotten hold of a new man to run the kitchen at the club and already we're seeing some welcomed changes. We've had cake a few times now. I think I may already have mentioned this, or maybe it was that I was groaning about the chow. But anyhow, today we even had pork chops, applesauce and green onions, items which we hardly remembered. Right after this guy took over, 2/3 of the cooks quit or were fired, I don't know which, but he's sure straightening it out and shaping it up. Yesterday you could even take an orange or two with you after your meal. Before that, they all used to find their way out the back door rather than to the members. The whole operation of this Club has smelled ever since I've been here—which has been ages now.

That's the latest from the far ends of the earth, honeybunch. Nothing very stimulating, I'm afraid. It won't be awfully long now before we can do away with this letter writing—then you can listen to my stimulating voice! Good night, my sweet girl. I love you with all my heart and always will.

Your Leo

15 Sep 66

My Honeybunch,

This won't be much of a letter tonight (again), but it's quite late already and in a few minutes Grenier, Green & myself will be heading for midnight chow. We've been pretty well tied up all night, 'till just a little while ago.

I got a special treat today—a tape from my favorite girl. I got to listen to it once, quick-like, during lunch time, but haven't had a chance to get back to it tonight. I hope that tomorrow night I'll have the chance to tape a letter, but if not I'll surely get it done this weekend.

Things keep growing and picking up around here. Just when you think you're about to catch up, in comes a bunch of new projects. We were cited again as the best Comm outfit in Vietnam, and each time we're praised we get more responsibilities and more work. The Group Commander said himself when he was here that we're given quite a bit more than any of the other outfits because they know we'll get it done. We even have things now that use to be the Army's responsibility. It also looks right now like we're going to take over a whole set-up presently run by some other outfit. Goody, goody, for the short time to go!

I've got a whole bunch of projects right now to get squared away before I leave here but, barring too much more put on me, I hope to pretty well have those squared away by 1 Oct. I started getting some of the troops in the act at this morning's staff meeting by telling them how APR's would hereafter be handled. It's going to make these supervisors get with the writing bit. I cited one write-up I got yesterday from one of our NCOs, about 2/3 of a sheet like this, and it had 26 misspelled words. Not simple errors but things like "vigusly" for vigorously, "comitabel" for commendable, and "tenicle" for technical. Too lazy to open a dictionary. Giving kids their spelling test is much easier!

Well sweet, I'm about to make it. I will try "reel' hard to get a tape done tomorrow night. We're getting there, sugargirl. Not too long ago even 39 days seemed like a long ways off, but we made it. Now I'm looking to get a specific departure date with flight reservations around the 25th. The picnic is almost over for both of us. We'll soon have to put up with each other again. What delicious torture! Good night, my wonderful wife.

Your Leo

19 Sep 66

My Honeybunch,

This past four or five days has made me think that everything has to be done before I go home, and it has to be done by me. I've been at it all day again today with another lengthy report, this one on air conditioners.

Fortunately though, things going at a brisk pace like this helps—doesn't give you quite as much time to sit and count days. I just tallied up—there are 29 of us leaving out of maintenance next month, and I guess each one is counting.   I was talking to Sgt Brewer at Group today. He was here on the inspection team. We came over on the same plane together and he said flight schedules were due at Group this afternoon or tomorrow. So, in a few days it should be shuttled down to us.

I mentioned in the tape last night, but I'll say it again in case the recorder is on the blink.   These people are up here from Saigon to check on a radar problem we were having. They said the 1st Air Calvary was going home next month and that all planes would be tied up taking out their 40,000 troops. Therefore, they were trying to get Air Force people out as early as they could. Of course, I'll count those days chopped off when I'm airborne.

Grenier has gone up north again, this time with those people from Saigon. He also took his replacement along with him. He figured he might be able to slip through the rest of his tour without any more trips, but no such luck.

I didn't get a brass table yet. Was figuring on getting it pretty soon. I didn't want it hanging around (no place to put it) and was going to ship it hold baggage. The thing I'm really sweating out now is getting hold of some beetle watches. I'd hate to disappoint the girls on that. You used to see them around quite a bit when I first got here, but now there hardly hasn't been any. At first, the Club used to get a couple hundred and sell them, but even then they'd get gobbled up by the guys who were at the Club during the day instead of at work. I haven't given up hope, however.

In the next week or so I'll have to get together whatever I want to ship back to the states as hold baggage. I don't want to carry any more than I have to. Not that I've got much more than I came with, because I haven't, but it sure would be clumsy hauling it half way around the world. That's another thing that has changed. Used to be that you'd turn it in to the AF here and they would fly it back. Now we have to turn it in to the Navy and they send it by ship. It may take them a month to load the ship, so there's no telling when it'll finally get to its destination. Oh well, I'm not figuring on moving too much more anyway.

Big John got back from Saigon this evening and all he could do was moan about how things were goofed up and everyone was going around in circles down there. It seems that every time someone comes back from there they say the same thing. I'll check it on my way out.

Well, sweet girl, we're just a bit closer to being together again. I'll be so glad to stop writing. Not only does being cooped up on base restrict the things to write about, it's also too hard to write about so many other things—like how much I miss you and how much I love you. Good night, my darling. Sleep good.

Your Leo

20 Sep 66

My Beloved,

I'll only have a few moments for some jottings right now as we have a Staff Meeting in twenty minutes. I've been yawning every thirty seconds right now, after having gone to bed at 2 a.m. last night. The meeting is at 7:30 p.m., so I don't know what time I'll get out tonight.

One of the two clerks, the best worker, is in here almost every night. I had to tell the other one to come in tonight. He's typing right now – and probably will have to do 70% of whatever he puts out over again. I told him to plan on being in to work most every night from now till I leave. That set good! He's one of those who never has time to do things right—but always has time to do them over.

Gren hit Dong Ha this morning early and he was back by lunch time. That should take care of his traveling for this tour, except for the one big trip—back home.

It's the old game again. Just got out of the staff meeting and, among other things, we're now embarking on another clean-up campaign. General Momeyer was down (He's 7th AF Commander) for two hours and I guess he did some ass chewing. He just left Training Command so he thinks these are all stateside bases. Didn't pay any attention to status of the F-4C's or anything; just looked at what needed to be painted, grass to be cut, trash emptied, etc. Let me tell you, it gets downright ridiculous and disgusting how much they'll go on a bender for things like that and yet do nothing about other problem areas. I'd mentioned before about nothing for the troops. With the town off limits about 6 months, I figured they'd get some type of program going. Instead there's nothing and every night there's a few more fights among those who have nothing else to do but drink. That's why I'd just as soon come back to the shop at night. About the only time anyone sees me in the barracks is when I get up in the morning.

I went to the BX this afternoon, but they didn't have much of anything. All I got was a couple boxes of saltines and a can of grapefruit sections. They didn't have too much of a selection of brass tables, so I'm going to try to get to the Marine BX at Hill 327 where they have a larger selection. I wanted to get this as soon as possible so I can get my baggage shipped before the last minute.

While I'm thinking of it, I wondered what I should draw, pay-wise, when I leave here. I can either draw my big travel pay, about $80, or advance pay. This payday you'll be getting your last $400 allotment check, plus the $300 I'll send. If I did draw a month's advance pay it would be somewhere around $400. Ah, it's nice to be making plans to go home.

Good night for now, my darling. What a wonderful feeling it'll be to hold you close to me again. I've missed you so terribly much during this long year. I love you, Don Leta, with all my heart.

Your Leo

"32"

22 Sep 66

My Beloved,

Got a special today—a triple letter from you, Karen and Stephanie. Also received a letter from Mom telling about the Bertone's homecoming.

There wasn't any mail yesterday, my love, and last night I was too shot for anything, even letter writing. You sounded sort of depressed in today's letter. I know my return won't solve all our problems, but things should brighten up a bit. As for going home, I'm afeered everyone scheduled to depart in October is just too hopped up awaiting port calls. Every day, ten times a day, people are asking when they'll be in, what dates they'll get, etc. I'll admit yours truly is among them. It doesn't do any good, however. They'll come in due time. The saying is that "the wheels of justice grind slowly." That may be so, but they'd win any race with the wheels of military red tape.

I was in the mess hall (club) last night about midnight when Carter came in. He's been working swings the past couple months. He said he was feeling old today. Had received a letter from his oldest daughter, 17 1/2, asking his permission to get married. He said, "That means pretty soon I'd be a grandfather." I think that's what bothers him more than anything—especially since he's two months younger than I am!

Speaking of getting old, I'm kind of sore all over myself. I'm getting to believe this is a young man's game—well, some of the young men anyhow. There are still so many around here that a little work and some long hours knock flat. Most of them start coming around after a while, though. Still, it'll be nice when I can get home and relax, doing things like washing & waxing the car, mowing the south 40, etc! I guess I'll make it a few more years. I'm still active enough to chase mommybunch around the house.

Three fights last night. Oh well, I guess that's what war is. Trouble is, some people find it difficult to identify the enemy. These fights took place, one each, in the Airman's, NCO, and Officer's Clubs! The reason I heard about it was that Capt Rayfield sat in on the daily Wing Conference for Maj. Groves, and he was telling us. Of all things, according to the Base Commander, the fight in the Officer's Club, between a Lt & a Capt, was over what song was going to be played on their juke box! What a war!!

Got hold of a box today to start packing my hold baggage. I'd like to get that out of the way before too much longer. I don't figure I'll have much laundry when I get home either. My shorts & T-Shirts are nearing their last wearing so I've bought new ones and plan on wearing the old one's when I leave here and the last few days here, throwing them away as I change.

I'll be doubly glad to leave here. Not only will I be going back to my love ones, but, I'll get away from this business. These 16-18 hour days get to you after a while. I just feel pooped out lately, even when I get up. I think a lot of it's psychological also; the pressure always seems to be on. There's nothing handled in a routine manner. Everything is an emergency.

Be sweet, my wonderful wife. Gosh but I miss you, Don Leta. I can't think of anything I've ever wanted more than to be back with you again, to hold you close and tell you I love you. You're so very much a part of me. By the time you get this letter we'll only have another 28 days or so to be apart, at the most. Even the minutes from the time I first see you upon arrival until I can take you in my arms will seem so long. Good night, my happiness.

Your Leo

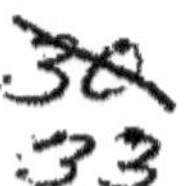

24 Sep 66

My Darling,

We received our port calls today, as you can see indicated above. They really put themselves out, letting us all leave on our DEROS or later. Grenier and Carter, who left the states a day before me, go back on the 24th. My flight is scheduled out of Saigon on the 28th, three days after my DEROS. I'd be curious to see what kind of shipping dates our Saigon Warriors got. Oh well, being at the most forward area you usually bring up the tail end in that kind of stuff. It's just like trying to get some of the BX goods they've got up here.

No letter from my sugarbun yesterday, nor did I write last night. Capt Rayfield, Green, Grenier & myself went out to Marble Mountain and we were a bit put out by the time we got out of there. We went up the actual mountain this time, past the Marine chopper facility. The mountain is made out of marble and most of the way up is by steps cut right out of the rock—324 of them if anyone cares to count. We had a couple Marines leading us up. The last few hundred feet is up with help of a rope and there was a Marine machine-gun crew on top. Along the way were a couple Buddhist pagodas we looked at. One was really something, built in a big cave, off of which run innumerable smaller caves. The main cave has a ceiling about 100 feet high, and the Buddha is carved right out of the marble, standing about 20 feet high. Reminded me a bit of the states as we left it, what with the Buddhist monk having his hand out for donations.

We came across three Viets about ¾ of the way up but they seemed to be clean. That's all we saw outside of a couple beggars near the pagodas. One of them seemed to have leprosy.

Did have a letter from my sweet girl when I got back today. Although it was a shorty, it's always so nice getting any word from you. Gosh but I miss you so. Even though an extra 3 days here isn't so bad, I had sort of been counting on getting out at least a couple of days early.

Figuring things out now, I don't believe there'll be any need to draw any extra money when I leave. I don't even think I'll need my travel pay. Besides the $700 you'll get next month, I should have around that much myself when I leave since it'll be so late in the month. I'll be money ordering most of that to you also as I don't want to carry it with me. It would make me feel too much like a capitalist!

It gets a little more discouraging here as time goes on. It's trying to fight a war with peacetime ideas. You get a tent or a hut or some mobile van and they want you to make it pretty! Paint, cut grass, plant flowers, tear down bunkers, build bunkers (pretty ones, with square corners), button your pockets, etc. My military fervor and motivation is wearing just a bit thin. Another thing, nobody can have a weapon. Don't worry about it, our fine combat-type Air Police will save us. We're one of the few outfits that have our own weapons since our duties take us all over the place.

"The 1972nd Comm Squadron
Deterrent Force"

Enough groaning and moaning for one letter. Better get it out of my system now so I can be sugar sweet when we're finally together again. Good night for now, my wonderful Don Leta. I love you, my dearest, with all of me, and being away from you for just one extra day is awful. All I can think of is holding you close to me and smothering you in kisses. Be sweet my happiness.

Your Leo

25 Sep 66

My dearest Don Leta,

Another sweet letter from my favorite wife today. Oh, how I wish I could hug you and squeeze you right now. I'm getting so anxious to be with you again. And don't worry about all the broken pieces. I imagine they would have happened even if I had been there, with no additional guarantee that my presence would have assured their being repaired. We'll be able to repair them together!

Also enclosed was the letter from Lt Druley. They must have a relatively small comm activity from the little bit of information furnished. I still can't see how they're authorized an E-8 in the 306 field. In the 4652 program at Ellsworth, I had 51 people. You asked about the 305X1's and 306X0's. These are data and crypto people, respectively. They normally put an "X" in there to show the whole field, taking in the 3 levels, 5 levels, etc. Otherwise they'd have to say 30531, 30551, 30571, etc.

Today's letter was a question letter. About hold baggage, I haven't shipped it yet. You have to do your own packing—crate, footlockers, or what have you. They inspect it first, however, to see that you're not shipping anything home that you're not supposed to. Then you either nail it shut or lock it. I haven't gotten any luggage to travel with yet, but will probably pick up a B-4 bag pretty soon.

With this departure date from Saigon of 28 October, that means I'll leave here 26 October, so I should wrap it up, as far as work goes, by October 20th. As of this minute, and provided I can make connections, I should be seeing my honeybunch on the 29th. The Captain said that since they were keeping me over 3 days past my DEROS, I could go to Nha Trang or Vung Tan at the rest camps and spend 3 days or so on the beach. Don't much figure I'll take him up on it, however. Besides the travel back and forth, it'll probably just make the time drag all the more. I'd just as soon the days pass as quickly as possible so I can get back with my wonderful wife.

I still miss you terribly, Don Leta. I must have said that over a hundred times by now, but it's as true as it ever was. I just don't have the words to say how much love is in my heart. Good night, my sweet. Take care of yourself.

Your Leo

31 (again!)

26 Sep 66

Hi Honeybunch,

Not too very much to report tonight, but I did want to get a little note off anyhow. Today has been pretty busy—again. We didn't see much of the sun, getting real heavy rains just before work this morning and clouds but no rain the rest of the day.

To fill your reading time, I enclosed the note from Lt Nelson and Capt Rayfield. Lt Nelson asked me what I'd done since I've been here so I furnished him two typewritten pages and three additional sheets, starting off with "I do hope you'll forgive the sparseness of information furnished, but my innate humility precludes my expounding too deeply on my many qualities!" You know—typical Dubois fashion.

There was a message from Col Schultz, the Group Commander, on the bulletin board this afternoon. He said that he was concerned over having so many people leaving after their DEROS and that he had taken the matter up with the Aerial Port people in Saigon. He said he was convinced that they were doing everything possible to get people out, but that there was just too many in October. There is a possibility that they will have more aircraft pressed into service and, if so, new port calls would be sent out. Even if nothing comes of it, I'm at least glad to see that the Group Commander was checking into it. It sounds like they must have gotten quite a few gripes over this batch.

No mail today, as a matter of fact hardly any came in for anyone, so nothing to report in that area. I wish there was more news, my sweet, but I'm at a loss. All I can do now is tell you for the umpteenth time how I miss you and love you. Won't this separation ever end? A whole month yet seems like such a long time. Good night, my sweet Don Leta. I love you, love you, love you.

Your Leo

29

28 Sep 66

My Darling,

I'm so tired about now that I know I won't get very far with this letter. The yawns just keep coming.

No mail yesterday, but there was a letter from you today. I must admit that I'm getting a bit weary of letter writing—though I still like to get some. Pretty soon you reach the saturation point where there just isn't much of anything to write about.

There is one bit of news, however. We received our Flight Orders today. I'll be leaving Da Nang for Saigon the morning of 26 October. Have to be at the port at 0530 that morning. Then, at 3:30 on the morning of the 28th, I have to be at the terminal in Saigon for the big ride. With the hours they've got, it's gonna be a hectic time. By then I don't imagine I'll feel like doing much sleeping anyhow. My flight number out of Saigon is W-244, which is a World Airlines 707 Jet, the same type aircraft I came over on.

One of the troops just got back from R&R to Hong Kong. I had asked him to check on beetle watches and it seems they're still out. They haven't had any for over a month since the shops in Switzerland were on their yearly one month vacation. I hate to disappoint the girls, but if I can't get hold of any I'll try to pick something up.

Well, my love, we've been delayed a couple days but we're moving again. Friday is my last pay formation here (other than just before I leave) and by the time you receive this, we'll already be in THE month. I can hardly wait to see you again. I love you so deeply, my honeybunch.

Your Leo

28

29 Sep 66

My Sugarbunch,

Got some more nice pictures today and I was amazed at the change in appearance of Lynn. She looks just precious in that one picture with you and Paul on the front steps. She looks so well filled out and alert. And of course, her mother doesn't look bad either. Yum yum!

It's coming promotion time again. We made 3 Staffs and 14 A1Cs this time. The Tech and Master promotions will be made 1 December. The selection board will meet on the 10th of October in Hawaii. I had been nominated the last go-round if you remember, but wasn't selected. This time Sgt Green was nominated and selected, so he's supposed to leave next week. The thing is, he doesn't care to go. So, I typed the enclosed and put it on Capt Rayfield's desk tonight. Oh well, it was good for a few chuckles anyhow! When he came back in, he read it and then carried on about how he didn't have anyone to spare, so he thought he'd go himself.

Not much else to report, my sweet. Pretty much routine today. I saw this one guy who came over with me and is assigned to the Wing. He leaves Monday, 3 October. He said this other guy who came over with us left this morning. We're the only outfit on the base that can't get out early, it seems. When we go out for port calls we put down the date available—and Group won't let it be more than 5 days prior to DEROS. 7th Air Force, on the other hand, will let their people forecast up to 29 days in advance. Oh well, it's almost over with.

Bed time once again, my beloved. I'm going to be counting those that I have left by myself. It's been real nice sleeping for about 10 days now, even though tonight is awfully muggy. We've had rain on and off all day. I'll be glad to get home where, for some mysterious and unknown reason, the thought of going to bed conjures up much more pleasant feelings. Good night, my love. Sweet dreams

Your Leo

CONTRIBUTION TO THE COST REDUCTION PROGRAM

PRESENT PRACTICE: A selected and representative number of senior NCOs are selected from units throughout the Pacific Command area to serve on the promotion board which is held at Wheeler AFB, Hawaii. This necessitates the removal of a usually important member of the organization and dispatching him some distance from his station from from 5 to 10 days. This has been known to happen even during periods of scheduled visits by very important personages (like General Klocko, for example). Such a TDY is often fraught with the dangers of extended TDY's as the result of the actions of the boards, or more often, as the result of a paucity of transportation.

RECOMMENDED CHANGE: If at all possible, send a fully qualified replacement who already has his replacement on board, is dedicated and will do anything to serve his organization, is familiar with personnel records, performance reports and selection boards, and has but a short time to go - even with his extended DEROS. (He can then go home from there!)

GAINS REALIZED:

1. A fully qualified representative on the promotion board, without the resulted loss of a key member of the "establishment".
2. Opportunity to get rid of certain people before some important General sees him and has his whole trip ruined.
3. Savings in time and money as the result of:
    a. The key NCO not having to travel TDY to Hawaii, spending approximately 5 days there, and then travelling back.
    b. The short time NCO completing two-thirds of his trip to the CONUS as part of this TDY. He can then proceed from there to the mainland.
    c. Release of a scheduled flight from Saigon to the states for the man who was already scheduled on that flight. This would enable another of our Vietnam veterans to acquire a seat which would take him back to his loved ones.
    d. The gratitude of one (1) each wife and six (6) each children.
    e. The opportunity of an old war horse to once again serve, even though the task may be distasteful and difficult. Someone has to do it!
    f. Availability of another bunk on Da Nang AB.
    g. Availability of one more seat at the movies when there's a good leg show.

1 October 66

My Beloved,

Does this month seem to be dragging by to you? October finally got here but it still seems so long 'till the end of the month.

The more we go on, the more they're trying to turn this into a stateside base. Granted, it needs to be straightened up a bit, but this is ridiculous. I had the chance to get the money orders this morning since everybody was having inspections. No line, so I got it over with right quick-like and was able to have them in the mail by noon. Anyhow, they're now having stand-by inspections in the barracks on Saturday mornings. I didn't have to stand it, but next week I'm on the inspection party. I joked about it before, but now I wouldn't doubt it if they decide to start parading next. The joke that was going around the last few days was that if we failed the inspection we'd be restricted to the base!

No mail from my sugargirl the last couple of days, so there should be a whole bunch tomorrow! Boy, I'm telling you, as time gets shorter and shorter, I hunger for you all the more. It'll be so nice being with you again Don Leta.

Ran into another troop I knew—this one from the 4504th MTW at Orlando. He's a Master now, was a Tech when I knew him. I don't believe you ever met him. His name is Komiotis and he was instructing for a while in the old 61C program. Worked for Hamline. Anyhow, he went back to the old 30470 AFSC, Radio Relay, and was here from the GEEIA squadron at Clark to do some modifications on some of our equipment. Now it doesn't look like they're going to do it for a while so he's supposed to leave in the morning.

Grenier, Carter and I were having coffee around 12:30 last night (this morning) and we remembered that there wasn't anyone else there that we recognized, out of about 30 people. We use to say that when we looked around and didn't see anyone who was here when we arrived then we knew we were getting short.

We lost three people out of maintenance within three days this week. Two emergency leaves and one compassionate reassignment. Neither of the two emergency leave cases should be back. One already had his assignment (to Alaska with Grenier in December.) I think I may have mentioned the other case—a TSgt who has only been here about five weeks. He should never have come here. It seems his wife was going blind, but he was afraid of being called chicken. I guess he'd rather be called stupid.

I spent a good part of the day today trying to get rice. We're trying to round up 10 bags to get some work done. Some of our people at outlying sites use it as barter materiel for local labor. There's no place where the natives would be able to spend piastres, so we give them rice.

My replacement is not making friends and influencing people very fast. To top it off, he's now barracks chief and the word is that you can't even wear loud shirts in there 'cause they're too noisy! A sense of humor he doesn't have.

Even his fellow NCOs moan, and if Grenier had too much longer I'm afraid they'd fall out back. Now they'll wish sweet, lovable Leo had stayed!

One of the guys who came over with us is in the Field Maintenance Squadron and he goes home next week, but not under the best circumstances. He came down with yellow jaundice (hepatitis) and the medics told him no liquor for a year and no intercourse for six months! The Flight Surgeon gave him a letter, stamped and everything, explaining to his wife so that she won't think there's some other reason! Once she see's his color I know she'll believe him. He caught it about 3 months ago. MSgt Scheirn, whom Big John replaced, had gone home that way also. Speaking of Big John, he's lost about 30 lbs. since he's been here and looks much better. He weighed 265 when he came in. I lost some weight at first but have since put it back on, so I'm pretty close to what I was when I came over.

It's after 1 a.m., so I guess I'd better call it quits for now. I've just been looking at the pictures again and that's always like adding fuel to a fire. How anxious I am to be with you again, honey bunch. It's been a long year. I'm feeling melancholy and yet romantic again tonight and could probably get to rambling on again. But I'm going to pass it up this time by just telling you that I love you with all my heart and I'm so very happy and proud that you're my wife.

Your Leo

2 Oct 66

My dearest Don Leta,

This was a nice Sunday 'cause I heard from my lovely wife again. How nice it'll be not to have to rely on the mailman to let us know about each other.

I also heard from Mom today, and enjoyed the letter from Marie that you had enclosed. Mom didn't have too much to report, other than the doctor being pleased with her progress on her latest visit. I think Viv was lucky to marry a guy like Angie. I don't know what she'd do if he was in the service and had to leave for a year. She's got the typical Dubois moodiness too. Oh well, let them all solve their own problems. Heavens knows we've all got some of our own.

So they put the mighty hand on Bob's shoulder. I didn't figure he'd get to spend too much time at Tinker. I also hope they don't ship out until we have the opportunity to get together. If Bob's assignment is with the Defense Communications Agency (DCA), chances are 10-to-1 that he'll be stationed in Saigon—one of the Saigon Warriors. They have a detachment at Da Nang—AF, and they are the overall circuit / facility control. We have our periodic arguments with them!

I do believe the airplane ticket I had gotten cost somewhere around the $46 you had quoted. I remember having to hunt you down to get the money to pay for it! Coming back there's no telling what it'll cost me since I've no idea how available military fares will be. There'll be a slew of us for one thing, plus it'll be on a weekend when air travel is the heaviest. Regardless, it shouldn't be too much. I will be paid up to date, as I mentioned, and with my travel pay that should be more than adequate.

It's a good thing I heard from you today as there'd be nothing to write about tonight. Got to bed at 3 a.m. yesterday and Grenier just now left and he notified me it was 2 a.m. Gonna have to hurry here so I can get to my scroungy bed. I sure wish you were in it. Good night, my darling. I love you and miss you as ever.

Your Leo

3 Oct 66

My Darling,

Another hectic day just about over with. Seems there's not too many of the other kind anymore. They've been doing nothing but dreaming up projects for the past couple weeks—many of them concerning things that should have been done eons ago, and Grenier and I are catching them all. At eleven o'clock this morning I was given a list of 5 things by Capt Rayfield. These were problem areas that he gave to the Commander so he could forward them to PACOM (Hawaii) as subjects to be discussed at the forthcoming Commander's Conference. Major Groves didn't want them that way. He wanted them in study form, with Problem, Discussion and Recommendation. Three of the five subjects I didn't even know anything about, but by talking to a few people we got something out by the 5 o'clock deadline. We keep moving anyhow.

Didn't expect any mail today—and didn't get any either. Another 20 days or so and I won't even have to worry over checking it. By the way, it's still a little early yet, but I wouldn't write any letter that wouldn't be posted by the morning of the 20th since the 25th will be my last chance to check mail since I'll leave Da Nang early the morning of the 26th.

I'm completely out of any news whatsoever, honeybunch, unless you'd like to hear about some of our technical problems. I'm sure that would thrill you!

Gosh, I wish this time would move a bit faster. I know it's going by pretty good, but when I stop like this and think about it, the time seems to stop too. Carter, Grenier and myself went down to the dispensary this afternoon and got all squared away on our final shots. I got a flu shot and the tine test for TB. All I have to do is go back Thursday to have the Tine test read.

Good night for now, my beloved. More and more (if possible) I yearn to be with you as time draws nearer. I've missed you so very much this long year, and my love for you has just built up to overflowing. Oh, Don Leta, I'm so happy that you're all mine. I think you're just the most wonderful person ever.

Your Leo

4 Oct 66

My dearest wife,

It's almost 9:30 now and I've just gotten back to the shop. I had lain on the bed after supper and conked out. We had our weekly meeting at 5:15 and Captain Rayfield said the Wing Commander reminded all units of the duty hours and that we were on a 56-hour week here. The Captain said he'd like to accommodate him but we can't afford to cut down. Last week I got 109 hours in.

Another nice letter made it in from my honeybunch today. This was when you had picked up the mail at mothers on your way to Fort Worth. I was surprised to hear you received one of them in only two days, much less three of them at once. I guess they spurt and sputter but most of the mail gets through.

Right now we're waiting on an aircraft bringing an antenna up from Saigon. We've got an emergency requirement up north. Green and I will take it up tonight if he can line up a chopper. He's been calling everyone but so far they're all pretty well loaded. The Marines are supposed to call if they have another flight going up. Otherwise, a couple other troops will probably take it up in the morning.

You know, that flight I'm scheduled to take out of here for Saigon on the 26th takes 5 ½ hours, and Saigon's only about 350 miles. Trouble is, it's the milk run—Saigon via Qui Nhon, Cam Rahn Bay and Pleiku. What I didn't need was to see any more of this country. Well, as of now I only have 21 more days in Da Nang, and it looks increasing like I'll be kept busy every one of them, with probably a little time to clear the base. The AFCS Commander is still due the 11th, and then Green will take off on the 12th for a week or so to Okinawa on a parts scrounging mission. His wife is Okinawan, though she's back in Florida. That mean's I'll take his job too during that period. We're due another E-8, radio type, by the name of Davis, in this month.

Well, my delicious sugar girl, there's a bit of rambling but no big news I guess. We'll just keep plodding along until the big day comes for us, which won't be too awfully long now. Just three more weekends apart, and we should be together on the 4th one. Good night once again, my happiness. All my love is yours, now and forever.

Your Leo

6 Oct 66

My dearest Don Leta,

There was no opportunity to write you last night, though I did manage to get a quick note off to Karen with my new departure date. I had Airman Canal mail it for me before I went out yesterday afternoon.

Did get a long letter from my honeybunch today, together with the housing application (which I filled out and mailed), the newspaper clipping of Pocakaren, and all sorts of ideas for spending money!

Grenier and I were called to the Orderly Room for a change of port calls yesterday morning. Group had moved Gren up from the 24th to the 19th, and me from the 28th to the 24th. I'll be on the same plane with Carter now. Now, instead of leaving here at 5:30 on the 26th, I'll depart at 10:00 on the 22nd. My flight out of Saigon will be leaving around 5:30, this time on Northwest Orient Airlines.

On the housing application, I would imagine the "30 days in advance" means 30 days prior to arrival in Altus. I dated it the 10th of October and asked for an occupancy date around 10-15 November. Also, I marked "4-bedroom" with "no" to whether I'd accept anything smaller. We can see what's what after we get there. I figure we might take a run up to check on housing status before I report in.

The price on the car doesn't sound too bad. Has daddy looked at it? Of course he won't be the one driving it (or paying for it) but I just wondered what he thought. As for ours, I've always been afraid of any car that starts losing oil. That can develop into some expensive problem. I don't imagine you let the air conditioning influence you in any way! It would be nice in that part of the country, however. I'd say right now to go ahead and take it. There's no telling how much longer he'd have it, even though if he's had it as long as you say, he may have it for a while yet. On the other hand, with the 67's out, it may go at reduced price.

There's a little thing about the financing figures that threw you off, I'm sure. Actually, the $82.98 GMAC charge, which looks like $1.04 more a month than our old $81.94 tab, is really $44.50 cheaper over a 3 year period! Sounds ridiculous, huh? I believe, however, that if you check our old mortgage you'll find that we made 36 payments of $81.94 PLUS one other payment. If that other payment had been added to the 36 monthly duns, we would have been paying $84.10 a month! In other words, about every $36 we pay in advance brings our payments down $1 per month—actually a couple cents more than that as we would pay interest on that $36. Hope I haven't confused you by this. My base pay is $487.20 and my allowances (quarters, rations, pro pay, clothing allowance) are an additional $190 –for a total $677.20.

On the Govt Employees financing, they send a bank draft whether you accept their contract or not. If you accept, you just cash it; otherwise you either return it or destroy it. I went ahead and filled out the application in case you're still checking rates, but there are a couple things you'd have to fill in. I've checked those with a pencil. I would think they'd be fairly close to bank rates.

I'm all squared away on shots now after having my negative reaction to the Tine test checked out. Carter's came out positive so he has to take x-rays tomorrow morning.

That's about all the big news, honeybunch, as I check once again and see I only have 15 days left in Da Nang and 17 in Vietnam. A good thing about leaving on a weekday also is that plane space out of Frisco should be better. They've had a number of articles in the S&S lately about that, and how the military was looking to have more of its schools end their courses in the middle of the week rather than on weekends.

The recommendation for the AF Commendation Medal that Lt. Carol had filled out has been scrapped. It wasn't supposed to go in until the end of my tour anyway. I understand I've been nominated for the Bronze Star.

It's that time again, sweetheart. When I came in this morning, Sgts Green & Boykin were just going out for a shower & breakfast after being up all night. The hours keep going. Major Groves was up here working himself until almost midnight tonight. Be sweet, my beloved. I love you with all my heart.

Your Leo

8 Oct 66

My Beloved,

If my figuring is correct, I should have between 6 and 11 more letters to write to my girl before I see her again, not counting this one. I now have only 13 days left on Da Nang and 15 in Vietnam.

We should get to Travis sometime on the morning of the 24th, providing this particular flight doesn't have any extended layovers anywhere. I know that coming over there were three main routes utilized—the one I was on (Travis-Japan-Phil-VN), one Travis-Alaska-Japan-Vietnam and the other via Hawaii-Guam-Philippines. Ours would not have gone to the P.I except for the fact that we couldn't come in 'till daylight. That restriction no longer holds. For instance, Grenier's plane leaves at 1:30 a.m. I'll plan on calling you as soon as I can; from Travis if possible. But now, don't get all excited if you don't hear from me promptly. There's no telling what will happen with flight schedules, delays, layovers, etc. Anyhow, I'll call you then and again when I have a flight to let you know the flight number and when it's due in TEXAS.

This has been another full day+. It's 11:30 P.M. now and I got myself some coffee and took a break to write this letter. With what I still have to accomplish tonight I imagine it'll be in the neighborhood of 3 a.m. before I sack out. I intend to sleep 'till about 9 or 10 though. This morning I overslept and it was a bad morning for it. We had another standby inspection and I was on the inspection party. The inspection was at 9 o'clock, but we had to meet with the Commander in the Orderly Room at 8:30. It was 8:15 when I got up, so you can imagine the hustling.

Then, this afternoon Capt Rayfield came up with six more projects that he wants completed prior to Gen Klocko's visit Tuesday. I don't know why the General couldn't wait until next month for his tour!

I guess I might finally make it with getting the girls a beetle watch. I hear they have them again in Hong Kong. One of our airmen is going Tuesday and I gave him money to get three of them. Hope he can get them as the girls seemed to be counting on it.

Good night for now, sweet girl. Gosh but I'm anxious to be with you and squeeze you close again. In two weeks—less by the time you get this—I'll be able to do it again. I've missed you so much this long year, my honeybunch. Love you, love you, love you.

Your Leo

9 Oct 66

My Darling,

Just a little note tonight as there's not much new to report. Just came back from midnight chow since we've still got a couple things to get squared away. It's 12:40 a.m. now, and the 4th game of the world series will be coming on in 5 minutes, so we'll be listening to that also. The first two games were in Los Angeles and broadcast time for those games was 3:45 A.M.!

I did get my plugs in today, however. We have this civilian here to write and film a story on Air Force Communications in Vietnam and the 1972nd was chosen to represent all comm. units here. This is supposed to be a 10-15 minute film for TV. Capt Rayfield spoke to him for a while and then turned him over to me. Grenier came into it too and we told some "war stories". Afterwards, I was carrying on with Capt Rayfield, telling him they wanted me to star in the film opposite Brigitte Bardot.

There's been quite a bit going on and we've gotten a lot done this week. I totaled my time for seven days and it's the longest I've put in yet—122 hours. Should make it to the sack by two tonight, after a good shower. I slept through 'till 9:30 this morning.

Only 12 more days in Da Nang, and an even two weeks in Vietnam. The big guns were booming earlier and I told them to knock it off. I don't know if they heard me. You just naturally get more apprehension as you get closer to leaving. Things have stayed relatively quiet for some time, however.

By the way, I haven't heard whether or not you received the money orders this month. I imagine you would have mentioned it by now if you hadn't, but I just want to make sure. Next Friday I have to go to Finance to get my pay record squared away and MPOs made up for what I'll draw prior to departure. I'll just take pay up to date (the 22nd) and my advance travel pay.

When there's 9, or 6, or even 3 months to go, you get lonesome but you're resolved that there's still quite a while to go. As it gets this close, however, it gets doubly hard because it seems the days can't go by fast enough. I'm so anxious to see you again, Don Leta. Gosh but I love you. Be sweet, my darling.

Your Leo

10/11 Oct 66

My Darling,

This is not going to be much of a letter I can tell you from the start. It's now 2:05 a.m. and I'm getting this done while Boykin is getting something ready for me to work on. We've had a bunch of stuff to get ready for General Klockos's visit, and on top of that Sec. McNamara is coming in so that causes additional confusion in communications circles.

I got a letter from my sweetheart today, and you answered a question I asked yesterday—about receiving the money orders.

I wish I had known earlier about Gary wanting a green beret. I'm sure I could have gotten him one. You can't get one in the BX or anywhere like that, but I could have gotten one from the troops. However, with only 11 more days in Da Nang, I doubt very much that I'll be out anymore to any of the SF camps.

Some more bum luck today. This guy was going to Hong Kong tomorrow (today) and was going to pick up beetle watches. Now they switched him around and he's not going 'til the 19th. Capt Rayfield said to have him get them anyhow and he'd mail them to me, so I guess I'll do that. He'd be coming back from Hong Kong the 24th, the day I'll be leaving Saigon.

Sgt Buck got his assignment today. His wife is at Altus. He came here from there and that's where he asked to go back to—so, naturally, he didn't get it. Instead, he got Robins AFB, Georgia, which means either 5th MOB or GEEIA. I haven't seen him but I imagine he's much unhappy. Five others, all operators, also got their orders – 3 to March and one each to Missouri and Michigan.

Well, I'm finished now. We made more charts for Major Grove's briefing tomorrow. I don't need any more visiting firemen for a while. I'm just going to finish this letter and go to bed. It's now 4:10. Pretty soon it'll be time to get up!

Hearing you carry on in today's letter about the racket the kids were all making, I could almost picture it in my mind. Still, it'll be nice being back there again. I just can hardly wait to hug you and kiss you and hold you close. Gosh but I love you and I've missed you so much this past year. The anticipation of these last few days has left me jittery and a bit nervous, I think. I've never wanted anything so much as to be with my sweet wife, my wonderful Don Leta.

Your Leo

12 Oct 66

My Darling,

Back to it once again after receiving a letter from my honeybunch today. Tonight, things are beginning to settle down again after a hectic period. We were saying a while ago that one of the hardest things once leaving here will be getting back to some semblance of a schedule. Here it is 12:30 a.m. and Grenier, Boykin, and I have just come back to the shop. After chow tonight I went to bed and woke up at 11:15. I don't know when I'll be able to get to sleep now.

We got through General Klockos visit in good shape and scored a few more points. When they were in here something or other was said and either Major Groves or Capt Rayfield commented about our feeling we were the best in Vietnam. General Shtogren, the Pacific Comm Area Commander (out of Hawaii) corrected him by saying to General Klocko "they're the best in PACAF." You could see our officers beaming.

We no sooner got through that episode when we got in to "Operation Anchor", concerning McNamara's visit to the Da Nang area. We were the Command Post for this operation. He came in about 4:30 this afternoon, toured the base, and then took off by copter to spend the night aboard a carrier. I guess they didn't trust our accommodations.

I got to chow down at 9 o'clock last night, just before they closed the chow line and stayed to watch a floor show. It wasn't too bad—a 3-piece combo and a girl singer. That was the first show I've watched at the club in about 8 months. Usually it's too crowded and full of drunks. Actually, there's nothing but men there but they still embarrass you by the way they act at times. Anyhow, last night I actually saw about 20-30 of them with tears in there eyes. I had a lump in my throat and was close to it myself. As a closing number, the group asked the G.I.'s to join them in "God Bless America". Everyone stood and you could feel the building shake from the voices. There was this one guy in the front, all drunked up and passed out, being held up under each arm by two of his buddies. He slowly opened his eyes and joined in.

Poor Capt Rayfield has been kind of shook up lately. On top of all the pressure from everything else going on, he's losing the bulk of his "old" NCOs. Sgt Green, who's been here almost 8 months, is being pulled by Group to go to Saigon. It's ridiculous with his only having 4 months to go. Then, with Demaree, Grenier and myself leaving, this leaves him with only two Masters out of the 9 Masters or above he's authorized. Of these, Sgt A__ leaves in December (and he's boozed up half the time). The only other one is my illustrious replacement, who few people get along with. The Capt had told Maj Groves he was still amazed at Grenier and I still putting in 16-18 hours a day when we're so short to going home. He said everyone else he sees around here just takes off the last couple weeks. At least it makes time go—plus which there's so much to do you can never get caught up.

Was in for midnight chow tonight and saw an old CINCPAC troop, TSgt H. He was a staff then and worked in the Admin Section. He's been in Vietnam 14 months, the first 12 at Bien Hoa, outside Saigon. He extended for 9 months over here so he could retire and work for RMK, the local civilian contractors. I say local, they're a stateside combine doing all this construction work for Uncle Sugar. Anyhow, he said his wife had left him and married some 24 year old guy in California. Last month he married a Vietnamese and she's in Saigon. Good luck to him!

We're in to Thursday now, and a week from Saturday I'll lift off from good old Da Nang. It's still hard to fully realize that a week from Monday or Tuesday we'll be together again. I'm so anxious for that time to come, my love.

Time again to say good night, my sweet. I still love you and miss you terribly and I always will. You've been so wonderful and good to me and for me.

<u>Your</u> Leo

14 Oct 66

My Honeybunch,

I was just talking to Grenier, who now has 32 hours left on Da Nang (it's now 10:30 P.M.) and he mentioned having written his last letter last night. Checking now, I see that if I wrote regularly I'd only have five more myself. I received a letter from you today written Sunday, the 9th, and I noticed you mentioned 3 more weeks so you hadn't received the change on my shipping date. I imagine it got there on Monday.

Things have slacked off just a bit now that our latest series of crisis has passed. And, of all things, last night I got 12 straight hours of sleep. Laid down at 7 P.M. and didn't budge until 7 A.M. I'm done for tonight also. Got a few things done and I've just been sitting around gabbing. Speaking of sleeping 12 hours last night, being up at all hours had become so common that Grenier asked me this morning where I was around 4 a.m. He was up—couldn't sleep. That's the way it got, too. At times there was so little sack time that when we tried to sleep we couldn't, and ended up outside sitting against the building and gabbing.

Had a visit from a friend today. MSgt Oliver, from Bien Hoa, had come over on the same plane with me from the states and we bunked together at Tan Son Nhut. He called from Base Ops and said he'd just be here a short while (about 30 minutes). He also asked if we had a Capt Rayfield. He was the Capt's FSgt on TDY in the Dominican Republic. A few minutes later Capt Rayfield came in so we got in the jeep and went to Base Ops. Oliver wasn't around though. Our Flight Facilities Officer said Oliver had called the shop back and left word for me that he'd be here a couple hours and would see me at the club. I took Capt Rayfield to the club and we had a reunion over Pepsi's. We then brought him to the shop to show him our operation. He said he'd heard we had a good set-up from the Group QC people. I guess quite a few outfits have had some of their people fired. We'd heard of some of them. They got rid of the Commander at Pleiku and sent some Lt Col down there to square the place away. Col Schultz supposedly told him to come up here to see how our Maintenance Control operated.

When Bien Hoa comm people got their port calls, they also were all after their DEROS. Their Commander sent them all back saying his people weren't leaving that late—to give him some other dates. Sure enough, they did. Oliver originally had 26 October, and it was changed to the 18th. Their CO obviously doesn't fear to speak out. Incidentally, Oliver had forecasted for Florida, with the Southeast as his area of choice. He got his area at least— Myrtle Beach AFB, South Carolina,—with duty station at Detachment 1, Luke AFB, Arizona!!

I hope Paul doesn't have more than a "bug" passing through. I'll be anxiously awaiting your next letter to hear how he is. On top of everything else, I know it won't make things any easier for you to have any of the kids sick.

How to Operate Maintenance Control

That about does it for this go-round, sweet girl. We have a few problems up north and some people are going up with the Captain but Gren and I are being left behind now. Good luck to 'em.

Just about ten days from now we should be back together again, honeybunch. I can hardly wait and just get more eager and anxious every day. I love you so much and all I can think of is our being together again. Good night, my happiness.

Your Leo

16 Oct 66

My Beloved,

As has happened so often in the history of man, a woman has come between the close relationship of two comrades. Grenier has gone home to his wife!

We stayed up all night, alternating between the club (open 24 hours a day for coffee & chow) and the stoop in front of the barracks. He had a show time of 5:30 A.M. at the terminal and finally left Da Nang at 7:45. His plane out of Saigon leaves at 1:30 a.m. Wednesday. Now, with today gone, I have five more days on Da Nang, leaving on the sixth. You can figure that I'll be leaving here at about midnight, your time on the 23rd. At this rate, I figure my last letter to you will probably be written this Wednesday.

I received both your and Karen's letters today. I could see you must have talked to her because she stated "If you do it, it will cause me to get noticed (LAUGH)," or words to that affect. I wouldn't mind too much speaking to her class, but only if it had been requested by the teacher—and not as a result of Karen's request. In essence, that is what I told her. I don't know if she'll show you my reply.

I'm glad Daddy mentioned the 4-barrel carburetor to you in case we bought that wagon. That is a gas burner and definitely something we can do without. That's stuff for hot rodders who like to goose it at high speeds. I'm done my fast living—in more ways than one.

Today was a scorcher, and it has been for a week now. We had been getting rain almost every day but all of a sudden it cleared up, and it's been dry and dusty since.

Nothing else new, my sweet, so this will be another in a long string of shorties. I look forward more and more every day to our being together again. Gosh, how I love you and miss you.

<u>Your</u> Leo

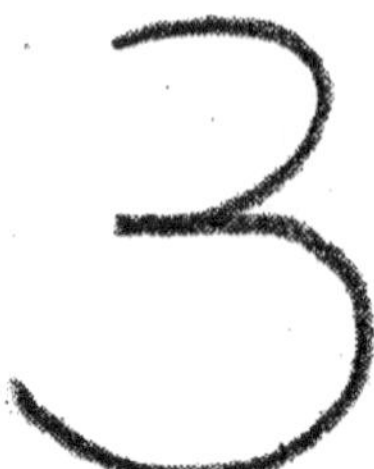

18 Oct 66

My Darling,

By the time you receive this, I should either be sitting in Saigon waiting on my flight, or already in the air and on my way. I've longed for that time forever, it seems. Right now I've only 3 days here—Wednesday, Thursday & Friday—and I'll be leaving Da Nang Saturday morning. I can already tell I'm about to leave—yesterday my work day was only 11 ½ hours long and today has only been a few minutes longer.

Received a letter from you today. I imagine there won't be more than one or two more from you. You made my mouth water in this one by telling me about the banana bread and rhubarb pie.

Today has been like the height of the monsoon season. We'd just been making comments the last couple days since there'd been no rain for about a week and the skies at night were full of stars while the days were scorchers. It's been pouring all day long (it's 11 P.M. now) and I would estimate, based on past rains, that we've probably had about 10 inches or so thus far. The water— or mud—is up to six inches deep between here and the barracks. When I cut out I intend to roll up my fatigues and go barefooted.

From what you reported about Karen and her teeth trouble, I guess we definitely will have to have something done about it, and it might just as well be done right as to try and find the easy or economical way out. It'll have to be another notch taken in the old belt.

TSgt Leschziner, who mans our Hue TROPO site, just came back from Clark and he saw Grenier at the terminal in Saigon but said he hardly had time to speak to him as he was catching a plane. Seems they had vacant seats on earlier flights and moved him up. His scheduled flight wasn't supposed to leave until 1:30 A.M. Wednesday, about 2 ½ hours from now.

I've just about cleared everything now, except for checking out of the Squadron. I've turned in my field gear (helmet, gas mask, etc.) and tomorrow I'll receive my security debriefing. After that I'm not allowed in the Comm Center, etc.

The weather doesn't look to good for it now, but tomorrow evening we're supposed to have a cookout near our line shack. The officers are splurging on chow and beer for them and the NCOs, with a similar deal later for the airmen. The old man wanted to do this as sort of a break after the hectic month we've been through. Captain Rayfield has charge of the meat and he chugged in this afternoon with more that 150 lbs. of beef.   Now it'll probably rain straight for a week!

Well, tomorrow night should be my last letter to you honeybunch. After that, I'd probably beat any letter home. So, when you get it you'll know I'll not be far behind. I can hardly wait now that the time is getting so close. Oh, how wonderful it'll be to hold you again and to kiss you. I've been saving for a whole year, double rations, and I'll probably want to do all my catching up in the first few moments. Gee, I love you so much, Don Leta. And the kids — how much they'll seem to have changed to me in a year's time. I could see it in the pictures, especially when comparing the first ones you sent with the latest ones. Good night, my sweet. Take extra good care of yourself for me

<u>Your</u> Leo

Epilogue

In the spring of 2004, Lanis called from a hospital in Fort Worth. She and the others had gathered to see Dad as his health was declining. Lanis told me, "Dad is speaking. You've got to come."

Lanis didn't mean that Dad had not been able to speak. Dad had congestive heart failure and suffered its syndrome of debilities, but he could speak and in fact had no trouble doing so. His usual speaking style was to pontificate, to offer his opinion as a final pronouncement, intoning, as it were, "Thus saith Leo". But now it was different. This episode with his heart frightened him and convinced him his time was short. He spoke to Lanis freely and tenderly that day, and addressed those who were there on subjects he usually treated from a distance.

I flew out from Maryland the next day. Paul was up from Austin and had bought a little tape recorder, so compelling was this chance to hear Dad's last words. Lanis had come from Delaware, Stephanie from New Mexico. Lynn and Mathew both lived in the Dallas-Fort Worth area. Thus all the living family gathered in his hospital room for a hasty reunion.

Our sister Karen was gone from us. As was our mother, Don Leta.

Once we were all present in that room, we gathered around Dad's wife Martha and gave her a gift. Seventeen years married and witnessing the death of another spouse, Martha was planning to quit her job to stay home and care for Leo. We had arranged for her a decorative wicker basket holding a bird on a nest. Along the back, we each tucked letters giving thanks for her. On the little bird's nest we placed "eggs", tightly-folded checks, gifts of money to buffer her transition.

Dad watched all this from his bed and cried out with a deep wail, thanking the Lord for us and moaning he was tired and wanted to go home. He spoke thanks that he had all of us around him and that he could see us practicing the giving of ourselves to others.

Several times that day Dad spoke of the tithe, another aspect of giving. He had read of the tithe practices of the different churches, he said. He agreed with one practice, that the believer should give half the tithe to the church and half as the individual determines. Dad spoke that day, moving from one subject to another, confirming to us again and for the last time the body of lessons he had taught us. *Bear in mind, children, you are at all times both a member and an individual. You are members of communities, be they your family, your church or society. Despite their flaws (they are our flaws) you belong and you owe them your support. Yet you are individuals, with individual responsibility before God to act.* God's measure—and Leo's—was the care of orphans and widows.

Homecoming; The Gun

The letter of October 18th, 1966, predicted one more letter, but in fact it was the last. I don't know what airport he flew into—I was only five years old. We met the airplane out on the concrete tarmac. The passengers filed down the stairs. Dad set the enormous B4 bag down and gave Mom a great big hug. For the first time, he kissed baby Lynn. We kids crowded around. I spied the B4 bag sitting there and wondered if my father had fulfilled his promise to me. The bag was large, but was it big enough to hold a rifle inside? Dad knelt down before me. I asked if he brought me a gun from Vietnam. His brow turned sad. He had asked, he told me, but his commander said no. They needed all the guns for the war.

The next day he took me to the store in Jacksboro to find a toy rifle. *Choose one.* I browsed all the stock, admiring the deluxe models. He did not voice a limit but he watched me. In the end I chose a less expensive one.

After Vietnam

After the tour in Vietnam, Leo wrapped up his twenty years at Altus Air Force Base in Oklahoma. Whenever asked about his career, he would say he had been in the Air Force for "twenty years, five months, twelve days, eight hours and forty five minutes . . . but who's counting?" To which one witty 30-year careerist once remarked, "What's the matter? You didn't like it?"

While at Altus for a year and a half, he took business and accounting courses and prepared to return to civilian life. Baby Mathew arrived. Dad found a job with defense contractor Raytheon. He worked logistics and purchasing for this electronics manufacturer, moving us to Billerica, Massachusetts, near the Rhode Island side of the family.

The big opportunity came with computers. Leo hired on with Xerox in 1969 and took the family to Rockville, Maryland, near Washington D.C. Xerox produced the big Sigma computers. NASA, the federal government in general, and the universities were the customers and they were buying mainframes like mad. Dad installed and maintained the machines. Specifically, he built service depots, leading squads of twenty-year-old technicians, running them around the clock to fix these complex, room-sized electronic systems. Ol' Sarge was in his element again.

The mainframe business boomed in those years. The big companies enlisted armies of salesmen. Proposals flew. Contracts were won. When tight install schedules faltered, fathers would bring their sons to the sites. We'd bolt cabinets together and pull cables under floors. The computer frames made ready on Saturday, the electronic brains went in Monday. Back on schedule. A customer could be invoiced without penalty. There was ever a reason to celebrate. Every month a party.

Ten years the family lived in Maryland. During this time, the older children finished high school, Karen, Stephanie, Lanis and Bryan. Don Leta went to work and quickly became an admired administrative assistant with the government.

Half-way through this period, though, the oil embargo and a downturn in the economy affected the computer business and our family fortunes. Xerox abandoned the big computers. Dad lost his job.

A familiar sight on and off the following years was Dad sitting at the table in the morning, a coffee cup at hand and a newspaper and pen. Instead of the crossword puzzle, Dad would circle the want ads. Leo held dozens of jobs from that point on. The jobs he preferred were in computer and communications services, often running technical service and repair groups. Many were tiny firms, obscure to begin with and not long lasting. He would apply and take jobs far afield, for it was not easy for a man near 50 to find the job he preferred. He was insurance salesman, office administrator, trade school counselor. Of course, I had often heard his ditch-digger speech. *All honest work is dignified. If you dig ditches, Son, dig ditches for the Lord!*

Leo lost patience for the nonsense of company life. He began quitting jobs.

In his letters from Vietnam, a singular word he applied to the stupidity of military life was "ridiculous". From time to time he would mention with humor the parking tickets issued in a war zone, the commander's big push to have all the vehicles washed, or the stateside paperwork. At the end of June, 1966, though, there was a sudden surge in his citations of the ridiculous and a frequent tone of disdain. His elevated sensitivity to the ridiculous continued through the rest of his letters. Likewise, his employment history from the mid-seventies on bore a thread of disgust. The fools were in charge and they weren't going to have Leo to kick around anymore. Still, every morning in my memory, he would don the business suit, give a firm handshake and smile and charge back out there. Optimism was his watchword. But Dad suspended one of his maxims. He no longer assured me, "A good worker will always have a job."

The saddest phrase I found in all the letters was "it looks like I'll be getting some backing", from November 12, 1965,

> . . . they haven't got a Maintenance Control other than in name
> so I was put in charge. . . I've only been at it 2 days but it looks
> like I'll be getting some backing. I told him if he wanted it to

remain only a recording and coordinating agency we could run it the way it was; but if he wanted to control maintenance I had to have more people, more room, more this and more that. He seems all for it. As a matter of fact, he was talking to the Seabees ten minutes later trying to get them to put up another Quonset for us.

Dear Lord, Leo built Maintenance Control at Da Nang. To the last days of his tour, he and Grenier were still putting in the long hours. He made it go! The best in the Pacific! Yet that phrase, "but it looks like I'll be getting some backing", that grieved me. In some unmentioned past situation he must have suffered the sting of backing denied. He would face a dry spell ahead, working for people from whom he would not be getting "some backing".

Karen

Daughter Karen began to display signs of depression in her early teen years. The letters reflected incidences of her moodiness and misbehavior. References to doctors and medicines tell that Leo and Don Leta were worried this was more than the ordinary "bad day". Leo implored, "Make sure you get the word to the Red Cross if anything goes wrong, and keep me advised of what develops. Don't just skip it over 'cause you don't want me to worry."

The early signs proved accurate. Karen's depression developed and deepened. Karen made several suicide attempts in the years that followed. She also had epilepsy and could not drive and so she further marked herself inferior to her contemporaries.

After high school, she lived at home and found employment in office work and accounting. Her volatile mood and abiding anger infected her relations with employers leading her so often to walk out or be dismissed. Mom and Dad, always near, helped her recover from each setback and encouraged her to step out again. She found an apartment across town, decorated it artfully and lived frugally.

Karen was a gifted artist skilled in detail and possessing an eye for style. She painted. She made handicrafts, God's-Eyes of colorful string construction, dried flowers, and so forth, and sold them at flea markets on Saturdays. She spent hours alone in coffee shops filling up her notebook, writing by fountain pen in her precise script. For pleasure, she worked out long algebra problems, evolving line upon line of equations neatly upon a clean page.

The bus was Karen's transportation or she would summon one of us to bring the family car. Our home phone would ring once. That was our signal to call her back, as she was conserving her monthly limit of outgoing phone calls. I'd snatch the car keys and take her to a greasy spoon. She would buy me a patty melt and we'd drink coffee for long hours and talk.

Though there were signs of hope—living independently, productive employment and marriage—she did not win against her troubles. Karen killed herself in the spring of 1979. She was twenty-six years old.

A Sign, Texas and Melancholy

The period of Karen's depression was about a decade and a half. Leo and Don Leta had consulted all the physicians but they were unable to heal. A beloved daughter in their own home, yet Leo could not reach her with a cure for her soul. He might as well have been ten thousand miles away again. He thought himself a stoic. Some night, after a long struggle to boost Karen's confidence and lift her out of a spell of depression, he must have privately come to a resignation that she might ultimately carry out suicide. When the phone call brought the news, Leo later said his first thought was, "It was as if she had died in her sleep".

Leo and Don Leta took Karen's death also as a sign from God that they were free to move to Texas. Dad had in his pocket an offer of promotion from his employer. If he would move to the corporate office, he would be promoted to the director of the national service division. To accept would mean removing support from Karen. But now the chapter had closed. They were free to go on. By autumn, Mom and Dad were in Texas with the three younger ones, Paul, 15, Lynn, 13, and Mathew, 11.

Leo's move to Texas did not brighten life. A sad and gloomy spell continued. His new job was short lived and the pattern of shifting employment resumed. To the younger children, Texas was dark, a Babylonian exile. The older children had memories of Dad outside playing ball with their friends. *Can your Dad come out and play?* The younger ones had no such experience. When we opened the box of letters forty years after his Vietnam tour, it was for Paul, Lynn and Mat as if gazing through a window and meeting a different man.

Don Leta

In 1985, Don Leta was diagnosed with melanoma cancer in her eye. Ocular melanoma was rare, aggressive and of unknown genesis. The accepted treatment was to immediately remove the eye. Don Leta chose instead a kind of radiation therapy in the hope of keeping her eye. The cancer spread, the radiation killed the bone around her eye and the eye had to come out in a short time anyway.

They say that there is no way to tell if removal of the eye would have been a better choice. Melanoma cells metastasize so easily, it might have been spread simply by the trauma of removal. Yet later, disfigured with tumors on the skin, her hair gone from the chemotherapy, Don Leta confessed it was her vanity that made her choose to keep the offending eye.

A death not sudden is a kind of grace. It is the chance to close matters in this world and, seeing clearly their emptiness, to be washed of a few more vanities   Don Leta approached death reconciled to God through Jesus Christ and at peace. Though she was forced to put off her outward beauty, her inward beauty was not extinguished. She even had a dream of assurance of the resurrection wherein she saw some of her relatives, those already deceased, appearing as healthy teenagers no matter their terrestrial ages. And they welcomed her.

One brisk day, we were walking in downtown Fort Worth. A gust of wind blew between the tall buildings and stole Mom's wig. We three chased after that curly wig, my wife and I and Mom, she with a few remaining tufts of hair, one cold glass eye, and her seeing eye filled with tears . . . of laughter.

A few days after Christmas, 1987, Don Leta died.

Martha

Proclaiming it clearly to all of us, Don Leta urged Leo to

re-marry right away. "You won't eat right and take care of your health, otherwise." Accordingly, Leo set out without delay. The Fort Worth Star Telegram bore the advertisement of "a definitely one-woman man" seeking one who's "warmth, sincerity and caring" were "better reflections of the truly loveable woman." Leo found Martha, married, and enjoyed a pleasant companionship for his remaining seventeen years. Martha's daughters and grandchildren gained Leo's affection and the benefit of his fatherly guidance.

A Regret

Don't live in the past, regretting what could have been. The Lord calls you today.   Hear his voice now and follow Him. Leo spoke this to people who were disabled in the present by self-pity over past mistakes. It was a warning to us, too. We would waste productive opportunity if we chose to wallow in our sorrows.

The only regret I remember Leo speaking was this: he wished he had been a teacher. He spoke fondly of his high school teachers, the Christian Brothers of Saint Raphael Academy. He enjoyed his role teaching religion classes for the high school students of our church. And "Sarge" was at all times teaching the young men in his squadron. His style of making authoritative pronouncements and his wit and grin proceeded from his joy of teaching.

Several men I work with have been taught by Leo's year of letters.   One man, Ken, said he would not have begun reading the letters except for my personal recommendation. Ken describes himself as "in the middle of his life". His time and attention is given to raising his teenagers to adulthood and providing for his wife. Ken cannot afford time to read anything but "how-to books", those kinds of books that help him achieve his specific goals.   Yet once he started reading, Ken declared Leo's letters a how-to book, "How to Tell Your Wife You Love Her".

Another man, Joe, read the letters. Amid the pressures coming from people he serves at work and his duties at home (he also has a son entering college), Joe found himself viewing his situations anew and asking himself, "What would Leo do?"

Indeed, Leo had always been and remains a teacher.

Lanis, Mathew, Paul, Bryan
Stephanie, Leo, Lynn
at Glen Rose, Texas, 2003

A little more and it will be time to rest.

      In July, 2004, the contest done, Leo went to sleep with his fathers. He had done his duty. He bore arms in the controversies of his day, served his earthly commanders, instructed those entrusted to his care, and loved his wife and children. His remains were interred with military honors at the Dallas-Fort Worth National Cemetery.

> Unless the Lord builds the house,
> They labor in vain who build it;
> Unless the Lord guards the city,
> The watchman stays awake in vain.
> It is vain for you to rise up early,
> To sit up late,
> To eat the bread of sorrows;
> For so He gives his beloved sleep.
>
> Behold, children are a heritage from the Lord,
> The fruit of the womb is his reward.
> Like arrows in the hands of a warrior,
> So are the children of one's youth.
> Happy is the man who has his quiver full of them;
> They shall not be ashamed,
> But shall speak with their enemies in the gate.

Psalm 127

R2